THE NIGGER OF THE "NARCISSUS"

AN AUTHORITATIVE TEXT
BACKGROUNDS AND SOURCES
REVIEWS AND CRITICISM

A NORTON CRITICAL EDITION

JOSEPH CONRAD

THE NIGGER OF THE "NARCISSUS"

AN AUTHORITATIVE TEXT
BACKGROUNDS AND SOURCES
REVIEWS AND CRITICISM

Edited by

ROBERT KIMBROUGH
UNIVERSITY OF WISCONSIN—MADISON

W·W· NORTON & COMPANY
New York

ACKNOWLEDGMENTS

William W. Bonney: "Semantic and Structural Indeterminacy in *The Nigger of the 'Narcissus'*: An Experiment in Reading," from *ELH*, 40 (1973), pp. 564–83. Copyright © The Johns Hopkins University Press. Reprinted by permission of the Johns Hopkins University Press and the author.

Joseph Conrad: From *A Conrad Memorial Library: The Collection of George T. Keating* (New York: Doubleday, 1929). From *Joseph Conrad's Letters to Cunninghame Graham*, edited by C. T. Watts (Cambridge: Cambridge University Press, 1969); reprinted by permission of Cambridge University Press. From *Joseph Conrad: Life and Letters*, edited by G. Jean-Aubry (New York: Doubleday, 1927); from *Letters from Joseph Conrad, 1895–1924*, edited by Edward Garnett (Indianapolis: Bobbs-Merrill, 1928); reprinted by permission of the Bobbs-Merril Company, Inc. From *The Mirror of the Sea*, by Joseph Conrad (London: J. M. Dent & Sons, Ltd., 1923, 1946). From *A Personal Record*, by Joseph Conrad (London: J. M. Dent & Sons, Ltd., 1923, 1946). "Stephen Crane" from *Last Essays*, by Joseph Conrad (London: J. M. Dent & Sons, Ltd., 1926). "Stephen Crane" from *Notes on Life and Letters*, by Joseph Conrad (New York: Doubleday, 1921). "To My Readers in America" from *Conrad's Manifesto: Preface to a Career*, by David R. Smith (Philadelphia: Gehenna Press, 1966).

Robert Foulke: "Postures of Belief in *The Nigger of the 'Narcissus'*" from *Modern Fiction Studies*, Vol. 17, Summer 1971, pp. 249–63. Copyright © 1977 by Purdue Research Foundation, West Lafayette, Indiana, U.S.A.

Albert J. Guerard: *"The Nigger of the 'Narcissus'"* reprinted by permission of the author and publishers from *Conrad the Novelist*, by Albert J. Guerard (Cambridge: Harvard University Press, 1958). Copyright © 1958 by the President and Fellows of Harvard College.

Gerald Morgan: "Narcissus Afloat," from *Bulletin of the Humanities Association of Canada (Bulletin de l'Association canadienne des Humanités)*, Vol. XV, No. 2 (Autumn 1964). Reprinted by permission of the author and the publisher.

Sanford Pinsker: "Selective Memory, Leisure and the Language of Joseph Conrad's *The Nigger of the 'Narcissus'*" from *Descant: Texas Christian University Literary Journal*, 15 (Summer 1971), pp. 38–48. Reprinted by permission of the publishers.

John E. Saveson: "Contemporary Psychology in *The Nigger of the 'Narcissus'*" from *Studies in Short Fiction*, 7 (Spring 1970), pp. 219–31. Reprinted by permission of the publishers.

Donald T. Torchiana: *"The Nigger of the 'Narcissus'*: Myth, Mirror, and Metropolis" from *Wascana Review*, II (1967), pp. 29–41. Reprinted by permission of the publishers.

Ian Watt: "Conrad Criticism and *The Nigger of the 'Narcissus'*" from *Nineteenth Century Fiction*, Vol. 12, No. 4, pp. 257–83. Copyright © 1958 by the Regents of the University of California. Copyright © 1974 by Ian Watt. Reprinted by permission of the Regents of the University of California and the author. "Conrad's Preface to *The Nigger of the 'Narcissus'*" from *Novel*, 8 (Winter 1974), pp. 101–15. Reprinted by permission of *Novel* and the author.

Paul L. Wiley: "A Tale of Passion" adapted, revised, and expanded from "Two Tales of Passion" *Conradiana*, 6 (1974), pp. 189–95. Reprinted by permission of *Conradiana*.

Norris W. Yates: "Social Comment in *The Nigger of the 'Narcissus'*" from *PMLA*, 79 (1964), pp. 183–85. Reprinted by permission of the Modern Language Association of America.

Library of Congress Cataloging in Publication Data

Conrad, Joseph, 1857–1924.
  The nigger of the "Narcissus."
  (Norton critical editions)
  Bibliography: p.
  1. Conrad, Joseph, 1857–1924. The nigger of the
Narcissus. I. Kimbrough, Robert. II. Title.
PR6005.04N5638 1979   823'.9'12   78-15249
ISBN 0-393-04517-X
ISBN 0-393-09019-1 pbk.

Contents

Reviews and Criticism

Preface

"By this book I stand or fall as an artist in prose." Joseph Conrad repeated this remark many times in conversation, correspondence, and print after finishing *The Nigger of the "Narcissus"* early in 1897. The act of writing the *"Narcissus"* established Conrad as a writer—in his own mind. Public fame was to be years away. Although his first two published works, *Almayer's Folly* (1895) and *An Outcast of the Islands* (1896), had gained the attention of important London literary figures, he still was unsure whether he should pursue fiction exclusively, forsaking his career as a sea captain. The completion of the manuscript of *The Nigger of the "Narcissus"* was the deciding factor.

So catalytic was this event, Conrad recalled in later years, that he immediately, instinctively turned to the writing of his manifesto as an artist—the justifiably famous "Preface," which has more to do with the art of fiction than with the story which it was intended to accompany. Actually, Conrad wrote the "Preface" some six months after *The Nigger of the "Narcissus."* But the recollection is more important than the fact, for the two works conjoined serve as Conrad's papers of certification for his new craft.

Because of the special nature of what Conrad called his "storm-piece" and because of the importance of the "Preface" in its own right, the three sections which make up the present book—the Text, Backgrounds and Sources, and Reviews and Criticism—depart slightly from the normal format of the Norton Critical Editions.

The Text

The text itself is freshly edited, based upon a full collation of all of the extant versions of the story. The annotation is light, restricted to the obsolete and the obscure. What has not been explained can be found in a dictionary or in the special Glossary of Nautical Terms.

The Textual Appendix has six parts. First come the materials on Textual History, the Present Text, and the Textual Notes, all of which are rather tortuous and quite extensive because of the complexities involved in tracing the evolution of Conrad's tale. Along with the Glossary, five illustrations have been provided which show the reader details Conrad assumed everyone could visualize. Finally, to facilitate further one's entrance into the sea-world of the text, Denis Murphy has written an essay which explains sailing terms and procedures while describing the dramatic storm at sea in chapter 3 (for Murphy's vivid account of his own disaster at sea in a small sailing boat, see *The Atlantic Monthly*, May 1976).

Murphy was, furthermore, of great assistance in the preparation of the Glossary. In addition to standard dictionaries and encyclopedias, I found the following particularly helpful: *The Sailor's Word-Book*, by Admiral W. H. Smyth (London, 1867); *Piloting, Seamanship, and Small Boat Handling* by Charles F. Chapman, M. E. (New York, 1969–70); and *The Lore of Ships*. compiled by Tre Tryckare and E. Gagner and Company (Nordbok ©, Gothenburg, Sweden, 1963)—a handsome, detailed book which is also the source of illustrations 4 and 5. The base drawing for the first three illustrations is the shipyard rigging plan of the *Narcissus* owned by Ugo Mursia of Milano, who has kindly granted permission for its use.

Backgrounds and Sources

Conrad's "Preface" is obviously the most important background item and appropriately comes right after the text of the story. Although this essay is usually placed before the story, it was originally intended as an "after-word," and so appeared in the fifth magazine installment. It was suppressed entirely in the first book editions of *The Nigger of the "Narcissus."* As does the story, the "Preface" provides textual problems which a responsible editor must attend. The present text was prepared by Thomas Lavoie, who also wrote the history and prepared the notes. Although Ian Watt's essay on the "Preface" is "critical," its inclusion here is more pertinent than in the Criticism section because of its explication of this landmark aesthetic statement.

Conrad's special American preface follows, along with a series of comments on the story from Conrad's letters and essays, bracketed by biographical pieces by Edward Garnett, his informal literary agent and advisor, and G. Jean-Aubry, his first formal biographer. The section closes with an extended essay—on the actual ship *Narcissus*, Conrad's connection with her, and his transformation of experience into art—specially written for this volume by Gerald Morgan.

Reviews and Criticism

After the presentation of a selection of initial reviews of Conrad's work, the first "modern" reaction is Albert Guerard's now classic essay. This is fitting, for Guerard is the most influential of all Conrad critics and scholars: most of us merely write expanded footnotes of explanation to his passing observations. The section ends with a short piece by another distinguished Conradian, Paul L. Wiley, specially adapted for this work, and with two essays, by John Howard Weston and Eugene B. Redmond, specially written for this edition.

The essays in between reflect a full range of interpretations and schools of criticism. All of the essays are reprinted in their entirety, except that page references to various editions of *The Nigger of the "Narcissus,"* the "Preface," and "To My Readers in America" have been removed, since all of those works are conveniently available here. Additional biographical and critical materials are included in the Bibliography which closes the book.

Preparing the text and researching the background for the present Norton Critical Edition has taken me to many libraries, which brought me in touch with many helpful people. I was allowed to use works from and consult works in: the Beinecke Rare Book and Manuscript Library of the Yale University Library, the library of the University of Illinois—Urbana, the Cambridge University Library, the British Museum, the University Library of the University of Wisconsin—Madison, the Philip H. and A.S.W. Rosenbach Foundation in Philadelphia, Colgate University Library, and the National Maritime Museum in Greenwich. I am grateful to all; Clive E. Driver, the director of the Rosenbach, Bruce M. Brown and Neill R. Joy at Colgate, and Mary Ollard at the Maritime were particularly generous.

Other numerous acknowledgments of gratitude could follow, but a few must. All typing was done in the Department of English of the University of Wisconsin—Madison. Collation in Philadelphia of the Rosenbach manuscript would not have been possible without the help of Dr. Beryl York Malawsky. Collation of all other states of the story was accomplished with the able assistance of Thomas Lavoie, who also did research on the backgrounds and made recommendations with regard to the essays. Renato Prinzhofer, faithful and creative translator of Conrad's works into Italian, enthusiastically shared knowledge and made suggestions during a visit with him in Milano. The final acknowledgment is both particular and general. Just as I was getting under way I received an invitation to participate in the International Conrad Conference in Kent, July 1974; the occasion, the place, and the people assured good sailing by providing opportune winds.

ROBERT KIMBROUGH

The Text of
The Nigger of
the "Narcissus"

A TALE OF THE SEA

. . . My Lord in his discourse discovered
a great deal of love to this ship.
DIARY OF SAMUEL PEPYS

TO
EDWARD GARNETT
THIS TALE
ABOUT MY FRIENDS
OF THE SEA

Chapter One

Mr. Baker, chief mate of the ship *Narcissus*, stepped in one stride out of his lighted cabin into the darkness of the quarter-deck. Above his head on the break of the poop, the night-watchman rang a double stroke. It was nine o'clock. Mr. Baker, speaking up to the man above him, asked: "Are all the hands aboard, Knowles?"

The man limped down the ladder, then said reflectively:

"I think so, sir. All our old chaps are there, and a lot of new men has come. . . . They must be all there."

"Tell the boatswain to send all hands aft," went on Mr. Baker; "and tell one of the youngsters to bring a good lamp here. I want to muster our crowd."

The main deck was dark aft, but half-way from forward, through the open doors of the forecastle, two streaks of brilliant light cut the shadow of the quiet night that lay upon the ship. A hum of voices was heard there, while port and starboard, in the illuminated doorways, silhouettes of moving men appeared for a moment, very black, without relief, like figures cut out of sheet tin. The ship was for sea. The carpenter had driven in the last wedge of the main-hatch battens, and, throwing down his maul, had wiped his face with great deliberation, just on the stroke of five. The decks had been swept, the windlass oiled and made ready to heave up the anchor; the big tow-rope lay in long bights along one side of the main deck, with one end carried up and hung over the bows, in readiness for the tug that would come paddling and hissing noisily, hot and smoky, in the limpid, cool quietness of the early morning. The captain was ashore, where he had been engaging some new hands to make up his full crew; and, the work of the day over, the ship's officers had kept out of the way, glad of a little breathing-time. Soon after dark the few liberty-men and the new hands began to arrive in shore-boats rowed by whiteclad Asiatics, who clamoured fiercely for payment before coming alongside the gangway-ladder. The feverish and shrill babble of Eastern language struggled against the masterful tones of tipsy seamen, who argued against brazen claims and dishonest hopes by profane shouts. The resplendent and bestarred peace of the East was torn into squalid tatters by howls of rage and shrieks of lament raised over sums ranging from five annas to half a rupee; and every soul afloat in Bombay Harbour[1] became aware that the new hands were joining the *Narcissus*.

Gradually the distracting noise had subsided. The boats came no longer in splashing clusters of three or four together, but dropped alongside singly, in a subdued buzz of expostulation cut short by a

1. The capital of the island of Bombay, major Indian seaport.
in western India, on the Arabian Sea; a

"Not a pice more! You go to the devil!" from some man staggering up the accommodation-ladder—a dark figure, with a long bag poised on the shoulder. In the forecastle the newcomers, upright and swaying amongst corded boxes and bundles of bedding, made friends with the old hands, who sat one above another in the two tiers of bunks, gazing at their future shipmates with glances critical but friendly. The two forecastle lamps were turned up high, and shed an intense hard glare; shore-going round hats were pushed far on the backs of heads, or rolled about on the deck amongst the chain-cables; white collars, undone, stuck out on each side of red faces; big arms in white sleeves gesticulated; the growling voices hummed steady amongst bursts of laughter and hoarse calls. "Here, sonny, take that bunk! . . . Don't you do it! . . . What's your last ship? . . . I know her. . . . Three years ago, in Puget Sound.[2] . . . This here berth leaks, I tell you! . . . Come on; give us a chance to swing that chest! . . . Did you bring a bottle, any of you shore toffs?[3] . . . Give us a bit of 'baccy. . . . I know her; her skipper drank himself to death. . . . He was a dandy boy! . . . Liked his lotion inside, he did! . . . No! . . . Hold your row, you chaps. . . . I tell you, you came on board a hooker,[4] where they get their money's worth out of poor Jack,[5] by—! . . ."

A little fellow, called Craik and nicknamed Belfast, abused the ship violently, romancing on principle, just to give the new hands something to think over. Archie, sitting aslant on his sea-chest, kept his knees out of the way, and pushed the needle steadily through a white patch in a pair of blue trousers. Men in black jackets and stand-up collars, mixed with men bare-footed, bare-armed, with coloured shirts open on hairy chests, pushed against one another in the middle of the forecastle. The group swayed, reeled, turning upon itself with the motion of a scrimmage,[6] in a haze of tobacco smoke. All were speaking together, swearing at every second word. A Russian Finn, wearing a yellow shirt with pink stripes, stared upwards, dreamy-eyed, from under a mop of tumbled hair. Two young giants with smooth, baby faces—two Scandinavians—helped each other to spread their bedding, silent and smiling placidly at the tempest of good-humoured and meaningless curses. Old Singleton, the oldest able seaman in the ship, sat apart on the deck right under the lamps, stripped to the waist, tattooed like a cannibal chief all over his powerful chest and enormous biceps. Between the blue and red

2. A large body of water opening to the Pacific Ocean in northwestern Washington.
3. Slang for a stylishly dressed, fashionable person, especially one who wants to be thought a member of the upper class.
4. Slang for a clumsy, old-fashioned vessel.

5. Slang for a sailor.
6. A term used in rugby for an ordered formation in which two opposing sets of front players pack themselves together with their heads down and try to push their opponents off the ball in order to kick it free to the back players.

patterns his white skin gleamed like satin; his bare back was propped against the heel of the bow-sprit, and he held a book at arm's length before his big, sunburnt face. With his spectacles and a venerable white beard, he resembled a learned and savage patriarch, the incarnation of barbarian wisdom serene in the blasphemous turmoil of the world. He was intensely absorbed, and, as he turned the pages, an expression of grave surprise would pass over his rugged features. He was reading *Pelham*.[7] The popularity of Bulwer Lytton in the forecastles of Southern-going ships is a wonderful and bizarre phenomenon. What ideas do his polished and so curiously insincere sentences awaken in the simple minds of the big children who people those dark and wandering places of the earth? What meaning can their rough, inexperienced souls find in the elegant verbiage of his pages? What excitement?—what forgetfulness? —what appeasement? Mystery! Is it the fascination of the incomprehensible? is it the charm of the impossible? Or are those beings who exist beyond the pale of life stirred by his tales as by an enigmatical disclosure of a resplendent world that exists within the frontier of infamy and filth, within that border of dirt and hunger, of misery and dissipation, that comes down on all sides to the water's edge of the incorruptible ocean, and is the only thing they know of life, the only thing they see of surrounding land—those lifelong prisoners of the sea? Mystery!

Singleton, who had sailed to the southward since the age of twelve, who in the last forty-five years had lived (as we had calculated from his papers) no more than forty months ashore—old Singleton, who boasted, with the mild composure of long years well spent, that generally from the day he was paid off from one ship till the day he shipped in another he seldom was in a condition to distinguish daylight—old Singleton sat unmoved in the clash of voices and cries, spelling through *Pelham* with slow labour, and lost in an absorption profound enough to resemble a trance. He breathed regularly. Every time he turned the book in his enormous and blackened hands the muscles of his big white arms rolled slightly under the smooth skin. Hidden by the white moustache, his lips, stained with tobacco-juice that trickled down the long beard, moved in inward whisper. His bleared eyes gazed fixedly from behind the glitter of black-rimmed glasses. Opposite to him, and on a level with his face, the ship's cat sat on the barrel of the windlass in the pose of a crouching chimera, blinking its green eyes at its old friend. It seemed to meditate a leap on to the old man's lap over the bent back of the ordinary seaman who sat at Singleton's feet. Young

7. *Pelham; or, Adventures of a Gentleman* (1828), by Edward Bulwer-Lytton (1803–73). A highly fashionable novel, it contributed greatly to the English concept of the dandy. Richard Dana, in *Two Years Before the Mast*, records that Lytton's books were popular on ships.

Charley was lean and long-necked. The ridge of his backbone made a chain of small hills under the old shirt. His face of a street-boy—a face precocious, sagacious, and ironic, with deep downward folds on each side of the thin, wide mouth—hung low over his bony knees. He was learning to make a lanyard knot with a bit of an old rope. Small drops of perspiration stood out on his bulging forehead; he sniffed strongly from time to time, glancing out of the corners of his restless eyes at the old seaman, who took no notice of the puzzled youngster muttering at his work.

The noise increased. Little Belfast seemed, in the heavy heat of the forecastle, to boil with facetious fury. His eyes danced; in the crimson of his face, comical as a mask, the mouth yawned black, with strange grimaces. Facing him, a half-undressed man held his sides, and, throwing his head back, laughed with wet eyelashes. Others stared with amazed eyes. Men sitting doubled up in the upper bunks smoked short pipes, swinging bare brown feet above the heads of those who, sprawling below on sea-chests, listened, smiling stupidly or scornfully. Over the white rims of berths stuck out heads with blinking eyes; but the bodies were lost in the gloom of those places, that resembled narrow niches for coffins in a white-washed and lighted mortuary. Voices buzzed louder. Archie, with compressed lips, drew himself in, seemed to shrink into a smaller space, and sewed steadily, industrious and dumb. Belfast shrieked like an inspired Dervish:[8] ". . . So I seez to him, boys, seez I, 'Beggin' your pardon, sorr,' seez I to that second mate of that steamer—'beggin' your-r-r pardon, sorr, the Board of Trade[9] must 'ave been drunk when they granted you your certificate!' 'What do you say, you—!' seez he, comin' at me like a mad bull . . . all in his white clothes; and I up with my tar-pot and capsizes it all over his blamed lovely face and his lovely jacket. . . . 'Take that!' seez I. 'I am a sailor, anyhow, you nosing, skipper-licking, useless, sooperfloos bridge-stanchion, you! That's the kind of man I am!' shouts I. . . . You should have seed him skip boys! Drowned, blind with tar, he was! So . . ."

"Don't 'ee believe him! He never upset no tar; I was there!" shouted somebody. The two Norwegians sat on a chest side by side, alike and placid, resembling a pair of love-birds on a perch, and with round eyes stared innocently; but the Russian Finn, in the racket of explosive shouts and rolling laughter, remained motionless, limp, and dull, like a deaf man without a backbone. Near him

8. A member of one of the various Muslim ascetic orders, some of which carry on ecstastic observances, such as violent dancing and whirling or vociferous chanting or singing.
9. The national ministry in England which supervises and encourages commerce and industry. One specific function is to examine officer candidates and issue certificates to the successful (see opening chapters of Conrad's *Chance*).

Archie smiled at his needle. A broad-chested, slow-eyed newcomer spoke deliberately to Belfast during an exhausted lull in the noise: "I wonder any of the mates here are alive yet with such a chap as you on board! I concloode they ain't that bad now, if you had the taming of them, sonny."

"Not bad! Not bad!" screamed Belfast. "If it wasn't for us sticking together. . . . Not bad! They ain't never bad when they ain't got a chawnce, blast their black 'arts. . . ." He foamed, whirling his arms, then suddenly grinned and, taking a tablet of black tobacco out of his pocket, bit a piece off with a funny show of ferocity. Another new hand—a man with shifty eyes and a yellow hatchet face, who had been listening open-mouthed in the shadow of the midship locker—observed in a squeaky voice: "Well, it's a 'omeward trip, anyhow. Bad or good, I can do it on my 'ed—s'long as I get 'ome. And I can look after my rights! I will show 'em!" All the heads turned towards him. Only the ordinary seaman and the cat took no notice. He stood with arms akimbo, a little fellow with white eyelashes. He looked as if he had known all the degradations and all the furies. He looked as if he had been cuffed, kicked, rolled in the mud; he looked as if he had been scratched, spat upon, pelted with unmentionable filth . . . and he smiled with a sense of security at the faces around. His ears were bending down under the weight of his battered felt hat. The torn tails of his black coat flapped in fringes about the calves of his legs. He unbuttoned the only two buttons that remained and every one saw that he had no shirt under it. It was his deserved misfortune that those rags which nobody could possibly be supposed to own looked on him as if they had been stolen. His neck was long and thin; his eyelids were red; rare hairs hung about his jaws; his shoulders were peaked and drooped like the broken wings of a bird; all his left side was caked with mud, which showed that he had lately slept in a wet ditch. He had saved his inefficient carcass from violent destruction by running away from an American ship[1] where, in a moment of forgetful folly, he had dared to engage himself; and he had knocked about for a fortnight ashore in the native quarter, cadging[2] for drinks, starving, sleeping on rubbish-heaps, wandering in sunshine: a startling visitor from a world of nightmares. He stood repulsive and smiling in the sudden silence. This clean white forecastle was his refuge; the place where he could be lazy; where he could wallow, and lie and eat—and curse the food he ate; where he could display his talents for shirking work, for cheating, for cadging; where he could find surely some one to wheedle and some one to bully—and

---

1. American ships were particularly noted for the harsh manner in which crews were treated.

2. British for begging or obtaining by begging.

where he would be paid for doing all this. They all knew him. Is there a spot on earth where such a man is unknown, an ominous survival testifying to the eternal fitness of lies and impudence? A taciturn long-armed shellback, with hooked fingers, who had been lying on his back smoking, turned in his bed to examine him dispassionately, then, over his head, sent a long jet of clear saliva towards the door. They all knew him! He was the man that cannot steer, that cannot splice, that dodges the work on dark nights; that, aloft, holds on frantically with both arms and legs, and swears at the wind, the sleet, the darkness; the man who curses the sea while others work. The man who is the last out and the first in when all hands are called. The man who can't do most things and won't do the rest. The pet of philanthropists and self-seeking landlubbers. The sympathetic and deserving creature that knows all about his rights, but knows nothing of courage, of endurance, and of the unexpressed faith, of the unspoken loyalty that knits together a ship's company. The independent offspring of the ignoble freedom of the slums full of disdain and hate for the austere servitude of the sea.

Some one cried at him: "What's your name?"—"Donkin," he said, looking round with cheerful effrontery.—"What are you?" asked another voice.—"Why, a sailor like you, old man," he replied, in a tone that meant to be hearty but was impudent.— "Blamme if you don't look a blamed sight worse than a broken-down fireman," was the comment in a convinced mutter. Charley lifted his head and piped in a cheeky voice: "He is a man and a sailor"—then, wiping his nose with the back of his hand, bent down industriously over his bit of rope. A few laughed. Others stared doubtfully. The ragged newcomer was indignant—"That's a fine way to welcome a chap into a fo'c'sle," he snarled. "Are you men or a lot of 'artless cannybals?"—"Don't take your shirt off for a word, shipmate," called out Belfast, jumping up in front, fiery, menacing, and friendly at the same time.—"Is that 'ere bloke blind?" asked the indomitable scarecrow, looking right and left with affected surprise. "Can't 'ee see I 'aven't got no shirt?"

He held both his arms out crosswise and shook the rags that hung over his bones with dramatic effect.

" 'Cos why?" he continued very loud. "The bloody Yankees been tryin' to jump my guts out 'cos I stood up for my rights like a good 'un. I am an Englishman, I am. They set upon me an' I 'ad to run. That's why. A'n't yer never seed a man 'ard up? Yah! What kind of blamed ship is this? I'm dead broke. I 'aven't got nothink. No bag, no bed, no blanket, no shirt—not a bloomin' rag but what I stand in. But I 'ad the 'art to stand up agin' them Yankees. 'As any of you 'art enough to spare a pair of old pants for a chum?"

He knew how to conquer the naive instincts of that crowd. In a moment they gave him their compassion, jocularly, contemptuously, or surlily; and at first it took the shape of a blanket thrown at him as he stood there with the white skin of his limbs showing his human kinship through the black fantasy of his rags. Then a pair of old shoes fell at his muddy feet. With a cry:—"From under," a rolled-up pair of canvas trousers, heavy with tar stains, struck him on the shoulder. The gust of their benevolence sent a wave of senti-mental pity through their doubting hearts. They were touched by their own readiness to alleviate a shipmate's misery. Voices cried:—"We will fit you out, old man." Murmurs:—"Never seed seech a hard case. . . . Poor beggar. . . . I've got an old singlet. . . . Will that be of any use to you? . . . Take it, matey. . . ." Those friendly murmurs filled the forecastle. He pawed around with his naked foot, gathering the things in a heap, and looked about for more. Unemotional Archie perfunctorily contributed to the pile an old cloth cap with the peak torn off. Old Singleton, lost in the serene regions of fiction, read on unheeding. Charley, pitiless with the wisdom of youth, squeaked:—"If you want brass buttons for your new unyforms I've got two for you." The filthy object of universal charity shook his fist at the youngster.—"I'll make you keep this 'ere fo'c'sle clean, young feller," he snarled viciously. "Never you fear. I will learn you to be civil to an able seaman, you ignerant ass." He glared harmfully, but saw Singleton shut his book, and his little beady eyes began to roam from berth to berth.—"Take that bunk by the door there—it's pretty fair," suggested Belfast. So advised, he gathered the gifts at his feet, pressed them in a bundle against his breast, then looked cautiously at the Russian Finn, who stood on one side with an unconscious gaze, contemplating, per-haps, one of those weird visions that haunt the men of his race.—"Get out of my road, Dutchy," said the victim of Yankee brutal-ity. The Finn did not move—did not hear. "Get out, blast ye," shouted the other, shoving him aside with his elbow. "Get out, you blanked deaf and dumb fool. Get out." The man staggered, recovered himself, and gazed at the speaker in silence.—"Those damned furriners should be kept under," opined the amiable Donkin to the forecastle. "If you don't teach 'em their place they put on you like anythink." He flung all his worldly possessions into the empty bedplace, gauged with another shrewd look the risks of the proceeding, then leaped up to the Finn, who stood pensive and dull.—"I'll teach you to swell around," he yelled. "I'll plug your eyes for you, you blooming square-head." Most of the men were now in their bunks and the two had the forecastle clear to them-selves. The development of the destitute Donkin aroused interest. He danced all in tatters before the amazed Finn, squaring from a distance at the heavy unmoved face. One or two men cried encouragingly: "Go it, Whitechapel!"[3] settling themselves luxuriously in their beds to survey the fight. Others shouted: "Shut yer row! . . . Go an' put yer 'ed in a bag! . . ." The hubbub was recommencing. Suddenly many heavy blows struck with a handspike on the deck above boomed like discharges of small cannon through the forecastle. Then the boatswain's voice rose outside the door with an authoritative note in its drawl;—"D'ye hear, below there? Lay aft! Lay aft to muster all hands!"

There was a moment of surprised stillness. Then the forecastle floor disappeared under men whose bare feet flopped on the planks as they sprang clear out of their berths. Caps were rooted for amongst tumbled blankets. Some, yawning, buttoned waistbands. Half-smoked pipes were knocked hurriedly against woodwork and stuffed under pillows. Voices growled:—"What's up? . . . Is there no rest for us?" Donkin yelped:—"If that's the way of this ship, we'll 'ave to change all that. . . . You leave me alone. . . . I will soon . . ." None of the crowd noticed him. They were lurching in twos and threes through the doors, after the manner of merchant Jacks who cannot go out of a door fairly, like mere landsmen. The votary of change followed them. Singleton, struggling into his jacket, came last, tall and fatherly, bearing high his head of a weatherbeaten sage on the body of an old athlete. Only Charley remained alone in the white glare of the empty place, sitting between the two rows of iron links that stretched into the narrow gloom forward. He pulled hard at the strands in a hurried endeavour to finish his knot. Suddenly he started up, flung the rope at the cat, and skipped after the black tom which went off leaping sedately over chain compressors, with its tail carried stiff and upright, like a small flag pole.

Outside the glare of the steaming forecastle the serene purity of the night enveloped the seamen with its soothing breath, with its tepid breath flowing under the stars that hung countless above the mastheads in a thin cloud of luminous dust. On the town side the blackness of the water was streaked with trails of light undulated gently on slight ripples, similar to filaments that float rooted to the shore. Rows of other lights stood away in straight lines as if drawn up on parade between towering buildings; but on the other side of the harbour sombre hills arched high their black spines, on which, here and there, the point of a star resembled a spark fallen from the sky. Far off, Byculla[4] way, the electric lamps at the dock gates shone on the end of lofty standards with a glow blinding and frigid like captive ghosts of some evil moons. Scattered all over the dark

3. A district in eastern London, then a desolate, lonely place inhabited chiefly by persons of low character.

4. A district in the center of Bombay Island, just west of the docks area.

polish of the roadstead, the ships at anchor floated in perfect stillness under the feeble gleam of their riding-lights, looming up,
opaque and bulky, like strange and monumental structures abandoned by men to an everlasting repose.

Before the cabin door Mr. Baker was mustering the crew. As they
stumbled and lurched along past the mainmast, they could see aft
his round, broad face with a white paper before it, and beside his
shoulder the sleepy head, with dropped eyelids, of the boy, who
held, suspended at the end of his raised arm, the luminous globe
of a lamp. Even before the shuffle of naked soles had ceased along
the decks, the mate began to call over the names. He called distinctly in a serious tone befitting this roll-call to unquiet loneliness, to inglorious and obscure struggle, or to the more trying endurance of small privations and wearisome duties. As the chief mate
read out a name, one of the men would answer: "Yes, sir!" or
"Here!" and, detaching himself from the shadowy mob of heads
visible above the blackness of starboard bulwarks, would step bare-
footed into the circle of light, and in two noiseless strides pass into
the shadows on the port side of the quarter-deck. They answered in
divers tones: in thick mutters, in clear, ringing voices; and some, as
if the whole thing had been an outrage on their feelings, used an
injured intonation: for discipline is not ceremonious in merchant
ships, where the sense of hierarchy is weak, and where all feel themselves equal before the unconcerned immensity of the sea and the
exacting appeal of the work.

Mr. Baker read on steadily:—"Hansen—Campbell—Smith—
Wamibo. Now, then, Wamibo. Why don't you answer? Always got
to call your name twice." The Finn emitted at last an uncouth
grunt, and, stepping out, passed through the patch of light, weird
and gaudy, with the face of a man marching through a dream. The
mate went on faster:—"Craik—Singleton—Donkin. . . . O Lord!"
he involuntarily ejaculated as the incredibly dilapidated figure
appeared in the light. It stopped; it uncovered pale gums and long,
upper teeth in a malevolent grin.—"Is there anything wrong with
me, Mister Mate?" it asked, with a flavour of insolence in the
forced simplicity of its tone. On both sides of the deck subdued tit-
ters were heard.—"That'll do. Go over," growled Mr. Baker, fixing
the new hand with steady blue eyes. And Donkin vanished suddenly
out of the light into the dark group of mustered men, to be slapped
on the back and to hear flattering whispers:—"He ain't afeard, he'll
give sport to 'em, see if he don't. . . . Reg'lar Punch and Judy
show.[5] . . . Did ye see the mate start at him? . . . Well! Damme, if
I ever! . . ."

5. A puppet show having a conventional
plot consisting primarily of slapstick
humor and the tragicomic misadventures
of a grotesque, hook-nosed, humpback
buffoon (Punch) and his wife (Judy).

The last man had gone over, and there was a moment of silence while the mate peered at his list.—"Sixteen, seventeen," he muttered. "I am one hand short, bo'sun," he said aloud. The big west-countryman at his elbow, swarthy and bearded like a gigantic Spaniard, said in a rumbling bass:—"There's no one left forward, sir. I had a look round. He ain't aboard, but he may turn up before daylight."—"Ay. He may or he may not," commented the mate. "Can't make out that last name. It's all a smudge. . . . That will do, men. Go below."

The distinct and motionless group stirred, broke up, began to move forward.

"Wait!" cried a deep, ringing voice.

All stood still. Mr. Baker, who had turned away yawning, spun round open-mouthed. At last furious, he blurted out:—"What's this? Who said 'Wait'? What . . ."

But he saw a tall figure standing on the rail. It came down and pushed through the crowd, marching with a heavy tread towards the light on the quarter-deck. Then again the sonorous voice said with insistence:—"Wait!" The lamplight lit up the man's body. He was tall. His head was away up in the shadows of lifeboats that stood on skids above the deck. The whites of his eyes and his teeth gleamed distinctly, but the face was indistinguishable. His hands were big and seemed gloved.

Mr. Baker advanced intrepidly. "Who are you? How dare you . . ." he began.

The boy, amazed like the rest, raised the light to the man's face. It was black. A surprised hum—a faint hum that sounded like the suppressed mutter of the word "Nigger"—ran along the deck and escaped out into the night. The nigger seemed not to hear. He balanced himself where he stood in a swagger that marked time. After a moment he said calmly:—"My name is Wait—James Wait."

"Oh!" said Mr. Baker. Then, after a few seconds of smouldering silence, his temper blazed out. "Ah! Your name is Wait. What of that? What do you want? What do you mean, coming shouting here?"

The nigger was calm, cool, towering, superb. The men had approached and stood behind him in a body. He overtopped the tallest by half a head. He said: "I belong to the ship." He enunciated distinctly, with soft precision. The deep, rolling tones of his voice filled the deck without effort. He was naturally scornful, unaffectedly condescending, as if from his height of six foot three he had surveyed all the vastness of human folly and had made up his mind not to be too hard on it. He went on:—"The captain shipped me this morning. I couldn't get aboard sooner. I saw you all aft as I came up the ladder, and could see directly you were mustering the crew. Naturally I called out my name. I thought you had it on your list, and would understand. You misapprehended." He stopped short. The folly around him was confounded. He was right as ever, and as ever ready to forgive. The disdainful tones had ceased, and, breathing heavily, he stood still, surrounded by all these white men. He held his head up in the glare of the lamp—a head vigorously modelled into deep shadows and shining lights—a head powerful and misshapen, with a tormented and flattened face—a face pathetic and brutal; the tragic, the mysterious, the repulsive mask of a nigger's soul.

Mr. Baker, recovering his composure, looked at the paper close. "Oh yes; that's so. All right, Wait. Take your gear forward," he said.

Suddenly the nigger's eyes rolled wildly, became all whites. He put his hand to his side and coughed twice, a cough metallic, hollow, and tremendously loud; it resounded like two explosions in a vault; the dome of the sky rang to it, and the iron plates of the ship's bulwarks seemed to vibrate in unison; then he marched off forward with the others. The officers lingering by the cabin door could hear him say: "Won't some of you chaps lend a hand with my dunnage? I've got a chest and a bag." The words, spoken sonorously, with an even intonation, were heard all over the ship, and the question was put in a manner that made refusal impossible. The short, quick shuffle of men carrying something heavy went away forward, but the tall figure of the nigger lingered by the main hatch in a knot of smaller shapes. Again he was heard asking: "Is your cook a coloured gentleman?" Then a disappointed and disapproving "Ah! h'm!" was his comment upon the information that the cook happened to be a mere white man. Yet, as they went all together towards the forecastle, he condescended to put his head through the galley door and boom out inside a magnificent "Good evening, doctor!"[6] that made all the saucepans ring. In the dim light the cook dozed on the coal locker in front of the captain's supper. He jumped up as if he had been cut with a whip, and dashed wildly on deck to see the backs of several men going away laughing. Afterwards, when talking about that voyage, he used to say:—"The poor felow had scared me. I thought I had seen the devil." The cook had been seven years in the ship with the same captain. He was a serious-minded man with a wife and three children, whose society he enjoyed on an average of one month out of twelve. When on shore he took his family to church twice every Sunday. At sea he went to sleep every evening with his lamp turned up full, a pipe in his mouth, and an open Bible in his hand. Some one had always to go during the night to put out the light, take the

6. Nickname (and function) of a cook aboard ship.

book from his hand, and the pipe from between his teeth. "For"—
Belfast used to say, irritated and complaining—"some night, you
stupid cookie, you'll swallow your ould clay, and we will have no
cook."—"Ah! sonny, I am ready for my Maker's call . . . wish you
all were," the other would answer with a benign serenity that was
altogether imbecile and touching. Belfast outside the gallery door
danced with vexation. "You holy fool! I don't want you to die," he
howled, looking up with furious, quivering face and tender eyes.
"What's the hurry? You blessed wooden-headed ould heretic, the
divvle will have you soon enough. Think of Us . . . of Us . . . of
Us!" And he would go away, stamping, spitting aside, disgusted and
worried; while the other, stepping out, saucepan in hand, hot, begrimed, and placid, watched with a superior cock-sure smile the back
of his "queer little man" reeling in a rage. They were great friends.

Mr. Baker, lounging over the after-hatch, sniffed the humid
night in the company of the second mate.—"Those West India
niggers run fine and large—some of them. . . . Ough! . . . Don't
they? A fine, big man that, Mr. Creighton. Feel him on a rope.
Hey? Ough! I will take him into my watch, I think." The second
mate, a fair, gentlemanly young fellow, with a resolute face and a
splendid physique, observed quietly that it was just about what he
expected. There could be felt in his tone some slight bitterness
which Mr. Baker very kindly set himself to argue away. "Come,
come, young man," he said, grunting between the words. "Come!
Don't be too greedy. You had that big Finn in your watch all the
voyage. I will do what's fair. You may have those two young Scandinavians and I . . . Ough! . . . I get the nigger, and will take that
. . . Ough! that cheeky costermonger[7] chap in a black frockcoat. I'll
make him . . . Ough! . . . make him toe the mark, or my . . .
Ough! . . . name isn't Baker. Ough! Ough! Ough!"

He grunted thrice—ferociously. He had that trick of grunting so
between his words and at the end of sentences. It was a fine, effective grunt that went well with his menacing utterance, with his
heavy, bull-necked frame, his jerky, rolling gait; with his big, seamed
face, his steady eyes, and sardonic mouth. But its effect had been
long ago discounted by the men. They liked him; Belfast—who
was a favourite, and knew it—mimicked him, not quite behind his
back. Charley—but with greater caution—imitated his rolling gait.
Some of his sayings became established, daily quotations in the forecastle. Popularity can go no further! Besides, all hands were ready to
admit that on a fitting occasion the mate could "jump down a fellow's throat in a reg'lar Western Ocean[8] style."

Now he was giving his last orders. "Ough! . . . You, Knowles!

7. British slang for a hawker of fruit,   8. The North Atlantic ocean.
vegetables, fish, etc.

Call all hands at four. I want . . . Ough! . . . to heave short before the tug comes. Look out for the captain. I am going to lie down in my clothes. . . . Ough! . . . Call me when you see the boat coming. Ough! Ough! . . . The old man is sure to have something to say when he gets aboard," he remarked to Creighton. "Well, good-night. . . . Ough! A long day before us to-morrow. . . . Ough! . . . Better turn in now. Ough! Ough!"

Upon the dark deck a band of light flashed, then a door slammed, and Mr. Baker was gone into his neat cabin. Young Creighton stood leaning over the rail, and looked dreamily into the night of the East. And he saw in it a long country lane, a lane of waving leaves and dancing sunshine. He saw stirring boughs of old trees outspread, and framing in their arch the tender, the caressing blueness of an English sky. And through the arch a girl in a light dress, smiling under a sunshade, seemed to be stepping out of the tender sky.

At the other end of the ship the forecastle, with only one lamp burning now, was going to sleep in a dim emptiness traversed by loud breathings, by sudden, short sighs. The double row of berths yawned black, like graves tenanted by uneasy corpses. Here and there a curtain of gaudy chintz, half drawn, marked the resting-place of a sybarite. A leg hung over the edge very white and lifeless. An arm stuck straight out with a dark palm turned up, and thick fingers half closed. Two light snores, that did not synchronise, quarrelled in funny dialogue. Singleton stripped again—the old man suffered much from prickly heat—stood cooling his back in the doorway, with his arms crossed on his bare and adorned chest. His head touched the beam of the deck above. The nigger, half undressed, was busy casting adrift the lashing of his box, and spreading his bedding in an upper berth. He moved about in his socks, tall and noiseless, with a pair of braces[9] beating about his calves. Amongst the shadows of stanchions and bowsprit, Donkin munched a piece of hard ship's bread, sitting on the deck with upturned feet and restless eyes; he held the biscuit up before his mouth in the whole fist and snapped his jaws at it with a raging face. Crumbs fell between his outspread legs. Then he got up.

"Where's our water-cask?" he asked in a contained voice.

Singleton, without a word, pointed with a big hand that held a short smouldering pipe. Donkin bent over the cask, drank out of the tin, splashing the water, turned round and noticed the nigger looking at him over the shoulder with calm loftiness. He moved up sideways.

"There's a blooming supper for a man," he whispered bitterly. "My dorg at 'ome wouldn't 'ave it. It's fit enouf for you an' me.

9. British for suspenders.

'Ere's a big ship's fo'c'sle! . . . Not a blooming scrap of meat in the kids. I've looked in all the lockers. . . ."

The nigger stared like a man addressed unexpectedly in a foreign language. Donkin changed his tone:—"Giv' us a bit of 'baccy, mate," he breathed out confidentially. "I 'aven't 'ad smoke or chew for the last month. I am rampin' mad for it. Come on, old man!"

"Don't be familiar," said the nigger. Donkin started and sat down on a chest near by, out of sheer surprise. "We haven't kept pigs together," continued James Wait in a deep undertone. "Here's your tobacco." Then, after a pause, he inquired:—"What ship?" —"*Golden State*," muttered Donkin indistinctly, biting the tobacco. The nigger whistled low.—"Ran?" he asked curtly. Donkin nodded: one of his cheeks bulged out. "In course I ran," he mumbled. "They booted the life out of one Dago chap on the passage 'ere, then started on me. I cleared out 'ere."—"Left your dunnage behind?"—"Yes, dunnage and money," answered Donkin, raising his voice a little; "I got nothink. No clothes, no bed. A bandy-legged little Irish chap 'ere 'as give me a blanket. . . . Think I'll go an' sleep in the fore topmast staysail to-night."

He went on deck trailing behind his back a corner of the blanket. Singleton, without a glance, moved slightly aside to let him pass. The nigger put away his shore togs and sat in clean working clothes on his box, one arm stretched over his knees. After staring at Singleton for some time he asked without emphasis: —"What kind of ship is this? Pretty fair? Eh?"

Singleton didn't stir. A long while after he said, with unmoved face:—"Ship! . . . Ships are all right. It is the men in them!"

He went on smoking in the profound silence. The wisdom of half a century spent in listening to the thunder of the waves had spoken unconsciously through his old lips. The cat purred on the windlass. Then James Wait had a fit of roaring, rattling cough, that shook him, tossed him like a hurricane, and flung him panting with staring eyes headlong on his sea-chest. Several men woke up. One said sleepily out of his bunk: " 'Struth! what a blamed row!"—"I have a cold on my chest," gasped Wait.—"Cold! you call it," grumbled the man; "should think 'twas something more. . . ."—"Oh! you think so," said the nigger, upright and loftily scornful again. He climbed into his berth and began coughing persistently, while he put his head out to glare all round the forecastle. There was no further protest. He fell back on the pillow, and could be heard there wheezing regularly like a man oppressed in his sleep.

Singleton stood at the door with his face to the light and his back to the darkness. And, alone in the dim emptiness of the sleeping forecastle he appeared bigger, colossal, very old; old as Father time himself, who should have come there into this place as quiet as a sepulchre to contemplate with patient eyes the short victory of sleep, the consoler. Yet he was only a child of time, a lonely relic of a devoured and forgotten generation. He stood, still strong, as ever unthinking; a ready man with a vast empty past and with no future, with his childlike impulses and his man's passions already dead within his tattooed breast. The men who could understand his silence were gone—those men who knew how to exist beyond the pale of life and within sight of eternity. They had been strong, as those are strong who know neither doubts nor hopes. They had been impatient and enduring, turbulent and devoted, unruly and faithful. Well-meaning people had tried to represent those men as whining over every mouthful of their food; as going about their work in fear of their lives. But in truth they had been men who knew toil, privation, violence, debauchery—but knew not fear, and had no desire of spite in their hearts. Men hard to manage, but easy to inspire; voiceless men—but men enough to scorn in their hearts the sentimental voices that bewailed the hardness of their fate. It was a fate unique and their own; the capacity to bear it appeared to them the privilege of the chosen! Their generation lived inarticulate and indispensable, without knowing the sweetness of affections or the refuge of a home—and died free from the dark menace of a narrow grave. They were the everlasting children of the mysterious sea. Their successors are the grown-up children of a discontented earth. They are less naughty, but less innocent; less profane, but perhaps also less believing; and if they had learned how to speak they have also learned how to whine. But the others were strong and mute; they were effaced, bowed and enduring, like stone caryatides that hold up in the night the lighted halls of a resplendent and glorious edifice. They are gone now—and it does not matter. The sea and the earth are unfaithful to their children: a truth, a faith, a generation of men goes—and is forgotten, and it does not matter! Except, perhaps, to the few of those who believed the truth, confessed the faith—or loved the men.

A breeze was coming. The ship that had been lying tide-rode swung to a heavier puff; and suddenly the slack of the chain-cable between the windlass and the hawse-pipe clinked, slipped forward an inch, and rose gently off the deck with a startling suggestion as of unsuspected life that had been lurking stealthily in the iron. In the hawse-pipe the grinding links sent through the ship a sound like a low groan of a man sighing under a burden. The strain came on the windlass, the chain tautened like a string, vibrated—and the handle of the screw-brake moved in slight jerks. Singleton stepped forward.

Till then he had been standing meditative and unthinking, reposeful and hopeless, with a face grim and blank—a sixty-year-old child of the mysterious sea. The thoughts of all his lifetime could have been expressed in six words, but the stir of those things that were as much part of his existence as his beating heart called up a gleam of alert understanding upon the sternness of his aged face. The flame of the lamp swayed, and the old man, with knitted and bushy eyebrows, stood over the brake, watchful and motionless in the wild saraband of dancing shadows. Then the ship, obedient to the call of her anchor, forged ahead slightly and eased the strain. The cable, relieved, hung down, and after swaying imperceptibly to and fro dropped with a loud tap on the hard wood planks. Singleton seized the high lever, and, by a violent throw forward of his body, wrung out another half-turn from the brake. He recovered himself, breathed largely, and remained for a while glaring down at the powerful and compact engine that squatted on the deck at his feet like some quiet monster—a creature amazing and tame.

"You . . . hold!" he growled at it masterfully, in the incult tangle of his white beard.

Chapter Two

Next morning, at daylight, the *Narcissus* went to sea.

A slight haze blurred the horizon. Outside the harbour the measureless expanse of smooth water lay sparkling like a floor of jewels, and as empty as the sky. The short black tug gave a pluck to windward, in the usual way, then let go the rope, and hovered for a moment on the quarter with her engines stopped; while the slim, long hull of the ship moved ahead slowly under lower topsails. The loose upper canvas blew out in the breeze with soft round contours, resembling small white clouds snared in the maze of ropes. Then the sheets were hauled home, the yards hoisted, and the ship became a high and lonely pyramid, gliding, all shining and white, through the sunlit mist. The tug turned short round and went away towards the land. Twenty-six pairs of eyes watched her low broad stern crawling languidly over the smooth swell between the two paddle-wheels that turned fast, beating the water with fierce hurry. She resembled an enormous and aquatic black beetle, surprised by the light, overwhelmed by the sunshine, trying to escape with ineffectual effort into the distant gloom of the land. She left a lingering smudge of smoke on the sky, and two vanishing trails of foam on the water. On the place where she had stopped a round patch of soot remained, undulating on the swell—an unclean mark of the creature's rest.

The *Narcissus* left alone, heading south, seemed to stand resplendent and still upon the restless sea, under the moving sun. Flakes of foam swept past her sides; the water struck her with flashing blows; the land glided away, slowly fading; a few birds screamed on motionless wings over the swaying mastheads. But soon the land disappeared, the birds went away; and to the west the pointed sail of an Arab dhow[1] running for Bombay, rose triangular and upright above the sharp edge of the horizon, lingered and vanished like an illusion. Then the ship's wake, long and straight, stretched itself out through a day of immense solitude. The setting sun, burning on the level of the water, flamed crimson below the blackness of heavy rain clouds. The sunset squall, coming up from behind, dissolved itself into the short deluge of a hissing shower. It left the ship glistening from trucks to water-line, and with darkened sails. She ran easily before a fair monsoon,[2] with her decks cleared for the night; and, moving along with her, was heard the sustained and monotonous swishing of the waves, mingled with the low whispers of men mustered aft for the setting of watches; the short plaint of some block aloft; or, now and then, a loud sigh of wind.

Mr. Baker, coming out of his cabin, called out the first name sharply before closing the door behind him. He was going to take charge of the deck. On the homeward passage, according to an old custom of the sea, the chief officer takes the first night-watch— from eight till midnight. So, Mr. Baker, after he had heard the last "Yes, sir!" said moodily, "Relieve the wheel and look-out"; and climbed with heavy feet the poop ladder to windward. Soon after Mr. Creighton came down, whistling softly, and went into the cabin. On the doorstep the steward lounged, in slippers, meditative, and with his shirt-sleeves rolled up to the armpits. On the main deck the cook, locking up the galley doors, had an altercation with young Charley about a pair of socks. He could be heard saying impressively, in the darkness amidships: "You don't deserve a kindness. I've been drying them for you, and now you complain about the holes—and you swear, too! Right in front of me! If I hadn't been a Christian—which you ain't, you young ruffian—I would give you a clout on the head. . . . Go away!" Men in couples or threes stood pensive or moved silently along the bulwarks in the waist. The first busy day of a homeward passage was sinking into the peace of resumed routine. Aft, on the high poop, Mr. Baker walked shuffling and grunted to himself in the pauses of his thoughts. Forward, the look-out man, erect between the flukes of the two anchors, hummed an endless tune, keeping his eyes fixed dutifully ahead in a vacant stare. A multitude of stars coming out into the clear night peopled the emptiness of the sky. They glittered, as if alive above the sea; they surrounded the running ship on all sides; more intense than the eyes of a staring crowd, and as inscrutable as the souls of men.

1. Coastal sailing vessel, with two or three triangular sails, about 85 feet long.
2. The seasonal wind of the Indian Ocean and southern Asia, blowing from the southwest in summer and from the northeast in winter.

The passage had begun, and the ship, a fragment detached from the earth, went on lonely and swift like a small planet. Round her the abysses of sky and sea met in an unattainable frontier. A great circular solitude moved with her, ever changing and ever the same, always monotonous and always imposing. Now and then another wandering white speck, burdened with life, appeared far off—disappeared; intent on its own destiny. The sun looked upon her all day, and every morning rose with a burning, round stare of undying curiosity. She had her own future; she was alive with the lives of those beings who trod her decks; like that earth which had given her up to the sea, she had an intolerable load of regrets and hopes. On her lived timid truth and audacious lies; and, like the earth, she was unconscious, fair to see—and condemned by men to an ignoble fate. The august loneliness of her path lent dignity to the sordid inspiration of her pilgrimage. She drove foaming to the southward, as if guided by the courage of a high endeavour. The smiling greatness of the sea dwarfed the extent of time. The days raced after one another, brilliant and quick like the flashes of a lighthouse, and the nights, uneventful and short, resembled fleeting dreams.

The men had shaken into their places, and the half-hourly voice of the bells ruled their life of unceasing care. Night and day the head and shoulders of a seaman could be seen aft by the wheel, outlined high against sunshine or starlight, very steady above the stir of revolving spokes. The faces changed, passing in rotation. Youthful faces, bearded faces, dark faces: faces serene, or faces moody, but all akin with the brotherhood of the sea; all with the same attentive expression of eyes, carefully watching the compass or the sails. Captain Allistoun, serious, and with an old red muffler round his throat, all day long pervaded the poop. At night, many times he rose out of the darkness of the companion, such as a phantom above a grave, and stood watchful and mute under the stars, his night-shirt fluttering like a flag—then, without a sound, sank down again. He was born on the shores of the Pentland Firth.[3] In his youth he attained the rank of harpooner in Peterhead whalers. When he spoke of that time his restless grey eyes became still and cold, like the loom of ice. Afterwards he went into the East Indian trade[4] for the sake of change. He had commanded the *Narcissus*

3. A channel northeast of Scotland, separating the Orkney Islands from the mainland. Regarding Allistoun's credentials as a seaman, C. F. Burgess (*The Fellowship of the Craft*, New York, 1976, pp. 112–13) writes that the Firth, where the North Sea and the Atlantic come into confluence, creates "perhaps the roughest and most treacherous waters for small boats to be found anywhere in the world. With the Firth as his 'nursery of the craft,' Allistoun was well equipped for anything the sea might have to offer him. . . . But the Firth was only the beginning of Allistoun's training for the sea. . . . Advanced training came in the Peterhead whalers, where Conrad reports, Allistoun attained the rank of harpooner, no modest feat for a relatively young man."

4. Trade with India through the English East India Company began in 1600. The Company itself was dissolved in 1873.

since she was built. He loved his ship, and drove her unmercifully; for his secret ambition was to make her accomplish some day a brilliantly quick passage which would be mentioned in nautical papers. He pronounced his owner's name with a sardonic smile, spoke but seldom to his officers, and reproved errors in a gentle voice, with words that cut to the quick. His hair was iron-grey, his face hard and of the colour of pump-leather. He shaved every morning of his life—at six—but once (being caught in a fierce hurricane eighty miles south-west of Mauritius)[5] he had missed three consecutive days. He feared naught but an unforgiving God, and wished to end his days in a little house, with a plot of ground attached—far in the country—out of sight of the sea.

He, the ruler of that minute world, seldom descended from the Olympian heights of his poop. Below him—at his feet, so to speak —common mortals led their busy and insignificant lives. Along the main deck, Mr. Baker grunted in a manner bloodthirsty and innocuous; and kept all our noses to the grindstone, being—as he once remarked—paid for doing that very thing. The men working about the deck were healthy and contented—as most seamen are, when once well out to sea. The true peace of God begins at any spot a thousand miles from the nearest land; and when He sends there the messengers of His might it is not in terrible wrath against crime, presumption, and folly, but paternally, to chasten simple hearts—ignorant hearts that know nothing of life, and beat undisturbed by envy or greed.

In the evening the cleared decks had a reposeful aspect, resembling the autumn of the earth. The sun was sinking to rest, wrapped in a mantle of warm clouds. Forward, on the end of the spare spars, the boatswain and the carpenter sat together with crossed arms; two men friendly, powerful, and deep-chested. Beside them the short, dumpy sailmaker—who had been in the Navy—related, between the whiffs of his pipe, impossible stories about Admirals. Couples tramped backwards and forwards, keeping step and balance without effort, in a confined space. Pigs grunted in the big pigsty. Belfast, leaning thoughtfully on his elbow, above the bars, communed with them through the silence of his meditation. Fellows with shirts open wide on sunburnt breasts sat upon the mooring bits, and all up the steps of the forecastle ladders. By the foremast a few discussed in a circle the characteristics of a gentleman. One said—"It's money as does it." Another maintained:—"No, it's the way they speak." Lame Knowles stumped up with an unwashed face (he had the distinction of being the dirty man of the forecastle), and, showing a few yellow fangs in a shrewd smile,

5. An island in the Indian Ocean, east of Madagascar.

explained craftily that he "had seen some of their pants." The back-sides of them—he had observed—were thinner than paper from constant sitting down in offices, yet otherwise they looked first-rate and would last for years. It was all appearance. "It was," he said, "bloomin' easy to be a gentleman when you had a clean job for life." They disputed endlessly, obstinate and childish; they repeated in shouts and with inflamed faces their amazing arguments; while the soft breeze, eddying down the enormous cavity of the foresail, distended above their bare heads, stirred the tumbled hair with a touch passing and light like an indulgent caress.

They were forgetting their toil, they were forgetting themselves. The cook approached to hear, and stood by, beaming with the inward consciousness of his faith, like a conceited saint unable to forget his glorious reward; Donkin, solitary and brooding over his wrongs on the forecastle-head, moved closer to catch the drift of the discussion below him; he turned his sallow face to the sea, and his thin nostrils moved, sniffing the breeze, as he lounged negligently by the rail. In the glow of sunset faces shone with interest, teeth flashed, eyes sparkled. The walking couples stood still suddenly, with broad grins; a man, bending over a wash-tub, sat up, entranced, with the soapsuds flecking his wet arms. Even the three petty officers listened leaning back, comfortably propped, and with superior smiles. Belfast left off scratching the ear of his favourite pig, and, open mouthed, tried with eager eyes to have his say. He lifted his arms, grimacing and baffled. From a distance Charley screamed at the ring:—"I know about gentlemen morn'n any of you. I've been intermit' with 'em. . . . I've blacked their boots." The cook, craning his neck to hear better, was scandalised. "Keep your mouth shut when your elders speak, you impudent young heathen—you." "All right, old Hallelujah, I'm done," answered Charley soothingly. At some opinion of dirty Knowles, delivered with an air of supernatural cunning, a ripple of laughter ran along, rose like a wave, burst with a startling roar. They stamped with both feet; they turned their shouting faces to the sky; many, spluttering, slapped their thighs; while one or two, bent double, gasped, hugging themselves with both arms like men in pain. The carpenter and the boatswain, without changing their attitude, shook with laughter where they sat; the sailmaker, charged with an anec-dote about a Commodore, looked sulky; the cook was wiping his eyes with a greasy rag; and lame Knowles, astonished at his own success, stood in their midst showing a slow smile.

Suddenly the face of Donkin leaning high-shouldered over the after-rail became grave. Something like a weak rattle was heard through the forecastle door. It became a murmur; it ended in a sighing groan. The washerman plunged both his arms into the tub abruptly; the cook became more crestfallen than an exposed back-slider; the boatswain moved his shoulders uneasily; the carpenter got up with a spring and walked away—while the sailmaker seemed mentally to give his story up, and began to puff at his pipe with sombre determination. In the blackness of the doorway a pair of eyes glimmered white, and big, and staring. Then James Wait's head protruding, became visible, as if suspended between the two hands that grasped a doorpost on each side of the face. The tassel of his blue woollen nightcap, cocked forward, danced gaily over his left eyelid. He stepped out in a tottering stride. He looked powerful as ever, but showed a strange and affected unsteadiness in his gait; his face was perhaps a trifle thinner, and his eyes appeared rather startlingly prominent. He seemed to hasten the retreat of departing light by his very presence; the setting sun dipped sharply, as though fleeing before our nigger; a black mist emanated from him; a subtle and dismal influence; a something cold and gloomy that floated out and settled on all the faces like a mourning veil. The circle broke up. The joy of laughter died on stiffened lips. There was not a smile left among all the ship's company. Not a word was spoken. Many turned their backs, trying to look unconcerned; others, with averted heads, sent half-reluctant glances out of the corners of their eyes. They resembled criminals conscious of misdeeds more than honest men distracted by doubt; only two or three stared frankly, but stupidly, with lips slightly open. All expected James Wait to say something, and, at the same time, had the air of knowing beforehand what he would say. He leaned his back against the doorpost, and with heavy eyes swept over them a glance domineering and pained, like a sick tyrant overawing a crowd of abject but untrustworthy slaves.

No one went away. They waited in fascinated dread. He said ironically, with gasps between the words:

"Thank you . . . chaps. You . . . are nice . . . and . . . quiet . . . you are! Yelling so . . . before . . . the door. . . ."

He made a longer pause, during which he worked his ribs in an exaggerated labour of breathing. It was intolerable. Feet were shuffled. Belfast let out a groan; but Donkin above blinked his red eyelids with invisible eyelashes, and smiled bitterly over the nigger's head.

The nigger went on again with surprising ease. He gasped no more, and his voice rang, hollow and loud, as though he had been talking in an empty cavern. He was contemptuously angry.

"I tried to get a wink of sleep. You know I can't sleep o' nights. And you come jabbering near the door here like a blooming lot of old women. . . . You think yourselves good shipmates. Do you? . . . Much you care for a dying man!"

Belfast spun away from the pigsty. "Jimmy," he cried tremulously, "if you hadn't been sick I would——"

He stopped. The nigger waited awhile, then said, in a gloomy tone:—"You would. . . . What? Go. an' fight another such one as yourself. Leave me alone. It won't be for long. I'll soon die. . . . It's coming right enough!"

Men stood around very still and with exasperated eyes. It was just what they had expected, and hated to hear, that idea of a stalking death, thrust at them many times a day like a boast and like a menace by this obnoxious nigger. He seemed to take a pride in that death which, so far, had attended only upon the ease of his life; he was overbearing about it, as if no one else in the world had ever been intimate with such a companion; he paraded it unceasingly before us with an affectionate persistence that made its presence indubitable, and at the same time incredible. No man could be suspected of such monstrous friendship! Was he a reality—or was he a sham—this ever-expected visitor of Jimmy's? We hesitated between pity and mistrust, while, on the slightest provocation, he shook before our eyes the bones of his bothersome and infamous skeleton. He was for ever trotting him out. He would talk of that coming death as though it had been already there, as if it had been walking the deck outside, as if it would presently come in to sleep in the only empty bunk; as if it had sat by his side at every meal. It interfered daily with our occupations, with our leisure, with our amusements. We had no songs and no music in the evening, because Jimmy (we all lovingly called him Jimmy, to conceal our hate of his accomplice) had managed, with that prospective decease of his, to disturb even Archie's mental balance. Archie was the owner of the concertina; but after a couple of stinging lectures from Jimmy he refused to play any more. He said:—"Yon's an uncanny joker. I dinna ken what's wrang wi' him, but there's something verra wrang, verra wrang. It's nae manner of use asking me. I won't play." Our singers became mute because Jimmy was a dying man. For the same reason no chap—as Knowles remarked—could "drive in a nail to hang his few poor rags upon," without being made aware of the enormity he committed in disturbing Jimmy's interminable last moments. At night, instead of the cheerful yell, "One bell! Turn out! Do you hear there? Hey! hey! hey! Show leg!" the watches were called man by man, in whispers, so as not to interfere with Jimmy's, possibly, last slumber on earth. True, he was always awake, and managed, as we sneaked out on deck, to plant in our backs some cutting remark that, for the moment, made us feel as if we had been brutes, and afterwards made us suspect ourselves of being fools. We spoke in low tones within that fo'c'sle as though it had been a church. We ate our meals in silence and dread, for

Jimmy was capricious with his food, and railed bitterly at the salt meat, at the biscuits, at the tea, as at articles unfit for human consumption—"let alone for a dying man!" He would say:—"Can't you find a better slice of meat for a sick man who's trying to get home to be cured—or buried? But there! If I had a chance, you fellows would do away with it. You would poison me. Look at what you have given me!" We served him in his bed with rage and humility, as though we had been the base courtiers of a hated prince; and he rewarded us by his unconciliating criticism. He had found the secret of keeping for ever on the run the fundamental imbecility of mankind; he had the secret of life, that confounded dying man, and he made himself master of every moment of our existence. We grew desperate, and remained submissive. Emotional little Belfast was for ever on the verge of assault or on the verge of tears. One evening he confided to Archie:—"For a ha'penny I would knock his ugly black head off—the skulking dodger!" And the straightforward Archie pretended to be shocked! Such was the infernal spell which that casual St. Kitt's[6] nigger had cast upon our guileless manhood! But the same night Belfast stole from the galley the officers' Sunday fruit pie, to tempt the fastidious appetite of Jimmy. He endangered not only his long friendship with the cook but also—as it appeared—his eternal welfare. The cook was overwhelmed with grief; he did not know the culprit, but he knew that wickedness flourished; he knew that Satan was abroad amongst those men, whom he looked upon as in some way under his spiritual care. Whenever he saw three or four of us standing together he would leave his stove, to run out and preach. We fled from him; and only Charley (who knew the thief) affronted the cook with a candid gaze which irritated the good man. "It's you, I believe," he groaned, sorrowful and with a patch of soot on his chin. "It's you. You are a brand for the burning! No more of YOUR socks in my galley." Soon, unofficially, the information was spread about that, should there be another case of stealing, our marmalade (an extra allowance: half a pound per man) would be stopped. Mr. Baker ceased to heap jocular abuse upon his favourites, and grunted suspiciously at all. The captain's cold eyes, high up on the poop, glittered mistrustful, as he surveyed us trooping in a small mob from halyards to braces for the usual evening pull at all the ropes. Such stealing in a merchant ship is difficult to check, and may be taken as a declaration by men of their dislike for their officers. It is a bad symptom. It may end in God knows what trouble. The *Narcissus* was still a peaceful ship, but mutual confidence was shaken. Donkin did not conceal his delight. We were dismayed.

Then illogical Belfast reproached our nigger with great fury.

6. A group of islands in the Barbadian West Indies.

James Wait, with his elbow on the pillow, choked, gasped out:—
"Did I ask you to bone the dratted thing? Blow your blamed pie. It
has made me worse—you little Irish lunatic, you!" Belfast, with
scarlet face and trembling lips, made a dash at him. Every man in the
forecastle rose with a shout. There was a moment of wild tumult.
Some one shrieked piercingly:—"Easy, Belfast! Easy! . . ." We
expected Belfast to strangle Wait without more ado. Dust flew. We
heard through it the nigger's cough, metallic and explosive like a
gong. Next moment we saw Belfast hanging over him. He was
saying plaintively:—"Don't! Don't, Jimmy! Don't be like that. An
angel couldn't put up with ye—sick as ye are." He looked round at
us from Jimmy's bedside, his comical mouth twitching, and through
tearful eyes; then he tried to put straight the disarranged blankets.
The unceasing whisper of the sea filled the forecastle. Was James
Wait frightened, or touched, or repentant? He lay on his back with
a hand to his side, and as motionless as if his expected visitor had
come at last. Belfast fumbled about his feet, repeating with emotion:—"Yes. We know. Ye are bad, but . . . Just say what ye want
done, and . . . We all know ye are bad—very bad. . . ." No! Decidedly James Wait was not touched or repentant. Truth to say, he
seemed rather startled. He sat up with incredible suddenness and ease.
"Ah! You think I am bad, do you?" he said gloomily, in his clearest baritone voice (to hear him speak sometimes you would never
think there was anything wrong with that man). "Do you? . . .
Well, act according! Some of you haven't sense enough to put a
blanket shipshape over a sick man. There! Leave it alone! I can die
anyhow!" Belfast turned away limping with a gesture of discourage-
ment. In the silence of the forecastle, full of interested men,
Donkin pronounced distinctly:—"Well, I'm blowed!" and snig-
gered. Wait looked at him. He looked at him in a quite friendly
manner. Nobody could tell what would please our incomprehensible invalid: but for us the scorn of that snigger was hard to bear.

Donkin's position in the forecastle was distinguished but
unsafe. He stood on the bad eminence of a general dislike. He was
left alone; and in his isolation he could do nothing but think of the
gales of the Cape of Good Hope[7] and envy us the possession of
warm clothing and waterproofs. Our sea-boots, our oilskin coats, our
well-filled sea-chests, were to him so many causes for bitter meditation; he had none of those things, and he felt instinctively that no
man, when the need arose, would offer to share them with him.
He was impudently cringing to us and systematically insolent to the
officers. He anticipated the best results, for himself, from such a
line of conduct—and was mistaken. Such natures forget that under
extreme provocation men will be just—whether they want to be so

7. The sea passage around the southernmost extremity of South Africa.

or not. Donkin's insolence to long-suffering Mr. Baker became at last intolerable to us, and we rejoiced when the mate, one dark night, tamed him for good. It was done neatly, with great decency and decorum, and with little noise. We had been called—just before midnight—to trim the yards, and Donkin—as usual—made insulting remarks. We stood sleepily in a row with the forebrace in our hands waiting for the next order, and heard in the darkness a scuffly trampling of feet, an exclamation of surprise, sounds of cuffs and slaps, suppressed, hissing whispers;—"Ah! Will you!" . . . "Don't! . . . Don't!" . . . "Then behave." . . . "Oh! Oh! . . ." Afterwards there were soft thuds mixed with the rattle of iron things as if a man's body had been tumbling helplessly amongst the main-pump rods. Before we could realise the situation, Mr. Baker's voice was heard very near and a little impatient;—"Haul away, men! Lay back on that rope!" And we did lay back on the rope with great alacrity. As if nothing had happened, the chief mate went on trimming the yards with his usual and exasperating fastidi-ousness. We didn't at the time see anything of Donkin, and did not care. Had the chief officer thrown him overboard, no man would have said as much as "Hallo! he's gone!" But, in truth, no great harm was done—even if Donkin did lose one of his front teeth. We preceived this in the morning, and preserved a ceremoni-ous silence: the etiquette of the forecastle commanded us to be blind and dumb in such a case, and we cherished the decencies of our life more than ordinary landsmen respect theirs. Charley, with unpardonable want of *savoir vivre*,[8] yelled out:—" 'Ave you been to your dentyst? . . . Hurt ye, didn't it?" He got a box on the ear from one of his best friends. The boy was surprised, and remained plunged in grief for at least three hours. We were sorry for him, but youth requires even more discipline than age. Donkin grinned ven-omously. From that day he became pitiless; told Jimmy that he was a "black fraud"; hinted to us that we were an imbecile lot, daily taken in by a vulgar nigger. And Jimmy seemed to like the fellow!

Singleton lived untouched by human emotions. Taciturn and unsmiling, he breathed amongst us—in that alone resembling the rest of the crowd. We were trying to be decent chaps, and found it jolly difficult; we oscillated between the desire of virtue and the fear of ridicule; we wished to save ourselves from the pain of remorse, but did not want to be made the contemptible dupes of our senti-ment. Jimmy's hateful accomplice seemed to have blown with his impure breath undreamt-of subtleties into our hearts. We were dis turbed and cowardly. That we knew. Singleton seemed to know nothing, understand nothing. We had thought him till then as wise as he looked, but now we dared, at times, suspect him of being

8. French for knowing the ways of the world and of polite society.

stupid—from old age. One day, however, at dinner, as we sat on our boxes round a tin dish that stood on the deck within the circle of our feet, Jimmy expressed his general disgust with men and things in words that were particularly disgusting. Singleton lifted his head. We became mute. The old man, addressing Jimmy, asked:— "Are you dying?" Thus interrogated, James Wait appeared horribly startled and confused. We all were startled. Mouths remained open; hearts thumped; eyes blinked; a dropped tin fork rattled in a dish; a man rose as if to go out, and stood still. In less than a minute Jimmy pulled himself together:—"Why? Can't you see I am?" he answered shakily. Singleton lifted a piece of soaked biscuit ("his teeth"—he declared—"had no edge on them now") to his lips.— "Well, get on with your dying," he said, with venerable mildness; "don't raise a blamed fuss with us over that job. We can't help you." Jimmy fell back in his bunk, and for a long time lay very still, wiping the perspiration off his chin. The dinner-tins were put away quickly. On deck we discussed the incident in whispers. Some showed a chuckling exultation. Many looked grave. Wamibo, after long periods of staring dreaminess, attempted abortive smiles; and one of the young Scandinavians, much tormented by doubt, ventured in the second dog-watch to approach Singleton (the old man did not encourage us much to speak to him) and ask sheepishly:— "You think he will die?" Singleton looked up.—"Why, of course he will die," he said deliberately. This seemed decisive. It was promptly imparted to every one by him who had consulted the oracle. Shy and eager, he would step up and with averted gaze recite his formula:—"Old Singleton says he will die." It was a relief! At last we knew that our compassion would not be misplaced, and we could again smile without misgivings—but we reckoned without Donkin. Donkin "didn't want to 'ave no truck with 'em dirty furriers." When Nilsen came to him with the news: "Singleton says he will die," he answered him by a spiteful "And so will you—you fat-headed Dutchman. Wish you Dutchmen were all dead—'stead comin' takin' our money inter your starvin' country." We were appalled. We perceived that after all Singleton's answer meant nothing. We began to hate him for making fun of us. All our certitudes were going; we were on doubtful terms with our officers; the cook had given us up for lost; we had overheard the boatswain's opinion that "we were a crowd of softies." We suspected Jimmy, one another, and even our very selves. We did not know what to do. At every insignificant turn of our humble life we met Jimmy overbearing and blocking the way, arm-in-arm with his awful and veiled familiar. It was a weird servitude.

It began a week after leaving Bombay and came on us stealthily like any other great misfortune. Every one had remarked that

Jimmy from the first was very slack at his work; but we thought it simply the outcome of his philosophy of life. Donkin said:—"You put no more weight on a rope than a bloody sparrer."[9] He disdained him. Belfast, ready for a fight, exclaimed provokingly:— "You don't kill yourself, old man!"—"Would you?" he retorted, with extreme scorn—and Belfast retired. One morning, as we were washing decks, Mr. Baker called to him:—"Bring your broom over here, Wait." He strolled languidly. "Move yourself! Ough!" grunted Mr. Baker; "what's the matter with your hind legs?" He stopped dead short. He gazed slowly with eyes that bulged out with an expression audacious and sad.—"It isn't my legs," he said, "it's my lungs." Everybody listened.—"What's . . . Ough! . . . What's wrong with them?" inquired Mr. Baker. All the watch stood around on the wet deck, grinning, and with brooms or buckets in their hands. He said mournfully:—"Going—or gone. Can't you see I'm a dying man? I know it!" Mr. Baker was disgusted.—"Then why the devil did you ship aboard here?"—"I must live till I die—mustn't I?" he replied. The grins became audible. "Go off the deck—get out of my sight," said Mr. Baker. He was nonplussed. It was a unique experience. James Wait, obedient, dropped his broom, and walked slowly forward. A burst of laughter followed him. It was too funny. All hands laughed. . . . They laughed! . . . Alas!

He became the tormentor of all our moments; he was worse than a nightmare. You couldn't see that there was anything wrong with him: a nigger does not show. He was not very fat—certainly—but then he was no leaner than other niggers we had known. He coughed often, but the most prejudiced person could perceive that, mostly, he coughed when it suited his purpose. He wouldn't, or couldn't, do his work—and he wouldn't lie-up. One day he would skip aloft with the best of them, and next time we would be obliged to risk our lives to get his limp body down. He was reported, he was examined; he was remonstrated with, threatened, cajoled, lectured. He was called into the cabin to interview the captain. There were wild rumours. It was said he had cheeked the old man; it was said he had frightened him. Charley maintained that the "skipper, weepin', 'as giv' 'im 'is blessin' an' a pot of jam." Knowles had it from the steward that the unspeakable Jimmy had been reeling against the cabin furniture; that he had groaned; that he had complained of general brutality and disbelief; and had ended by coughing all over the old man's meteorological journals which were then spread on the table. At any rate, Wait returned forward supported by the steward, who, in a pained and shocked voice, entreated us:—"Here! Catch hold of him, one of you. He is to lie-up." Jimmy drank a tin mugful of coffee, and, after bullying first one and then another, went to bed.

9. Sparrow.

He remained there most of the time, but when it suited him would come on deck and appear amongst us. He was scornful and brooding; he looked ahead upon the sea, and no one could tell what was the meaning of that black man sitting apart in a meditative attitude and as motionless as a carving.

He refused steadily all medicine; he threw sago[1] and cornflour overboard till the steward got tired of bringing it to him. He asked for paregoric. They sent him a big bottle; enough to poison a wilderness of babies. He kept it between his· mattress and the deal lining of the ship's side; and nobody ever saw him take a dose. Donkin abused him to his face, jeered at him while he gasped; and the same day Wait would lend him a warm jersey. Once Donkin reviled him for half an hour; reproached him with the extra work his malingering gave to the watch; and ended by calling him "a black-faced swine." Under the spell of our accursed perversity we were horror-struck. But Jimmy positively seemed to revel in that abuse. It made him look cheerful—and Donkin had a pair of old sea boots thrown at him. "Here, you East-end[2] trash," boomed Wait, "you may have that."

At last Mr. Baker had to tell the captain that James Wait was disturbing the peace of the ship. "Knock discipline on the head—he will, Ough," grunted Mr. Baker. As a matter of fact, the starboard watch came as near as possible to refusing duty, when ordered one morning by the boatswain to wash out their forecastle. It appears Jimmy objected to a wet floor—and that morning we were in a compassionate mood. We thought the boatswain a brute, and, practically, told him so. Only Mr. Baker's delicate tact prevented an all-fired row; he refused to take us seriously. He came bustling forward, and called us many unpolite names, but in such a, hearty and seamanlike manner that we began to feel ashamed of ourselves. In truth, we thought him much too good a sailor to annoy him willingly: and after all Jimmy might have been a fraud —probably was! The forecastle got a clean up that morning; but in the afternoon a sick-bay was fitted up in the deck-house. It was a nice little cabin opening on deck, and with two berths. Jimmy's belongings were transported there, and then—notwithstanding his protests—Jimmy himself. He said he couldn't walk. Four men carried him on a blanket. He complained that he would have to die there alone, like a dog. We grieved for him, and were delighted to have him removed from the forecastle. We attended him as before.

1. A starchy foodstuff, like corn flour, used in the making of puddings. Paregoric is a medicine derived from opium, used largely to relieve pain and curb diarrhea.

2. The eastern section of London; primarily a region of poor streets, inhabited largely by a "marine" population whose life and activity centers in the Docks.

The galley was next door, and the cook looked in many times a day. Wait became a little more cheerful. Knowles affirmed having heard him laugh to himself in peals one day. Others had seen him walking about on deck at night. His little place, with the door ajar on a long hook, was always full of tobacco smoke. We spoke through the crack cheerfully, sometimes abusively, as we passed by, intent on our work. He fascinated us. He would never let doubt die. He overshadowed the ship. Invulnerable in his promise of speedy corruption he trampled on our self-respect; he demonstrated to us daily our want of moral courage; he tainted our lives. Had we been a miserable gang of wretched immortals, unhallowed alike by hope and fear, he could not have lorded it over us with a more pitiless assertion of his sublime privilege.

Chapter Three

Meantime the *Narcissus*, with square yards, ran out of the fair monsoon. She drifted slowly, swinging round and round the compass, through a few days of baffling light airs. Under the patter of short warm showers, grumbling men whirled the heavy yards from side to side; they caught hold of the soaked ropes with groans and sighs, while their officers, sulky and dripping with rain water, unceasingly ordered them about in wearied voices. During the short respites they looked with disgust into the smarting palms of their stiff hands, and asked one another bitterly:—"Who would be a sailor if he could be a farmer?" All the tempers were spoilt, and no man cared what he said. One black night, when the watch, panting in the heat and half-drowned with the rain, had been through four mortal hours hunted from brace to brace, Belfast declared that he would "chuck the sea for ever and go in a steamer." This was excessive, no doubt. Captain Allistoun, with great self-control, would mutter sadly to Mr. Baker:—"It is not so bad—not so bad," when he had managed to shove, and dodge, and manoeuvre his smart ship through sixty miles in twenty-four hours. From the doorstep of the little cabin, Jimmy, chin in hand, watched our distasteful labours with insolent and melancholy eyes. We spoke to him gently—and out of his sight exchanged sour smiles.

Then, again, with a fair wind and under a clear sky, the ship went on piling up the South Latitude.[1] She passed outside Madagascar[2] and Mauritius without a glimpse of the land. Extra lashings were put on the spare spars. Hatches were looked to. The steward in his leisure moments and with a worried air tried to fit

1. Southern hemisphere, between the South Pole and the equator.

2. An island in the Indian Ocean off the southeastern coast of Africa.

washboards to the cabin doors. Stout canvas was bent with care. Anxious eyes looked to the westward, towards the cape of storms.[3] The ship began to dip into a south-west swell, and the softly luminous sky of low latitudes took on a harder sheen from day to day above our heads: it arched high above the ship, vibrating and pale, like an immense dome of steel, resonant with the deep voice of freshening gales. The sunshine gleamed cold on the white curls of black waves. Before the strong breath of westerly squalls the ship, with reduced sail, lay slowly over, obstinate and yielding. She drove to and fro in the unceasing endeavour to fight her way through the invisible violence of the winds: she pitched headlong into dark smooth hollows; she struggled upwards over the snowy ridges of great running seas; she rolled restless, from side to side, like a thing in pain. Enduring and valiant, she answered to the call of men; and her slim spars waving for ever in abrupt semicircles, seemed to beckon in vain for help towards the stormy sky.

It was a bad winter off the Cape that year. The relieved helmsmen came off flapping their arms, or ran stamping hard and blowing into swollen, red fingers. The watch on deck dodged the sting of cold sprays or, crouching in sheltered corners, watched dismally the high and merciless seas boarding the ship time after time in unappeasable fury. Water tumbled in cataracts over the forecastle doors. You had to dash through a waterfall to get into your damp bed. The men turned in wet and turned out stiff to face the redeeming ruthless exactions of their glorious and obscure fate. Far aft, and peering watchfully to windward, the officers could be seen through the mist of squalls. They stood by the weather-rail, holding on grimly, straight and glistening in their long coats; and in the disordered plunges of the hard-driven ship, they appeared high up, attentive, tossing violently above the grey line of a clouded horizon in motionless attitudes.

They watched the weather and the ship as men on shore watch the momentous chances of fortune. Captain Allistoun never left the deck, as though he had been part of the ship's fittings. Now and then the steward, shivering, but always in shirt sleeves, would struggle towards him with some hot coffee, half of which the gale blew out of the cup before it reached the master's lips. He drank what was left gravely in one long gulp, while heavy sprays pattered loudly on his oilskin coat, the seas swishing broke about his high boots; and he never took his eyes off the ship. He kept his gaze riveted upon her as a loving man watches the unselfish toil of a delicate woman upon the slender thread of whose existence is hung the

3. Name given to the Cape of Good Hope by its discoverer, the Portugese navigator Bartholomeu Dias, in 1486. Later called the Cape of Good Hope because of its commercial importance as the new route to the East.

whole meaning and joy of the world. We all watched her. She was beautiful and had a weakness. We loved her no less for that. We admired her qualities aloud, we boasted of them to one another, as though they had been our own, and the consciousness of her only fault we kept buried in the silence of our profound affection. She was born in the thundering peal of hammers beating upon iron, in black eddies of smoke, under a grey sky, on the banks of the Clyde.[4] The clamorous and sombre stream gives birth to things of beauty that float away into the sunshine of the world to be loved by men. The *Narcissus* was one of that perfect brood. Less perfect than many perhaps, but she was ours, and, consequently, incomparable. We were proud of her. In Bombay, ignorant landlubbers alluded to her as that "pretty grey ship." Pretty! A scurvy meed of commendation! We knew she was the most magnificent sea-boat ever launched. We tried to forget that, like many good sea-boats, she was at times rather a crank. She was exacting. She wanted care in loading and handling, and no one knew exactly how much care would be enough. Such are the imperfections of mere men! The ship knew, and sometimes would correct the presumptuous human ignorance by the wholesome discipline of fear. We had heard ominous stories about past voyages. The cook (officially a seaman, but in reality no sailor)—the cook, when unstrung by some misfortune, such as the rolling over of a saucepan, would mutter gloomily while he wiped the floor:—"There! Look at what she has done! Some voy'ge she will drown all hands! You'll see if she won't." To which the steward, snatching in the galley a moment to draw breath in the hurry of his worried life, would remark philosophically:—"Those that see won't tell, anyhow. I don't want to see it." We derided those fears. Our hearts went out to the old man when he pressed her hard so as to make her hold her own, hold to every inch gained to windward; when he made her, under reefed sails, leap obliquely at enormous waves. The men, knitted together aft into a ready group by the first sharp order of an officer coming to take charge of the deck in bad weather:—"Keep handy the watch," stood admiring her valiance. Their eyes blinked in the wind; their dark faces were wet with drops of water more salt and bitter than human tears; beards and moustaches, soaked, hung straight and dripping like fine seaweed. They were fantastically misshapen; in high boots, in hats like helmets, and swaying clumsily, stiff and bulky in glistening oilskins,[5] they resembled men strangely equipped for some fabulous adventure. Whenever she rose easily to a towering green sea, elbows dug ribs, faces brightened, lips murmured:—"Didn't she do

4. Location of the shipbuilding yards on the Clyde River in southern Scotland.
5. Cotton fabric made waterproof by treatment; usually a long, full-cut raincoat worn by sailors for protection against rain.

it cleverly," and all the heads turning like one watched with sardonic grins the foiled wave go roaring to leeward, white with the
foam of a monstrous rage. But when she had not been quick
enough and, struck heavily, lay over trembling under the blow, we
clutched at ropes, and looking up at the narrow bands of drenched
and strained sails waving desperately aloft, we thought in our
hearts:—"No wonder. Poor thing!"

The thirty-second day out of Bombay began inauspiciously. In
the morning a sea smashed one of the galley doors. We dashed in
through lots of steam and found the cook very wet and indignant
with the ship:—"She's getting worse every day. She's trying to
drown me in front of my own stove!" He was very angry. We pacified him, and the carpenter, though washed away twice from there,
managed to repair the door. Through that accident our dinner was
not ready till late, but it didn't matter in the end because Knowles,
who went to fetch it, got knocked down by a sea and the dinner
went over the side. Captain Allistoun, looking more hard and thin-
lipped than ever, hung on to full topsails and foresail, and would
not notice that the ship, asked to do too much, appeared to lose
heart altogether for the first time since we knew her. She refused to
rise, and bored her way sullenly through the sea. Twice running, as
though she had been blind or weary of life, she put her nose deliberately into a big wave and swept the decks from end to end. As the
boatswain observed with marked annoyance, while we were splashing about in a body to try and save a worthless wash-tub:—"Every
blooming thing in the ship is going overboard this afternoon." Venerable Singleton broke his habitual silence and said, with a glance
aloft:—"The old man's in a temper with the weather, but it's no
good bein' angry with the winds of heaven." Jimmy had shut his
door, of course. We knew he was dry and comfortable within his
little cabin, and in our absurd way were pleased one moment, exasperated the next, by that certitude. Donkin skulked shamelessly,
uneasy and miserable. He grumbled;—"I'm perishin' with cold outside in bloomin' wet rags, an' that 'ere black sojer sits dry on a
blamed chest full of bloomin' clothes; blank his black soul!" We
took no notice of him; we hardly gave a thought to Jimmy and his
bosom friend. There was no leisure for idle probing of hearts. Sails
blew adrift. Things broke loose. Cold and wet, we were washed
about the deck while trying to repair damages. The ship tossed
about, shaken furiously, like a toy in the hand of a lunatic. Just at
sunset there was a rush to shorten sail before the menace of a
sombre hail cloud. The hard gust of wind came brutal like the blow
of a fist. The ship relieved of her canvas in time received it pluckily:
she yielded reluctantly to the violent onset; then, coming up with a
stately and irresistible motion, brought her spars to windward in the

teeth of the screeching squall. Out of the abysmal darkness of the black cloud overhead white hail streamed on her, rattled on the rigging, leaped in handfuls off the yards, rebounded on the deck—round and gleaming in the murky turmoil like a shower of pearls. It passed away. For a moment a livid sun shot horizontally the last rays of sinister light between the hills of steep rolling waves. Then a wild night rushed in—stamped out in a great howl that dismal remnant of a stormy day.

There was no sleep on board that night. Most seamen remember in their life one or two such nights of a culminating gale. Nothing seems left of the whole universe but darkness, clamour, fury—and the ship. And like the last vestige of a shattered creation she drifts, bearing an anguished remnant of sinful mankind, through the distress, tumult, and pain of an avenging terror. No one slept in the forecastle. The tin oil-lamp suspended on a long string, smoking, described wide circles; wet clothing made dark heaps on the glistening floor; a thin layer of water rushed to and fro. In the bed-places men lay booted, resting on elbows and with open eyes. Hung-up suits of oilskin swung out and in, lively and disquieting like reckless ghosts of decapitated seamen dancing in a tempest. No one spoke and all listened. Outside the night moaned and sobbed to the accompaniment of a continuous loud tremor as of innumerable drums beating far off. Shrieks passed through the air. Tremendous dull blows made the ship tremble while she rolled under the weight of the seas toppling on her deck. At times she soared up swiftly as if to leave this earth for ever, then during interminable moments fell through a void with all the hearts on board of her standing still, till a frightful shock, expected and sudden, started them off again with a big thump. After every dislocating jerk of the ship, Wamibo, stretched full length, his face on the pillow, groaned slightly with the pain of his tormented universe. Now and then, for the fraction of an intolerable second, the ship, in the fiercer burst of a terrible uproar, remained on her side, vibrating and still, with a stillness more appalling than the wildest motion. Then upon all those prone bodies a stir would pass, a shiver of suspense. A man would protrude his anxious head and a pair of eyes glistened in the sway of light, glaring wildly. Some moved their legs a little as if making ready to jump out. But several, motionless on their backs and with one hand gripping hard the edge of the bunk, smoked nervously with quick puffs, staring upwards; immobilised in a great craving for peace.

At midnight, orders were given to furl the fore and mizzen-topsails. With immense efforts men crawled aloft through a merciless buffeting, saved the canvas, and crawled down almost exhausted, to bear in panting silence the cruel battering of the seas. Perhaps for the first time in the history of the merchant service the watch, told to go below, did not leave the deck, as if compelled to remain there by the fascination of a venomous violence. At every heavy gust men, huddled together, whispered to one another:—"It can blow no harder"—and presently the gale would give them the lie with a piercing shriek, and drive their breath back into their throats. A fierce squall seemed to burst asunder the thick mass of sooty vapours; and above the wrack of torn clouds glimpses could be caught of the high moon rushing backwards with frightful speed over the sky, right into the wind's eye. Many hung their heads, muttering that it "turned their inwards out" to look at it. Soon the clouds closed up and the world again became a raging, blind darkness that howled, flinging at the lonely ship salt sprays and sleet.

About half-past seven the pitchy obscurity round us turned a ghastly grey, and we knew that the sun had risen. This unnatural and threatening daylight, in which we could see one another's wild eyes and drawn faces, was only an added tax on our endurance. The horizon seemed to have come on all sides within arm's length of the ship. Into that narrowed circle furious seas leaped in, struck, and leaped out. A rain of salt, heavy drops flew aslant like mist. The main-topsail had to be goose-winged, and with stolid resignation every one prepared to go aloft once more; but the officers yelled, pushed back, and at last we understood that no more men would be allowed to go on the yard than were absolutely necessary for the work. As at any moment the masts were likely to be jumped out or blown overboard, we concluded that the captain didn't want to see all his crowd go over the side at once. That was reasonable. The watch then on duty, led by Mr. Creighton, began to struggle up the rigging. The wind flattened them against the ratlines; then, easing a little, would let them ascend a couple of steps; and again, with a sudden gust, pin all up the shrouds the whole crawling line in attitudes of crucifixion. The other watch plunged down on the main deck to haul up the sail. Men's heads bobbed up as the water flung them irresistibly from side to side. Mr. Baker grunted encouragingly in our midst, spluttering and blowing amongst the tangled ropes like an energetic porpoise. Favoured by an ominous and untrustworthy lull, the work was done without any one being lost either off the deck or from the yard. For the moment the gale seemed to take off, and the ship, as if grateful for our efforts, plucked up heart and made better weather of it.

At eight the men off duty, watching their chance, ran forward over the flooded deck to get some rest. The other half of the crew remained aft for their turn of "seeing her through her trouble," as they expressed it. The two mates urged the master to go below. Mr. Baker grunted in his ear:—"Ough! surely now . . . Ough! . . . confidence in us . . . nothing more to do . . . she must lay it out or go. Ough! Ough!" Tall young Mr. Creighton smiled down at him cheerfully:—" . . . She's as right as a trivet![6] Take a spell, sir." He looked at them stonily with bloodshot, sleepless eyes. The rims of his eyelids were scarlet, and he moved his jaws unceasingly with a slow effort, as though he had been masticating a lump of indiarubber. He shook his head. He repeated:—"Never mind me. I must see it out—I must see it out," but he consented to sit down for a moment on the skylight, with his hard face turned unflinchingly to windward. The sea spat at it—and stoical, it streamed with water as though he had been weeping. On the weather side of the poop the watch, hanging on to the mizzen-rigging and to one another, tried to exchange encouraging words. Singleton, at the wheel, yelled out: —"Look out for yourselves!" His voice reached them in a warning whisper. They were startled.

A big, foaming sea came out of the mist; it made for the ship, roaring wildly, and in its rush it looked as mischievous and discomposing as a madman with an axe. One or two, shouting, scrambled up the rigging; most, with a convulsive catch of the breath, held on where they stood. Singleton dug his knees under the wheel-box, and carefully eased the helm to the headlong pitch of the ship, but without taking his eyes off the coming wave. It towered close-to and high, like a wall of green glass topped with snow. The ship rose to it as though she had soared on wings, and for a moment rested poised upon the foaming crest as if she had been a great sea-bird. Before we could draw breath a heavy gust struck her, another roller took her unfairly under the weather bow, she gave a toppling lurch, and filled her decks. Captain Allistoun leaped up, and fell; Archie rolled over him, screaming:—"She will rise!" She gave another lurch to leeward; the lower deadeyes dipped heavily; the men's feet flew from under them, and they hung kicking above the slanting poop. They could see the ship putting her side in the water, and shouted all together:—"She's going!" Forward the forecastle doors flew open, and the watch below were seen leaping out one after another, throwing their arms up; and, falling on hands and knees, scrambled aft on all fours along the high side of the deck, sloping more than the roof of a house. From leeward the seas rose, pursuing them; they looked wretched in a hopeless struggle, like vermin fleeing before a flood; they fought up the weather ladder of the poop one after another, half naked and staring wildly; and as soon as they got up they shot to leeward in clusters, with closed eyes, till they brought up heavily with their ribs against the iron stanchions of the rail, when, groaning, they rolled in a confused mass. The

6. A three-footed or three-legged stand or support, especially one of iron placed over a fire to support cooking vessels.

immense volume of water thrown forward by the last scend of the ship had burst the lee door of the forecastle. They could see their chests, pillows, blankets, clothing, come out floating upon the sea. While they struggled back to windward they looked in dismay. The straw beds swam high, the blankets, spread out, undulated; while the chests, waterlogged and with a heavy list, pitched heavily like dismasted hulks, before they sank; Archie's big coat passed with out-spread arms, resembling a drowned seaman floating with his head under water. Men were slipping down while trying to dig their fingers into the planks; others jammed in corners, rolled enormous eyes. They all yelled unceasingly:—"The masts! Cut! Cut! . . ." A black squall howled low over the ship, that lay on her side with the weather yard-arms pointing to the clouds; while the tall masts, inclined nearly to the horizon, seemed to be of an immeasurable length. The carpenter let go his hold, rolled against the skylight, and began to crawl to the cabin entrance, where a big axe was kept ready for just such an emergency. At that moment the topsail sheet parted, the end of the heavy chain racketed aloft, and sparks of red fire streamed down through the flying sprays. The sail flapped once with a jerk that seemed to tear our hearts out through our teeth, and instantly changed into a bunch of fluttering narrow ribbons that tied themselves into knots and became quiet along the yard. Captain Allistoun struggled, managed to stand up with his face near the deck, upon which men swung on the ends of ropes, like nest robbers upon a cliff, One of his feet was on somebody's chest; his face was purple; his lips moved. He yelled also; he yelled, bending down:—"No! No!" Mr. Baker, one leg over the binnacle-stand, roared out:—"Did you say no? Not cut?" He shook his head madly. "No! No!" Between his legs the crawling carpenter heard, collapsed at once, and lay full length in the angle of the skylight. Voices took up the shout—"No! No!" Then all became still. They waited for the ship to turn over altogether, and shake them out into the sea; and upon the terrific noise of wind and sea not a murmur of remonstrance came out from those men, who each would have given ever so many years of life to see "them damned sticks go over-board!" They all believed it their only chance; but a little hard-faced man shook his grey head and shouted "No!" without giving them as much as a glance. They were silent, and gasped. They gripped rails, they had wound ropes'-ends under their arms, they clutched ring-bolts, they crawled in heaps where there was foothold; they held on with both arms; hooked themselves to anything to windward with elbows, with chins, almost with their teeth: and some, unable to crawl away from where they had been flung, felt the sea leap up, striking against their backs as they struggled upwards. Singleton had stuck to the wheel. His hair flew out in the wind; the gale seemed to take its lifelong adversary by the beard and shake his old head. He wouldn't let go, and, with his knees forced between the spokes, flew up and down like a man on a bough. As Death appeared unready, they began to look about. Donkin, caught by one foot in a loop of some rope, hung, head down, below us, and yelled, with his face to the deck:—"Cut! Cut!" Two men lowered themselves cautiously to him; others hauled on the rope. They caught him up, shoved him into a safer place, held him. He shouted curses at the master, shook his fist at him with horrible blasphemies, called upon us in filthy words to "Cut! Don't mind that murdering fool! Cut, some of you!" One of his rescuers struck him a back-handed blow over the mouth; his head banged on the deck, and he became suddenly very quiet, with a white face, breathing hard, and with a few drops of blood trickling from his cut lip. On the lee side another man could be seen stretched out as if stunned; only the washboard prevented him from going over the side. It was the steward. We had to sling him up like a bale, for he was paralysed with fright. He had rushed up out of the pantry when he felt the ship go over, and had rolled down helplessly, clutching a china mug. It was not broken. With difficulty we tore it away from him, and when he saw it in our hands he was amazed. "Where did you get that thing?" he kept on asking us in a trembling voice. His shirt was blown to shreds; the ripped sleeves flapped like wings. Two men made him fast, and, doubled over the rope that held him, he resembled a bundle of wet rags. Mr. Baker crawled along the line of men, asking—"Are you all there?" and looking them over. Some blinked vacantly, others shook convulsively; Wamibo's head hung over his breast; and in painful attitudes, cut by lashings, exhausted with clutching, screwed up in corners, they breathed heavily. Their lips twitched, and at every sickening heave of the overturned ship they opened them wide as if to shout. The cook, embracing a wooden stanchion, unconsciously repeated a prayer. In every short interval of the fiendish noises around he could be heard there, without cap or slippers, imploring in that storm the Master of our lives not to lead him into temptation. Soon he also became silent. In all that crowd of cold and hungry men, waiting wearily for a violent death, not a voice was heard; they were mute, and in sombre thoughtfulness listened to the horrible imprecations of the gale.

Hours passed. They were sheltered by the heavy inclination of the ship from the wind that rushed in one long unbroken moan above their heads, but cold rain showers fell at times into the uneasy calm of their refuge. Under the torment of that new infliction a pair of shoulders would writhe a little. Teeth chattered. The sky was clearing, and bright sunshine gleamed over the ship. After

every burst of battering seas, vivid and fleeting rainbows arched over
the drifting hull in the flick of sprays. The gale was ending in a
clear blow, which gleamed and cut like a knife. Between two
bearded shellbacks Charley, fastened with somebody's long muffler
to a deck ring-bolt, wept quietly, with rare tears wrung out by bewil-
derment, cold, hunger, and general misery. One of his neighbours
punched him in the ribs, asking roughly:—"What's the matter with
your cheek? In fine weather there's no holding you, youngster."
Turning about with prudence, he worked himself out of his coat
and threw it over the boy. The other man closed up, muttering:—
" 'Twill make a bloomin' man of you, sonny." They flung their
arms over and pressed against him. Charley drew his feet up and his
eyelids dropped. Sighs were heard, as men, perceiving that they
were not to be "drowned in a hurry," tried easier positions. Mr.
Creighton, who had hurt his leg, lay amongst us with compressed
lips. Some fellows belonging to his watch set about securing him
better. Without a word or a glance he lifted his arms one after
another to facilitate the operation, and not a muscle moved in his
stern, young face. They asked him with solicitude:—"Easier now,
sir?" He answered with a curt:—"That'll do." He was a hard young
officer, but many of his watch used to say they liked him well
enough because he had "such a gentlemanly way of damning us up
and down the deck." Others, unable to discern such fine shades of
refinement, respected him for his smartness. For the first time since
the ship had gone on her beam ends Captain Allistoun gave a short
glance down at his men. He was almost upright—one foot against
the side of the skylight, one knee on the deck; and with the end of
the vang round his waist swung back and forth with his gaze fixed
ahead, watchful, like a man looking out for a sign. Before his eyes
the ship, with half her deck below water, rose and fell on heavy seas
that rushed from under her, flashing in the cold sunshine. We
began to think she was wonderfully buoyant—considering. Confident voices were heard shouting—"She'll do, boys!" Belfast
exclaimed with fervour:—"I would giv' a month's pay for a draw at
a pipe!" One or two, passing dry tongues on their salt lips, muttered
something about a "drink of water." The cook, as if inspired, scrambled up with his breast against the poop water-cask and looked in.
There was a little at the bottom. He yelled, waving his arms, and
two men began to crawl backwards and forwards with the mug. We
had a good mouthful all round. The master shook his head impatiently, refusing. When it came to Charley one of his neighbours
shouted:—"That bloomin' boy's asleep." He slept as though he had
been dosed with narcotics. They let him be. Singleton held to the
wheel with one hand while he drank, bending down to shelter his
lips from the wind. Wamibo had to be poked and yelled at before

he saw the mug held before his eyes. Knowles said sagaciously:—
"It's better'n a tot[7] o' rum." Mr. Baker grunted:—"Thank ye."
Mr. Creighton drank and nodded. Donkin gulped greedily, glaring
over the rim. Belfast made us laugh when with grimacing mouth he
shouted:—"Pass it this way. We're all taytottlers here." The
master, presented with the mug again by a crouching man, who
screamed up at him;—"We all had a drink, captain," groped for it
without ceasing to look ahead, and handed it back stiffly as though
he could not spare half a glance away from the ship. Faces brightened. We shouted to the cook:—"Well done, doctor!" He sat to
leeward, propped by the water-cask and yelled back abundantly, but
the seas were breaking in thunder just then, and we only caught
snatches that sounded like:—"Providence" and "born again." He
was at his old game of preaching. We made friendly but derisive
gestures at him, and from below he lifted one arm, holding on with
the other, moved his lips; he beamed up to us, straining his voice—
earnest, and ducking his head before the sprays.

Suddenly some one cried:—"Where's Jimmy?" and we were
appalled once more. On the end of the row the boatswain shouted
hoarsely:—"Has any one seed him come out?" Voices exclaimed
dismally:—"Drowned—is he? . . . No! In his cabin! . . . Good
Lord! . . . Caught like a bloomin' rat in a trap. . . . Couldn't open
his door. . . . Ay! She went over too quick and the water jammed it.
. . . Poor beggar! . . . No help for 'im. . . . Let's go and see. . . ."
"Damn him, who could go?" screamed Donkin.—"Nobody expects
you to," growled the man next to him: "you're only a thing."—"Is
there half a chance to get at 'im?" inquired two or three men
together. Belfast untied himself with blind impetuosity, and all at
once shot down to leeward quicker than a flash of lightning. We
shouted all together with dismay; but with his legs overboard he
held and yelled for a rope. In our extremity nothing could be terrible; so we judged him funny kicking there, and with his scared face.
Some one began to laugh, and, as if hysterically infected with
screaming merriment, all those haggard men went off laughing,
wild-eyed, like a lot of maniacs tied up on a wall. Mr. Baker swung
off the binnacle-stand and tendered him one leg. He scrambled up
rather scared, and consigning us with abominable words to the
"divvle." "You are . . . Ough! You're a foul-mouthed beggar,
Craik," grunted Mr. Baker. He answered, stuttering with indignation:—"Look at 'em, sorr. The bloomin' dirty images! laughing at a
chum going overboard. Call themselves men, too." But from the
break of the poop the boatswain called out:—"Come along," and
Belfast crawled away in a hurry to join him. The five men, poised
and gazing over the edge of the poop, looked for the best way to get

7. British for a small portion of a beverage, especially liquor.

forward. They seemed to hesitate. The others, twisting in their lashings, turning painfully, stared with open lips. Captain Allistoun saw
nothing; he seemed with his eyes to hold the ship up in a super-
human concentration of effort. The wind screamed loud in sunshine;
columns of spray rose straight up; and in the glitter of rainbows
bursting over the trembling hull the men went over cautiously, disappearing from sight with deliberate movements.

They went swinging from belaying pin to cleat above the seas
that beat the half-submerged deck. Their toes scraped the planks.
Lumps of green cold water toppled over the bulwark and on their
heads. They hung for a moment on strained arms, with the breath
knocked out of them, and with closed eyes—then, letting go with
one hand, balanced with lolling heads, trying to grab some rope or
stanchion further forward. The long-armed and athletic boatswain
swung quickly, gripping things with a fist hard as iron, and remembering suddenly snatches of the last letter from his "old woman."
Little Belfast scrambled in a rage, spluttering "Cursed nigger."
Wamibo's tongue hung out with excitement; and Archie, intrepid
and calm, watched his chance to move with intelligent coolness.

When above the side of the house, they let go one after another,
and, falling heavily, sprawled, pressing their palms to the smooth
teak wood. Round them the backwash of waves seethed white and
hissing. All the doors had become trap-doors, of course. The first
was the galley door. The galley extended from side to side, and they
could hear the sea splashing with hollow noises in there. The next
door was that of the carpenter's shop. They lifted it, and looked
down. The room seemed to have been devastated by an earthquake.
Everything in it had tumbled on the bulkhead facing the door, and
on the other side of that bulkhead there was Jimmy, dead or alive.
The bench, a half-finished meat-safe, saws, chisels, wire rods, axes,
crowbars, lay in a heap besprinkled with loose nails. A sharp adze
stuck up with a shining edge that gleamed dangerously down there
like a wicked smile. The men clung to one another, peering. A sickening, sly lurch of the ship nearly sent them overboard in a body.
Belfast howled "Here goes!" and leaped down. Archie followed can-
nily, catching at shelves that gave way with him, and eased himself
in a great crash of ripped wood. There was hardly room for three
men to move. And in the sunshiny blue square of the door, the
boatswain's face, bearded and dark, Wamibo's face, wild and pale,
hung over—watching.

Together they shouted: "Jimmy! Jim!" From above the boatswain
contributed a deep growl: "You . . . Wait!" In a pause, Belfast
entreated: "Jimmy, darlin', are ye aloive?" The boatswain said
"Again! All together, boys!" All yelled excitedly. Wamibo made
noises resembling loud barks. Belfast drummed on the side of the

bulkhead with a piece of iron. All ceased suddenly. The sound of screaming and hammering went on, thin and distinct—like a solo after a chorus. He was alive. He was screaming and knocking below us with the hurry of a man prematurely shut up in a coffin. We went to work. We attacked with desperation the abominable heap of things heavy, of things sharp, of things clumsy to handle. The boatswain crawled away to find somewhere a flying end of a rope; and Wamibo, held back by shouts:—"Don't jump! . . . Don't come in here, muddle head!"—remained glaring above us—all shining eyes, gleaming fangs, tumbled hair; resembling an amazed and half-witted fiend gloating over the extraordinary agitation of the damned. The boatswain adjured us to "bear a hand," and a rope descended. We made things fast to it and they went up spinning, never to be seen by man again. A rage to fling things overboard possessed us. We worked fiercely, cutting our hands and speaking brutally to one another. Jimmy kept up a distracting row; he screamed piercingly, without drawing breath, like a tortured woman; he banged with hands and feet. The agony of his fear wrung our hearts so terribly that we longed to abandon him, to get out of that place deep as a well and swaying like a tree, to get out of his hearing, back on the poop where we could wait passively for death in incomparable repose. We shouted to him to "shut up, for God's sake." He redoubled his cries. He must have fancied we could not hear him. Probably he heard his own clamour but faintly. We could picture him crouching on the edge of the upper berth, letting out with both fists at the wood, in the dark, and with his mouth wide open for that unceasing cry. Those were loathsome moments. A cloud driving across the sun would darken the doorway menacingly. Every movement of the ship was pain. We scrambled about with no room to breathe, and felt frightfully sick. The boatswain yelled down at us:—"Bear a hand! Bear a hand! We two will be washed away from here directly if you ain't quick!" Three times a sea leaped over the high side and flung bucketfuls of water on our heads. Then Jimmy, startled by the shock, would stop his noise for a moment—waiting for the ship to sink, perhaps—and began again, distressingly loud, as if invigorated by the gust of fear. At the bottom the nails lay in a layer several inches thick. It was ghastly. Every nail in the world, not driven in firmly somewhere, seemed to have found its way into that carpenter's shop. There they were, of all kinds, the remnants of stores from seven voyages. Tin-tacks, copper tacks (sharp as needles), pump nails, with big heads, like tiny iron mushrooms; nails, without any heads (horrible); French nails polished and slim. They lay in a solid mass more inabordable[8] than a hedgehog. We hesitated, yearning for a shovel, while Jimmy below us yelled as though

8. Inaccessible.

he had been flayed. Groaning, we dug our fingers in, and very much hurt, shook our hands, scattering nails and drops of blood. We passed up our hats full of assorted nails to the boatswain, who, as if performing a mysterious and appeasing rite, cast them wide upon a raging sea.

We got to the bulkhead at last. Those were stout planks. She was a ship, well finished in every detail—the *Narcissus* was. They were the stoutest planks ever put into a ship's bulkhead—we thought—and then we perceived that, in our hurry, we had sent all the tools overboard. Absurd little Belfast wanted to break it down with his own weight, and with both feet leaped straight up like a springbok,[9] cursing the Clyde shipwrights for not scamping their work. Incidentally he reviled all North Britain, the rest of the earth, the sea—and all his companions. He swore, as he alighted heavily on his heels, that he would never, never any more associate with any fool that "hadn't savee enough to know his knee from his elbow." He managed by his thumping to scare the last remnant of wits out of Jimmy. We could hear the object of our exasperated solicitude darting to and fro under the planks. He had cracked his voice at last, and could only squeak miserably. His back or else his head rubbed the planks, now here, now there, in a puzzling manner. He squeaked as he dodged the invisible blows. It was more heart-rending even than his yells. Suddenly Archie produced a crowbar. He had kept it back; also a small hatchet. We howled with satisfaction. He struck a mighty blow and small chips flew at our eyes. The boatswain above shouted:—"Look out! Look out there. Don't kill the man. Easy does it!" Wamibo, maddened with excitement, hung head down and insanely urged us:—"Hoo! Strook 'im! Hoo! Hoo!" We were afraid he would fall in and kill one of us, and hurriedly we entreated the boatswain to "shove the blamed Finn overboard." Then, all together, we yelled down at the planks:—"Stand from under! Get forward," and listened. We only heard the deep hum and moan of the wind above us, the mingled roar and hiss of the seas. The ship, as if overcome with despair, wallowed lifelessly, and our heads swam with that unnatural motion. Belfast clamoured:—"For the love of God, Jimmy, where are ye? . . . Knock! Jimmy darlint! . . . Knock! You bloody black beast! Knock!" He was as quiet as a dead man inside a grave; and, like men standing above a grave, we were on the verge of tears—but with vexation, the strain, the fatigue; with the great longing to be done with it, to get away, and lie down to rest somewhere where we could see our danger and breathe. Archie shouted:—"Gi'e me room!" We crouched behind him, guarding our heads, and he struck time after time in the

9. A gazelle of southern Africa noted for its habit of springing into the air when alarmed.

joint of planks. They cracked. Suddenly the crowbar went half-way in through a splintered oblong hole. It must have missed Jimmy's head by less than an inch. Archie withdrew it quickly, and that infamous nigger rushed at the hole, put his lips to it, and whispered "Help" in an almost extinct voice; he pressed his head to it, trying madly to get out through that opening one inch wide and three inches long. In our disturbed state we were absolutely paralysed by his incredible action. It seemed impossible to drive him away. Even Archie at last lost his composure. "If ye don't clear oot I'll drive the crowbar thro' your head," he shouted in a determined voice. He meant what he said, and his earnestness seemed to make an impression on Jimmy. He disappeared suddenly, and we set to prising and tearing at the planks with the eagerness of men trying to get at a mortal enemy, and spurred by the desire to tear him limb from limb. The wood split, cracked, gave way. Belfast plunged in head and shoulders and groped viciously. "I've got 'im! Got 'im," he shouted. "Oh! There! . . . He's gone; I've got 'im! . . . Pull at my legs! . . . Pull!" Wamibo hooted unceasingly. The boatswain shouted directions:—"Catch hold of his hair, Belfast; pull straight up, you two! . . . Pull fair!" We pulled fair. We pulled Belfast out with a jerk, and dropped him with disgust. In a sitting posture purple-faced, he sobbed despairingly:—"How can I hold on to 'is blooming short wool?" Suddenly Jimmy's head and shoulders appeared. He stuck half-way, and with rolling eyes foamed at our feet. We flew at him with brutal impatience, we tore the shirt off his back, we tugged at his ears, we panted over him; and all at once he came away in our hands as though somebody had let go his legs. With the same movement, without a pause, we swung him up. His breath whistled, he kicked our upturned faces, he grasped two pairs of arms above his head, and he squirmed up with such precipitation that he seemed positively to escape from our hands like a bladder full of gas. Streaming with perspiration, we swarmed up the rope, and, coming into the blast of cold wind, gasped like men plunged into icy water. With burning faces we shivered to the very marrow of our bones. Never before had the gale seemed to us more furious, the sea more mad, the sunshine more merciless and mocking, and the position of the ship more hopeless and appalling. Every movement of her was ominous of the end of her agony and of the beginning of ours. We staggered away from the door, and, alarmed by a sudden roll, fell down in a bunch. It appeared to us that the side of the house was more smooth than glass and more slippery than ice. There was nothing to hang on to but a long brass hook used sometimes to keep back an open door. Wamibo held on to it and we held on to Wamibo, clutching our Jimmy. He had completely collapsed now. He did not seem to have the strength to close his hand. We stuck to him blindly in our fear. We were not afraid of Wamibo letting go (we remembered that the brute was stronger than any three men in the ship), but we were afraid of the hook giving way, and we also believed that the ship had made up her mind to turn over at last. But she didn't. A sea swept over us. The boatswain spluttered:—"Up and away. There's a lull. Away aft with you, or we will all go to the devil here." We stood up surrounding Jimmy. We begged him to hold up, to hold on, at least. He glared with his bulging eyes, mute as a fish, and with all the stiffening knocked out of him. He wouldn't stand; he wouldn't even as much as clutch at our necks; he was only a cold black skin loosely stuffed with soft cotton wool; his arms and legs swung jointless and pliable; his head rolled about; the lower lip hung down, enormous and heavy. We pressed round him, bothered and dismayed; sheltering him, we swung here and there in a body; and on the very brink of eternity we tottered all together with concealing and absurd gestures, like a lot of drunken men embarrassed with a stolen corpse.

Something had to be done. We had to get him aft. A rope was tied slack under his armpits, and, reaching up at the risk of our lives, we hung him on the foresheet cleat. He emitted no sound; he looked as ridiculously lamentable as a doll that had lost half its sawdust, and we started on our perilous journey over the main deck, dragging along with care that pitiful, that limp, that hateful burden. He was not very heavy, but had he weighed a ton he could not have been more awkward to handle. We literally passed him from hand to hand. Now and then we had to hang him up on a handy belaying-pin, to draw a breath and reform the line. Had the pin broken he would have irretrievably gone into the Southern Ocean, but he had to take his chance of that; and after a little while, becoming apparently aware of it, he groaned slightly, and with a great effort whispered a few words. We listened eagerly. He was reproaching us with our carelessness in letting him run such risks: "Now, after I got myself out from there," he breathed out weakly. "There" was his cabin. And he got himself out. We had nothing to do with it apparently! . . . No matter. . . . We went on and let him take his chances, simply because we could not help it; for though at that time we hated him more than ever—more than anything under heaven—we did not want to lose him. We had so far saved him; and it had become a personal matter between us and the sea. We meant to stick to him. Had we (by an incredible hypothesis) undergone similar toil and trouble for an empty cask, that cask would have become as precious to us as Jimmy was. More precious, in fact, because we would have had no reason to hate the cask. And we hated James Wait. We could not get rid of the monstrous suspicion that this astounding black man was shamming sick, had been malingering heartlessly in the face of our toil, of our scorn, of our patience—and now was malingering in the face of our devotion—in the face of death. Our vague and imperfect morality rose with disgust at his unmanly lie. But he stuck to it manfully— amazingly. No! It couldn't be. He was at all extremity. His cantankerous temper was only the result of the provoking invincibleness of that death he felt by his side. Any man may be angry with such a masterful chum. But, then, what kind of men were we—with our thoughts! Indignation and doubt grappled within us in a scuffle that trampled upon the finest of our feelings. And we hated him because of the suspicion; we detested him because of the doubt. We could not scorn him safely—neither could we pity him without risk to our dignity. So we hated him, and passed him carefully from hand to hand. We cried, "Got him?"—"Yes. All right. Let go." And he swung from one enemy to another, showing about as much life as an old bolster would do. His eyes made two narrow white slits in the black face. The air escaped through his lips with a noise like the sound of bellows. We reached the poop ladder at last, and it being a comparatively safe place, we lay for a moment in an exhausted heap to rest a little. He began to mutter. We were always incurably anxious to hear what he had to say. This time he mumbled peevishly, "It took you some time to come. I began to think the whole smart lot of you had been washed overboard. What kept you back? Hey? Funk?" We said nothing. With sighs we started again to drag him up. The secret and ardent desire of our hearts was the desire to beat him viciously with our fists about the head; and we handled him as tenderly as though he had been made of glass. . . .

The return on the poop was like the return of wanderers after many years amongst people marked by the desolation of time. Eyes were turned slowly in their sockets, glancing at us. Faint murmurs were heard, "Have you got 'im after all?" The well-known faces looked strange and familiar; they seemed faded and grimy; they had a mingled expression of fatigue and eagerness. They seemed to have become much thinner during our absence, as if all these men had been starving for a long time in their abandoned attitudes. The captain, with a round turn of a rope on his wrist, and kneeling on one knee, swung with a face cold and stiff; but with living eyes he was still holding the ship up, heeding no one, as if lost in the unearthly effort of that endeavour. We fastened up James Wait in a safe place. Mr. Baker scrambled along to lend a hand. Mr. Creighton, on his back, and very pale, muttered, "Well done," and gave us, Jimmy, and the sky a scornful glance, then closed his eyes slowly. Here and there a man stirred a little, but most of them remained

apathetic, in cramped positions, muttering between shivers. The sun
was setting. A sun enormous, unclouded, and red, declining low as
if bending down to look into their faces. The wind whistled across
long sunbeams that, resplendent and cold, struck full on the dilated
pupils of staring eyes without making them wink. The wisps of hair
and the tangled beards were grey with the salt of the sea. The faces
were earthy, and the dark patches under the eyes extended to the
ears, smudged into the hollows of sunken cheeks. The lips were
livid and thin, and when they moved it was with difficulty, as
though they had been glued to the teeth. Some grinned sadly in the
sunlight, shaking with cold. Others were sad and still. Charley, subdued by the sudden disclosure of the insignificance of his youth,
darted fearful glances. The two smoothfaced Norwegians resembled
decrepit children, staring stupidly. To leeward, on the edge of the
horizon, black seas leaped up towards the glowing sun. It sank
slowly, round and blazing, and the crests of waves splashed on the
edge of the luminous circle. One of the Norwegians appeared to
catch sight of it, and, after giving a violent start, began to speak.
His voice, startling the others, made them stir. They moved their
heads stiffly, or, turning with difficulty, looked at him with surprise,
with fear, or in grave silence. He chattered at the setting sun, nodding his head, while the big seas began to roll across the crimson
disc; and over miles of turbulent waters the shadows of high waves
swept with a running darkness the faces of men. A crested roller
broke with a loud hissing roar, and the sun, as if put out, disappeared. The chattering voice faltered, went out together with the
light. There were sighs. In the sudden lull that follows the crash of
a broken sea a man said wearily, "Here's that blooming Dutchman
gone off his chump."[1] A seaman, lashed by the middle, tapped the
deck with his open hand with unceasing quick flaps. In the gathering greyness of twilight a bulky form was seen rising aft, and began
marching on all fours with the movements of some big, cautious
beast. It was Mr. Baker passing along the line of men. He grunted
encouragingly over every one, felt their fastenings. Some, with half-
open eyes, puffed like men oppressed by heat; others mechanically
and in dreamy voices answered him, "Ay! ay! sir!" He went from
one to another grunting, "Ough! . . . See her through it yet;" and
unexpectedly, with loud, angry outbursts, blew up Knowles for cutting off a long piece from the fall of the relieving tackle. "Ough! . . .
Ashamed of yourself . . . Relieving tackle . . . Don't you know
better! . . . Ough! . . . Able seaman! Ough!" The lame man was
crushed. He muttered, "Get som'think for a lashing for myself, sir."
—"Ough! Lashing . . . yourself. Are you a tinker or a sailor . . .
What? Ough! . . . May want that tackle directly . . . Ough! . . .

1. British slang for crazy, mentally deranged.

More use to the ship than your lame carcass. Ough! . . . Keep it! . . .
Keep it, now you've done it." He crawled away slowly, muttering
to himself about some men being "worse than children." It had
been a comforting row. Low exclamations were heard: "Hallo . . .
Hallo." . . . Those who had been painfully dozing asked with convulsive starts, "What's up? . . . What is it?" The answers came
with unexpected cheerfulness: "The mate is going bald-headed for
lame Jack about something or other." "No!" . . . "What 'as he
done?" Some one even chuckled. It was like a whiff of hope, like a
reminder of safe days. Donkin, who had been stupefied with fear,
revived suddenly and began to shout:—" 'Ear 'im; that's the way
they tawlk to us. Vy donch 'ee 'it 'im—one ov yer? 'It 'im! 'It 'im!
Comin' the mate over us. We are as good men as 'ee! We're all
goin' to 'ell now. We 'ave been starved in this rotten ship, an' now
we're goin' to be drowned for them black-'earted bullies! 'It 'im!"
He shrieked in the deepening gloom, he blubbered and sobbed,
screaming:—" 'It 'im! 'It 'im!" The rage and fear of his disregarded
right to live tried the steadfastness of hearts more than the menacing shadows of the night that advanced through the unceasing clamour of the gale. From aft Mr. Baker was heard:—"Is one of you
men going to stop him—must I come along?" "Shut up!" . . .
"Keep quiet!" cried various voices, exasperated, trembling with cold.
— "You'll get one across the mug from me directly," said an invisible seaman, in a weary tone. "I won't let the mate have the trouble." He ceased and lay still, with the silence of despair. On the
black sky the stars, coming out, gleamed over an inky sea that, spec-
kled with foam, flashed back at them the evanescent and pale light
of a dazzling whiteness born from the black turmoil of the waves.
Remote in the eternal calm they glittered hard and cold above the
uproar of the earth; they surrounded the vanquished and tormented
ship on all sides: more pitiless than the eyes of a triumphant mob,
and as unapproachable as the hearts of men.

The icy south wind howled exultingly under the sombre splendour of the sky. The cold shook the men with a resistless violence
as though it had tried to shake them to pieces. Short moans were
swept, unheard, off the stiff lips. Some complained in mutters of
"not feeling themselves below the waist"; while those who had
closed their eyes imagined they had a block of ice on their chests.
Others, alarmed at not feeling any pain in their fingers, beat the
deck feebly with their hands—obstinate and exhausted. Wamibo
stared vacant and dreamy. The Scandinavians kept on a meaningless
mutter through chattering teeth. The spare Scotchmen, with determined efforts, kept their lower jaws still. The West-country men lay
big and stolid in an invulnerable surliness. A man yawned and
swore in turns. Another breathed with a rattle in his throat. Two

elderly hard-weather shellbacks, fast side by side, whispered dismally to one another about the landlady of a boarding-house in Sunderland,[2] whom they both knew. They extolled her motherliness and her liberality; they tried to talk about the joint of beef and the big fire in the downstairs kitchen. The words, dying faintly on their lips, ended in light sighs. A sudden voice cried into the cold night, "O Lord!" No one changed his position or took any notice of the cry. One or two passed, with a repeated and vague gesture, their hand over their faces, but most of them kept very still. In the benumbed immobility of their bodies they were excessively wearied by their thoughts, which rushed with the rapidity and vividness of dreams. Now and then, by an abrupt and startling exclamation, they answered the weird hail of some illusion; then, again, in silence contemplated the vision of known faces and familiar things. They recalled the aspect of forgotten shipmates and heard the voice of dead-and-gone skippers; they remembered the noise of gaslit streets, the steamy heat of tap-rooms, or the scorching sunshine of calm days at sea.

Mr. Baker left his insecure place, and crawled, with stoppages, along the poop. In the dark and on all fours he resembled some carnivorous animal prowling amongst corpses. At the break, propped to windward of a stanchion, he looked down on the main deck. It seemed to him that the ship had a tendency to stand up a little more. The wind had eased a little, he thought, but the sea ran as high as ever. The waves foamed viciously, and the lee side of the deck disappeared under a hissing whiteness as of boiling milk, while the rigging sang steadily with a deep vibrating note, and, at every upward swing of the ship, the wind rushed with a long-drawn clamour amongst the spars. Mr. Baker watched very still. A man near him began to make a blabbing noise with his lips, all at once and very loud, as though the cold had broken brutally through him. He went on:—"Ba—ba—ba—brrr—brr—ba—ba."—"Stop that!" cried Mr. Baker, groping in the dark. "Stop it!" He went on shaking the leg he found under his hand.—"What is it, sir?" called out Belfast, in the tone of a man awakened suddenly; "we are looking after that 'ere Jimmy."—"Are you? Ough! Don't make that row then. Who's that near you?"—"It's me—the boatswain, sir," growled the West-country man; "we are trying to keep life in that poor devil." —"Ay, ay!" said Mr. Baker. "Do it quietly, can't you."—"He wants us to hold him up above the rail," went on the boatswain, with irritation, "says he can't breathe here under our jackets."—"If we lift 'im, we drop 'im overboard," said another voice, "we can't feel our hands with cold."—"I don't care. I am choking!" exclaimed James Wait in a clear tone.—"Oh no, my son," said the boatswain desper-

2. A shipping center in northern England, on the North Sea.

ately, "you don't go till we all go on this fine night."—"You will see yet many a worse," said Mr. Baker cheerfully.—"It's no child's play, sir!" answered the boatswain. "Some of us farther aft, here, are in a pretty bad way."—"If the blamed sticks had been cut out of her she would be running along on her bottom now like any decent ship, an' giv' us all a chance," said some one, with a sigh.— "The old man wouldn't have it . . . much he cares for us," whispered another.—"Care for you!" exclaimed Mr. Baker angrily. "Why should he care for you? Are you a lot of women passengers to be taken care of? We are here to take care of the ship—and some of you ain't up to that. Ough! . . . What have you done so very smart to be taken care of? Ough! . . . Some of you can't stand a bit of a breeze without crying over it."—"Come, sorr. We ain't so bad," protested Belfast, in a voice shaken by shivers; "we ain't . . . brrr . . ."—"Again," shouted the mate, grabbing at the shadowy form; "again! . . . Why, you're in your shirt! What have you done?"— "I've put my oilskin and jacket over that half-dead nayg-gur—and he says he chokes," said Belfast complainingly.—"You wouldn't call me nigger if I wasn't half dead, you Irish beggar!" boomed James Wait vigorously.—"You . . . brrr . . . You wouldn't be white if you were ever so well . . . I will fight you . . . brrrr . . . in fine weather . . . brrr . . . with one hand tied behind my back . . . brrrrr . . ."—"I don't want your rags—I want air," gasped out the other faintly, as if suddenly exhausted.

The sprays swept over whistling and pattering. Men disturbed in their peaceful torpor by the pain of quarrelsome shouts, moaned, muttering curses. Mr. Baker crawled off a little way to leeward where a water-cask loomed up big, with something white against it. "Is it you, Podmore?" asked Mr. Baker. He had to repeat the question twice before the cook turned, coughing feebly.—"Yes, sir. I've been praying in my mind for a quick deliverance; for I am prepared for any call. . . . I——"—"Look here, cook," interrupted Mr. Baker, "the men are perishing with cold."—"Cold!" said the cook mournfully; "they will be warm enough before long."—"What?" asked Mr. Baker, looking along the deck into the faint sheen of frothing water.—"They are a wicked lot," continued the cook solemnly, but in an unsteady voice, "about as wicked as any ship's company in this sinful world! Now, I"—he trembled so that he could hardly speak; his was an exposed place, and in a cotton shirt, a thin pair of trousers, and with his knees under his nose, he received, quaking, the flicks of stinging, salt drops; his voice sounded exhausted—"now, I—any time. . . . My eldest youngster, Mr. Baker . . . a clever boy . . . last Sunday on shore before this voyage he wouldn't go to church, sir. Says I, 'You go and clean yourself, or I'll know the reason why!' What does he do? . . . Pond,

Mr. Baker—fell into the pond in his best rig, sir! . . . Accident? . . .
'Nothing will save you, fine scholar though you are!' says I. . . .
Accident! . . . I whopped him, sir, till I couldn't lift my arm. . . ."
His voice faltered. "I whopped 'im!" he repeated, rattling his teeth;
then, after a while, let out a mournful sound that was half a groan,
half a snore. Mr. Baker shook him by the shoulders. "Hey! Cook!
Hold up, Podmore! Tell me—is there any fresh water in the galley
tank? The ship is lying along less, I think; I would try to get forward. A little water would do them good. Hallo! Look out! Look
out!" The cook struggled.—"Not you, sir—not you!" He began to
scramble to windward. "Galley! . . . my business!" he shouted.—
"Cook's going crazy now," said several voices. He yelled:—"Crazy,
am I? I am more ready to die than any of you, officers incloosive—
there! As long as she swims I will cook! I will get you coffee."—
"Cook, ye are a gentleman!" cried Belfast. But the cook was already
going over the weather ladder. He stopped for a moment to shout
back on the poop:—"As long as she swims I will cook!" and disappeared as though he had gone overboard. The men who had heard
sent after him a cheer that sounded like a wail of sick children. An
hour or more afterwards some one said distinctly: "He's gone for
good."—"Very likely," assented the boatswain; "even in fine
weather he was as smart about the deck as a milch-cow[3] on her first
voyage. We ought to go and see." Nobody moved. As the hours
dragged slowly through the darkness Mr. Baker crawled back and
forth along the poop several times. Some men fancied they had
heard him exchange murmurs with the master, but at that time the
memories were incomparably more vivid than anything actual, and
they were not certain whether the murmurs were heard now or
many years ago. They did not try to find out. A mutter more or less
did not matter. It was too cold for curiosity, and almost for hope.
They could not spare a moment or a thought from the great mental
occupation of wishing to live. And the desire of life kept them alive,
apathetic and enduring under the cruel persistence of wind and
cold; while the bestarred black dome of the sky revolved slowly
above the ship, that drifted, bearing their patience and their suffering, through the stormy solitude of the sea.

Huddled close to one another, they fancied themselves utterly
alone. They heard sustained loud noises, and again bore the pain of
existence through long hours of profound silence. In the night
they saw sunshine, felt warmth, and suddenly, with a start, thought
that the sun would never rise upon a freezing world. Some heard
laughter, listened to songs; others, near the end of the poop, could
hear loud human shrieks, and opening their eyes, were surprised to

3. A cow that is raised for her milk   ships in order to supply the crew with
rather than her beef and taken on board   fresh milk.

hear them still, though very faint, and far away. The boatswain said:—"Why, it's the cook, hailing from forward, I think." He hardly believed his own words or recognised his own voice. It was a long time before the man next to him gave a sign of life. He punched hard his other neighbour and said;—"The cook's shouting!" Many did not understand, others did not care; the majority farther aft did not believe. But the boatswain and another man had the pluck to crawl away forward to see. They seemed to have been gone for hours, and were very soon forgotten. Then suddenly men who had been plunged in a hopeless resignation became as if possessed with a desire to hurt. They belaboured one another with fists. In the darkness they struck persistently anything soft they could feel near, and, with a greater effort than for a shout, whispered excitedly—"They've got some hot coffee. . . . Boss'en got it. . . ." "No! . . . Where?" . . . "It's coming! Cook made it." James Wait moaned. Donkin scrambled viciously, caring not where he kicked, and anxious that the officers should have none of it. It came in a pot, and they drank in turns. It was hot, and while it blistered the greedy palates, it seemed incredible. The men sighed out parting with the mug:—"How 'as he done it?" Some cried weakly;—"Bully for you, doctor!"

He had done it somehow. Afterwards Archie declared that the thing was "meeraculous." For many days we wondered, and it was the one ever-interesting subject of conversation to the end of the voyage. We asked the cook, in fine weather, how he felt when he saw his stove "reared up on end." We inquired, in the north-east trade[4] and on serene evenings, whether he had to stand on his head to put things right somewhat. We suggested he had used his breadboard for a raft, and from there comfortably had stoked his grate; and we did our best to conceal our admiration under the wit of fine irony. He affirmed not to know anything about it, rebuked our levity, declared himself, with solemn animation, to have been the object of a special mercy for the saving of our unholy lives. Fundamentally he was right, no doubt; but he need not have been so offensively positive about it—he need not have hinted so often that it would have gone hard with us had he not been there, meritorious and pure, to receive the inspiration and the strength for the work of grace. Had we been saved by his recklessness or his agility, we could have at length become reconciled to the fact; but to admit our obligation to anybody's virtue and holiness alone was as difficult for us as for any other handful of mankind. Like many benefactors of humanity, the cook took himself too seriously, and reaped the reward of irreverence. We were not ungrateful, however. He re-

4. Winds from ENE, having a steady general direction from the northeast in north latitude.

mained heroic. His saying—*the* saying of his life—became proverbial in the mouths of men as are the sayings of conquerors or sages. Later, whenever one of us was puzzled by a task and advised to relinquish it, he would express his determination to persevere and to succeed by the words:—"As long as she swims I will cook!"

The hot drink helped us through the bleak hours that precede the dawn. The sky low by the horizon took on the delicate tints of pink and yellow like the inside of a rare shell. And higher, where it glowed with a pearly sheen, a small black cloud appeared, like a forgotten fragment of the night set in a border of dazzling gold. The beams of light skipped on the crests of waves. The eyes of men turned to the eastward. The sunlight flooded their weary faces. They were giving themselves up to fatigue as though they had done for ever with their work. On Singleton's black oilskin coat the dried salt glistened like hoarfrost. He hung on by the wheel, with open and lifeless eyes. Captain Allistoun, unblinking, faced the rising sun. His lips stirred, opened for the first time in twenty-four hours, and with a fresh firm voice he cried, "Wear ship!"

The commanding sharp tones made all these torpid men start like a sudden flick of a whip. Then again, motionless where they lay, the force of habit made some of them repeat the order in hardly audible murmurs. Captain Allistoun glanced down at his crew, and several, with trembling fingers and hopeless movements, tried to cast themselves adrift. He repeated impatiently, "Wear ship. Now then, Mr. Baker, get the men along. What's the matter with them?"—"Wear ship. Do you hear there?—Wear ship!" thundered out the boatswain suddenly. His voice seemed to break through a deadly spell. Men began to stir and crawl.—"I want the fore-top-mast stay sail run up smartly," said the master, very loudly; "if you can't manage it standing up you must do it lying down—that's all. Bear a hand!"—"Come along! Let's give the old girl a chance," urged the boatswain.—"Ay! ay! Wear ship!" exclaimed quavering voices. The forecastle men, with reluctant faces, prepared to go forward. Mr. Baker pushed ahead, grunting, on all fours to show the way, and they followed him over the break. The others lay still with a vile hope in their hearts of not being required to move till they got saved or drowned in peace.

After some time they could be seen forward appearing on the forecastle head, one by one in unsafe attitudes; hanging on to the rails clambering over the anchors; embracing the cross-head of the windlass or hugging the fore-capstan. They were restless with strange exertions, waved their arms, knelt, lay flat down, staggered up, seemed to strive their hardest to go overboard. Suddenly a small white piece of canvas fluttered amongst them, grew larger, beating. Its narrow head rose in jerks—and at last it stood distended and triangular in the sunshine.—"They have done it!" cried the voices aft. Captain Allistoun let go the rope he had round his wrist and rolled to leeward headlong. He could be seen casting the lee main braces off the pins while the backwash of waves splashed over him.— "Square the main yard!" he shouted up to us—who stared at him in wonder. We hesitated to stir. "The main brace, men. Haul! haul anyhow! Lay on your backs and haul!" he screeched, half drowned down there. We did not believe we could move the main yard, but the strongest and the less discouraged tried to execute the order. Others assisted half-heartedly. Singleton's eyes blazed suddenly as he took a fresh grip of the spokes. Captain Allistoun fought his way up to windward.—"Haul, men! Try to move it! Haul, and help the ship." His hard face worked suffused and furious. "Is she going off, Singleton?" he cried.—"Not a move yet, sir," croaked the old seaman in a horribly hoarse voice.—"Watch the helm, Singleton," spluttered the master. "Haul, men! Have you no more strength than rats? Haul, and earn your salt." Mr. Creighton, on his back, with a swollen leg and a face as white as a piece of paper, blinked his eyes; his bluish lips twitched. In the wild scramble men grabbed at him, crawled over his hurt leg, knelt on his chest. He kept perfectly still, setting his teeth without a moan, without a sigh. The master's ardour, the cries of that silent man inspired us. We hauled and hung in bunches on the rope. We heard him say with violence to Donkin, who sprawled abjectly on his stomach,—"I will brain you with this belaying-pin if you don't catch hold of the brace," and that victim of men's injustice, cowardly and cheeky, whimpered:—"Are you goin' to murder us now?" while with sudden desperation he gripped the rope. Men sighed, shouted, hissed meaningless words, groaned. The yards moved, came slowly square against the wind, that hummed loudly on the yard-arms.—"Going off, sir," shouted Singleton, "she's just started."—"Catch a turn with that brace. Catch a turn!" clamoured the master. Mr. Creighton, nearly suffocated and unable to move, made a mighty effort, and with his left hand managed to nip the rope.—"All fast!" cried some one. He closed his eyes as if going off into a swoon, while huddled together about the brace we watched with sacred looks what the ship would do now.

She went off slowly as though she had been weary and disheartened like the men she carried. She paid off very gradually, making us hold our breath till we choked, and as soon as she had brought the wind abaft the beam she started to move, and fluttered our hearts. It was awful to see her, nearly overturned, begin to gather way and drag her submerged side through the water. The dead-eyes of the rigging churned the breaking seas. The lower half of the deck was full of mad whirlpools and eddies; and the long line of the lee rail could be seen showing black now and then in the swirls of a field of foam as dazzling and white as a field of snow. The wind sang shrilly amongst the spars; and at every slight lurch we expected her to slip to the bottom sideways from under our backs. When dead before it she made the first distinct attempt to stand up, and we encouraged her with a feeble and discordant howl. A great sea came running up aft and hung for a moment over us with a curling top; then crashed down under the counter and spread out on both sides into a great sheet of bursting froth. Above its fierce hiss we heard Singleton's croak:—"She is steering!" He had both his feet now planted firmly on the grating, and the wheel spun fast as he eased the helm.—"Bring the wind on the port quarter and steady her!" called out the master, staggering to his feet, the first man up from amongst our prostrate heap. One or two screamed with excitement:—"She rises!" Far away forward, Mr. Baker and three others were seen erect and black on the clear sky, lifting their arms, and with open mouths as though they had been shouting all together. The ship trembled, trying to lift her side, lurched back, seemed to give up with a nerveless dip, and suddenly with an unexpected jerk swung violently to windward, as though she had torn herself out from a deadly grasp. The whole immense volume of water, lifted by her deck, was thrown bodily across to starboard. Loud cracks were heard. Iron ports breaking open thundered with ringing blows. The water topped over the starboard rail with the rush of a river falling over a dam. The sea on deck, and the seas on every side of her, mingled together in a deafening roar. She rolled violently. We got up and were helplessly run or flung about from side to side. Men, rolling over and over, yelled,—"The house will go!"—"She clears herself!" Lifted by a towering sea she ran along with it for a moment, spouting thick streams of water through every opening of her wounded sides. The lee braces having been carried away or washed off the pins, all the ponderous yards on the fore swung from side to side and with appalling rapidity at every roll. The men forward were seen crouching here and there with fearful glances upwards at the enormous spars that whirled about over their heads. The torn canvas and the ends of broken gear streamed in the wind like wisps of hair. Through the clear sunshine, over the flashing turmoil and uproar of the seas, the ship ran blindly, dishevelled and headlong, as if fleeing for her life; and on the poop we spun, we tottered about, distracted and noisy. We all spoke at once in a thin babble; we had the aspects of invalids and the gestures of maniacs. Eyes shone, large and haggard, in smiling, meagre faces that seemed to have been dusted over with powdered chalk. We stamped, clapped our hands, feeling ready to jump and do anything; but in reality hardly able to keep our feet. Captain Allistoun, hard and slim, gesticulated madly from the poop at Mr. Baker: "Steady these fore-yards! Steady them the best you can!" On the main deck, men excited by his cries, splashed, dashing aimlessly here and there with the foam swirling up to their waists. Apart, far aft, and alone by the helm, old Singleton had deliberately tucked his white beard under the top button of his glistening coat. Swaying upon the din and tumult of the seas, with the whole battered length of the ship launched forward in a rolling rush before his steady old eyes, he stood rigidly still, forgotten by all, and with an attentive face. In front of his erect figure only the two arms moved crosswise with a swift and sudden readiness, to check or urge again the rapid stir of circling spokes. He steered with care.

Chapter Four

On men reprieved by its disdainful mercy, the immortal sea confers in its justice the full privilege of desired unrest. Through the perfect wisdom of its grace they are not permitted to meditate at ease upon the complicated and acrid savour of existence. They must without pause justify their life to the eternal pity that commands toil to be hard and unceasing, from sunrise to sunset, from sunset to sunrise; till the weary succession of nights and days tainted by the obstinate clamour of sages, demanding bliss and an empty heaven, is redeemed at last by the vast silence of pain and labour, by the dumb fear and the dumb courage of men obscure, forgetful, and enduring.

The master and Mr. Baker coming face to face stared for a moment, with the intense and amazed looks of men meeting unexpectedly after years of trouble. Their voices were gone, and they whispered desperately at one another.—"Any one missing?" asked Captain Allistoun.—"No. All there,"—"Anybody hurt?"—"Only the second mate."—"I will look after him directly. We're lucky." —"Very," articulated Mr. Baker faintly. He gripped the rail and rolled bloodshot eyes. The little grey man made an effort to raise his voice above a dull mutter, and fixed his chief mate with a cold gaze, piercing like a dart.—"Get sail on the ship," he said, speaking authoritatively and with an inflexible snap of his thin lips. "Get sail on her as soon as you can. This is a fair wind. At once, sir—don't give the men time to feel themselves. They will get done up and stiff, and we will never . . . We must get her along now" . . . He reeled to a long heavy roll; the rail dipped into the glancing hissing water. He caught a shroud, swung helplessly against the mate . . . "Now we have a fair wind at last——Make——sail." His head rolled from shoulder to shoulder. His eyelids began to beat rapidly. "And the pumps——pumps, Mr. Baker." He peered as though the face within a foot of his eyes had been half a mile off. "Keep the men on the move to——to get her along," he mumbled in a drowsy tone, like a man going off into a doze. He pulled himself together suddenly. "Mustn't stand. Won't do," he said, with a painful attempt at a smile. He let go his hold, and, propelled, by the dip of the ship, ran aft unwillingly, with small steps, till he brought up against the binnacle stand. Hanging on there, he looked up in an aimless manner at Singleton, who, unheeding him, watched anxiously the end of the jib-boom.—"Steering gear works all right?" he asked. There was a noise in the old seaman's throat, as though the words had been rattling together before they could come out.— "Steers . . . like a little boat," he said, at last, with hoarse tenderness, without giving the master as much as half a glance—then, watchfully, spun the wheel down, steadied, flung it back again. Captain Allistoun tore himself away from the delight of leaning against the binnacle, and began to walk the poop, swaying and reeling to preserve his balance. . . .

The pump-rods, clanking, stamped in short jumps while the flywheels turned smoothly, with great speed, at the foot of the mainmast, flinging back and forth with a regular impetuosity two limp clusters of men clinging to the handles. They abandoned themselves, swaying from the hip with twitching faces and stony eyes. The carpenter, sounding from time to time, exclaimed mechanically: "Shake her up! Keep her going!" Mr. Baker could not speak, but found his voice to shout; and under the goad of his objurgations, men looked to the lashings, dragged out new sails; and, thinking themselves unable to move, carried heavy blocks aloft—overhauled the gear. They went up the rigging with faltering and desperate efforts. Their heads swam as they shifted their hold, stepped blindly on the yards like men in the dark; or trusted themselves to the first rope at hand with the negligence of exhausted strength. The narrow escapes from falls did not disturb the languid beat of their hearts; the roar of the seas seething far below them sounded continuous and faint like an indistinct noise from another world; the wind filled their eyes with tears, and with heavy gusts tried to push them off from where they swayed in insecure positions. With streaming faces and blowing hair they flew up and down between sky and water, bestriding the ends of yard-arms, crouching on footropes, embracing lifts to have their hands free, or standing up against chain ties. Their thoughts floated vaguely between the desire of rest and the desire of life, while their stiffened fingers cast off head-earrings, fumbled for knives, or held with tenacious grip against the violent shocks of beating canvas. They glared savagely at one another, made frantic signs with one hand while they held their life in the other, looked down on the narrow strip of flooded deck, shouted along to leeward: "Light-to!" . . . "Haul out!" . . . "Make fast!" Their lips moved, their eyes started, furious and eager with the desire to be understood, but the wind tossed their words unheard upon the disturbed sea. In an unendurable and unending strain they worked like men driven by a merciless dream to toil in an atmosphere of ice or flame. They burnt and shivered in turns. Their eyeballs smarted as if in the smoke of a conflagration; their heads were ready to burst with every shout. Hard fingers seemed to grip their throats. At every roll they thought: Now I must let go. It will shake us all off—and thrown about aloft they cried wildly: "Look out, there—catch the end." . . . "Reeve clear." . . . "Turn this block. . . ." They nodded desperately; shook infuriated faces. "No! No! From down up." They seemed to hate one another with a deadly hate. The longing to be done with it all gnawed their breasts, and the wish to do things well was a burning pain. They cursed their fate, contemned their life, and wasted their breath in deadly imprecations upon one another. The sailmaker, with his bald head bared, worked feverishly, forgetting his intimacy with so many admirals. The boatswain, climbing up with marlinspikes and bunches of spunyarn rovings, or kneeling on the yard and ready to take a turn with the midship-stop, had acute and fleeting visions of his old woman and the youngsters in a moorland village. Mr. Baker, feeling very weak, tottered here and there, grunting and inflexible, like a man of iron. He waylaid those who, coming from aloft, stood gasping for breath. He ordered, encouraged, scolded. "Now then— to the main topsail now! Tally on to that gantline. Don't stand about there!"—"Is there no rest for us?" muttered voices. He spun round fiercely, with a sinking heart.—"No! No rest till the work is done. Work till you drop. That's what you're here for." A bowed seaman at his elbow gave a short laugh.—"Do or die," he croaked bitterly, then spat into his broad palms, swung up his long arms, and grasping the rope high above his head sent out a mournful, wailing cry for a pull all together. A sea boarded the quarterdeck and sent the whole lot sprawling to leeward. Caps, handspikes floated. Clenched hands, kicking legs, with here and there a spluttering face, stuck out of the white hiss of foaming water. Mr. Baker, knocked down with the rest, screamed—"Don't let go that rope! Hold on to it! Hold!" And sorely bruised by the brutal fling, they held on to it, as though it had been the fortune of their life. The ship ran, rolling heavily, and the topping crests glanced past port and starboard flashing their white heads. Pumps were freed. Braces were rove. The three topsails and foresail were set. She spurted faster over the water, outpacing the swift rush of waves. The menacing thunder of distanced seas rose behind her—filled the air with the tremendous vibrations of its voice. And devastated, battered and wounded she drove foaming to the northward, as though inspired by the courage of a high endeavour. . . .

The forecastle was a place of damp desolation. They looked at their dwelling with dismay. It was slimy, dripping; it hummed hollow with the wind, and was strewn with shapeless wreckage like a half-tide cavern in a rocky and exposed coast. Many had lost all they had in the world, but most of the starboard watch had preserved their chests; thin streams of water trickled out of them, however. The beds were soaked; the blankets spread out and saved by some nail squashed under foot. They dragged wet rags from evil-smelling corners, and wringing the water out, recognised their property. Some smiled stiffly. Others looked round blank and mute. There were cries of joy over old waistcoats, and groans of sorrow over shapeless things found among the splinters of smashed bed boards. One lamp was discovered jammed under the bowsprit. Charley whimpered a little. Knowles stumped here and there, sniffing, examining dark places for salvage. He poured dirty water out of a boot, and was concerned to find the owner. Those who, overwhelmed by their losses, sat on the forepeak hatch, remained elbows on knees, and, with a fist against each cheek, disdained to look up. He pushed it under their noses. "Here's a good boot. Yours?" They snarled, "No—get out." One snapped at him, "Take it to hell out of this." He seemed surprised. "Why? It's a good boot," but, remembering suddenly that he had lost every stitch of his clothing, he dropped his find and began to swear. In the dim light cursing voices clashed. A man came in and, dropping his arms, stood still, repeating from the doorstep, "Here's a bloomin' old go! Here's a bloomin' old go!" A few rooted anxiously in flooded chests for tobacco. They breathed hard, clamoured with heads down. "Look at that, Jack!" . . . "Here! Sam! Here's my shore-going rig spoilt for ever." One blasphemed tearfully, holding up a pair of dripping trousers. No one looked at him. The cat came out from somewhere. He had an ovation. They snatched him from hand to hand, caressed him in a murmur of pet names. They wondered where he had "weathered it out"; disputed about it. A squabbling argument began. Two men brought in a bucket of fresh water, and all crowded round it; but Tom, lean and mewing, came up with every hair astir and had the first drink. A couple of hands went aft for oil and biscuits.

Then in the yellow light and in the intervals of mopping the deck they crunched hard bread, arranging to "worry through somehow." Men chummed as to beds. Turns were settled for wearing boots and having the use of oilskin coats. They called one another "old man" and "sonny" in cheery voices. Friendly slaps resounded. Jokes were shouted. One or two stretched on the wet deck, slept with heads pillowed on their bent arms, and several, sitting on the hatch, smoked. Their weary faces appeared through a thin blue haze, pacified and with sparkling eyes. The boatswain put his head through the door. "Relieve the wheel, one of you"—he shouted inside—"it's six. Blamme if that old Singleton hasn't been there more'n thirty hours. You are a fine lot." He slammed the door again. "Mate's watch on deck," said some one. "Hey, Donkin, it's your relief!" shouted three or four together. He had crawled into an empty bunk and on wet planks lay still. "Donkin, your wheel." He made no sound. "Donkin's dead," guffawed some one. "Sell 'is bloomin' clothes," shouted another. "Donkin, if ye don't go to the bloomin' wheel they will sell your clothes—d'ye hear?" jeered a third. He groaned from his dark hole. He complained about pains in all his bones, he whimpered pitifully. "He won't go," exclaimed a contemptuous voice; "your turn, Davis." The young seaman rose painfully, squaring his shoulders. Donkin stuck his head out, and it appeared in the yellow light fragile and ghastly. "I will giv' yer a pound of tobaccer," he whined in a conciliating voice, "so soon as I draw it from aft. I will—s'elp me. . . ." Davis swung his arm backhanded and the head vanished. "I'll go," he said, "but you will pay for it." He walked unsteady but resolute to the door. "So I will," yelped Donkin, popping out behind him. "So I will—s'elp me . . . a pound . . . three bob they chawrge." Davis flung the door open. "You will pay my price . . . in fine weather," he shouted over his shoulder. One of the men unbuttoned his wet coat rapidly, threw it at his head. "Here, Taffy—take that, you thief!" "Thank you!" he cried from the darkness above the swish of rolling water. He could be heard splashing; a sea came on board with a thump. "He's got his bath already," remarked a grim shellback. "Ay, ay!" grunted others. Then, after a long silence, Wamibo made strange noises. "Hallo, what's up with you?" said some one grumpily. "He says he would have gone for Davy," explained Archie, who was the Finn's interpreter generally. "I believe him!" cried voices. . . . "Never mind, Dutchy. . . . You'll do, muddle-head. . . . Your turn will come soon enough. . . . You don't know when ye're well off." They ceased and all together turned their faces to the door. Singleton stepped in, advanced two paces, and stood swaying slightly. The sea hissed, flowed roaring past the bows, and the forecastle trembled, full of deep murmurs; the lamp flared, swinging like a pendulum. He looked with a dreamy and puzzled stare, as though he could not distinguish the still men from their restless shadows. There were awestruck exclamations:—"Hallo, hallo." . . . "How does it look outside now, Singleton?" Those who sat on the hatch lifted their eyes in silence, and the next oldest seaman in the ship (those two understood one another, though they hardly exchanged three words in a day) gazed up at his friend attentively for a moment, then, taking a short clay pipe out of his mouth, offered it without a word. Singleton put out his arm towards it, missed, staggered, and suddenly fell forward, crashing down, stiff and headlong like an uprooted tree. There was a swift rush. Men pushed, crying:—"He's done!" . . . "Turn him over!" . . . "Stand clear, there!" Under a crowd of startled faces bending over him he lay on his back, staring upwards in a continuous and intolerable manner. In the breathless silence of a general consternation, he said in a grating murmur:—"I am all right," and clutched with his hands. They helped him up. He mumbled despondently:—"I am getting old . . . old."—"Not you," cried Belfast, with ready tact. Supported on all sides, he hung his head.—"Are you better?" they asked. He glared at them from under his eyebrows with large black eyes, spreading over his chest the bushy whiteness of a beard long and thick.—"Old! old!" he repeated sternly. Helped along, he reached his bunk. There was in it a slimy soft heap of something that smelt, as does, at dead low water, a muddy foreshore. It was his soaked straw bed. With a convulsive effort he pitched himself on it, and in the darkness of the narrow place could be heard growling angrily, like an irritated and savage animal uneasy in its den:—"Bit of breeze . . . small thing . . . can't stand up . . . old!" He slept at last, high-booted, sou'wester on head, and his oilskin clothes rustled, when with a deep sighing groan he turned over. Men conversed about him in quiet concerned whispers. "This will break 'im up." . . . "Strong as a horse." . . . "Ay. But he ain't what he used to be." . . . In sad murmurs they gave him up. Yet at midnight he turned out to duty as if nothing had been the matter, and answered to his name with a mournful "Here!" He brooded alone more than ever, in an impenetrable silence and with a saddened face. For many years he had heard himself called "Old Singleton," and had serenely accepted the qualification, taking it as a tribute of respect due to a man who through half a century had measured his strength against the favours and the rages of the sea. He had never given a thought to his mortal self. He lived unscathed, as though he had been indestructible, surrendering to all the temptations, weathering many gales. He had panted in sunshine, shivered in the cold; suffered hunger, thirst, debauch; passed through many trials—known all the furies. Old! It seemed to him he was broken at last. And like a man bound treacherously while he sleeps, he woke up fettered by the long chain of disregarded years. He had to take up at once the burden of all his existence, and found it almost too heavy for his strength. Old! He moved his arms, shook his head, felt his limbs. Getting old . . . and then? He looked upon the immortal sea with the awakened and groping perception of its heartless might; he saw it unchanged, black and foaming under the eternal scrutiny of the stars; he heard its impatient voice calling for him out of a pitiless vastness full of unrest, of turmoil, and of terror. He looked afar upon it, and he saw an immensity tormented and blind, moaning and furious, that claimed all the days of his tenacious life, and, when life was over, would claim the worn-out body of its slave. . . .

This was the last of the breeze. It veered quickly, changed to a black south-easter, and blew itself out, giving the ship a famous shove to the northward into the joyous sunshine of the trade. Rapid and white she ran homewards in a straight path, under a blue sky and upon the plain of a blue sea. She carried Singleton's completed wisdom, Donkin's delicate susceptibilities, and the conceited folly of us all. The hours of ineffective turmoil were forgotten; the fear and anguish of these dark moments were never mentioned in the glowing peace of fine days. Yet from that time our life seemed to start afresh as though we had died and had been resuscitated. All the first part of the voyage, the Indian Ocean on the other side of the Cape, all that was lost in a haze, like an ineradicable suspicion of some previous existence. It had ended—then there were blank hours: a livid blur — and again we lived! Singleton was possessed of sinister truth; Mr. Creighton of a damaged leg; the cook of fame— and shamefully abused the opportunities of his distinction. Donkin had an added grievance. He went about repeating with insistence: —"'E said 'e would brain me—did yer 'ear? They are goin' to murder us now for the least little thing." We began at last to think it was rather awful. And we were conceited! We boasted of our pluck, of our capacity for work, of our energy. We remembered honourable episodes: our devotion, our indomitable perseverance— and were proud of them as though they had been the outcome of our unaided impulses. We remembered our danger, our toil—and conveniently forgot our horrible scare. We decried our officers— who had done nothing—and listened to the fascinating Donkin. His care for our rights, his disinterested concern for our dignity, were not discouraged by the invariable contumely of our words, by the disdain of our looks. Our contempt for him was unbounded— and we could not but listen with interest to that consummate artist. He told us we were good men—a "bloomin' condemned lot of good men." Who thanked us? Who took any notice of our wrongs? Didn't we lead a "dorg's loife for two poun' ten[1] a month"? Did we think that miserable pay enough to compensate us for the risk to our lives and for the loss of our clothes? "We've lost every rag!" he cried. He made us forget that he, at any rate, had lost nothing of his own. The younger men listened, thinking—this 'ere Donkin's a

1. Monthly rate of pay: two pounds and ten shillings ("old" money).

long-headed chap, though no kind of man, anyhow. The Scandinavians were frightened at his audacities; Wamibo did not understand; and the older seamen thoughtfully nodded their heads,
making the thin gold earrings glitter in the fleshy lobes of hairy
ears. Severe, sunburnt faces were propped meditatively on tattooed
forearms. Veined, brown fists held in their knotted grip the dirty
white clay of smouldering pipes. They listened, impenetrable,
broad-backed, with bent shoulders, and in grim silence. He talked
with ardour, despised and irrefutable. His picturesque and filthy
loquacity flowed like a troubled stream from a poisoned source. His
beady little eyes danced, glancing right and left, ever on the watch
for the approach of an officer. Sometimes Mr. Baker going forward
to take a look at the head sheets would roll with his uncouth gait
through the sudden stillness of the men; or Mr. Creighton limped
along, smooth-faced, youthful, and more stern than ever, piercing
our short silence with a keen glance of his clear eyes. Behind his
back Donkin would begin again darting stealthy, sidelong looks.—
" 'Ere's one of 'em. Some of yer 'as made 'im fast that day. Much
thanks yer got for it. Ain't 'ee a-driven' yer wusse'n ever? . . . Let
'im slip overboard. . . . Vy not? It would 'ave been less trouble. Vy
not?" He advanced confidentially, backed away with great effect; he
whispered, he screamed, waved his miserable arms no thicker than
pipe-stems—stretched his lean neck—spluttered—squinted. In the
pauses of his impassioned orations the wind sighed quietly aloft, the
calm sea unheeded murmured in a warning whisper along the ship's
side. We abominated the creature and could not deny the luminous
truth of his contentions. It was all so obvious. We were indubitably
good men; our deserts were great and our pay small. Through our
exertions we had saved the ship and the skipper would get the
credit of it. What had he done? we wanted to know. Donkin asked:
—"What 'ee could do without hus?" and we could not answer. We
were oppressed by the injustice of the world, surprised to perceive
how long we had lived under its burden without realising our unfortunate state, annoyed by the uneasy suspicion of our undiscerning
stupidity. Donkin assured us it was all our "good 'eartedness," but
we would not be consoled by such shallow sophistry. We were men
enough to courageously admit to ourselves our intellectual shortcomings; though from that time we refrained from kicking him,
tweaking his nose, or from accidentally knocking him about, which
last, after we had weathered the Cape, had been rather a popular
amusement. Davis ceased to talk at him provokingly about black
eyes and flattened noses. Charley, much subdued since the gale, did
not jeer at him. Knowles deferentially and with a crafty air pro-
pounded questions such as:—"Could we all have the same grub as
the mates? Could we all stop ashore till we got it? What would be

the next thing to try for if we got that?" He answered readily with contemptuous certitude; he strutted with assurance in clothes that were much too big for him as though he had tried to disguise himself. These were Jimmy's clothes mostly—though he would accept anything from anybody; but nobody, except Jimmy, had anything to spare. His devotion to Jimmy was unbounded. He was for ever dodging in the little cabin, ministering to Jimmy's wants, humouring his whims, submitting to his exacting peevishness, often laughing with him. Nothing could keep him away from the pious work of visiting the sick, especially when there was some heavy hauling to be done on deck. Mr. Baker had on two occasions jerked him out from there by the scruff of the neck to our inexpressible scandal. Was a sick chap to be left without attendance? Were we to be illused for attending a shipmate?—"What?" growled Mr. Baker, turning menacingly at the mutter, and the whole half-circle like one man stepped back a pace. "Set the topmast stunsail. Away aloft, Donkin, overhaul the gear," ordered the mate inflexibly. "Fetch the sail along; bend the down-haul clear. Bear a hand." Then, the sail set, he would go slowly aft and stand looking at the compass for a long time, careworn, pensive, and breathing hard as if stifled by the taint of unaccountable ill-will that pervaded the ship. "What's up amongst them?" he thought. "Can't make out this hanging back and growling. A good crowd, too, as they go nowadays." On deck the men exchanged bitter words, suggested by a silly exasperation against something unjust and irremediable that would not be denied, and would whisper into their ears long after Donkin had ceased speaking. Our little world went on its curved and unswerving path carrying a discontented and aspiring population. They found comfort of a gloomy kind in an interminable and conscientious analysis of their unappreciated worth; and inspired by Donkin's hopeful doctrines they dreamed enthusiastically of the time when every lonely ship would travel over a serene sea, manned by a wealthy and well-fed crew of satisfied skippers.

It looked as if it would be a long passage. The south-east trades, light and unsteady, were left behind; and then, on the equator and under a low grey sky, the ship, in close heat, floated upon a smooth sea that resembled a sheet of ground glass. Thunder squalls hung on the horizon, circled round the ship, far off and growling angrily, like a troop of wild beasts afraid to charge home. The invisible sun, sweeping above the upright masts, made on the clouds a blurred stain of rayless light, and a similar patch of faded radiance kept pace with it from east to west over the unglittering level of the waters. At night, through the impenetrable darkness of earth and of heaven, broad sheets of flame waved noiselessly; and for half a second the becalmed craft stood out with its masts and rigging, with every sail and every rope distinct and black in the centre of a fiery outburst, like a charred ship enclosed in a globe of fire. And, again, for long hours, she remained lost in a vast universe of night and silence where gentle sighs wandering here and there like forlorn souls, made the still sails flutter, as in sudden fear, and the ripple of a beshrouded ocean whisper its compassion afar—in a voice mournful, immense, and faint. . . .

When the lamp was put out, and through the door thrown wide open, Jimmy, turning on his pillow, could see vanishing beyond the straight line of top-gallant rail, the quick, repeated visions of a fabulous world made up of leaping fire and sleeping water. The lightning gleamed in his big sad eyes that seemed in a red flicker to burn themselves out in his black face, and then he would lie blinded and invisible in the midst of an intense darkness. He could hear on the quiet deck soft footfalls, the breathing of some man lounging on the doorstep; the low creak of swaying masts; or the calm voice of the watch-officer reverberating aloft, hard and loud, amongst the unstirring sails. He listened with avidity, taking a rest in the attentive perception of the slightest sound from the fatiguing wanderings of his sleeplessness. He was cheered by the rattling of blocks, reassured by the stir and murmur of the watch, soothed by the slow yawn of some sleepy and weary seaman settling himself deliberately for a snooze on the planks. Life seemed an indestructible thing. It went on in darkness, in sunshine, in sleep; tireless, it hovered affectionately round the imposture of his ready death. It was bright, like the twisted flare of lightning, and more full of surprises than the dark night. It made him safe, and the calm of its overpowering darkness was as precious as its restless and dangerous light.

But in the evening, in the dog-watches, and even far into the first night-watch, a knot of men could always be seen congregated before Jimmy's cabin. They leaned on each side of the door peacefully interested, and with crossed legs; they stood astride the doorstep discoursing, or sat in silent couples on his sea-chest; while against the bulwark along the spare topmast, three or four in a row stared meditatively; with their simple faces lit up by the projected glare of Jimmy's lamp. The little place, repainted white, had, in the night, the brilliance of a silver shrine where a black idol, reclining stiffly under a blanket, blinked its weary eyes and received our homage. Donkin officiated. He had the air of a demonstrator showing a phenomenon, a manifestation bizarre, simple, and meritorious that, to the beholders, should be a profound and an everlasting lesson. "Just look at 'im, 'ee knows what's what—never fear!" he exclaimed now and then, flourishing a hand hard and fleshless like the claw of a snipe. Jimmy, on his back, smiled with reserve and without moving a limb. He affected the languor of extreme weakness, so as to make it manifest to us that our delay in hauling him out from his horrible confinement, and then that night spent on the poop among our selfish neglect of his needs, had "done for him." He rather liked to talk about it, and of course we were always interested. He spoke spasmodically, in fast rushes with long pauses between, as a tipsy man walks. . . . "Cook had just given me a pannikin of hot coffee. . . . Slapped it down there, on my chest—banged the door to. . . . I felt a heavy roll coming; tried to save my coffee, burnt my fingers . . . and fell out of my bunk. . . . She went over so quick. . . . Water came in through the ventilator. . . . I couldn't move the door . . . dark as a grave . . . tried to scramble up into the upper berth. . . . Rats . . . a rat bit my finger as I got up. . . . I could hear him swimming below me. . . . I thought you would never come. . . . I thought you were all gone overboard . . . of course. . . . Could hear nothing but the wind. . . . Then you came . . . to look for the corpse, I suppose. A little more and . . ."

"Man! But ye made a rare lot of noise in here," observed Archie thoughtfully.

"You chaps kicked up such a confounded row above. . . . Enough to scare any one. . . . I didn't know what you were up to. . . . Bash in the blamed planks . . . my head. . . . Just what a silly, scary gang of fools would do. . . . Not much good to me, anyhow. . . . Just as well . . . drown. . . . Pah."

He groaned, snapped his big white teeth, and gazed with scorn. Belfast lifted a pair of dolorous eyes, with a broken-hearted smile, clenched his fists stealthily; blue-eyed Archie caressed his red whiskers with a hesitating hand; the boatswain at the door stared a moment, and brusquely went away with a loud guffaw. Wamibo dreamed. . . . Donkin felt all over his sterile chin for the few rare hairs, and said, triumphantly, with a sidelong glance at Jimmy:—"Look at 'im! Wish I was 'arf has 'ealthy as 'ee is—I do." He jerked a short thumb over his shoulder towards the after end of the ship. "That's the blooming way to do 'em!" he yelped, with forced heartiness. Jimmy said;—"Don't be a dam' fool." in a pleasant voice. Knowles, rubbing his shoulder against the doorpost, remarked shrewdly:—"We can't all go an' be took sick—it would be mutiny."—"Mutiny—gawn!" jeered Donkin; "there's no boomin' law against bein' sick."—"There's six weeks' hard for refoosing dooty," argued Knowles. "I mind I once seed in Cardiff[2] the crew of an overloaded ship—leastways she weren't overloaded, only a fatherly old gentleman with a white beard and an umbreller came along the quay and talked to the hands. Said as how it was crool hard to be

---

2. **A seaport city in southeastern Wales noted for coal shipping and shipbuilding.**

drownded in winter just for the sake of a few pounds more for the owner—he said. Nearly cried over them—he did; and he had a square mainsail coat, and a gaff-topsail hat too—all proper. So they chaps they said they wouldn't go to be drownded in winter—depending upon that 'ere Plimsoll man[3] to see 'em through the court. They thought to have a bloomin' lark and two or three days' spree. And the beak[4] giv' 'em six weeks coss the ship warn't overloaded. Anyways they made it out in court that she wasn't. There wasn't one overloaded ship in Penarth Dock[5] at all. 'Pears that old coon he was only on pay and allowance from some kind people, under orders to look for overloaded ships, and he couldn't see no further than the length of his umbreller. Some of us in the boarding-house, where I live when I'm looking for a ship in Cardiff, stood by to duck that old weeping spunger in the dock. We kept a good look out, too—but he topped his boom[6] directly he was outside the court. . . . Yes. They got six weeks' hard. . . ."

They listened, full of curiosity, nodding in the pauses their rough pensive faces. Donkin opened his mouth once or twice, but restrained himself. Jimmy lay still with open eyes and not at all interested. A seaman emitted the opinion that after a verdict of atrocious partiality, "the bloomin' beaks go an' drink at the skipper's expense." Others assented. It was clear, of course. Donkin said:—"Well, six weeks ain't much trouble. You sleep all night in, reg'lar, in chokey.[7] Do it on my 'ead." "You are used to it ainch'ee, Donkin?" asked somebody. Jimmy condescended to laugh. It cheered up every one wonderfully. Knowles, with surprising mental agility, shifted his ground. "If we all went sick what would become of the ship? eh?" He posed the problem and grinned all round.— "Let 'er go to 'ell," sneered Donkin. "Damn 'er. She ain't yourn." —"What? Just let her drift?" insisted Knowles in a tone of unbelief.—"Ay! Drift, an' be blowed," affirmed Donkin, with fine recklessness. The other did not see it—meditated.—"The stores would run out," he muttered, "and . . . never get anywhere . . . and what about pay-day?" he added, with greater assurance.—"Jack likes a good pay-day," exclaimed a listener on the doorstep. "Ay, because then the girls put one arm round his neck an' t'other in his pocket, and call him ducky. Don't they, Jack?"—"Jack, you're a terror with the gals."—"He takes three of 'em in tow at once, like one of 'em Watkinses[8] two-funnel tugs waddling away with three schooners behind."—"Jack, you're a lame scamp."—"Jack, tell us about that one with a blue eye and a black eye. Do."—"There's plenty of girls

3. Samuel Plimsoll, an English shipping reformer known as "the sailor's friend." See Yates's essay in Criticism.
4. British slang for a judge or magistrate.
5. A seaport in southeastern Wales.
6. Got boozed up.
7. British slang for a jail, prison.
8. William Watkins founded one of the first steam tugboat companies on the Thames in 1833; which soon became and still is the largest.

with one black eye along the Highway by . . ." "No, that's a spe-
shul one—come, Jack." Donkin looked severe and disgusted; Jimmy
very bored; a grey-haired sea-dog shook his head slightly, smiling at
the bowl of his pipe, discreetly amused. Knowles turned about
bewildered; stammered first at one, then at another—'No! . . . I
never! . . . can't talk sensible sense 'midst you. . . . Always on the
kid." He retired bashfully—muttering and pleased. They laughed,
hooting in the crude light, around Jimmy's bed, where on a white
pillow his hollowed black face moved to and fro restlessly. A puff of
wind came, made the flame of the lamp leap, and outside, high up,
the sails fluttered, while near by the block of the foresheet struck a
ringing blow on the iron bulwark. A voice far off cried, "Helm up!"
another, more faint, answered, "Hard up, sir!" They became silent
—waited expectantly. The grey-haired seaman knocked his pipe on
the doorstep and stood up. The ship leaned over gently, and the sea
seemed to wake up, murmuring drowsily. "Here's a little wind
comin'," said some one very low. Jimmy turned over slowly to face
the breeze. The voice in the night cried loud and commanding:—
"Haul the spanker out." The group before the door vanished out of
the light. They could be heard tramping aft while they repeated
with varied intonations:—"Spanker out!" . . . "Out spanker, sir!"
Donkin remained alone with Jimmy. There was silence. Jimmy
opened and shut his lips several times as if swallowing draughts of
fresher air; Donkin moved the toes of his bare feet and looked at
them thoughtfully.

"Ain't you going to give them a hand with the sail?" asked
Jimmy.

"No. If six ov 'em ain't 'nough beef to set that blamed, rotten
spanker, they ain't fit to live," answered Donkin in a bored, far-
away voice, as though he had been talking from the bottom of a
hole. Jimmy considered the conical, fowl-like profile with a queer
kind of interest; he was leaning out of his bunk with the calculating, uncertain expression of a man who reflects how best to lay hold
of some strange creature that looks as though it could sting or bite.
But he said only:—"The mate will miss you—and there will be ruc-
tions."

Donkin got up to go. "I will do for 'em some dark night; see if I
don't," he said over his shoulder.

Jimmy went on quickly:—"You're like a poll-parrot, like a screech-
in' poll-parrot." Donkin stopped and cocked his head attentively
on one side. His big ears stood out, transparent and veined, resembling the thin wings of a bat.

"Yuss!" he said, with his back towards Jimmy.

"Yes! Chatter out all you know—like . . . like a dirty white cock-
atoo."

Donkin waited. He could hear the other's breathing, long and slow; the breathing of a man with a hundredweight or so on the breastbone. Then he asked calmly:—"What do I know?"

"What? . . . What I tell you . . . not much. What do you want . . . to talk about my health so . . ."

"It's a bloomin' imposyshun. A bloomin', stinkin', first-class imposyshun—but it don't tyke me in. Not it."

Jimmy kept still. Donkin put his hands in his pockets, and in one slouching stride came up to the bunk.

"I talk—what's the odds. They ain't men 'ere—sheep they are. A driven lot of sheep. I 'old you up. . . . Vy not? You're well orf."

"I am . . . I don't say anything about that. . . ."

"Well. Let 'em see it. Let 'em larn what a man can do. I am a man, I know all about yer. . . ." Jimmy threw himself farther away on the pillow; the other stretched out his skinny neck, jerked his birdface down at him as though pecking at the eyes. "I am a man. I've seen the inside of every chokey in the Colonies rather'n give up my rights. . . ."

"You are a jail-prop," said Jimmy weakly.

"I am . . . an' proud of it too. You! You 'aven't the bloomin' nerve—so you inventyd this 'ere dodge. . . ." He paused; then with marked afterthought accentuated slowly:—"Yer ain't sick—are yer?"

"No," said Jimmy firmly. "Been out of sorts now and again this year," he mumbled, with a sudden drop in his voice.

Donkin closed one eye, amicable and confidential. He whispered: —"Ye 'ave done this afore, 'aven'tchee?" Jimmy smiled—then as if unable to hold back he let himself go:—"Last ship—yes. I was out of sorts on the passage. See? It was easy. They paid me off in Calcutta,[9] and the skipper made no bones about it either. . . . I got my money all right. Laid up fifty-eight days! The fools! O Lord! The fools! Paid right off." He laughed spasmodically. Donkin chimed in giggling. Then Jimmy coughed violently. "I am as well as ever," he said, as soon as he could draw breath.

Donkin made a derisive gesture. "In course," he said profoundly. "any one can see that."—"They don't," said Jimmy, gasping like a fish.—"They would swallow any yarn," affirmed Donkin.—"Don't you let on too much," admonished Jimmy in an exhausted voice.— "Your little gyme? Eh?" commented Donkin jovially. Then with sudden disgust; "Yer all for yerself, s'long as ye're right. . . ."

So charged with egoism James Wait pulled the blanket up to his chin and lay still for a while. His heavy lips protruded in an ever-lasting black pout. "Why are you so hot on making trouble?" he asked, without much interest.

9. A seaport in northeastern India which was the largest port of trade in Asia during the 1880s.

" 'Cos it's a bloomin' shayme. We are put upon . . . bad food, bad pay . . . I want us to kick up a bloomin' row; a blamed 'owling row that would make 'em remember! Knocking people about . . . brain us . . . indeed! Ain't we men?" His altruistic indignation blazed. Then he said calmly:—"I've been airing yer clothes."—"All right," said Jimmy languidly, "bring them in."—"Giv' us the key of your chest, I'll put 'em away for yer," said Donkin, with friendly eagerness.—"Bring 'em in, I will put them away myself," answered James Wait, with severity. Donkin looked down, muttering. . . . "What d'you say? What d'you say?" inquired Wait anxiously.— "Nothink. The night's dry, let 'em 'ang out till the morning," said Donkin, in a strangely trembling voice, as though restraining laughter or rage. Jimmy seemed satisfied.—"Give me a little water for the night in my mug—there," he said. Donkin took a stride over the doorstep.—"Git it yerself," he replied in a surly tone. "You can do it, unless you *are* sick."—"Of course I can do it," said Wait, "only . . ."—"Well, then, do it," said Donkin viciously, "if yer can look after yer clothes, yer can look after yerself." He went on deck without a look back.

Jimmy reached out for the mug. Not a drop. He put it back gently, with a faint sigh—and closed his eyes. He thought:—That lunatic Belfast will bring me some water if I ask. Fool. I am very thirsty. . . . It was very hot in the cabin, and it seemed to turn slowly round, detach itself from the ship, and swing out smoothly into a luminous, arid space where a black sun shone, spinning very fast. A place without any water! No water! A policeman with the face of Donkin drank a glass of beer by the side of an empty well, and flew away flapping vigorously. A ship whose mastheads protruded through the sky and could not be seen, was discharging grain, and the wind whirled the dry husks in spirals along the quay of a dock with no water in it. He whirled along with the husks—very tired and light. All his inside was gone. He felt lighter than the husks—and more dry. He expanded his hollow chest. The air streamed in, carrying away in its rush a lot of strange things that resembled houses, trees, people, lamp-posts. . . . No more! There was no more air— and he had not finished drawing his long breath. But he was in jail! They were locking him up. A door slammed. They turned the key twice, flung a bucket of water over him—Phoo! What for?

He opened his eyes, thinking the fall had been very heavy for an empty man—empty—empty. He was in his cabin. Ah! All right! His face was streaming with perspiration, his arms heavier than lead. He saw the cook standing in the doorway, a brass key in one hand and a bright tin hook-pot in the other.

"I have locked up the galley for the night," said the cook, beaming benevolently. "Eight bells just gone. I brought you a pot of cold tea for your night's drinking, Jimmy. I sweetened it with some white cabin sugar, too. Well—it won't break the ship."

He came in, hung the pot on the edge of the bunk, asked perfunctorily, "How goes it?" and sat down on the box.—"H'm," grunted Wait inhospitably. The cook wiped his face with a dirty cotton rag, which, afterwards, he tied round his neck.—"That's how them firemen do in steamboats," he said serenely, and much pleased with himself. "My work is as heavy as theirs—I'm thinking —and longer hours. Did you ever see them down the stokehold? Like fiends they look—firing—firing—firing—down there."

He pointed his forefinger at the deck. Some gloomy thought darkened his shining face, fleeting, like the shadow of a travelling cloud over the light of a peaceful sea. The relieved watch tramped noisily forward, passing in a body across the sheen of the doorway. Some one cried, "Good night!" Belfast stopped for a moment and looked at Jimmy, quivering and speechless with repressed emotion. He gave the cook a glance charged with dismal foreboding, and vanished. The cook cleared his throat. Jimmy stared upwards and kept as still as a man in hiding.

The night was clear, with a gentle breeze. Above the mastheads the resplendent curve of the Milky Way spanned the sky like a triumphal arch of eternal light, thrown over the dark pathway of the earth. On the forecastle head a man whistled with loud precision a lively jig, while another could be heard faintly, shuffling and stamping in time. There came from forward a confused murmur of voices, laughter—snatches of song. The cook shook his head, glanced obliquely at Jimmy, and began to mutter. "Ay. Dance and sing. That's all they think of. I am surprised that Providence don't get tired. . . . They forget the day that's sure to come . . . but you. . . ."

Jimmy drank a gulp of tea hurriedly, as though he had stolen it, and shrank under his blanket, edging away towards the bulkhead. The cook got up, closed the door, then sat down again and said distinctly:—

"Whenever I poke my galley fire I think of you chaps—swearing, stealing, lying, and worse—as if there was no such thing as another world. . . . Not bad fellows, either, in a way," he conceded slowly; then, after a pause of regretful musing, he went on in a resigned tone:—"Well, well. They will have a hot time of it. Hot! Did I say? The furnaces of one of them White Star boats[1] ain't nothing to it."

He kept very quiet for a while. There was a great stir in his brain;

1. The White Star Line was founded in Liverpool in the 1850s and in 1870 successfully and dramatically initiated "express luxury" service to New York. Merged with the Cunard Line in the 1930s.

an addled vision of bright outlines; an exciting row of rousing songs and groans of pain. He suffered, enjoyed, admired, approved. He was delighted, frightened, exalted—as on that evening (the only time in his life—twenty-seven years ago; he loved to recall the number of years) when as a young man he had—through keeping bad company—become intoxicated in an East-end music-hall. A tide of sudden feeling swept him clean out of his body. He soared. He contemplated the secret of the hereafter. It commended itself to him. It was excellent; he loved it, himself, all hands, and Jimmy. His heart overflowed with tenderness, with comprehension, with the desire to meddle, with anxiety for the soul of that black man, with the pride of possessed eternity, with the feeling of might. Snatch him up in his arms and pitch him right into the middle of salvation . . . the black soul—blacker—body—rot—Devil. No! Talk—strength—Samson. . . . There was a great din as of cymbals in his ears; he flashed through an ecstatic jumble of shining faces, lilies, prayer-books, unearthly joy, white skirts, gold harps, black coats, wings. He saw flowing garments, clean shaved faces, a sea of light —a lake of pitch. There were sweet scents, a smell of sulphur—red tongues of flame licking a white mist. An awesome voice thundered! . . . It lasted three seconds.

"Jimmy!" he cried in an inspired tone. Then he hesitated. A spark of human pity glimmered yet through the infernal fog of his supreme conceit.

"What?" said James Wait unwillingly. There was a silence. He turned his head just the least bit, and stole a cautious glance. The cook's lips moved without a sound; his face was rapt, his eyes turned up. He seemed to be mentally imploring deck beams, the brass hook of the lamp, two cockroaches.

"Look here," said Wait. "I want to go to sleep. I think I could."

"This is no time for sleep!" exclaimed the cook, very loud. He had prayerfully divested himself of the last vestige of his humanity. He was a voice—a fleshless and sublime thing, as on that memorable night—the night when he went walking over the sea to make coffee for perishing sinners. "This is no time for sleeping," he repeated, with exaltation. "*I* can't sleep."

"Don't care damn," said Wait, with factitious energy. "*I* can. Go an' turn in."

"Swear . . . in the very jaws! . . . In the very jaws! Don't you see the everlasting fire . . . don't you feel it? Blind, chockfull of sin! Repent, repent! I can't bear to think of you. I hear the call to save you. Night and day. Jimmy, let me save you!" The words of entreaty and menace broke out of him in a roaring torrent. The cockroaches ran away. Jimmy perspired, wriggling stealthily under his blanket. The cook yelled. . . . "Your days are numbered! . . ."—

"Get out of this," boomed Wait courageously.—"Pray with me! . . ."
—"I won't! . . ." The little cabin was as hot as an oven. It contained an immensity of fear and pain; an atmosphere of shrieks and
moans; prayers vociferated like blasphemies and whispered curses.
Outside, the men called by Charley, who informed them in tones of
delight that there was a holy row going on in Jimmy's place,
crowded before the closed door, too startled to open it. All hands
were there. The watch below had jumped out on deck in their
shirts, as after a collision. Men running up, asked:—"What is it?"
Others said:—"Listen!" The· muffled screaming went on:—"On
your knees! On your knees!"—"Shut up!"—"Never! You are delivered
into my hands. . . . Your life has been saved. . . . Purpose. . . .
Mercy. . . . Repent."—"You are a crazy fool! . . ."—"Account of
you . . . you . . . Never sleep in this world, if I . . ."—"Leave off."
—"No! . . . stokehold . . . only think! . . ." Then an impassioned
screeching babble where words pattered like hail.—"No!" shouted
Wait.—"Yes. You are! . . . No help. . . . Everybody says so."—
"You lie!"—"I see you dying this minnyt . . . before my eyes . . . as
good as dead already."—"Help!" shouted Jimmy piercingly.—"Not
in this valley . . . look upwards," howled the other.—"Go away!
Murder! Help!" clamoured Jimmy. His voice broke. There were
moanings, low mutters, a few sobs.

"What's the matter now?" said a seldom-heard voice.—"Fall
back, men! Fall back, there!" repeated Mr. Creighton sternly, pushing through.—"Here's the old man," whispered some.—"The
cook's in there, sir," exclaimed several, backing away. The door clat-
tered open; a broad stream of light darted out on wondering faces; a
warm whiff of vitiated air passed. The two mates towered head and
shoulders above the spare, grey-haired man who stood revealed
between them, in shabby clothes, stiff and angular, like a small
carved figure, and with a thin, composed face. The cook got up
from his knees. Jimmy sat high in the bunk, clasping his drawn-up
legs. The tassel of the blue night-cap almost imperceptibly trembled
over his knees. They gazed astonished at his long, curved back,
while the white corner of one eye gleamed blindly at them. He was
afraid to turn his head, he shrank within himself; and there was an
aspect astounding and animal-like in the perfection of his expectant
immobility. A thing of instinct—the unthinking stillness of a scared
brute.

"What are you doing here?" asked Mr. Baker sharply.—"My
duty," said the cook, with ardour.—"Your . . . what?" began the
mate. Captain Allistoun touched his arm lightly.—"I know his
caper," he said in a low voice. "Come out of that, Podmore," he
ordered, aloud.

The cook wrung his hands, shook his fists above his head, and his arms dropped as if too heavy. For a moment he stood distracted and speechless.—"Never," he stammered, "I . . . he . . . I."—"What—do—you—say?" pronounced Captain Allistoun. "Come out at once —or . . ." "I am going," said the cook, with a hasty and sombre resignation. He strode over the doorstep firmly—hesitated—made a few steps. They looked at him in silence.—"I make you responsible!" he cried desperately, turning half round. "That man is dying. I make you . . ."—"You there yet?" called the master in a threatening tone.—"No, sir," he exclaimed hurriedly in a startled voice. The boatswain led him away by the arm; some one laughed; Jimmy lifted his head for a stealthy glance, and in one unexpected leap sprang out of his bunk; Mr. Baker made a clever catch and felt him very limp in his arms; the group at the door grunted with surprise. —"He lies," gasped Wait, "he talked about black devils—he is a devil—a white devil—I am all right." He stiffened himself, and Mr. Baker, experimentally, let him go. He staggered a pace or two; Captain Allistoun watched him with a quiet and penetrating gaze; Belfast ran to his support. He did not appear to be aware of any one near him; he stood silent for a moment, battling single-handed with a legion of nameless terrors, amidst the eager looks of excited men who watched him far off, utterly alone in the impenetrable solitude of his fear. The sea gurgled through the scuppers as the ship heeled over to a short puff of wind.

"Keep him away from me," said James Wait at last in his fine baritone voice, and leaning with all his weight on Belfast's neck. "I've been better this last week . . . I am well . . . I was going back to duty . . . to-morrow—now if you like—Captain." Belfast hitched his shoulders to keep him upright.

"No," said the master, looking at him, fixedly.

Under Jimmy's armpit Belfast's red face moved uneasily. A row of eyes, gleaming, stared on the edge of light. They pushed one another with elbows, turned their heads, whispered. Wait let his chin fall on his breast and, with lowered eyelids, looked round in a suspicious manner.

"Why not?" cried a voice from the shadows, "the man's all right, sir."

"I am all right," said Wait, with eagerness. "Been sick . . . better . . . turn-to now." He sighed.—"Howly Mother!" exclaimed Belfast, with a heave of the shoulders, "stand up, Jimmy."—"Keep away from me, then," said Wait, giving Belfast a petulant push, and reeling fetched against the door-post. His cheekbones glistened as though they had been varnished. He snatched off his night-cap, wiped his perspiring face with it, flung it on the deck. "I am coming out," he declared, without stirring.

"No. You don't," said the master curtly. Bare feet shuffled, disapproving voices murmured all round; he went on as if he had not heard:—"You have been skulking nearly all the passage and now you want to come out. You think you are near enough to the pay-table now. Smell the shore, hey?"

"I've been sick . . . now—better," mumbled Wait, glaring in the light.—"You have been shamming sick," retorted Captain Allistoun, with severity. "Why . . ." He hesitated for less than half a second. "Why, anybody can see that. There's nothing the matter with you, but you choose to lie-up to please yourself—and now you shall lie-up to please me. Mr. Baker, my orders are that this man is not to be allowed on deck to the end of this passage."

There were exclamations of surprise, triumph, indignation. The dark group of men swung across the light. "What for?" "Told you so . . ." "Bloomin' shame . . ."—"We've got to say somethink about that," screeched Donkin from the rear.—"Never mind, Jimmy, we will see you righted," cried several together. An elderly seaman stepped to the front. "D'ye mean to say, sir," he asked ominously, "that a sick chap ain't allowed to get well in this 'ere hooker?" Behind him Donkin whispered excitedly amongst a staring crowd where no one spared him a glance, but Captain Allistoun shook a forefinger at the angry bronzed face of the speaker.—"You —you hold your tongue," he said warningly.—"This isn't the way," clamoured two or three younger men.—"Are we bloomin' mash-eens?" inquired Donkin in a piercing tone, and dived under the elbows of the front rank.—"Soon show 'm we ain't boys . . ."— "The man's a man if he is black."—"We ain't goin' to work this bloomin' ship shorthanded if Snowball's all right . . ."—"He says he is."—"Well then, strike, boys, strike!"—"That's the bloomin' ticket." Captain Allistoun said sharply to the second mate: "Keep quiet, Mr. Creighton," and stood composed in the tumult, listening with profound attention to mixed growls and screeches, to every exclamation and every curse of the sudden outbreak. Somebody slammed the cabin door to with a kick; the darkness full of menacing mutters leaped with a short clatter over the streak of light, and the men became gesticulating shadows that growled, hissed, laughed excitedly. Mr. Baker whispered:—"Get away from them, sir." The big shape of Mr. Creighton hovered silently about the slight figure of the master.—"We have been imposed upon all this voyage," said a gruff voice, "but this 'ere fancy takes the cake."—"That man is a shipmate."—"Are we bloomin' kids?"—"The port watch will refuse duty." Charley carried away by his feelings whistled shrilly, then yelped:— "Giv'us our Jimmy!" This seemed to cause a variation in the disturbance. There was a fresh burst of squabbling uproar. A lot of quarrels were set going at once.—"Yes."—"No."—"Never been sick."—"Go for them to once."—"Shut yer mouth, youngster—this is men's work."—"Is it?" muttered Captain Allistoun bitterly. Mr. Baker grunted: "Ough! They're gone silly. They've been simmering for the last month."—"I did notice," said the master.—"They have started a row amongst themselves now," said Mr. Creighton, with disdain, "better get aft, sir. We will soothe them."—"Keep your temper, Creighton," said the master. And the three men began to move slowly towards the cabin door.

In the shadows of the fore rigging a dark mass stamped, eddied, advanced, retreated. There were words of reproach, encouragement, unbelief, execration. The elder seamen, bewildered and angry, growled their determination to go through with something or other; but the younger school of advanced thought exposed their and Jimmy's wrongs with confused shouts, arguing amongst themselves. They clustered round that moribund carcass, the fit emblem of their aspirations, and encouraging one another they swayed, they tramped on one spot, shouting that they would not be "put upon." Inside the cabin, Belfast, helping Jimmy into his bunk, twitched all over in his desire not to miss all the row, and with difficulty restrained the tears of his facile emotion. James Wait, flat on his back under the blanket, gasped complaints.—"We will back you up, never fear," assured Belfast, busy about his feet.—"I'll come out to-morrow morning——take my chance——you fellows must——" mumbled Wait, "I come out to-morrow——skipper or no skipper." He lifted one arm with great difficulty, passed the hand over his face; "Don't you let that cook . . ." he breathed out.—"No, no," said Belfast, turning his back on the bunk, "I will put a head on him if he comes near you."—"I will smash his mug!" exclaimed faintly Wait, enraged and weak; "I don't want to kill a man, but . . ." He panted fast like a dog after a run in sunshine. Some one just outside the door shouted. "He's as fit as any ov us!" Belfast put his hand on the door-handle.—"Here!" called James Wait hurriedly and in such a clear voice that the other spun round with a start. James Wait, stretched out black and deathlike in the dazzling light, turned his head on the pillow. His eyes stared at Belfast, appealing and impudent. "I am rather weak from lying-up so long," he said distinctly. Belfast nodded. "Getting quite well now," insisted Wait. —"Yes. I noticed you getting better this . . . last month," said Belfast looking down. "Hallo! What's this?" he shouted and ran out.

He was flattened directly against the side of the house by two men who lurched against him. A lot of disputes seemed to be going on all round. He got clear and saw three indistinct figures standing alone in the fainter darkness under the arched foot of the mainsail, that rose above their heads like a convex wall of a high edifice. Donkin hissed:—"Go for them . . . it's dark!" The crowd took a short run aft in a body—then there was a check. Donkin, agile and thin, flitted past with his right arm going like a windmill—and then stood still suddenly with his arm pointing rigidly above his head. The hurtling flight of some heavy object was heard; it passed between the heads of the two mates, bounded heavily along the deck, struck the after hatch with a ponderous and deadened blow. The bulky shape of Mr. Baker grew distinct. "Come to your senses, men!" he cried, advancing at the arrested crowd. "Come back, Mr. Baker!" called the master's quiet voice. He obeyed unwillingly. There was a minute of silence, then a deafening hubbub arose. Above it Archie was heard energetically:—"If ye do oot ageen I wull tell!" There were shouts. "Don't!"—"Drop it!"—"We ain't that kind!" The black cluster of human forms reeled against the bulwark, back again towards the house. Ringbolts rang under stumbling feet.—"Drop it!"—"Let me!"—"No!"—"Curse you . . . hah!" Then sounds as of some one's face being slapped; a piece of iron fell on the deck; a short scuffle, and some one's shadowy body scuttled rapidly across the main hatch before the shadow of a kick. A raging voice sobbed out a torrent of filthy language. . . . "Throwing things—good God!" grunted Mr. Baker in dismay.—"That was meant for me," said the master quietly; "I felt the wind of that thing; what was it—an iron belaying-pin?"—"By Jove!" muttered Mr. Creighton. The confused voices of men talking amidships mingled with the wash of the sea, ascended between the silent and distended sails—seemed to flow away into the night, farther than the horizon, higher than the sky. The stars burned steadily over the inclined mastheads. Trails of light lay on the water, broke before the advancing hull, and, after she had passed, trembled for a long time as if in awe of the murmuring sea.

Meantime the helmsman, anxious to know what the row was about, had let go the wheel, and, bent double, ran with long stealthy footsteps to the break of the poop. The Narcissus, left to herself, came up gently to the wind without any one being aware of it. She gave a slight roll, and the sleeping sails woke suddenly, coming all together with a mighty flap against the masts, then filled again one after another in a quick succession of loud reports that ran down the lofty spars, till the collapsed mainsail flew out last with a violent jerk. The ship trembled from trucks to keel; the sails kept on rattling like a discharge of musketry; the chain sheets and loose shackles jingled aloft in a thin peal; the gin blocks groaned. It was as if an invisible hand had given the ship an angry shake to recall the men that peopled her decks to the sense of reality, vigilance, and duty.—"Helm up!" cried the master sharply. "Run aft, Mr. Creighton, and see what that fool there is up to."—"Flatten in the head sheets. Stand by the weather fore-braces," growled Mr. Baker. Startled men ran swiftly repeating the orders. The watch below, abandoned all at once by the watch on deck, drifted towards the forecastle in twos and threes, arguing noisily as they went—"We shall see to-morrow!" cried a loud voice, as if to cover with a menacing hint an inglorious retreat. And then only orders were heard, the falling of heavy coils of rope, the rattling of blocks. Singleton's white head flitted here and there in the night, high above the deck, like the ghost of a bird.—"Going off, sir!" shouted Mr. Creighton from aft.—"Full again."—"All right. . . ."—"Ease off the head sheets. That will do the braces. Coil the ropes up," grunted Mr. Baker, bustling about.

Gradually the tramping noises, the confused sound of voices, died out, and the officers, coming together on the poop, discussed the events. Mr. Baker was bewildered and grunted; Mr. Creighton was calmly furious; but Captain Allistoun was composed and thoughtful. He listened to Mr. Baker's growling argumentation, to Creighton's interjected and severe remarks, while looking down on the deck he weighed in his hand the iron belaying-pin—that a moment ago had just missed his head—as if it had been the only tangible fact of the whole transaction. He was one of those commanders who speak little, seem to hear nothing, look at no one—and know everything, hear every whisper, see every fleeting shadow of their ship's life. His two big officers towered above his lean, short figure; they talked over his head; they were dismayed, surprised, and angry, while between them the little quiet man seemed to have found his taciturn serenity in the profound depths of a larger experience. Lights were burning in the forecastle; now and then a loud gust of babbling chatter came from forward, swept over the decks, and became faint, as if the unconscious ship, gliding gently through the great peace of the sea, had left behind and for ever the foolish noise of turbulent mankind. But it was renewed again and again. Gesticulating arms, profiles of heads with open mouths appeared for a moment in the illuminated squares of doorways; black fists darted —withdrew. . . . "Yes. It was most damnable to have such an unprovoked row sprung on one," assented the master. . . . A tumult of yells rose in the light, abruptly ceased. . . . He didn't think there would be any further trouble just then. . . . A bell was struck aft, another, forward, answered in a deeper tone, and the clamour of ringing metal spread round the ship in a circle of wide vibrations that ebbed away into the immeasurable night of an empty sea. . . . Didn't he know them! Didn't he! In past years. Better men, too. Real men to stand by one in a tight place. Worse than devils too sometimes—downright, horned devils. Pah! This—nothing. A miss as good as a mile. . . . The wheel was being relieved in the usual way.—"Full and by," said, very loud, the man going off.—"Full and by," repeated the other, catching hold of the spokes.—"This head wind is my trouble," exclaimed the master, stamping his foot in sudden anger; "head wind! all the rest is nothing." He was calm again in a moment. "Keep them on the move to-night, gentlemen; just to let them feel we've got hold all the time—quietly, you know. Mind you keep your hands off them, Creighton. Tomorrow I will talk to them like a Dutch Uncle. A crazy crowd of tinkers! Yes, tinkers! I could count the real sailors amongst them on the fingers of one hand. Nothing will do but a row—if—you—please." He paused. "Did you think I had gone wrong there, Mr. Baker?" He tapped his forehead, laughed short. "When I saw him standing there, three parts dead and so scared—black amongst that gaping lot—no grit to face what's coming to us all—the notion came to me all at once, before I could think. Sorry for him—as you would be for a sick brute. If ever creature was in a mortal funk to die! . . . I thought I would let him go out in his own way. Kind of impulse. It never came into my head, those fools. . . . H'm! Stand to it now —of course." He stuck the belaying-pin in his pocket, seemed ashamed of himself, then sharply:—"If you see Podmore at his tricks again tell him I will have him put under the pump. Had to do it once before. The fellow breaks out like that now and then. Good cook tho'." He walked away quickly, came back to the companion. The two mates followed him through the starlight with amazed eyes. He went down three steps, and changing his tone, spoke with his head near the deck:—"I shan't turn in to-night, in case of anything; just call out if . . . Did you see the eyes of that sick nigger, Mr. Baker? I fancied he begged me for something. What? Past all help. One lone black beggar amongst the lot of us, and he seemed to look through me into the very hell. Fancy, this wretched Podmore! Well, let him die in peace. I am master here after all. Let him be. He might have been half a man once. . . . Keep a good look-out." He disappeared down below, leaving his mates facing one another, and more impressed than if they had seen a stone image shed a miraculous tear of compassion over the incertitudes of life and death. . . .

In the blue mist spreading from twisted threads that stood upright in the bowls of pipes, the forecastle appeared as vast as a hall. Between the beams a heavy cloud stagnated; and the lamps surrounded by halos burned each at the core of a purple glow in two lifeless flames without rays. Wreaths drifted in denser wisps. Men sprawled about on the deck, sat in negligent poses, or, bending a knee, drooped with one shoulder against a bulkhead. Lips moved, eyes flashed, waving arms made sudden eddies in the smoke. The murmur of voices seemed to pile itself higher and higher as if unable to run out quick enough through the narrow doors. The watch below in their shirts, and striding on long white legs, resembled raving somnambulists; while now and then one of the watch on deck would rush in, looking strangely overdressed, listen a moment, fling a rapid sentence into the noise and run out again; but a few remained near the door, fascinated, and with one ear turned to the deck. "Stick together, boys," roared Davis. Belfast tried to make himself heard. Knowles grinned in a slow, dazed way. A short fellow with a thick clipped beard kept on yelling periodically:—"Who's afeard? Who's afeard?" Another one jumped up, excited, with blazing eyes, sent out a string of unattached curses and sat down quietly. Two men discussed familiarly, striking one another's breast in turn, to clinch arguments. Three others, with their heads in a bunch, spoke all together with a confidential air, and at the top of their voices. It was a stormy chaos of speech where intelligible fragments tossing, struck the ear. One could hear:—"In the last ship"—"Who cares? Try it on any one of us if——." "Knock under"—"Not a hand's turn"—"He says he is all right"—"I always thought"—"Never mind. . . ." Donkin, crouching all in a heap against the bowsprit, hunched his shoulder blades as high as his ears, and hanging a peaked nose, resembled a sick vulture with ruffled plumes. Belfast, straddling his legs, had a face red with yelling, and with arms thrown up, figured a Maltese cross. The two Scandinavians, in a corner, had the dumbfounded and distracted aspect of men gazing at a cataclysm. And, beyond the light, Singleton stood in the smoke, monumental, indistinct, with his head touching the beam; like a statue of heroic size in the gloom of a crypt.

He stepped forward, impassive and big. The noise subsided like a broken wave: but Belfast cried once more with uplifted arms:—"The man is dying, I tell ye!" then sat down suddenly on the hatch and took his head between his hands. All looked at Singleton, gazing upwards from the deck, staring out of dark corners, or turning their heads with curious glances. They were expectant and appeased as if that old man, who looked at no one, had possessed the secret of their uneasy indignations and desires, a sharper vision, a clearer knowledge. And indeed standing there amongst them, he had the uninterested appearance of one who had seen multitudes of ships, had listened many times to voices such as theirs, had already seen all that could happen on the wide seas. They heard his voice rumble in his broad chest as though the words had been rolling towards them out of a rugged past. "What do you want to do?" he asked. No one answered. Only Knowles muttered—"Ay, ay," and somebody said low:—"It's a bloomin' shame." He waited, made a contemptuous gesture.— "I have seen rows aboard ship before some of you were born," he said slowly, "for something or nothing; but never for such a thing."—"The man is dying, I tell ye," repeated

Belfast woefully, sitting at Singleton's feet.—"And a black fellow, too," went on the old seaman, "I have seen them die like flies." He stopped, thoughtful, as if trying to recollect gruesome things, details of horrors, hecatombs of niggers. They looked at him fascinated. He was old enough to remember slavers, bloody mutinies, pirates perhaps; who could tell through what violences and terrors he had lived! What would he say? He said:—"You can't help him; die he must." He made another pause. His moustache and beard stirred. He chewed words, mumbled behind tangled white hairs; incomprehensible and exciting, like an oracle behind a veil. . . .—"Stop ashore—sick.—Instead—bringing all this head wind. Afraid. The sea will have her own.—Die in sight of land. Always so. They know it—long passage—more days, more dollars.—You keep quiet.—What do you want? Can't help him." He seemed to wake up from a dream. "You can't help yourselves," he said austerely. "Skipper's no fool. He has something in his mind. Look out—I say! I know 'em!" With eyes fixed in front he turned his head from right to left, from left to right, as if inspecting a long row of astute skippers.—" 'Ee said 'ee would brain me!" cried Donkin in a heartrending tone. Singleton peered downwards with puzzled attention, as though he couldn't find him.—"Damn you!" he said vaguely, giving it up. He radiated unspeakable wisdom, hard unconcern, the chilling air of resignation. Round him all the listeners felt themselves somehow completely enlightened by their disappointment, and mute, they lolled about with the careless ease of men who can discern perfectly the irremediable aspect of their existence. He, profound and unconscious, waved his arm once, and strode out on deck without another word.

Belfast was lost in a round-eyed meditation. One or two vaulted heavily into upper berths, and, once there, sighed; others dived head first inside lower bunks—swift, and turning round instantly upon themselves, like animals going into lairs. The grating of a knife scraping burnt clay was heard. Knowles grinned no more. Davis said, in a tone of ardent conviction:—"Then our skipper's looney." Archie muttered:—"My faith! we haven't heard the last of it yet!"

Four bells were struck.—"Half our watch below gone!" cried Knowles in alarm, then reflected. "Well, two hours' sleep is something towards a rest," he observed consolingly. Some already pretended to slumber; and Charley, sound asleep, suddenly said a few slurred words in an arbitrary, blank voice.—"This blamed boy has worrums!" commented Knowles from under a blanket, in a learned manner. Belfast got up and approached Archie's berth.—"We pulled him out," he whispered sadly.—"What?" said the other, with sleepy discontent.—"And now we will have to chuck him overboard," went on Belfast, whose lower lip trembled.—"Chuck

what?" asked Archie.—"Poor Jimmy," breathed out Belfast.—"He
be blowed!" said Archie with untruthful brutality, and sat up in his
bunk; "It's all through him. If it hadn't been for me, there would
have been murder on board this ship!"—" 'Tain't his fault, is it?"
argued Belfast, in a murmur; "I've put him to bed . . . an' he ain't
no heavier than an empty beef-cask." he added, with tears in his
eyes. Archie looked at him steadily, then turned his nose to the
ship's side with determination. Belfast wandered about as though
he had lost his way in the dim forecastle, and nearly fell over
Donkin. He contemplated him from on high for a while. "Ain't ye
going to turn in?" he asked. Donkin looked up hopelessly.—"That
black'earted Scotch son of a thief kicked me!" he whispered from
the floor, in a tone of utter desolation.—"And a good job, too!"
said Belfast, still very depressed. "You were as near hanging as
damn-it to-night, sonny. Don't you play any of your murthering
games around my Jimmy! You haven't pulled him out. You just
mind! 'Cos if I start to kick you"—he brightened up a bit—"if I
start to kick you, it will be Yankee fashion—to break something!"
He tapped lightly with his knuckles the top of the bowed head.
"You moind that, my bhoy!" he concluded cheerily. Donkin let it
pass.—"Will they split on me?" he asked, with pained anxiety.—
"Who—split?" hissed Belfast, coming back a step. "I would split
your nose this minnyt if I hadn't Jimmy to look after! Who d'ye
think we are?" Donkin rose and watched Belfast's back lurch
through the doorway. On all sides invisible men slept, breathing
calmly. He seemed to draw courage and fury from the peace around
him. Venomous and thin-faced, he glared from the ample misfit of
borrowed clothes as if looking for something he could smash. His
heart leaped wildly in his narrow chest. They slept! He wanted to
wring necks, gouge eyes, spit on faces. He shook a dirty pair of
meagre fists at the smoking lights. "Ye're no men!" he cried, in a
deadened tone. No one moved. "Yer 'aven't the pluck of a mouse!"
His voice rose to a husky screech. Wamibo darted out a dishevelled
head, and looked at him wildly. "Ye're sweepings ov ships! I 'ope
you will all rot before you die!" Wamibo blinked, uncomprehend-
ing but interested. Donkin sat down heavily; he blew with force
through quivering nostrils, he ground and snapped his teeth, and,
with the chin pressed hard against the breast, he seemed busy gnaw-
ing his way through it, as if to get at the heart within. . . .

In the morning the ship, beginning another day of her wandering
life, had an aspect of sumptuous freshness, like the spring-time of
the earth. The washed decks glistened in a long clear stretch; the
oblique sunlight struck the yellow brasses in dazzling splashes,
darted over the polished rods in lines of gold, and the single drops

of salt water forgotten here and there along the rail were as limpid as drops of dew, and sparkled more than scattered diamonds. The sails slept, hushed by a gentle breeze. The sun, rising lonely and splendid in the blue sky, saw a solitary ship gliding close-hauled on the blue sea.

The men pressed three deep abreast of the mainmast and opposite the cabin door. They shuffled, pushed, had an irresolute mien and stolid faces. At every slight movement Knowles lurched heavily on his short leg. Donkin glided behind backs, restless and anxious, like a man looking for an ambush. Captain Allistoun came out on the quarter-deck suddenly. He walked to and fro before the front. He was grey, slight, alert, shabby in the sunshine, and as hard as adamant. He had his right hand in the side-pocket of his jacket, and also something heavy in there that made folds all down that side. One of the seamen cleared his throat ominously.—"I haven't till now found fault with you men," said the master, stopping short. He faced them with his worn, steely gaze, that by a universal illusion looked straight into every individual pair of the twenty pairs of eyes before his face. At his back Mr. Baker, gloomy and bullnecked, grunted low; Mr. Creighton, fresh as paint, had rosy cheeks and a ready, resolute bearing. "And I don't now," continued the master; "but I am here to drive this ship and keep every man-jack aboard of her up to the mark. If you knew your work as well as I do mine, there would be no trouble. You've been braying in the dark about 'See to-morrow morning!' Well, you see me now. What do you want?" He waited, stepping quickly to and fro, giving them searching glances. What did they want? They shifted from foot to foot, they balanced their bodies; some, pushing back their caps, scratched their heads. What did they want? Jimmy was forgotten; no one thought of him, alone forward in his cabin, fighting great shadows, clinging to brazen lies, chuckling painfully over his transparent deceptions. No, not Jimmy; he was more forgotten than if he had been dead. They wanted great things. And suddenly all the simple words they knew seemed to be lost forever in the immensity of their vague and burning desire. They knew what they wanted, but they could not find anything worth saying. They stirred on one spot, swinging, at the end of muscular arms, big tarry hands with crooked fingers. A murmur died out.—"What is it—food?" asked the master, "you know the stores have been spoiled off the Cape." —"We know that, sir," said a bearded shell-back[2] in the front rank.—"Work too hard—eh? Too much for your strength?" he asked again. There was an offended silence.—"We don't want to go shorthanded, sir," began at last Davis in a wavering voice, "and this 'ere black— . . ."—"Enough!" cried the master. He stood scanning

2. An old, experienced sailor.

them for a moment, then walking a few steps this way and that began to storm at them coldly, in gusts violent and cutting like the gales of those icy seas that had known his youth.—"Tell you what's the matter? Too big for your boots. Think yourselves damn good men. Know half your work. Do half your duty. Think it too much. If you did ten times as much it wouldn't be enough."—"We did our best by her, sir," cried some one with shaky exasperation.— "Your best!" stormed on the master. "You hear a lot on shore, don't you? They don't tell you there your best isn't much to boast of. I tell you—your best is no better than bad. You can do no more? No, I know, and I say nothing. But you stop your caper or I will stop it for you. I am ready for you! Stop it!" He shook a finger at the crowd. "As to that man," he raised his voice very much; "as to that man, if he puts his nose out on deck without my leave I will clap him in irons. There!" The cook heard him forward, ran out of the galley lifting his arms, horrified, unbelieving, amazed, and ran in again. There was a moment of profound silence during which a bow-legged seaman, stepping aside, expectorated decorously into the scupper. "There is another thing," said the master calmly. He made a quick stride and with a swing took an iron belaying-pin out of his pocket. "This!" His movement was so unexpected and sudden that the crowd stepped back. He gazed fixedly at their faces, and some at once put on a surprised air as though they had never seen a belaying-pin before. He held it up. "This is my affair. I don't ask you any questions, but you all know it; it has got to go where it came from." His eyes became angry. The crowd stirred uneasily. They looked away from the piece of iron, they appeared shy, they were embarrassed and shocked as though it had been something horrid, scandalous, or indelicate, that in common decency should not have been flourished like this in broad daylight. The master watched them attentively. "Donkin," he called out in a short, sharp tone.

Donkin dodged behind one, then behind another, but they looked over their shoulders and moved aside. The ranks kept on opening before him, closing behind, till at last he appeared alone before the master as though he had come up through the deck. Captain Allistoun moved close to him. They were much of a size, and at short range the master exchanged a deadly glance with the beady eyes. They wavered.—"You know this," asked the master.— "No, I don't," answered the other with a cheeky trepidation.— "You are a cur. Take it," ordered the master. Donkin's arms seemed glued to his thighs; he stood, eyes front, as if drawn on parade.[3] "Take it," repeated the master, and stepped closer; they breathed on one another. "Take it," said Captain Allistoun again, making a menacing gesture. Donkin tore away one arm from his side.—"Vy

3. Standing at attention in a military formation.

are yer down on me?" he mumbled with effort and as if his mouth had been full of dough.—"If you don't . . ." began the master. Donkin snatched at the pin as though his intention had been to run away with it, and remained stock still holding it like a candle. "Put it back where you took it from," said Captain Allistoun, looking at him fiercely. Donkin stepped back opening wide eyes. "Go, you blackguard, or I will make you," cried the master, driving him slowly backwards by a menacing advance. He dodged, and with the dangerous iron tried to guard his head from a threatening fist. Mr. Baker ceased grunting for a moment.—"Good! By Jove," murmured appreciatively Mr. Creighton in the tone of a connoisseur.—"Don't tech me," snarled Donkin, backing away.—"Then go. Go faster." —"Don't yer 'it me. . . . I will pull yer up afore the magistryt. . . . I'll show yer up." Captain Allistoun made a long stride, and Donkin, turning his back fairly, ran off a little, then stopped and over his shoulder showed yellow teeth.—"Farther on, fore-rigging," urged the master, pointing with his arm.—"Are yer goin' to stand by and see me bullied," screamed Donkin at the silent crowd that watched him. Captain Allistoun walked at him smartly. He started off again with a leap, dashed at the fore-rigging, rammed the pin into its hole violently. "I'll be even with yer yet," he screamed at the ship at large and vanished beyond the foremast. Captain Allistoun spun round and walked back aft with a composed face, as though he had already forgotten the scene. Men moved out of his way. He looked at no one.—"That will do, Mr. Baker. Send the watch below," he said quietly. "And you men try to walk straight for the future," he added in a calm voice. He looked pensively for a while at the backs of the impressed and retreating crowd. "Breakfast, steward," he called in a tone of relief through the cabin door. —"I didn't like to see you—Ough!—give that pin to that chap, sir," observed Mr. Baker; "he could have bust—Ough!—bust your head like an eggshell with it."—"Oh! he!" muttered the master absently. "Queer lot," he went on in a low voice. "I suppose it's all right now. Can never tell tho', nowadays, with such a . . . Years ago —I was a young master then—one China voyage I had a mutiny; real mutiny, Baker. Different men, tho'. I knew what they wanted: they wanted to broach the cargo and get at the liquor. Very simple. . . . We knocked them about for two days, and when they had enough—gentle as lambs. Good crew. And a smart trip I made." He glanced aloft at the yards braced sharp up. "Head wind day after day," he exclaimed bitterly. "Shall we never get a decent slant this passage?"—"Ready, sir," said the steward, appearing before them as if by magic and with a stained napkin in his hand. —"Ah! All right. Come along, Mr. Baker—it's late—with all this nonsense."

Chapter Five

A heavy atmosphere of oppressive quietude pervaded the ship. In the afternoon men went about washing clothes and hanging them out to dry in the unprosperous breeze with the meditative languor of disenchanted philosophers. Very little was said. The problem of life seemed too voluminous for the narrow limits of human speech, and by common consent it was abandoned to the great sea that had from the beginning enfolded it in its immense grip; to the sea that knew all, and would in time infallibly unveil to each the wisdom hidden in all the errors, the certitude that lurks in doubts, the realm of safety and peace beyond the frontiers of sorrow and fear. And in the confused current of impotent thoughts that set unceasingly this way and that through bodies of men, Jimmy bobbed up upon the surface, compelling attention, like a black buoy chained to the bottom of a muddy stream. Falsehood triumphed. It triumphed through doubt, through stupidity, through pity, through sentimentalism. We set ourselves to bolster it up, from compassion, from recklessness, from a sense of fun. Jimmy's steadfastness to his untruthful attitude in the face of the inevitable truth had the proportions of a colossal enigma—of a manifestation grand and incomprehensible that at times inspired a wondering awe; and there was also, to many, something exquisitely droll in fooling him thus to the top of his bent.[1] The latent egoism of tenderness to suffering appeared in the developing anxiety not to see him die. His obstinate non-recognition of the only certitude whose approach we could watch from day to day was as disquieting as the failure of some law of nature. He was so utterly wrong about himself that one could not but suspect him of having access to some source of supernatural knowledge. He was absurd to the point of inspiration. He was unique, and as fascinating as only something inhuman could be; he seemed to shout his denials already from beyond the awful border. He was becoming immaterial like an apparition; his cheekbones rose, the forehead slanted more; the face was all hollows, patches of shade; and the fleshless head resembled a disinterred black skull, fitted with two restless globes of silver in the sockets of eyes. He was demoralising. Through him we were becoming highly humanised, tender, complex, excessively decadent: we understood the subtlety of his fear, sympathised with all his repulsions, shrinkings, evasions, delusions—as though we had been over-civilised, and rotten, and without any knowledge of the meaning of life. We had the air of being initiated in some infamous mysteries; we had the profound grimaces of conspirators, exchanged meaning glances, significant

1. Capacity or endurance.

short words. We were inexpressibly vile and very much pleased with ourselves. We lied to him with gravity, with emotion, with unction, as if performing some moral trick with a view to an eternal reward. We made a chorus of affirmation to his wildest assertions, as though he had been a millionaire, a politician, or a reformer—and we a crowd of ambitious lubbers.[2] When we ventured to question his statements we did it after the manner of obsequious sycophants, to the end that his glory should be augmented by the flattery of our dissent. He influenced the moral tone of our world as though he had it in his power to distribute honours, treasures, or pain; and he could give us nothing but his contempt. It was immense; it seemed to grow gradually larger, as his body day by day shrank a little more, while we looked. It was the only thing about him—of him—that gave the impression of durability and vigour. It lived within him with an unquenchable life. It spoke through the eternal pout of his black lips; it looked at us through the impertinent mournfulness of his languid and enormous stare. We watched him intently. He seemed unwilling to move, as if distrustful of his own solidity. The slightest gesture must have disclosed to him (it could not surely be otherwise) his bodily weakness, and caused a pang of mental suffering. He was chary of movements. He lay stretched out, chin on blanket, in a kind of sly, cautious immobility. Only his eyes roamed over faces; his eyes disdainful, penetrating and sad.

It was at that time that Belfast's devotion—and also his pugnacity—secured universal respect. He spent every moment of his spare time in Jimmy's cabin. He tended to him, talked to him; was as gentle as a woman, as tenderly gay as an old philanthropist, as sentimentally careful of his nigger as a model slave-owner. But outside he was irritable, explosive as gunpowder, sombre, suspicious, and never more brutal than when most sorrowful. With him it was a tear and a blow: a tear for Jimmy, a glow for any one who did not seem to take a scrupulously orthodox view of Jimmy's case. We talked about nothing else. The two Scandinavians, even, discussed the situation—but it was impossible to know in what spirit, because they quarrelled in their own language. Belfast suspected one of them of irreverence, and in this incertitude thought that there was no option but to fight them both. They became very much terrified by his truculence, and henceforth lived amongst us, dejected, like a pair of mutes. Wamibo never spoke intelligibly, but he was as smileless as an animal—seemed to know much less about it all than the cat—and consequently was safe. Moreover he had belonged to the chosen band of Jimmy's rescuers, and was above suspicion. Archie was silent generally, but often spent an hour or so talking to Jimmy quietly with an air of proprietorship. At any

2. Awkward, unskilled seamen; hence, landlubbers.

time of the day and often through the night some man could be seen sitting on Jimmy's box. In the evening, between six and eight, the cabin was crowded, and there was an interested group at the door. Every one stared at the nigger.

He basked in the warmth of our interest. His eyes gleamed ironically, and in a weak voice he reproached us with our cowardice. He would say, "If you fellows had stuck out for me I would be now on deck." We hung our heads. "Yes, but if you think I am going to let them put me in irons just to show you sport. . . . Well, no. . . . It ruins my health, this lying up, it does. You don't care." We were as abashed as if it had been true. His superb impudence carried all before it. We would not have dared to revolt. We didn't want to, really. We wanted to keep him alive till home—to the end of the voyage.

Singleton as usual held aloof, appearing to scorn the insignificant events of an ended life. Once only he came along, and unexpectedly stopped in the doorway. He peered at Jimmy in profound silence, as if desirous to add that black image to the crowd of Shades that peopled his old memory. We kept very quiet, and for a long time Singleton stood there as though he had come by appointment to call for some one, or to see some important event. James Wait lay perfectly still, and apparently not aware of the gaze scrutinising him with a steadiness full of expectation. There was a sense of a contest in the air. We felt the inward strain of men watching a wrestling bout. At last Jimmy with perceptible apprehension turned his head on the pillow.—"Good evening," he said in a conciliating tone.— "H'm," answered the old seaman, grumpily. For a moment longer he looked at Jimmy with severe fixity, then suddenly went away. It was a long time before any one spoke in the little cabin, though we all breathed more freely as men do after an escape from some dangerous situation. We all knew the old man's ideas about Jimmy, and nobody dared to combat them. They were unsettling, they caused pain; and, what was worse, they might have been true for all we knew. Only once did he condescend to explain them fully, but the impression was lasting. He said that Jimmy was the cause of head winds. Mortally sick men—he maintained—linger till the first sight of land, and then die; and Jimmy knew that the very first land would draw his life from him. It is so in every ship. Didn't we know it? He asked us with austere contempt: what did we know? What would we doubt next? Jimmy's desire encouraged by us and aided by Wamibo's (he was a Finn—wasn't he? Very well!) by Wamibo's spells delayed the ship in the open sea. Only lubberly fools couldn't see it. Whoever heard of such a run of calms and head winds? It wasn't natural. . . . We could not deny that it was strange. We felt uneasy. The common saying, "More days, more dollars," did not give the usual comfort because the stores were running short. Much had been spoiled off the Cape, and we were on half allowance of biscuit. Peas, sugar, and tea had been finished long ago. Salt meat was giving out. We had plenty of coffee but very little water to make it with. We took up another hole in our belts and went on scraping, polishing, painting the ship from morning to night. And soon she looked as though she had come out of a band-box;[3] but hunger lived on board of her. Not dead starvation, but steady, living hunger that stalked about the decks, slept in the forecastle; the tormentor of waking moments, the disturber of dreams. We looked to windward for signs of change. Every few hours of night and day we put her round with the hope that she would come up on that tack at last! She didn't. She seemed to have forgotten the way home; she rushed to and fro, heading north-west, heading east; she ran backwards and forwards, distracted like a timid creature at the foot of a wall. Sometimes, as if tired to death, she would wallow languidly for a day in the smooth swell of an unruffled sea. All up the swinging masts the sails thrashed furiously through the hot stillness of the calm. We were weary, hungry, thirsty; we commenced to believe Singleton, but with unshaken fidelity dissembled to Jimmy. We spoke to him with jocose allusiveness, like cheerful accomplices in a clever plot; but we looked to the westward over the rail with longing eyes for a sign of hope, for a sign of fair wind; even if its first breath should bring death to our reluctant Jimmy. In vain! The universe conspired with James Wait. Light airs from the northward sprang up again; the sky remained clear; and round our weariness the glittering sea, touched by the breeze, basked voluptuously in the great sunshine, as though it had forgotten our life and trouble.

Donkin looked out for a fair wind along with the rest. No one knew the venom of his thoughts now. He was silent, and appeared thinner, as if consumed slowly by an inward rage at the injustice of men and of fate. He was ignored by all and spoke to no one, but his hate for every man dwelt in his furtive eyes. He talked with the cook only, having somehow persuaded the good man that he—Donkin—was a much calumniated and persecuted person. Together they bewailed the immorality of the ship's company. There could be no greater criminals than we, who by our lies conspired to send the unprepared soul of a poor ignorant black man to everlasting perdition. Podmore cooked what there was to cook, remorsefully, and felt all the time that by preparing the food of such sinners he imperilled his own salvation. As to the Captain—he had sailed with him for seven years, now, he said, and would not have believed it

3. A small box of cardboard or very thin wood covered with paper, for carrying or storing collars, caps, and hats.

possible that such a man. . . . "Well. Well. . . . There it was. . . .
Can't get out of it. Judgment capsized all in a minute. . . . Struck
in all his pride. . . . More like a sudden visitation than anything
else." Donkin, perched sullenly on the coal-locker, swung his legs
and concurred. He paid in the coin of spurious assent for the privilege to sit in the galley; he was disheartened and scandalised; he
agreed with the cook; could find no words severe enough to criticise
our conduct, and when in the heat of reprobation he swore at us,
Podmore, who would have liked to swear also if it hadn't been for
his principles, pretended not to hear. So Donkin, unrebuked, cursed
enough for two, cadged for matches, borrowed tobacco, and loafed
for hours, very much at home, before the stove. From there he
could hear us on the other side of the bulkhead, talking to Jimmy.
The cook knocked the saucepans about, slammed the oven door,
muttered prophecies of damnation for all the ship's company; and
Donkin, who did not admit of any hereafter (except for purposes of
blasphemy) listened, concentrated and angry, gloating fiercely over
a called-up image of infinite torment—as men gloat over the
accursed images of cruelty and revenge, of greed, and of power. . . .

On clear evenings the silent ship, under the cold sheen of the
dead moon, took on a false aspect of passionless repose, resembling
the winter of the earth. Under her a long band of gold barred the
black disc of the sea. Footsteps echoed on her quiet decks. The
moonlight clung to her like a frosted mist, and the white sails stood
out in dazzling cones as of stainless snow. In the magnificence of
the phantom rays the ship appeared pure like a vision of ideal
beauty, illusive like a tender dream of serene peace. And nothing in
her was real, nothing was distinct and solid but the heavy shadows
that filled her decks with their unceasing and noiseless stir: the
shadows darker than the night and more restless than the thoughts
of men.

Donkin prowled spiteful and alone amongst the shadows, thinking that Jimmy too long delayed to die. That evening land had
been reported from aloft, and the master, while adjusting the tubes
of the long glass, had observed with quiet bitterness to Mr. Baker
that, after fighting our way inch by inch to the Western Islands,[4]
there was nothing to expect now but a spell of calm. The sky was
clear and the barometer high. The light breeze dropped with the
sun; and an enormous stillness, forerunner of a night without wind,
descended upon the heated waters of the ocean. As long as daylight
lasted the hands collected on the forecastle-head watched on the
eastern sky the island of Flores,[5] that rose above the level expanse
of the sea with irregular and broken outlines like a sombre ruin

4. The Azores, west of Portugal.   5. One of the Azores.

upon a vast and deserted plain. It was the first land seen for nearly four months. Charley was excited, and in the midst of general indulgence took liberties with his betters. Men, strangely elated without knowing why, talked in groups, and pointed with bared arms. For the first time that voyage Jimmy's sham existence seemed for a moment forgotten in the face of a solid reality. We had got so far anyhow. Belfast discoursed, quoting imaginary examples of short homeward runs from the Islands. "Them smart fruit schooners do it in five days," he affirmed. "What do you want?—only a good little breeze." Archie maintained. that seven days was the record passage, and they disputed amicably with insulting words. Knowles declared he could already smell home from there, and with a heavy list on his short leg laughed fit to split his sides. A group of grizzled sea-dogs[6] looked out for a time in silence and with grim absorbed faces. One said suddenly—" 'Tain't far to London now."—"My first night ashore, blamme if I haven't steak and onions for supper . . . and a pint of bitter," said another.—"A barrel ye mean," shouted some one.—"Ham an' eggs three times a day. That's the way I live!" cried an excited voice. There was a stir, appreciative murmurs; eyes began to shine; jaws champed; short nervous laughs were heard. Archie smiled with reserve all to himself. Singleton came up, gave a careless glance, and went down again without saying a word, indifferent, like a man who had seen Flores an incalculable number of times. The night travelling from the East blotted out of the limpid sky the purple stain of the high land. "Dead calm," said somebody quietly. The murmur of lively talk suddenly wavered, died out; the clusters broke up; men began to drift away one by one, descending the ladders slowly and with serious faces as if sobered by that reminder of the dependence upon the invisible. And when the big yellow moon ascended gently above the sharp rim of the clear horizon it found the ship wrapped up in a breathless silence; a fearless ship that seemed to sleep profoundly, dreamlessly on the bosom of the sleeping and terrible sea.

Donkin chafed at the peace—at the ship—at the sea that stretching away on all sides merged into the illimitable silence of all creation. He felt himself pulled up sharp by unrecognised grievances. He had been physically cowed, but his injured dignity remained indomitable, and nothing could heal his lacerated feelings. Here was land already—home very soon—a bad pay-day—no clothes—more hard work. How offensive all this was. Land! The land that draws away life from sick sailors. That nigger there had money—clothes —easy times; and would not die. Land draws life away. . . . He felt tempted to go and see whether it did. Perhaps already. . . . It would be a bit of luck. There was money in the beggar's chest. He stepped

6. Old, experienced sailors.

briskly out of the shadows into the moonlight, and instantly, his craving, hungry face from sallow became livid. He opened the door of the cabin and had a shock. Sure enough, Jimmy was dead! He moved no more than a recumbent figure with clasped hands, carved on the lid of a stone coffin. Donkin glared with avidity. Then Jimmy, without stirring, blinked his eyelids, and Donkin had another shock. Those eyes were rather startling. He shut the door behind his back with gentle care, looking intently the while at James Wait as though he had come in there at a great risk to tell some secret of startling importance. Jimmy did not move but glanced languidly out of the corners of his eyes.—"Calm?" he asked. "Yuss," said Donkin, very disappointed, and sat down on the box.

Jimmy was used to such visits at all times of night or day. Men succeeded one another. They spoke in clear voices, pronounced cheerful words, repeated old jokes, listened to him; and each, going out, seemed to leave behind a little of his own vitality, surrender some of his own strength, renew the assurance of life—the indestructible thing! He did not like to be alone in his cabin, because, when he was alone, it seemed to him as if he hadn't been there at all. There was nothing. No pain. Not now. Perfectly right—but he couldn't enjoy his healthful repose unless some one was by to see it. This man would do as well as anybody. Donkin watched him stealthily:—"Soon home now," observed Wait.—"Vy d'yer whisper?" asked Donkin with interest, "can't yer speak up?" Jimmy looked annoyed and said nothing for a while; then in a lifeless unringing voice:—"Why should I shout? You ain't deaf that I know."—"Oh! I can 'ear right enough," answered Donkin in a low tone, and looked down. He was thinking sadly of going out when Jimmy spoke again.—"Time we did get home . . . to get something decent to eat . . . I am always hungry." Donkin felt angry all of a sudden. —"What about me." he hissed, "I am 'ungry too an' got ter work. You, 'ungry!"—"Your work won't kill you," commented Wait feebly; "there's a couple of biscuits in the lower bunk there—you may have one. I can't eat them." Donkin dived in, groped in the corner and when he came up again his mouth was full. He munched with ardour. Jimmy seemed to doze with open eyes. Donkin finished his hard bread and got up.—"You're not going?" asked Jimmy, staring at the ceiling.—"No," said Donkin impulsively, and instead of going out leaned his back against the closed door. He looked at James Wait, and saw him long, lean, dried up, as though all his flesh had shrivelled on his bones in the heat of a white furnace; the meagre fingers of one hand moved lightly upon the edge of the bunk playing an endless tune. To look at him was irritating and fatiguing; he could last like this for days; he was out-

rageous—belonging wholly neither to death nor life, and perfectly
invulnerable in his apparent ignorance of both. Donkin felt
tempted to enlighten him.—"What are yer thinkin' of?" he asked
surlily. James Wait had a grimacing smile that passed over the
deathlike impassiveness of his bony face, incredible and frightful as
would, in a dream, have been the sudden smile of a corpse.

"There is a girl," whispered Wait. . . . "Canton Street[7] girl.—
She chucked a third engineer of a Rennie boat[8]—for me. Cooks
oysters just as I like. . . . She says—she would chuck—any toff—for
a coloured gentleman. . . . That's me. I am kind to wimmen," he
added, a shade louder.

Donkin could hardly believe his ears. He was scandalised—
"Would she? Yer wouldn't be any good to 'er," he said with unre-
strained disgust. Wait was not there to hear him. He was swaggering
up the East India Dock Road; saying kindly, "Come along for a
treat," pushing glass swing-doors, posing with superb assurance in
the gaslight above a mahogany counter.—"D'yer think yer will ever
get ashore?" asked Donkin angrily. Wait came back with a start.—
"Ten days," he said promptly, and returned at once to the regions
of memory that know nothing of time. He felt untired, calm, and
safely withdrawn within himself beyond the reach of every grave
incertitude. There was something of the immutable quality of eternity in the slow moments of his complete restfulness. He was very
quiet and easy amongst his vivid reminiscences which he mistook
joyfully for images of an undoubted future. He cared for no one.
Donkin felt this vaguely as a blind man feeling in his darkness the
fatal antagonism of all the surrounding existences, that to him shall
for ever remain unrealisable, unseen, and enviable. He had a desire
to assert his importance, to break, to crush; to be even with everybody for everything; to tear the veil, unmask, expose, leave no
refuge—a perfidious desire of truthfulness! He laughed in a mocking splutter and said:

"Ten days. Strike me blind if I ever! . . . You will be dead by this
time to-morrow p'r'aps. Ten days!" He waited for a while. "D'ye
'ear me? Blamme if yer don't look dead already."

Wait must have been collecting his strength, for he said, almost
aloud—"You're a stinking, cadging liar. Every one knows you."
And sitting up, against all probability, startled his visitor horribly.
But very soon Donkin recovered himself. He blustered.

"What? What? Who's a liar? You are—the crowd are—the
skipper—everybody. I ain't! Putting on airs! Who's yer?" He nearly

<hr />

7. Just north of and running parallel to
East India Dock Road, which services
two main basins on the Thames.
8. Steam, screw-driven ships of the
Royal Navy. John Rennie (1761–1821),
famous civil engineer and bridge designer, introduced steam to the British
navy; his son George (1791–1866) was
an engine designer and shipbuilder for
the Royal Navy.

choked himself with indignation. "Who's yer to put on airs," he repeated trembling. " 'Ave one—'ave one, says 'ee—an' cawn't eat 'em 'isself. Now I'll 'ave both. By Gawd—I will! Yer nobody!"

He plunged into the lower bunk, rooted in there and brought to light another dusty biscuit. He held it up before Jimmy—then took a bite defiantly.

"What now?" he asked with feverish impudence. "Yer may take one—says yer. Why not giv' me both? No. I'm a mangy dorg. One fur a mangy dorg. I'll tyke both. Can yer stop me? Try. Come on. Try."

Jimmy was clasping his legs and hiding his face on the knees. His shirt clung to him. Every rib was visible. His emaciated back was shaken in repeated jerks by the panting catches of his breath.

"Yer won't. Yer can't! What did I say?" went on Donkin fiercely. He swallowed another dry mouthful with a hasty effort. The other's silent helplessness, his weakness, his shrinking attitude exasperated him. "Ye're done!" he cried. "Who's yer to be lied to; to be waited on 'and an' foot like a bloomin' ymperor. Yer nobody! Yer no one at all!" he spluttered with such a strength of unerring conviction that it shook him from head to foot in coming out, and left him vibrating like a released string.

James Wait rallied again. He lifted his head and turned bravely at Donkin, who saw a strange face, an unknown face, a fantastic and grimacing mask of despair and fury. Its lips moved rapidly; and hollow, moaning, whistling sounds filled the cabin with a vague mutter full of menace, complaint and desolation, like the far-off murmur of a rising wind. Wait shook his head; rolled his eyes; he denied, cursed, threatened—and not a word had the strength to pass beyond the sorrowful pout of those black lips. It was incomprehensible and disturbing: a gibberish of emotions, a frantic dumb show of speech pleading for impossible things, promising a shadowy vengeance. It sobered Donkin into a scrutinising watchfulness.

"Yer can't oller. See? What did I tell yer?" he said slowly after a moment of attentive examination. The other kept on headlong and unheard, nodding passionately, grinning with grotesque and appalling flashes of big white teeth. Donkin, as if fascinated by the dumb eloquence and anger of that black phantom, approached, stretching his neck out with distrustful curiosity; and it seemed to him suddenly that he was looking only at the shadow of a man crouching high in the bunk on the level with his eyes.—"What? What?" he said. He seemed to catch the shape of some words in the continuous panting hiss. "Yer will tell Belfast! Will yer? Are yer a bloomin' kid?" He trembled with alarm and rage. "Tell yer gran'mother! Yer afeard! Who's yer ter be afeard more'n any one?" His passionate sense of his own importance ran away with a last remnant of caution. "Tell an' be damned! Tell, if yer can!" he cried. "I've been treated worser'n a dorg by your blooming back-lickers. They 'as set me on, only to turn aginst me. I am the only man 'ere. They clouted me, kicked me—an' yer laffed—yer black, rotten incumbrance, you! Yer will pay fur it. They giv' yer their grub, their water —yer will pay fur it to me, by Gawd! Who axed me ter 'ave a drink of water? They put their bloomin' rags on yer that night, an' what did they giv' ter me—a clout on the bloomin' mouth—blast their . . . S'elp me! . . . Yer will pay fur it with yer money. I'm goin' ter 'ave it in a minnyt; as soon as ye're dead, yer bloomin' useless fraud. That's the man I am. An' ye're a thing—a bloody thing! Yah—you corpse!"

He flung at Jimmy's head the biscuit he had been all the time clutching hard, but it only grazed, and striking with a loud crack the bulkhead beyond burst like a hand-grenade into flying pieces. James Wait, as if wounded mortally, fell back on the pillow. His lips ceased to move and the rolling eyes became quiet and stared upwards with an intense and steady persistence. Donkin was surprised; he sat suddenly on the chest, and looked down, exhausted and gloomy. After a moment, he began to mutter to himself, "Die, you beggar—die. Somebody'll come in . . . I wish I was drunk . . . Ten days . . . oysters . . ." He looked up and spoke louder. "No . . . No more for yer . . . no more bloomin' gals that cook oysters. . . . Who's yer? It's my turn now . . . I wish I was drunk; I would soon giv' you a leg up. That's where yer bound to. Feet fust, through a port . . . Splash! Never see yer any more. Overboard! Good 'nuff fur yer."

Jimmy's head moved slightly and he turned his eyes to Donkin's face; a gaze unbelieving, desolated and appealing, of a child frightened by the menace of being shut up alone in the dark. Donkin observed him from the chest with hopeful eyes; then, without rising, tried the lid. Locked. "I wish I was drunk," he muttered and getting up listened anxiously to the distant sound of footsteps on the deck. They approached—ceased. Some one yawned interminably just outside the door, and the footsteps went away shuffling lazily. Donkin's fluttering heart eased its pace, and when he looked towards the bunk again Jimmy was staring as before at the white beam.—"'Ow d'yer feel now?" he asked.—"Bad," breathed out Jimmy.

Donkin sat down patient and purposeful. Every half-hour the bells spoke to one another ringing along the whole length of the ship. Jimmy's respiration was so rapid that it couldn't be counted, so faint that it couldn't be heard. His eyes were terrified as though he had been looking at unspeakable horrors; and by his face one could see that he was thinking of abominable things. Suddenly with an incredibly strong and heart-breaking voice he sobbed out:

"Overboard! . . . I! . . . My God!"

Donkin writhed a little on the box. He looked unwillingly. James Wait was mute. His two long bony hands smoothed the blanket upwards, as though he had wished to gather it all up under his chin. A tear, a big solitary tear, escaped from the corner of his eye and, without touching the hollow cheek, fell on the pillow. His throat rattled faintly.

And Donkin watching the end of that hateful nigger, felt the anguishing grasp of a great sorrow on his heart at the thought that he himself, some day, would have to go through it all—just like this —perhaps! His eyes became moist. "Poor beggar," he murmured. The night seemed to go by in a flash; it seemed to him he could hear the irremediable rush of precious minutes. How long would this blooming affair last? Too long surely. No luck. He could not restrain himself. He got up and approached the bunk. Wait did not stir. Only his eyes appeared alive and his hands continued their smoothing movement with a horrible and tireless industry. Donkin bent over.

"Jimmy," he called low. There was no answer, but the rattle stopped. "D'yer see me?" he asked trembling. Jimmy's chest heaved. Donkin, looking away, bent his ear to Jimmy's lips, and heard a sound like the rustle of a single dry leaf driven along the smooth sand of a beach. It shaped itself.

"Light . . . the lamp . . . and . . . go," breathed out Wait.

Donkin, instinctively, glanced over his shoulder at the brilliant flame; then, still looking away, felt under the pillow for the key. He got it at once and for the next few minutes remained on his knees shakily but swiftly busy inside the box. When he got up, his face— for the first time in his life—had a pink flush—perhaps of triumph.

He slipped the key under the pillow again, avoiding to glance at Jimmy, who had not moved. He turned his back squarely from the bunk, and started to the door as though he were going to walk a mile. At his second stride he had his nose against it. He clutched the handle cautiously, but at that moment he received the irresistible impression of something happening behind his back. He spun round as though he had been tapped on the shoulder. He was just in time to see Wait's eyes blaze up and go out at once, like two lamps overturned together by a sweeping blow. Something resembling a scarlet thread hung down his chin out of the corner of his lips—and he had ceased to breathe.

Donkin closed the door behind him gently but firmly. Sleeping men, huddled under jackets, made on the lighted deck shapeless dark mounds that had the appearance of neglected graves. Nothing had been done all through the night and he hadn't been missed. He stood motionless and perfectly astounded to find the world outside as he had left it; there was the sea, the ship—sleeping men; and he wondered absurdly at it, as though he had expected to find the men dead, familiar things gone for ever: as though, like a wanderer returning after many years, he had expected to see bewildering changes. He shuddered a little in the penetrating freshness of the air, and hugged himself forlornly. The declining moon drooped sadly in the western board as if withered by the cold touch of a pale dawn. The ship slept. And the immortal sea stretched away, immense and hazy, like the image of life, with a glittering surface and lightless depths. Donkin gave it a defiant glance and slunk off noiselessly as if judged and cast out by the august silence of its might.

Jimmy's death, after all, came as a tremendous surprise. We did not know till then how much faith we had put in his delusions. We had taken his chances of life so much at his own valuation that his death, like the death of an old belief, shook the foundations of our society. A common bond was gone; the strong, effective and respectable bond of a sentimental lie. All that day we mooned at our work, with suspicious looks and a disabused air. In our hearts we thought that in the matter of his departure Jimmy had acted in a perverse and unfriendly manner. He didn't back us up, as a shipmate should. In going he took away with himself the gloomy and solemn shadow in which our folly had posed, with humane satisfaction, as a tender arbiter of fate. And now we saw it was no such thing. It was just common foolishness; a silly and ineffectual meddling with issues of a majestic import—that is, if Podmore was right. Perhaps he was? Doubt survived Jimmy; and, like a community of banded criminals disintegrated by a touch of grace, we were profoundly scandalised with each other. Men spoke unkindly to their best chums. Others refused to speak at all. Singleton only was not surprised. "Dead—is he? Of course," he said, pointing at the island right abeam; for the calm still held the ship spell-bound within sight of Flores. Dead—of course. *He* wasn't surprised. Here was the land, and there, on the fore-hatch and waiting for the sailmaker—there was the corpse. Cause and effect. And for the first time that voyage, the old seaman became quite cheery and garrulous, explaining and illustrating from the stores of experience how, in sickness, the sight of an island (even a very small one) is generally more fatal than the view of a continent. But he couldn't explain why.

Jimmy was to be buried at five, and it was a long day till then—a day of mental disquiet and even of physical disturbance. We took no interest in our work and, very properly, were rebuked for it. This, in our constant state of hungry irritation, was exasperating. Donkin worked with his brow bound in a dirty rag, and looked so ghastly that Mr. Baker was touched with compassion at the sight of this plucky suffering.—"Ough! You, Donkin! Put down your work and go lay-up this watch. You look ill."—"I am bad, sir—in my 'ead," he said in a subdued voice, and vanished speedily. This annoyed many, and they thought the mate "bloomin' soft to-day." Captain Allistoun could be seen on the poop watching the sky to the southwest, and it soon got to be known about the decks that the barometer had begun to fall in the night, and that a breeze might be expected before long. This, by a subtle association of ideas, led to violent quarrelling as to the exact moment of Jimmy's death. Was it before or after "that 'ere glass started down"? It was impossible to know, and it caused much contemptuous growling at one another. All of a sudden there was a great tumult forward. Pacific Knowles and good-tempered Davis had come to blows over it. The watch below interfered with spirit, and for ten minutes there was a noisy scrimmage round the hatch, where, in the balancing shade of the sails, Jimmy's body, wrapped up in a white blanket, was watched over by the sorrowful Belfast, who, in his desolation, disdained the fray. When the noise had ceased, and the passions had calmed into surly silence, he stood up at the head of the swathed body, lifting both arms on high, cried with pained indignation:—"You ought to be ashamed of yourselves! . . ." We were.

Belfast took his bereavement very hard. He gave proofs of unextinguishable devotion. It was he, and no other man, who would help the sailmaker to prepare what was left of Jimmy for a solemn surrender to the insatiable sea. He arranged the weights carefully at the feet: two holystones, an old anchor-shackle without its pin, some broken links of a worn-out stream cable. He arranged them this way, then that. "Bless my soul! you aren't afraid he will chafe his heel?" said the sailmaker, who hated the job. He pushed the needle, puffing furiously, with his head in a cloud of tobacco smoke; he turned the flaps over, pulled at the stitches, stretched at the canvas.—"Lift his shoulders. . . . Pull to you a bit. . . . So—o—o. Steady." Belfast obeyed, pulled, lifted, overcome with sorrow, dropping tears on the tarred twine.—"Don't you drag the canvas too taut over his poor face, Sails," he entreated tearfully. "What are you fashing[9] yourself for? He will be comfortable enough," assured the sailmaker, cutting the thread after the last stitch, which came about the middle of Jimmy's forehead. He rolled up the remaining canvas, put away the needles. "What makes you take on so?" he asked. Belfast looked down at the long package of grey sailcloth.—

9. Scottish for being troubled or worrying.

"I pulled him out," he whispered, "and he did not want to go. If I had sat up with him last night he would have kept alive for me . . . but something made me tired." The sailmaker took vigorous draws at his pipe and mumbled;—"When I . . . West India Station . . . In the *Blanche*[1] frigate . . . Yellow Jack[2] . . . sewed in twenty men a week . . . Portsmouth[3]—Devonport[4] men—townies—knew their fathers, mothers, sisters—the whole boiling of 'em. Thought nothing of it. And these niggers like this one—you don't know where it comes from. Got nobody. No use to nobody. Who will miss him?"—"I do—I pulled him out," mourned Belfast dismally.

On two planks nailed together and apparently resigned and still under the folds of the Union Jack with a white border, James Wait, carried aft by four men, was deposited slowly, with his feet point-ing at an open port. A swell had set in from the westward, and fol-lowing on the roll of the ship, the red ensign, at half-mast, darted out and collapsed again on the grey sky, like a tongue of flickering fire; Charley tolled the bell; and at every swing to starboard the whole vast semicircle of steely waters visible on that side seemed to come up with a rush to the edge of the port, as if impatient to get at our Jimmy. Every one was there but Donkin, who was too ill to come; the Captain and Mr. Creighton stood bareheaded on the break of the poop; Mr. Baker, directed by the master, who had said to him gravely:—"You know more about the prayer book than I do," came out of the cabin door quickly and a little embarrassed. All the caps went off. He began to read in a low tone, and with his usual harmlessly menacing utterance, as though he had been for the last time reproving confidentially that dead seaman at his feet. The men listened in scattered groups; they leaned on the fife rail, gazing on the deck; they held their chins in their hands thoughtfully, or, with crossed arms and one knee slightly bent, hung their heads in an attitude of upright meditation. Wamibo dreamed. Mr. Baker read on, grunting reverently at the turn of every page. The words, missing the unsteady hearts of men, rolled out to wander without a home upon the heartless sea; and James Wait, silenced for ever, lay un-critical and passive under the hoarse murmur of despair and hopes.

Two men made ready and waited for those words that send so many of our brothers to their last plunge. Mr. Baker began the passage. "Stand by," muttered the boatswain. Mr. Baker read out: "To the deep," and paused. The men lifted the inboard end of the

1. Originally called the *Tilkhurst*; Con-rad signed on at the age of twenty-seven in April 1885 as second mate, for voyage to Calcutta, signing off in June 1886 (see Jerry Allen, *The Sea Years of Joseph Conrad*, New York, 1965, p. 322).
2. Yellow fever; also the term for the yellow quarantine flag with the letter

"Q" which signifies there is disease on board ship.
3. A chief British naval station and sea-port situated on Portsea Island in the English Channel in southern England.
4. A seaport in southwestern England, in the county of Devonshire.

planks, the boatswain snatched off the Union Jack, and James Wait did not move.—"Higher," muttered the boatswain angrily. All the heads were raised; every man stirred uneasily, but James Wait gave no sign of going. In death and swathed up for all eternity, he yet seemed to cling to the ship with the grip of an undying fear. "Higher! Lift!" whispered the boatswain fiercely.—"He won't go," stammered one of the men shakily, and both appeared ready to drop everything. Mr. Baker waited, burying his face in the book, and shuffling his feet nervously. All the men looked profoundly disturbed; from their midst a faint humming noise spread out—growing louder. . . . "Jimmy!" cried Belfast in a wailing tone, and there was a second of shuddering dismay.

"Jimmy, be a man!" he shrieked passionately. Every mouth was wide open, not an eyelid winked. He stared wildly, twitching all over; he bent his body forward like a man peering at an horror. "Go!" he shouted, and sprang out of the crowd with his arm extended. "Go, Jimmy!—Jimmy, go! Go!" His fingers touched the head of the body, and the grey package started reluctantly to whizz off the lifted planks all at once, with the suddenness of a flash of lightning. The crowd stepped forward like one man; a deep Ah—h—h! came out vibrating from the broad chests. The ship rolled as if relieved of an unfair burden; the sails flapped. Belfast, supported by Archie, gasped hysterically; and Charley, who anxious to see Jimmy's last dive, leaped headlong on the rail, was too late to see anything but the faint circle of a vanishing ripple.

Mr. Baker, perspiring abundantly, read out the last prayer in a deep rumour of excited men and fluttering sails. "Amen!" he said in an unsteady growl, and closed the book.

"Square the yards!" thundered a voice above his head. All hands gave a jump; one or two dropped their caps; Mr. Baker looked up surprised. The master, standing on the break of the poop, pointed to the westward. "Breeze coming," he said. "Man the weather braces." Mr. Baker crammed the book hurriedly into his pocket.— "Forward, there—let go the foretack!" he hailed joyfully, bareheaded and brisk; "Square the foreyard, you port watch!"—"Fair wind—fair wind," muttered the men going to the braces.—"What did I tell you?" mumbled old Singleton, flinging down coil after coil with hasty energy; "I knowed it—he's gone, and here it comes."

It came with the sound of a lofty and powerful sigh. The sails filled, the ship gathered way, and the waking sea began to murmur sleepily of home to the ears of men.

That night, while the ship rushed foaming to the northward before a freshening gale, the boatswain unbosomed himself to the petty officers' berth:—"The chap was nothing but trouble," he said, "from the moment he came aboard—d'ye remember—that night in Bombay? Been bullying all that softy crowd—cheeked the old man —we had to go fooling all over a half-drowned ship to save him. Dam' nigh a mutiny all for him—and now the mate abused me like a pickpocket for forgetting to dab a lump of grease on them planks. So I did, but you ought to have known better, too, than to leave a nail sticking up—hey, Chips,"

"And you ought to have known better than to chuck all my tools overboard for 'im, like a skeary greenhorn," retorted the morose carpenter. "Well—he's gone after 'em now," he added in an unforgiving tone.—"On the China Station,[5] I remember once, the Admiral he says to me . . ." began the sailmaker.

A week afterwards the Narcissus entered the chops of the Channel.[6]

Under white wings she skimmed low over the blue sea like a great tired bird speeding to its nest. The clouds raced with her mastheads; they rose astern enormous and white, soared to the zenith, flew past, and, falling down the wide curve of the sky, seemed to dash headlong into the sea—the clouds swifter than the ship, more free, but without a home. The coast to welcome her stepped out of space into the sunshine. The lofty headlands trod masterfully into the sea; the wide bays smiled in the light; the shadows of homeless clouds ran along the sunny plains, leaped over valleys, without a check darted up the hills, rolled down the slopes; and the sunshine pursued them with patches of running brightness. On the brows of dark cliffs white lighthouses shone in pillars of light. The Channel glittered like a blue mantle shot with gold and starred by the silver of the capping seas. The Narcissus rushed past the headlands and the bays. Outward-bound vessels crossed her track, lying over, and with their masts stripped for a slogging fight with the hard sou'wester. And, inshore, a string of smoking steamboats waddled, hugging the coast, like migrating and amphibious monsters, distrustful of the restless waves.

At night the headlands retreated, the bays advanced into one unbroken line of gloom. The lights of the earth mingled with the lights of heaven; and above the tossing lanterns of a trawling fleet a great lighthouse shone steadily, like an enormous riding light burning above a vessel of fabulous dimensions. Below its steady glow, the coast, stretching away straight and black, resembled the high side of an indestructible craft riding motionless upon the immortal and unresting sea. The dark land lay alone in the midst of waters,

5. Service with the Royal Navy in the China Sea.
6. The English Channel, the strait between southern England and northern France which connects the Atlantic Ocean and the North Sea.

like a mighty ship bestarred with vigilant lights—a ship carrying the burden of millions of lives—a ship freighted with dross and with jewels, with gold and with steel. She towered up immense and strong, guarding priceless traditions and untold suffering, sheltering glorious memories and base forgetfulness, ignoble virtues and splendid transgressions. A great ship! For ages had the ocean battered in vain her enduring sides; she was there when the world was vaster and darker, when the sea was great and mysterious, and ready to surrender the prize of fame to audacious men. A ship mother of fleets and nations! The great flagship of the race; stronger than the storms! and anchored in the open sea.

The *Narcissus*, heeling over to off-shore gusts, rounded the South Foreland,[7] passed through the Downs,[8] and, in tow, entered the river.[9] Shorn of the glory of her white wings, she wound obediently after the tug through the maze of invisible channels. As she passed them the red-painted light-vessels, swung at their moorings, seemed for an instant to sail with great speed in the rush of tide, and the next moment were left hopelessly behind. The big buoys on the tails of banks slipped past her sides very low, and, dropping in her wake, tugged at their chains like fierce watchdogs. The reach narrowed; from both sides the land approached the ship. She went steadily up the river. On the riverside slopes the houses appeared in groups—seemed to stream down the declivities at a run to see her pass, and, checked by the mud of the foreshore, crowded on the banks. Farther on, the tall factory chimneys appeared in insolent bands and watched her go by, like a straggling crowd of slim giants, swaggering and upright under the black plummets of smoke, cavalierly aslant. She swept round the bends; an impure breeze shrieked a welcome between her stripped spars; and the land, closing in, stepped between the ship and the sea.

A low cloud hung before her—a great opalescent and tremulous cloud, that seemed to rise from the steaming brows of millions of men. Long drifts of smoky vapours soiled it with livid trails; it throbbed to the beat of millions of hearts, and from it came an immense and lamentable murmur—the murmur of millions of lips praying, cursing, sighing, jeering—the undying murmur of folly, regret, and hope exhaled by the crowds of the anxious earth. The *Narcissus* entered the cloud; the shadows deepened; on all sides there was the clang of iron, the sound of mighty blows, shrieks, yells. Black barges drifted stealthily on the murky stream. A mad jumble of begrimed walls loomed up vaguely in the smoke, bewil-

7. The southern of two headlands in Kent, near Dover.
8. An anchorage or sea space in the English Channel between the eastern coast of Kent and the Goodwin Sands, stretching from the South to the North Foreland.
9. The Thames, connecting London with the North Sea.

dering and mournful, like a vision of disaster. The tugs backed and filled in the stream, to hold the ship steady at the dock gates; from her bows two lines went through the air whistling, and struck at the land viciously, like a pair of snakes. A bridge broke in two before her, as if by enchantment; big hydraulic capstans began to turn all by themselves, as though animated by a mysterious and unholy spell. She moved through a narrow lane of water between two low walls of granite, and men with check-ropes in their hands kept pace with her, walking on the broad flagstones. A group waited impatiently on each side of the vanished bridge: rough heavy men in caps; sallow-faced men in high hats; two bareheaded women; ragged children, fascinated, and with wide eyes. A cart coming at a jerky trot pulled up sharply. One of the women screamed at the silent ship—"Hallo, Jack!" without looking at any one in particular, and all hands looked at her from the forecastle head.—"Stand clear! Stand clear of that rope!" cried the dockmen, bending over stone posts. The crowd murmured, stamped where they stood.—"Let go your quarter-checks! Let go!" sang out a ruddy-faced old man on the quay. The ropes splashed heavily falling in the water, and the *Narcissus* entered the dock.

The stony shores ran away right and left in straight lines, enclosing a sombre and rectangular pool. Brick walls rose high above the water—soulless walls, staring through hundreds of windows as troubled and dull as the eyes of over-fed brutes. At their base monstrous iron cranes crouched, with chains hanging from their long necks, balancing cruel-looking hooks over the decks of lifeless ships. A noise of wheels rolling over stones, the thump of heavy things falling, the racket of feverish winches, the grinding of strained chains, floated on the air. Between high buildings the dust of all the continents soared in short flights; and a penetrating smell of perfumes and dirt, of spices and hides, of things costly and of things filthy, pervaded the space, made for it an atmosphere precious and disgusting. The *Narcissus* came gently into her berth; the shadows of soulless walls fell upon her, the dust of all the continents leaped upon her deck, and a swarm of strange men, clambering up her sides, took possession of her in the name of the sordid earth. She had ceased to live.

A toff in a black coat and high hat scrambled with agility, came up to the second mate, shook hands, and said:—"Hallo, Herbert," It was his brother. A lady appeared suddenly. A real lady, in a black dress and with a parasol. She looked extremely elegant in the midst of us, and as strange as if she had fallen there from the sky. Mr. Baker touched his cap to her. It was the master's wife. And very soon the Captain, dressed very smartly and in a white shirt, went with her over the side. We didn't recognise him at all till, turning on the quay, he called to Mr. Baker:—"Don't forget to wind up the chronometers to-morrow morning." An underhand lot of seedy-looking chaps with shifty eyes wandered in and out of the forecastle looking for a job—they said.—"More likely for something to steal," commented Knowles cheerfully. Poor beggars! Who cared? Weren't we home! But Mr. Baker went for one of them who had given him some cheek, and we were delighted. Everything was delightful.—"I've finished aft, sir," called out Mr. Creighton.—"No water in the well, sir," reported for the last time the carpenter, sounding-rod in hand. Mr. Baker glanced along the decks at the expectant group of sailors, glanced aloft at the yards.—"Ough! That will do, men," he grunted. The group broke up. The voyage was ended.

Rolled-up beds went flying over the rail; lashed chests went sliding down the gangway—mighty few of both at that. "The rest is having a cruise off the Cape," explained Knowles enigmatically to a dock-loafer with whom he had struck a sudden friendship. Men ran, calling to one another, hailing utter strangers to "lend a hand with the dunnage," then with sudden decorum approached the mate to shake hands before going ashore.—"Good-bye, sir," they repeated in various tones. Mr. Baker grasped hard palms. grunted in a friendly manner at every one, his eyes twinkled.—"Take care of your money, Knowles. Ough! Soon get a nice wife if you do." The lame man was delighted.—"Good-bye, sir," said Belfast, with emotion, wringing the mate's hand, and looked up with swimming eyes. "I thought I would take 'im ashore with me," he went on plaintively. Mr. Baker did not understand, but said kindly:—"Take care of yourself, Craik," and the bereaved Belfast went over the rail mourning and alone.

Mr. Baker, in the sudden peace of the ship, moved about solitary and grunting, trying door handles, peering into dark places, never done—a model chief mate! No one waited for him ashore. Mother dead; father and two brothers, Yarmouth[1] fishermen, drowned together on the Dogger Bank[2]; sister married and unfriendly. Quite a lady. Married to the leading tailor of a little town, and its leading politician, who did not think his sailor brother-in-law quite respectable enough for him. Quite a lady, quite a lady, he thought, sitting down for a moment's rest on the quarter-hatch. Time enough to go ashore and get a bite and sup, and a bed somewhere. He didn't like to part with a ship. No one to think about then. The darkness of a misty evening fell, cold and damp, upon the deserted deck; and Mr. Baker sat smoking, thinking of all the successive ships to whom

1. A seaport in eastern England, in the county of Norfolk, situated on a narrow strip of land between the North Sea and the river Yare.

2. A submerged sand bank about sixty miles east of England, in the middle of the North Sea.

through many long years he had given the best of a seaman's care. And never a command in sight. Not once!—"I haven't somehow the cut of a skipper about me," he meditated placidly, while the ship-keeper (who had taken possession of the galley), a wizened old man with bleared eyes, cursed him in whispers for "hanging about so." —"Now, Creighton," he pursued the unenvious train of thought, "quite a gentleman . . . swell friends . . . will get on. Fine young fellow . . . a little more experience." He got up and shook himself. "I'll be back first thing to-morrow morning for the hatches. Don't you let them touch anything before I come, shipkeeper," he called out. Then, at last, he also went ashore—a model chief mate!

The men scattered by the dissolving contact of the land came together once more in the shipping office.—"The Narcissus pays off," shouted outside a glazed door a brass-bound old fellow, with a crown and the capitals B.T. on his cap. A lot trooped in at once but many were late. The room was large, whitewashed, and bare; a counter surmounted by a brass-wire grating fenced off a third of the dusty space, and behind the grating a pasty-faced clerk, with his hair parted in the middle, had the quick, glittering eyes and the vivacious, jerky movements of a caged bird. Poor Captain Allistoun also in there and sitting before a little table with piles of gold and notes on it, appeared subdued by his captivity. Another Board of Trade bird was perching on a high stool near the door: an old bird that did not mind the chaff of elated sailors. The crew of the Narcissus, broken up into knots, pushed in the corners. They had new shore togs, smart jackets that looked as if they had been shaped with an axe, glossy trousers that seemed made of crumpled sheet-iron, collarless flannel shirts, shiny new boots. They tapped on shoulders, button-holed one another, asked:—"Where did you sleep last night?" whispered gaily, slapped their thighs with bursts of sub-dued laughter. Most had clean radiant faces; only one or two turned up dishevelled and sad; the two young Norwegians looked tidy, meek, and altogether of a promising material for the kind ladies who patronise the Scandinavian Home.[3] Wamibo, still in his working clothes, dreamed, upright and burly in the middle of the room, and, when Archie came in, woke up for a smile. But the wide-awake clerk called out a name, and the paying-off business began.

One by one they came up to the pay-table to get the wages of their glorious and obscure toil. They swept the money with care into broad palms, rammed it trustfully into trousers' pockets, or, turning their backs on the table, reckoned with difficulty in the hollow of their stiff hands.—"Money right? Sign the release. There —there," repeated the clerk impatiently. "How stupid those sailors

3. The Scandinavian Sailor's Temperance Home, by West India Dock, founded in 1880 and directed by Agnes Hedenström.

are!" he thought. Singleton came up, venerable—and uncertain as to daylight; brown drops of tobacco juice hung in his white beard; his hands, that never hesitated in the great light of the open sea, could hardly find the small pile of gold in the profound darkness of the shore. "Can't write?" said the clerk, shocked. "Make a mark then." Singleton painfully sketched in a heavy cross, blotted the page. "What a disgusting old brute," muttered the clerk. Somebody opened the door for him, and the patriarchal seaman passed through unsteadily, without as much as a glance at any of us.

Archie displayed a pocket-book. He was chaffed. Belfast, who looked wild, as though he had already luffed up[4] through a public-house[5] or two, gave signs of emotion and wanted to speak to the captain privately. The master was surprised. They spoke through the wires, and we could hear the captain saying:—"I've given it up to the Board of Trade." "I should've liked to get something of his," mumbled Belfast. "But you can't, my man. It's given up, locked and sealed, to the Marine Office,"[6] expostulated the master; and Belfast stood back, with drooping mouth and troubled eyes. In a pause of the business we heard the master and the clerk talking. We caught: "James Wait—deceased—found no papers of any kind—no relations—no trace—the Office must hold his wages then." Donkin entered. He seemed out of breath, was grave, full of business. He went straight to the desk, talked with animation to the clerk, who thought him an intelligent man. They discussed the account, dropping h's against one another as if for a wager—very friendly. Captain Allistoun paid. "I give you a bad discharge," he said quietly. Donkin raised his voice;—"I don't want your bloomin' discharge —keep it. I'm goin' ter 'ave a job ashore." He turned to us. "No more bloomin' sea fur me," he said aloud. All looked at him. He had better clothes, had an easy air, appeared more at home than any of us; he stared with assurance, enjoying the effect of his declaration. "Yuss. I 'ave friends well off. That's more'n you got. But I am a man. Ye're shipmates for all that. Who's comin' fur a drink?"

No one moved. There was a silence; a silence of blank faces and stony looks. He waited a moment, smiled bitterly, and went to the door. There he faced round once more. "You won't? You bloomin' lot of 'ypocrites. No? What 'ave I done to yer? Did I bully yer? Did I 'urt yer? Did I? . . . You won't drink? . . . No! . . . Then may ye die of thirst, every mother's son of yer! Not one of yer 'as the sperrit of a bug. Ye're the scum of the world. Work and starve!"

He went out, and slammed the door with such violence that the old Board of Trade bird nearly fell off his perch.

"He's mad," declared Archie. "No! No! He's drunk," insisted

4. When applied to sails means to shake, from being set too close to the wind.
5. "Pub," an English bar, tavern, or inn.
6. A part of the Board of Trade, on Tower Hill, in Saint Katharine Dock House, which supervised the way ships' crews were handled: the signing, shipping, sailing, and paying off.

Belfast, lurching about, and in a maudlin tone. Captain Allistoun sat smiling thoughtfully at the cleared pay-table.

Outside, on Tower Hill,[7] they blinked, hesitated clumsily, as if blinded by the strange quality of the hazy light, as if discomposed by the view of so many men; and they who could hear one another in the howl of gales seemed deafened and distracted by the dull roar of the busy earth.—"To the Black Horse![8] To the Black Horse!" cried some. "Let us have a drink together before we part." They crossed the road, clinging to one another. Only Charley and Belfast wandered off alone. As I came up I saw a red-faced, blowsy woman, in a grey shawl, and with dusty, fluffy hair, fall on Charley's neck. It was his mother. She slobbered over him:—"Oh, my boy! My boy!"— "Leggo of me," said Charley, "Leggo, Mother!" I was passing him at the time, and over the untidy head of the blubbering woman he gave me a humorous smile and a glance ironic, courageous, and profound, that seemed to put all my knowledge of life to shame. I nodded and passed on, but heard him say again, good-naturedly:— "If you leggo of me this minyt—ye shall 'ave a bob[9] for a drink out of my pay." In the next few steps I came upon Belfast. He caught my arm with tremulous enthusiasm.—"I couldn't go wi' 'em," he stammered, indicating by a nod our noisy crowd, that drifted slowly along the other sidewalk. "When I think of Jimmy . . . Poor Jim! When I think of him I have no heart for drink. You were his chum, too . . . but I pulled him out . . . didn't I? Short wool he had. . . . Yes. And I stole the blooming pie. . . . He wouldn't go. . . . He wouldn't go for nobody." He burst into tears. "I never touched him—never—never!" he sobbed. "He went for me like . . . like . . . a lamb."

I disengaged myself gently. Belfast's crying fits generally ended in a fight with some one, and I wasn't anxious to stand the brunt of his inconsolable sorrow. Moreover, two bulky policemen stood near by, looking at us with a disapproving and incorruptible gaze.—"So long!" I said, and went on my way.

But at the corner I stopped to take my last look at the crew of the Narcissus. They were swaying irresolute and noisy on the broad flagstones before the Mint.[1] They were bound for the Black Horse, where men, in fur caps, with brutal faces and in shirt sleeves, dispense out of varnished barrels the illusions of strength, mirth, happiness; the illusion of splendour and poetry of life, to the paid-off

7. The hill rising above and behind the ancient Tower of London on the Thames next to Saint Katharine's Dock.
8. A pub formerly facing the Board of Trade on a street next to Tower Hill, now replaced by a "roundabout," or traffic circle.
9. British for a shilling.
1. On Tower Hill, to the northeast of the Tower; until just recently the gold, silver, and bronze coins current in the United Kingdom were struck there.

crews of southern-going ships. From afar I saw them discoursing, with jovial eyes and clumsy gestures, while the sea of life thundered into their ears ceaseless and unheeded. And swaying about there on the white stones, surrounded by the hurry and clamour of men, they appeared to be creatures of another kind—lost, alone, forgetful, and doomed; they were like castaways, like reckless and joyous castaways, like mad castaways making merry in the storm and upon an insecure ledge of a treacherous rock. The roar of the town resembled the roar of topping breakers, merciless and strong, with a loud voice and cruel purpose; but overhead the clouds broke; a flood of sunshine streamed down the walls of grimy houses. The dark knot of seamen drifted in sunshine. To the left of them the trees in Tower Gardens[2] sighed, the stones of the Tower gleaming, seemed to stir in the play of light, as if remembering suddenly all the great joys and sorrows of the past, the fighting prototypes of these men; press-gangs;[3] mutinous cries; the wailing of women by the riverside, and the shouts of men welcoming victories. The sunshine of heaven fell like a gift of grace on the mud of the earth, on the remembering and mute stones, on greed, selfishness; on the anxious faces of forgetful men. And to the right of the dark group the stained front of the Mint, cleansed by the flood of light, stood out for a moment dazzling and white like a marble palace in a fairy tale. The crew of the *Narcissus* drifted out of sight.

I never saw them again. The sea took some, the steamers took others, the graveyards of the earth will account for the rest. Singleton has no doubt taken with him the long record of his faithful work into the peaceful depths of an hospitable sea. And Donkin, who never did a decent day's work in his life, no doubt earns his living by discoursing with filthy eloquence upon the right of labour to live. So be it! Let the earth and the sea each have its own.

A gone shipmate, like any other man, is gone for ever; and I never met one of them again. But at times the spring-flood of memory sets with force up the dark River of the Nine Bends.[4] Then on the waters of the forlorn stream drifts a ship—a shadowy ship manned by a crew of Shades. They pass and make a sign, in a shadowy hail. Haven't we, together and upon the immortal sea, wrung out a meaning from our sinful lives? Good-bye, brothers! You were a good crowd. As good a crowd as ever fisted with wild cries the beating canvas of a heavy foresail; or tossing aloft, invisible in the night, gave back yell for yell to a westerly gale.

THE END

2. The public gardens between the north moat of the Tower itself and Tower Hill.
3. Parties of seamen, under officers, empowered to draft other men for naval service.
4. Conrad's private mythologizing of a merged Thames and Styx, the river of the dead.

Textual Appendix

Textual History

After writing and underscoring "The End" at the close of the holograph of *The Nigger of the "Narcissus,"* Conrad added, "Stanford-le-hope .19 Feb. 1897," thus ending a story begun in Britanny some eight months earlier. But Conrad had returned to England in September 1896 with only ten pages completed.[1] By November he had written enough to enable his friend and literary adviser, Edward Garnett, to bring the work to the attention of S. S. Pawling of the publishing house of William Heinemann and William E. Henly, editor of the *New Review* (owned by Heinemann).[2] Both showed immediate interest and verbally agreed to publish, although Conrad went on to finish the story before final details for serial and book publication were completed.

The manuscript (M) was typewritten and corrected (T) in the spring of 1897, and the story was set in type during the early summer. On July 29 seven copies (D) were run, five for the purpose of copyright deposit in British libraries and two for presentation, to his friend Garnett's mother and to his early supporter W. H. Chesson. (Other complete sets were probably run for eventual use as copy texts for the first American (A) and English (E) editions.) The type was then used, after appropriate divisions had been made, for five monthly installments to run in the *New Review* (P) from August through December.[3] Heinemann arranged for American rights with Dodd, Meade and Company and the book appeared in New York as *The Children of the Sea* on November 30, 1897. Heinemann's edition appeared December 2, 1897, but was dated 1898.

1. Essential details can be found in Edward Garnett, ed., *Letters from Joseph Conrad: 1895–1924* (1928), Thomas J. Wise, *A Bibliography of the Writings of Conrad, 1895–1921* (1921, 2nd ed. 1961), and George T. Keating, *A Conrad Memorial Library* (1929).

2. Edward Garnett (as well as W. H. Chesson, mentioned below), of the publishing house of T. Fisher Unwin, had been instrumental in getting Conrad's first novel, *Almayer's Folly,* published in 1895. Garnett and Chesson urged Conrad to take up writing as a career, and when Unwin showed only minimal interest in *The Nigger of the "Narcissus,"* Garnett, even though employed by Unwin, acted as Conrad's informal agent. Pawling, second only to Heinemann in the firm, gave Conrad generous terms. Henley (1849–1903), known to American students as the poet of "Invictus," was a much respected literary leader and arbiter whose approval meant much to Conrad. See Backgrounds and Sources.

3. Although the version of the story in the *New Review* (P) appears in five installments, it does not preserve the five chapter divisions of all other states of the story, which vary in length. In order to appear in segments of from twenty to twenty-five pages for each issue, the se-

rial form of the story was redivided into eight sections. Whether or not Conrad was consulted in the establishment of the resulting new rhythm, we do not know. But, on August 9, 1897, Conrad asked R. B. Cunninghame Graham not to read *The Nigger* in the forthcoming serial form, but to wait until November, when Conrad would send him a copy of the whole story: "The installment plan ruins it" (see below, p. 181).

The August issue contains chapter one as section I and the part of chapter two ending "that snigger was hard to bear" (24.32) as section II.

The September issue starts section III at this point and continues for the whole number (ignoring the beginning of chapter three [29.14], ending with "as though he had been made of glass" (45.29).

The October issue starts section IV at this point, and section V with the beginning of chapter four, but ends at "well-fed crew of satisfied skippers" (63.33).

The November issue starts section VI at this point, and section VII with the beginning of chapter five, but ends at "his eyes disdainful, penetrating and sad" (86.23).

The December issue starts section VIII at this point, running to the ending of the story.

Thus, in less than a year *The Nigger of the "Narcissus"* was extant in six states: the manuscript (M) January 1897, the typescript (T) Spring 1897, the copyright deposit copies (D) July 1897, the serial form in the *New Review* (P) August–December 1897, the first American edition (A) November 1897, and the first English edition (E) December 1897. The relationships which exist among these six states are cloudy, to say the least.[4] The partially extant typescript (T) follows the manuscript (M) and was corrected by Conrad, but it does not itself lead directly to any of the three main branches from the manuscript: D-P, A, and E (for example Singleton remains Sullivan in typescript, as he is in manuscript). That P differs from D only at chapter breaks and at beginnings and endings of paragraphs proves they are related mainly because of the practical need to preserve the type as set (indeed, it cannot be proved that the variants are from Conrad or a house editor). A and E are more nearly alike than either is to the D-P pairing, yet are sufficiently different to preclude the assumption of an exactly common source. A and E are decidedly superior to M, T, D, and P.

Fortunately for an editor, the story of transmittal does not end here, for two authoritative states follow. In April 1916, Conrad took a copy (Y) of the 1910 Heinemann Popular Edition (which was printed from the unmodified plates of E) and turned it into—to use his words—the "Corrected Text for the corrected edition." The "corrected edition" was to be the definitive, limited Collected Edition (H) published by Heinemann in 1921. Thus by accident or by purpose, Conrad selected E as the working text for the copy text Y of the collected edition H. Subsequent Dent (London) and Doubleday (New York) editions are dependent variously on E, Y, and H, but none has Conrad's authority.[5]

The eight major states of the story are:

M: The 194-page manuscript entitled "The Nigger of the 'Narcissus,'" owned by the Philip H. & A. S. W. Rosenbach Foundation in Philadelphia, is complete except for a short, lost insert corresponding to 90.26 of the present text. Numbered consecutively and divided into five successive sections, the manuscript is another testimonial to Conrad's early mastery of a natural architectonic. The whole story flows through its evolutionary contours from beginning to end. There are no stops, no redirections, only pauses along the way to refine a phrase, reorder a sentence, or regroup a paragraph. Nothing remains suppressed; reworked parts are crossed out, then recopied for the ease of typing. Here and there a word is changed or a clause is dropped. The whole is there, the changes themselves being examples of minor change, the only kind to be found in all later states of the story.

T: The typescript exists in two fragments, thirty-eight pages, pp. 59 to 96, in the Henry A. Colgate collection in the Case Library of Colgate University and p. 97 at the Rosenbach Foundation. Conrad corrected

4. For a full accounting which comes to a different conclusion from the present see Kenneth W. Davis and Donald W. Rude, "The Transmission of the Text of *The Nigger of the "Narcissus,"* Conrad-*iana*, V (1973), 2, 20–45.
5. See Robert Kimbrough, ed., *The Heart of Darkness* (revised, 1971), pp. 80–81, and Thomas C. Moser, *Lord Jim* (1968), pp. 255–57.

typos (missed some), changed words, and tinkered with punctuation (but seemed content to let the haphazard "style" of the manuscript pretty much stand). (The extant fragments correspond to pp. 42.19 to 72.44 and 72.44 to 73.35 of the present text. See Textual Notes for 72.44.)

D: Seven copies of *The Nigger of the "Narcissus": A Tale of the Forecastle* were printed, five for copyright deposit in British libraries and two for presentation to Chesson and Mrs. Richard Garnett, Edward's mother, whose maiden name was Singleton and in honor of whom Conrad changed the original name of Sullivan (which twice survives in D). Conrad corrected these mistakes in the Garnett copy, which is at Colgate, as well as some fifteen others, all of which were incorporated into A and E, and hence H. The punctuation of D (and P) moves away from M and T, but without an extant intermediate source we cannot determine to what extent this reflects Conrad's design.

P: The last three installments of *The Nigger of the "Narcissus": A Tale of the Forecastle* (not the same as the last three chapters: see note 3, above) contain a number of unique readings, which make them look suspiciously like house changes rather than authorial. Although none have been adopted, all are included in the Textual Notes.

A: Has no unique readings in the text, but was first published as *The Children of the Sea: A Tale of the Forecastle,* on the American publisher's insistence that nobody would buy or read a book with the word nigger in its title.

E: *The Nigger of the "Narcissus": A Tale of the Sea* has some grammatical and usage changes which reflect suggested corrections offered Conrad; this is, therefore, the most polished version before H.

Y: Although at base a reprint of E, this is the most interesting version for the obvious reason that it is Conrad's copy text for H. Now housed in the Keating Collection in the Beinecke Library at Yale University.

H: Conrad considered the 1921 Heinemann Collected Edition to contain the definitive versions of his work.

(M was consulted in Philadelphia; T was consulted in Hamilton, New York; D was consulted at the British Museum, Cambridge University, and Colgate University; P was consulted at the University of Wisconsin–Madison; A was consulted at the British Museum; E was consulted at the British Museum and at the University of Wisconsin–Madison; Y was consulted through a microfilm provided by Yale University; and H was loaned by the University of Illinois–Urbana.)

Present Text

The copy text for the present Norton Critical Edition is **H**, the 1921 Heinemann edition. However, all states of the text have been examined and collated, which has led to a number of emendations, all listed below and all justified in the Textual Notes (except for typographical errors). Some introduce readings from **Y** not caught by the house editor, and some bring in earlier authoritative changes either made by Conrad or intended, as testified by written remarks. The numbers refer to the page and line of the present edition, followed (in boldface type) by the reading used in this edition, followed by the reading preserved in **H**.

9.17 **bare-footed** barefooted
14.12 **asked** said
14.14 **out** hout
14.15 **out** hout
14.18 **Irish** Hirish
15.35 **chain** chain cable
17.18 **passage** trip
17.21 **look-out'';** look-out;"
17.35 **the peace** the dull peace
18.19 **uneventful** eventful
30.35 **shirt sleeves** short sleeves
31.21 **officially** technically
35.23 **glass** grass
42.41 **lie down** lay down
44.21 **cleat** cleet
46.40–47.2 [Ellipses replace internal dashes in Baker's speeches.]
47.36 **swept, unheard,** swept unheard
48.16 **skippers; they** skippers. They
48.27 **sang** sank
49.43 **this** his
57.45 **battered and** battered, and
59.42 **hallo.'' . . .** hallo'' . . .
60.17 **does, at dead low water,** does at dead low water
60.25 **up.'' . . . "Strong as a horse.''** up'' . . . "Strong as a horse"
63.43 **and of heaven** and heaven
64.2 **globe** glove
65.16 **of course. . . .** of course . . .

68.19 **I am . . . an'** I am...an'
69.30 **dock** deck
73.12 **made** make
74.11 **not to be allowed** not allowed to be
74.16 **Jimmy,** Jim—
74.25 **'m** 'im
74.38 **imposed** himposed
76.11 **"Don't"—"Drop it!"** "Don't" "Drop it!"
76.14 **Drop it!"—"Let me!"** Drop it!" "Let me!"
77.8 **All right. . . .** All right . . .
77.33 **withdrew. . . .** withdrew . . .
78.13 **as** like
83.11 **and I say nothing** and say nothing
84.34 **Years ago—I was** Years ago; I was
89.19 [Space added in accordance with Conrad's notation in Y.]
89.39 **sun;** sun.
92.26 **as** like
93.18 **Yer nobody!** Yer nobody
93.30 **disturbing:** disturbing:
94.10 **soon as ye're** soon has ye're
94.12 **thing!** thing.
94.25 **bound to.** bound to go.
105.33 **Ye're** Yer

Textual Notes

The following textual notes have been selected from the variants discovered in collating all of the separate states of the story. Those included have been chosen to indicate peculiarities of various editions, as well as to show how Conrad worked this way toward achieving what he considered to be his final text. The numbers refer to the page and line of the present text where the boldface reading that follows can be found. Variant readings, given in regular type, are preceded by capital letters indicating the sources. Italics indicate manuscript readings rejected by Conrad. Editorial comments are enclosed in brackets. An **H** appearing alone indicates that a change made by Conrad in **Y** was not picked up by the Heinemann typesetter.

1.1 Mr. Baker, chief mate M Mr. Baker the chief mate
1.6 said reflectively: M doubtfully: **DP** said deliberately:
1.16 silhouettes of moving men M passing men
1.18 The carpenter * * * stroke of five. M Ever since five in the afternoon the carpenter had finished battening down the main hatch.
1.25 limpid, M pellucid,
1.27 hands M hands *out of an American ship.*
1.33 tipsy seamen, M obscure and typsy sea kings,
1.39 distracting noise M unholy noise
1.41 buzz of expostulation M buzz of *profanity*
2.8 shore-going round hats DPAE shore-going hard hats **M** shore going hats
2.36 Singleton M Sullivan [throughout the entire manuscript]
3.7 grave surprise M puzzled surprise
3.17 by an enigmatical disclosure of a resplendant world that M by the pompous ring of the incomprehensible fairy tale telling of a world fabulous and splendid that
3.27 old years well spent, M of serene old age,
3.40 old friend. It seemed M old friend. The tip of its black tail moved and it seemed
5.14 I can do it on my 'ed— M I can do it all on my 'ed— **DPAE** I can do it hall on my 'ed—
5.23 felt hat. MDPAE hard hat.
5.23 saw that he MDPAE saw he
5.37 nightmares. M scarecrows.
6.2 a spot on earth M a ship
6.24 look a blamed sight worse than M look like **DPAE** look a dam sight worse than
6.30 fo'c'sle," MDP foc'sle," [and throughout]
6.39 [In all versions until Conrad corrected **Y**, he gave Donkin an *h* before each initial vowel: *hout, hup, Henglishman,* etc. These changes will not hereafter be listed.]

7.7 pair of canvas trousers, MDAPE pair of trousers,
8.5 many heavy blows M three heavy blows
8.28 which went MDPAE that went
8.29 with its tail DPAE with the tail
9.26 Hansen MDPAE Hanssen
9.36 forced simplicity M affected simplicity
9.40 whispers:—"He ain't MDPAE [following "whispers:—"and preceding " 'He"] Round him men muttered to one another:
10.10 distinct and motionless group M motionless group of indistinct men **DPAE** indistinct and motionless group
10.12 deep, ringing voice. M resounding voice.
10.15 Who said 'Wait'? MDP Who said wait?
10.30 where he stood in a swagger that M where he stood *from foot to foot*
11.9 the repulsive MDP and repulsive
12.22 some slight bitterness M a little bitterness **DP** just a little bitterness
12.38 his rolling gait. MDPAE his walk.
12.40 further! AE farther!
13.2 lie MDPAE lay
13.5 gets MDPAE comes
13.9 slammed, MDP banged,
13.14 a light dress, MDPAE a clear dress,
13.32 calves. MDPAE heels.
13.43 blooming DP bloomin'
14.1 blooming DP bloomin'
14.10 inquired:— MDPAE asked:—
14.12 asked H said
14.14 out H hout
14.15 out H hout
14.18 Irish H Hirish
14.27 It is the men in them! M They are what men make 'em.
15.10 impatient M *violent*
15.11 unruly M *rebellious*
15.16 voiceless men—but men M in-

articulate men, *no spite in their hearts,* but men

15.33 confessed the faith— M sacrificed to the faith—

17.18 passage H trip

17.35 the peace H the dull peace

17.36 shuffling and grunted M D P shuffling; grunting **A E** shuffling; grunted

18.19 uneventful H eventful

18.28 serious, M D P grave,

18.33 Pentland Firth. M *Firth of Forth.*

18.34 Peterhead M *Dundee*

18.35 grey M D P blue

18.36 Indian M D P India

19.15 busy and insignificant lives. M regular and futile lives.

19.26 aspect, resembling the M D P aspect like the

19.31 related, M *discussed,* **M D P** invented,

20.9 distended above M D P A E that stood out distended above

20.45 the tub M D P his tub

21.27 over them M D P A E over us

22.5 still and M D P A E still, breathing lightly, and

22.14 us M *them*

22.19 our eyes M *their* eyes

22.37 yell, "One bell! Turn out! Do you hear there? Hey! hey! hey! Show leg!" the M D P yell, "Turn out! Do you hear there? Turn out!" the

23.16 skulking M bloody

26.11 answered shakily. M answered shakily but roughly.

26.31 Nilsen M D P A E Neillssen

26.32 Singleton D Sullivan

26.35 Singleton's D Sullivan's

29.27 "chuck the sea M D P A E "chuck going to sea

30.28 coats; and in the M D P A E coats; then, at times, in the

30.35 shirt sleeves, M D P A E shirt sleeves, H short sleeves

30.40 He kept M D P A E He watched her every motion; he kept

30.41 man watches M D P A E man who watches

31.5 affection. She was born M affection. She was a bad cargo-carrier but a lovable ship. She was born

31.13 A scurvey meed of commendation! M A scurvey commendation! [but something like "meed" is inserted between and raised above "scurvey commendation"] **D P** scurvey commendation!

31.21 officially H technically

32.8 inauspiciously. M D A unsuspiciously.

33.7 stamped out in a great howl P and in a great howl stamped out

34.7 vapours; and above the wrack of torn M D P vapours; they broke for a moment. Above the torn

34.28 duty, led by Mr. Creighton, began M D P duty began

36.9 under water. Men were M under water. Clinging to another man's leg,

he was heard to mutter: "Another pound gone." Men were

36.13 weather yard-arms M D P lower yard-arms

36.21 changed into M D P became

36.23 struggled, M D P scrambled,

36.35 damned sticks M D P A damned, bloody sticks

37.21 it away from M D P A E it from

37.23 asking us in M D P A E asking in

38.21 but M D P and

38.21 used to say M D P said

38.28 waist M wrist

39.43 crawled away M D P scrambled

39.43 five men, M three men,

40.17 rage, spluttering M D P A E rageously, muttering

40.17 "Cursed nigger M D P A "Bloody nigger

41.1 All ceased M D P We ceased

41.9 glaring above us—all M D P glaring, all

41.18 hearts so terribly that we M hearts so we **D P** hearts, so that we

42.19 ted solicitude [Colgate typescript begins here.]

42.41 lay M D E H lay **T P A** lie

44.15 sheltering him, we M T D P protecting him we

44.16 concealing M T D P sheltering

44.30 a little while, M D a while, **T P** awhile,

45.18 face. The air M face. He breathing slowly, and the air **T D P A E** face. He breathed slowly, and the air

45.45 most of them M T D P A E most

47.36 swept, unheard, H swept unheard

47.40 exhausted. M [Reference to "Sullivan and the master" preserving "an erect attitude" crossed out in manuscript.]

48.11 which M T D P A E that

48.16 skippers; they H skippers. They

48.27 sang M D P A E sang **H** sank

49.3 farther M T D P A E further

49.43 this M T D P A E this **H** his

49.44 church, M T D P service,

51.7 farther M T D P A E further

51.10 who M T D P A E that

52.3 Later, M T D P A E Later on,

52.23 trembling M T D P A E fumbling

53.27 to murder T D P A E ter murder

53.35 swoon, M T D P faint,

53.38 been weary and disheartened like M been as weary and hopeless as **T D P** been as weary and disheartened as

54.18 The ship M T D P She

55.16 existence. They M T D P A E existence, lest they should remember, and perchance, regret the reward of a cup of inspiring bitterness, tasted so often, and so often withdrawn from be-

fore their stiffening but reluctant lips.
They
56.31 at hand M T D P A E to hand
57.6 ice or flame. M T D P flame or
ice.
57.45 battered and H battered, and
58.14 among the splinters M T amongst
black splinters **D P A E** amongst the
black splinters
58.36 men brought in a M T D P A E
men came in with a
58.38 A couple of hands went M A
couple went **T D P A E A** couple
of men went
59.4 door. "Relieve M door. Behind
him the darkness sang a loud bass note
and the seas swished over the deck.
He said "Hallo, in there! Relieve
59.15 Davis M T D P A E Davies
59.19 Davis M T D P A E Davies
59.23 Davis M T D P A E Davies
59.39 of deep murmurs M of a trembling deep rumour **T D P A E** of a
deep rumour
59.42 exclamations M T D P A E murmurs
60.17 as does M T D P A E like does
60.17 does, at dead low water, H does
at dead low water
60.22 last, high-booted, M T D P A E
last. He breathed heavily, high-booted,
60.39 man bound treacherously M *man
bound treacherously* man drugged,
and bound treacherously
**61.18 like an ineradicable suspicion of
some previous existence. M** like a
dream of another existence.
61.41 two M T D P three
62.1 man, anyhow. The M T D P man
anyhow; the
62.40 Davis M T D P A E Davies
62.44 questions such as:— P questions:—
62.44 grub M wages
63.43 and of heaven H and heaven
64.2 globe M T D P A E globe **H**
glove
64.13 lie M D A E lay
65.1 a limb. He affected [On top of
manuscript page 113 Conrad wrestles
for a long time with Wait's experience
with death after the rescue; some
clauses and phrases: "He observed a
greater reticence as to his intimate relations with the invincible death, and
at the very time when we all began to
see it plainly enough standing by his
side" / "Any wind?" / "I want to get
home to be buried" / "cured".
65.7 as M like
65.13 bit my finger M T D P bit me
in the finger
**66.15 boom directly he was outside the
court. . . . Yes. They got M T D P**
boom, and ran off free directly he was
outside the court . . . But they got
**66.30 'ell," sneered Donkin. "Damn'er.
M T D P** 'ell. Damn'er
66.39 at once, M T P A E to once,
**67.8 on a white pillow his hollowed
black face moved to and fro restlessly.**

P his hollowed black face moved to
and fro restlessly on a white pillow.
67.37 'em some M T D P A E 'im hon
some
68.13 farther M T D P A E further
68.26 this M T D P A E hit
68.32 chimed in giggling M T D P A E
chummed giggling
68.41 and lay still for a while. M T
and meditated.
69.1 put upon M T D P A E put hon
69.5 airing yer M T D P A E a-hair-
ing ov yer
69.28 mastheads T D P masts
69.30 dock M T D P A E dock **H**
deck
69.31 husks M T D P dust
69.36 jail! M T jail. **E** goal!
**69.44 have locked up the galley for
M T D P A E** have been locking up
for
70.16 looked at M T D P A E looked
in at
70.16 with P as with **M T D A E** as
if with
70.20 breeze. Above M T D P A E
breeze. The ship heeled over a little,
slipping quietly over a sombre sea,
towards the inaccessible and festal
splendour of a black horizon pierced
by points of flickering fire. Above
70.28 that Providence M T D P A E
the Providence
71.3 as M T D A E like
71.4 twenty-seven M T D P thirty-
seven
71.17 skirts, M T shirts,
71.27 without a sound; M T D P A E
inaudibly;
71.34 went walking over M T D P A E
went over
71.40 everlasting fire M T D P A E
fire
**71.40 sin! Repent, repent! I can't bear
to think of you. I hear M T D P A E**
sin. I can see it for you. I can't bear
it. I hear
72.6 a holy row M T D P A E a row
72.7 crowded M T D P A E pushed
72.13 crazy fool! M T D P bloody
fool!
72.17 Wait.— D P A E Jim.— **M**
Jimmy. **T** Jimm—
72.19 already." T D P A E now."
72.36 himself; and there M *himself;
a man overwhelmed by shame, or sorrow or, perhaps. by fear.* And there
72.44 aloud. [Last word in the Colgate
typescript, page 96; the single Rosenbach typed page picks up here as page
97 with: "The cook." Line twenty-
four of page 128 of the manuscript between "aloud." and "The cook" has
the number 97 written in, the only
place in the manuscript so marked, and
typed page 97 is on regular-size paper,
not the legal size of the surviving Colgate pages 59 to 96. Even though the
same typewriter seems to have been
used, this sole surviving page of this
"new" batch of typing is further curi-

ous because it has more Conrad corrections on it than any of the other typed pages, 59 to 96. He even used the back of the sheet to rework several times the passage at 73.17.]

73.1 head, and his arms dropped as if too heavy. For a M head. For a

73.4 said the cook with a hasty and sombre resignation. He strode over the doorstep firmly—hesitated—made a few steps. They looked at him in silence.— "I make M said the cook quickly. He became dismal suddenly and his arms fell along his body. He stepped out—hesitated—walked off a few steps. "I make

73.9 "No, sir," he exclaimed hurriedly in a startled voice. The boatswain led him away by the arm; some one laughed; Jimmy lifted his head for a stealthy glance, M "No sir!" he cried and vanished. Someone laughed. Jimmy lifted his head cautiously

73.12 made M D P A E made H make

73.17 Belfast ran to his support. He did not appear to be aware of anyone near him; he stood silent for a moment, battling single-handed with a legion of nameless terrors, amidst the eager looks of excited men who watched him far off, utterly alone in the impenetrable solitude of his fear. The sea M Belfast ran up to support him; he did not seem to be aware of it. Men breathed in the darkness. The sea T D P A E Belfast ran to support him. He did not appear to be * * * solitude of his fear. Heavy breathing stirred the darkness. The sea

73.25 neck M shoulder

73.35 a voice [Rosenbach typescript ends here.]

73.44 declared, M D P A E said,

74.11 not allowed to be on M D P A E not to be allowed on

74.16 Jimmy, we H Jim—we

74.25 'm H 'im

74.38 imposed H himposed

75.5 soothe them." M quiet them."

76.3 some heavy M D P A E some small, heavy

76.13 house. Ringbolts M D P A E house. Shadowy figures could be seen tottering, falling, leaping up. Ringbolts

76.24 farther M D P A E further

76.29 Meantime the helmsman, M Meantime *the ship pushed quietly through the water closehauled on the starboard tack*

77.9 ropes up," M D P A E ropes,"

77.20 and know M D P and who know

78.13 as [At the suggestion of W. H. Chesson, Conrad in January 1898 changed in his copy of E *like* to *as* five times, only three of which were included in subsequent editions.] H like

78.29 wretched M damned

78.30 all. Let M D P A E all. Say what I like. Let

78.43 murmur M D P rumour

79.1 while now M *while* now D P now

79.3 moment, M D P while,

80.4 niggers. They looked at him fascinated. M D P niggers; and they looked at him absorbed.

80.17 in front he M D P in front of him, he

80.32 like animals going into lairs. M like dogs going into kennels.

80.33 Davis M D P A E Davies

80.36 below M D P A E below is

81.14 still very depressed M still dismal P still very much depressed

81.20 moind that, my M D P A E moind, my

81.38 with the chin P with his chin

82.11 out on the quarter-deck suddenly. M D P A E out suddenly.

82.17 by a universal M by universal D P A E by an universal

82.18 twenty pairs [In Y Conrad wrote *four* in the margin.]

82.39 have M D P A E had

82.40 shell-back M sea dog

82.43 Davis M D P A E Davies

83.11 And I say nothing H And say nothing

84.16 "Farther M D P A E "Further

84.37 broach the cargo M D P A E broach cargo

84.41 "Shall M D P A E "Will

85.1 [No section V in M.]

85.9 doubts, the realm M D P doubts, the essential logic of accidents, the realm

85.27 suspect him of having M suspect *him* D P suspect that he had

85.38 as though we had been M as though *we had ceased to be men; as though in the light of his fear death had ceased to be contemptible.*

86.16 the impertinent mournfulness of his languid and enormous stare. We watched him intently. He M the profound impertinence of his large eyes, that stood out of his head like the eyes of crabs. We watched him intently. Nothing else stirred. He D P A E the profound impertinence of his large eyes, that stood far out of his head like the eyes of crabs. We watched them intently. Nothing else of him stirred. He

86.26 tended to him, M D P A E tended him,

86.28 his nigger M *our* the his

87.23 of a contest M D P A E of tussle

87.37 the very first land M D P A E the land

88.23 longing M D P A E mournful

88.34 man dwelt in his furtive eyes. M D P A E man looked out through his eyes.

88.39 the unprepared soul M D P A E the soul

88.42 sailed M been D P A E lived

89.1 was. M D P A E is.

89.11 tobacco, and M D P A E tobacco,
89.12 very M D P A E and very
89.18 as men P just as men **M D A E** like men
89.21 took on a M D P A E took on the
89.28 heavy M D P moving
89.30 darker M D P A E blacker
89.33 die. That evening land M D P A E die. Just before dark, land
89.39 sun; H sun,
90.8 runs M D P A E passages
90.10 record M D P A E shortest
90.22 careless M D P A E negligent
90.26 the murmur of [etc.] **M** *The murmur of talk died out. Men began to descend the ladders looking grave. Belfast went to give Jimmy the news. He sat chattering in the cabin for a long time and in his excitement forgot himself so far as to mention a doctor. "Who wants a doctor?" asked Wait in a strong offended voice. "Well: for your cold" muttered Belfast* [Conrad's revision of this passage (90.26–33) was taped into the manuscript, but is now missing, leaving only this cancellation.]
90.31 wrapped up P wrapped
90.35 of all P of
90.40 Land! D P A E Land
91.9 there at a great risk to tell some secret of startling importance. M there to tell a tremendous secret. **D P** there at some risk to tell a tremendous secret.
91.12 very P deeply
91.14 Jimmy was used to such visits at all times of M D P A E Jimmy breathed with composure. He was used to such visits at any time of
92.15 the East D P East
92.21 and safely M D P A E and as if safely
92.26 as [see note **78.13**] **H** like
92.26 feeling M D P A E may feel
92.28 unrealisable, M D P A E irrealisable,
92.38 Wait M D P A E Jimmy
93.18 Yer nobody! H Yer nobody.
93.22 James Wait M D P A E Jimmy
93.28 threatened M D P A E menaced
93.30 disturbing; H disturbing;
93.31 promising M D P A E threatening
94.10 soon as ye're H soon has ye're
94.12 thing! H thing.
94.16 if M D P A E though
94.25 leg up. M D P A E leg hup haloft.
94.25 bound to. H bound to go.
94.26 Splash! D P Splash.
95.4 James Wait M D P A E Jimmy
95.13 became P got
95.17 restrain M D P contain
95.18 appeared P seemed
95.19 horrible and tireless P horrible
95.27 brilliant M D P A E blazing
95.29 minutes remained on his knees shakily but swiftly busy inside the box. M D P A E minutes was shakily and swiftly busy about the box.
95.39 Wait's M D P A E Jimmy's
95.40 resembling M P like
96.1 that had the appearance of M that resembled small **D P** that had the aspect of
96.13 depths. Donkin M depths; exacting tears and toils; promising empty, inspiring and terrible—everchanging and always the same. Donkin **D P A E** depths; promising, empty, inspiring—terrible. Donkin
96.28 common foolishness; M blamed foolishness;
97.1 and, very properly, were rebuked for it. P and were rebuked very properly for it.
97.9 sky to the southwest, M D P A E sky cloud over from the southwest,
97.17 Davis M D P A E Davies
97.27 who M D P that
97.33 said the M D P said impatiently the
97.37 pulled, lifted, overcome M D P overcome
97.41 which M D P A E that
98.6 a week M D P A E a day
98.22 master, M D P Captain,
98.23 said to him M D P told him
98.28 groups; they leaned M groups. They pressed their caps with both hands to their breasts; they leaned
98.31 meditation. Wamibo dreamed. Mr. M P meditation. Mr.
98.34 James Wait, silenced * * * hopes. M *Wait's overbearing voice now silenced forever could find no fault with the cry of despair or the whisper of hope.*
99.5 to cling to the ship M D P A E to hang on to
99.16 and sprang out of the crowd with his own arm extended. M D P A E and leaped off with his own arm thrown out.
99.18 reluctantly to whizz off the lifted planks all at once, with M reluctantly, to all at once whizz off the tilted planks with **D P A E** reluctantly, all at once to whizz off the lifted planks with
99.32 said, "Man the weather braces." Mr. M D P A E said, "square the yards. Look alive, men!" Mr.
100.9 morose M D P moody
100.33 restless waves. M D P open waters.
100.34 one M D P an
100.37 like an D A E such as an
101.5 forgetfulness, ignoble M forgetfulness, courage and fear, sloth and endeavor, ignoble [Garnett had marked in margin of M: "?too much of this?"]
101.10 nations! The M nations; the **D P** nations: the
101.11 storms! M D P storms,
101.17 an instant M D P a moment
101.25 Farther M D P A E Further

101.35 murmur * * * murmur M D P
rumour * * * rumour
102.1 tugs backed M D P A E tugs,
panting furiously, backed
103.2 "Don't forget to M D P A E
"Remember to
103.4 forecastle M [First wrote *focs'l*
but expanded it to *forecastle*.]
103.11 group of sailors, M D P A E
groups of men,
103.13 group M D P A E groups
103.35 town, and its leading politician,
M D P town, a leading Liberal, ˙
103.36 sailor M D P seaman
103.41 fell, cold and damp, upon
M D P fell upon
103.42 whom P which
104.25 broken M E broke
104.30 thighs with M D P A E thighs,
stamped with
104.31 turned up M D P A E were
104.34 who M D P A E that
105.2 hung in his M D P A E mascu-
lated his
105.10 displayed M D P A E had

105.22 was grave, M D P grave,
105.33 Ye're H Yer
105.43 declared M D P A E said
105.43 Archie. "No! No! He's M D P
Archie. "He's
106.14 at the time, M at the moment
D P at that moment,
106.25 pie. * * * He burst M pie . . .
I could do anything wi' 'im. Couldn't
I . . . He went for me; he would go
for nobody." . . He burst
106.31 inconsolable M D P incomprehensible
106.33 went on my way. M D P A E
went off.
107.32 met M D P A E saw
107.36 hail. Haven't we, M hail. Good
bye brothers. Haven't we
107.38 were a good crowd. M were
as good a crowd as ever.
107.39 the beating canvas of a heavy
foresail; or M the heavy canvas of a
storm-foresail; or
107.39 or D P and

Glossary of Nautical Terms

Numbers in parentheses indicate Illustrations.

ABAFT. Toward the stern.

ACCOMMODATION LADDER. Portable steps from the gangway down to the waterline.

ADRIFT. Broken free from moorings or fastenings.

AFT (AFTER). Near the stern.

ALOFT. Above the deck, usually high in the upper masts, yards, and rigging (1, 2, 3, and 4).

AMIDSHIP(S). In the center of of the vessel, either with regard to length or breadth.

ASTERN. In the direction of the stern. The opposite of ahead/forward.

ATHWART (ACROSS). Therefore "athwart-ships," means across the length of a vessel. The opposite of fore-and-aft.

BACKSTAY. A long rope extending from a mast head (above the lower mast) to the side of the ship (3).

BALLAST. Heavy material—iron, lead, or stone—placed in the bottom of the hold, to keep a vessel steady.

BARE-POLES. The condition of a vessel when she has no sails set.

BARQUE (BARK). A small ship, square-sterned, without head-rails; also, a three-masted vessel with fore-and-aft sails on her mizzen mast (i.e., no square sails).

BATTENS. Narrow pieces of wood used for confining the edges of the hatchcovers. Hence, verb "batten" means to cover and fasten the hatches or other openings.

BEAM. The greatest width of a ship.

BEAMS. Strong pieces of timber stretching across the vessel, to support the decks. "Gone on her beam ends": tilted so far that the deck is practically vertical.

BEATING TO WIND. Going to the direction of the wind, by alternate tacks.

BELAY. To make a rope or line fast by turns around a piece of wood or iron without hitching it.

BELAYING PIN. A short piece of wood or iron to "belay" ropes to.

BELLS. To tell time, sounded each half-hour over a four-hour period, from "one bell" to "eight bells." Also used for fog or distress signals.

BEND. To make fast. "To bend a sail" is to tie it to a spar.

BERTH. Anchorage or mooring space assigned to a vessel.

BIGHT. A loop of rope, line, or chain.

BINNACLE. A case or box holding the compass, fitted with a lamp for night.

BLOCK. A piece of machinery enclosing one or more freely rotating, grooved pulleys, about which ropes or chains pass to form a hoisting or hauling tackle.

BOATSWAIN ("BO'SUN"). A ship's officer who has charge of the rigging and who calls the crew to duty.

BOLSTER. A circular casting on the side of a vessel, through which an anchor chain passes.

BOOM. A long spar used to extend the foot of a sail (1).

BOTTLE. An old English term for a boat.

BOTTLESCREW (TURNBUCKLE). A metal sleeve threaded inside, into which are inserted a right-hand-threaded prong at one end and a left-hand-threaded prong at the other; thus whatever is linked by the sleeve or "bottle" is tautened when the sleeve is turned one way, slackened when it is turned the other way.

BOW. BOWSPRIT. HEEL OF THE BOWSPRIT. Front of a ship (1, 2, and 3).

BOWSPRIT. The jib boom (1 and 5).

BRACE. A rope by which a yard is worked or turned about.

BREAK OF THE POOP. At the foremost part where it meets the maindeck.

BRIDGE. A walkway which extends across the rear deck above the aft rail, offering a commanding position of the ship.

BULKHEADS. Walls forming rooms or compartments below deck, which also serve to prevent water from filling all areas of any deck level all at once.

BULWARKS. A kind of low wooden fence around the main deck, with openings to allow water to run off during heavy weather.

BUNTLINE. A rope attached to the foot-rope of a topsail to aid in furling it. "To bunt a sail" is to haul up the middle part in furling it (4).

BUTTOCK. The breadth of a ship across the stern below the poop.

CABINS. Officers' quarters (5).

CABLE. A rope or chain for securing a vessel at anchor. A "stream cable" is used to move or hold the ship temporarily in a river or harbor, sheltered from the wind and sea.

CAPSIZE. To overturn.

CAPSTAN. A vertical drum revolving on a spindle perpendicular to the deck, used for pulling and raising objects, especially the anchor.

CASTAWAY. A shipwrecked person; hence anything thrown away at sea.

CHAIN-CABLE. Anchor chain.

CHAIN COMPRESSOR. An iron lever by means of which the chain cable can be checked or stopped as it runs out (5).

CHAIN TIE. A chain for hoisting a yard at its middle and hauled upon by the halyard tackle.

CHIEF MATE. The officer of a merchant vessel next in command beneath the captain.

CHRONOMETER. An accurate navigational clock indicating Greenwich mean time, used to determine the longitude at sea by means of a timepiece and observation of the heavenly bodies.

CLEAT. An anvil-shaped deck fitting of wood or metal used for securing lines.

CLEW. A lower corner of square sails, and the "after" corner of fore-and-aft sails.

CLOSE-HAULED. As close to the wind as a vessel will sail, with sails as flat as possible.

COEFFICIENT OF FINENESS. The relation between the shape of a hull and a rectangular block having the same dimensions, expressed in decimal points of the block's volume. For example: a hull 200' x 30' x 20', with a volume of only 72,000 cubic feet, has a Coefficient of 0.6 relative to the block of 120,000 cubic feet.

COMPANION (COMPANIONWAY). A covered stairway: also called "ladder."

COUNTER. The portion of a ship from the waterline to the angle of the stern (1).

"CRACK-ON-SAIL." To put up all of the sails.

CROSSJACK ("CROJECK"). The first sail above deck on the mizzenmast (1 and 2).

DEADEYE. A circular block of wood, with holes through it, for the lanyards of rigging to reeve through, and with a groove round it for an iron strap (5). Lower deadeyes hold the shrouds to the deck railing.

DOCK. Large basin either permanently filled with water (wet dock) or capable of being filled and drained (dry dock).

DOGWATCH. Four-hour duty period from 1600 hours to 2200 hours (4–8 P.M.), divided into "first dog" and "second dog."

DOWNHAUL. Line, rope, or wire used to pull (haul) downwards.

DRAFT. The depth of water required to float a vessel.

DUNNAGE. Any waste or extra material used in securing or protecting stocked supplies aboard ship, such as boards, mats, straps, etc. Also, slang for sailor's personal gear.

EARING. A small piece of rope used to tie a sail to its yard.

FIFE RAIL. A rail surrounding the mast for use in holding the pins, to which some of the rigging is attached.

FIREMAN. A man assigned to the care and operation of a ship's boilers; a stoker. There are first- and second-class firemen.

FLATTEN IN. To pull the lower corner of a sail as nearly amidships as possible.

FLUKES. The broad arms of an anchor which form the holding edges when the anchor is down on the ocean floor.

FLYWHEEL. A heavy disk or wheel rotating on a shaft so that its momentum gives almost uniform rotational speed to the shaft and to all connected machinery.

FOOT. The lower end of a mast or sail.

FOOTROPE. The rope suspended a few feet beneath a yard, bowsprit, jib boom, or spanker to give a footing for men handling sails. Also, the portion of the rope to which the lower edge of a sail is sewn.

FORE (FORWARD). At or toward the bow of a vessel. FORE-RIGGING, FORE-SAIL, FORESHEET, FORE-TOPMAST, etc. (1, 2, and 3).

FORECASTLE. That part of the upper deck forward of the foremast; and, the forward part under the deck where the sailors live ("fo'c'sle") (5).

FOREMAST. Front, first mast (1).

FORESAIL. First sail above deck on the foremast (2).

FOUNDER. To sink below the surface of the sea, as happens when a vessel fills with water.

FULL-RIGGER. See SQUARE-RIGGED.

FURL. To roll up and tie a sail to its yard or boom (hence, to make up a bundle (4).

GAFF. A spar, to which is tied the head of a fore-and-aft sail.

GALLEY. Kitchen.

GANGWAY. A cut in the bulwarks allowing easy entrance onto the main deck.

GANTLINE. A rope-and-block attached to the head of a lower mast used to begin the rigging of a ship my making the initial hoists.

GIN BLOCK. A block having a large pulley in an open metal frame, used especially to support a cargo tackle.

GOOSE-WING. To furl the weather half of a lower topsail (4).

GUNWALE ("GUN'L"). The upper rail of a boat or vessel.

HALYARD. A light line (rope) used for hoisting.

HATCH. A square opening cut in the deck to get below to quarters or storage holds.

HAUL OUT (LIGHT TO). To pass along the job of reefing (taking in) a sail along its yard from windward to leeward.

HAWSE-PIPES. The heavy castings through which the anchor chain runs to prevent the cable from cutting the wood (5).

HEAD. Front or top. HEEL. Rear or bottom.

HEADSHEETS. Lines controlling the headsails (jibs) which are in front of the foremast (2).

HELM. The entire steering apparatus of a ship, but especially the wheel or "stick" (tiller) held by the helmsman.

HIGH POOP. The deck behind the mizzenmast (1).

HOLD. A storage compartment below deck.

HOLYSTONE. A small stone used with sand and water to scrub wooden decks, to remove stains.

HULK. A store-vessel condemned as unfit for the risks of the sea.

HULL. The body of a ship exclusive of masts, sails, yards, and rigging.

IRON. Anchor.

JIB. Any of various triangular sails set forward of the foresails on the jib-boom (1 and 2). Also called HEADSAIL.

JUMP OUT. For a mast to pull or pop out of its footing at the coat (1).

KEEL. The lowest and principal timber of a vessel, running fore-and-aft its whole length, and supporting the whole frame. It is composed of several pieces, placed lengthwise, and scarfed and bolted together.

KEELSON. An internal keel, laid upon the middle of the floor-timbers, immediately over the keel, and serving to bind all together by means of long bolts driven from without, and clinched on the upper side of the keelson.

KID. A tublike wooden container for serving food.

KNIGHT-HEADS. Timbers next to the stem (the bow), the ends of which come up through the deck and form a support for the bowsprit.

LANYARDS. Ropes reeved through deadeyes for setting up rigging. Also a rope made fast to anything to secure it.

LASHING. The wrapping material around things tied down by line or wire.

LEE. The side opposite to that from which the wind blows; if a vessel has the wind on her starboard side, that will be the "weather" side and port will be the "lee" side.

LIFT. A line (rope) from the masthead to each end of a yard to support the yardarms (1 and 3).

LIGHT TO. See HAUL OUT.

MAIN DECK. Uppermost complete deck running the length and breadth of a ship.

MAINMAST. Middle mast (1).

MAINSAIL. First sail above deck on the mainmast (2).

MAST. A spar set upright from the deck, to support rigging, yards, and sails: foremast, mainmast, mizzenmast (1). Each mast is subdivided: lower, top, top gallant, royal, skysail.

MAST HEAD. Top of one of the sections of mast making up the total mast (1).

MAKE FAST. To belay (secure) a rope with turns around a pin or cleat.

MARLINSPIKE. Tapered steel tool for separating wire or rope in splicing.

MASTHEAD. The top of a mast (1).

MIZZENMAST. Rear mast (1).

MOORING BITS. Frames made up of two upright pieces of timber in the fore-part of a ship to fasten cables to when riding at anchor.

NIP. A short turn in a rope.

ORDINARY SEAMAN. A seaman insufficiently skilled to be classified as an able-bodied seaman. A rating next below seaman.

PANTRY. Special kitchen for preparing officers' food.

PETTY OFFICERS. In rank and responsibility, between the ships' officers (master and mates) and the crew (seamen): boatswain, carpenter, sailmaker. The cook and steward are special crew.

PIN. Belaying pin.

POOP. A raised deck running from the mizzenmast to the stern, containing accommodations for the master and officers (1 and 5).

PORT. Left. Also various-sized openings in side of ship for windows, guns, or taking in cargo.

QUARTER. Literally the rear one-fourth of a ship, but usually means 45° to the rear of the beam: hence, port-quarter and starboard-quarter in the after section of a ship.

QUARTERDECK. An upper deck running from the mainmast to the mizzenmast (1).

QUARTER CHECKS. The ropes put out from the poop or quarterdeck when a ship is in port to keep her stern centered between the dock walls, which otherwise she might scrape; when they are "let go" by the dockers they are hauled back on board the ship.

QUAY. A wharf.

RATLINE. Any of the small ropes or lines that cross the shrouds horizontally and serve as steps for going aloft (3).

REACH. A straight portion between the curves (bends) of a stream or river.

REEF. To reduce the area of a sail exposed to the wind by partially rolling it up and tying it to the yard (4).

REEVE. To pass the end of a rope through a block, or an aperture.

RIDING LIGHT. A white-all-around light hoisted in the bow indicating that a vessel is anchored.

RIGGING. The general term for all the ropes of a vessel. Also, the common term for the shrouds with their ratlines; as the main rigging, mizzen rigging, etc. (3).

RINGBOLT. A deck bolt with an eye at the end for attaching a ring to which to fasten tackle.

ROADSTEAD. A partially sheltered area of water near a shore in which vessels may ride at anchor.

ROVE. A small copper ring or washer over which the end of a nail is clinched. Also, another name for earing, or a short piece of rope. Therefore, an older past-tense form meaning "tied down."

ROYAL. The light sail above the topgallant (2).

SCEND. To lurch forward from the motion of a heavy sea; the heaving motion of a vessel; the forward impulse imparted by the motion of a sea against a vessel.

SCREW. A manually rotated deck machine for lifting large loads; a cargo winch.

SCUPPER. An opening in the bulwarks on exposed decks, funneling sea water, overboard; or, below decks, an opening funneling the water through the side.

SEAMAN. Crewman on a ship; sailor.

SECOND MATE. Next in command following the first or chief mate.

SHACKLE. A U-shaped metal fitting, closed at the open ends with a pin, used to fasten ends of wire and chain, usually to the deck.

SHEETS. Ropes used to set the angle of a sail, to keep the clews of the sails in place. With square sails, the sheets run through each yardarm. With boom sails, they haul the sails to the desired position. (Also, slang for "sails.")

SHIFTING. Changing or altering the position of a sail, topmast, spar, etc.

SHIP. A vessel with three or four masts, and with topmasts and yards. Also, to enter on board a vessel. Also, to fix anything in its proper place.

SHIPKEEPER. A caretaker placed on board in charge of a vessel when it is in harbor without a crew.

SHORTEN. To take in (roll up) canvas to reduce the exposed area of sail.

SHROUDS. Ropes on each side of a vessel, reaching from the mastheads to the vessel's sides, to support the masts (3).

SICKBAY. Infirmary or first-aid station.

SKIDS. Fittings on deck designed to hold and support a boat.

SKYLIGHT. Glazed opening on top deck that allows light to pass to deck below. It is usually hinged, to admit air in fine weather.

SPANKER. A fore-and-aft sail on the aftermost lower mast of a sailing vessel having three or more masts (2).

SPAR. A stout, rounded wood or metal piece; hence, the general term for masts, yards, booms, gaffs, etc. (1).

SQUARE-RIGGED. Literally a ship with square sails, but usually means a big, fully outfitted ship such as the *Narcissus* (1, 2, and 3).

SQUARING THE BRACES. Bringing the yards perpendicular to the ship's length.

STANCHIONS. Upright posts of wood or iron, placed so as to support the beams of a vessel. Also, upright pieces of timber, placed at intervals along the sides of a vessel, to support the bulwarks and rail. Also, any fixed, upright support.

STARBOARD. Right.

STAY. A long rope extending from the upper end (head) of each mast toward the stem (bow) of the ship (1 and 3).

STAYSAIL. Any sail hoisted on a stay, for example, a triangular sail between two masts (2 and 4).

STERN. Rear of the ship.

STEWARD. Officers' waiter and general factotum.

STICK. Mast.

STOP. Small length of rope, line, yard used for tying.

STUDDING SAIL (SCUDDING SAIL). Fine-weather sail set outside a square sail.

STUNSAIL. A light sail, sometimes set on the exterior of a sail, and extended by horizontal spars or poles when the wind is fair.

SWEATING-UP. Setting or hoisting taut sail, so as to increase speed.

TACK. To change direction by pointing the bow into and across the wind, thus changing the side exposed to the wind. (The opposite of "wearing.") Hence, zigzagging toward a set point when unable to steer directly toward it.

TACKLE (as in "fall of the relieving tackle"). Any arrangement of line and blocks to gain a mechanical advantage in a ship's "rigging." A fall is a rope which, with blocks, is part of the "tackle." A "relieving tackle" is a tackle used to reduce strain on the wheel ropes in heavy weather; they are hooked to the tiller.

TAFFRAIL. A curved railing on the captain's balcony over the stern of a ship.

TIDE-RODE. Term applied to a moored vessel when her head is pointing in the direction from which a tidal current is flowing.

TONNAGE/TONS. A "ton" is both 100 cubic feet and 2240 pounds. GROSS TONNAGE is the enclosed *space* (internal capacity) of a ship. NET TONNAGE is the *space* left for cargo after the ship's supplies and crew's gear have been stowed. DISPLACEMENT TONNAGE is the *weight* of the ship calculated by the sea water displaced when afloat. DEADWEIGHT TONNAGE is the difference in *weight* between loaded and unloaded hence indicates the weight of cargo which can be shipped.

TOPGALLANT. The third sail above deck (2).

TOPMAST. The mast next above a lower mast, usually formed as a separate spar from the lower mast and used to support the yards or rigging of a topsail or topsails. SPARE TOPMAST: one which is kept in reserve in case of an emergency (1).

TOPSAIL. The second sail above the deck (2).

TRUCK. A circular or square piece of wood fixed on the head of a mast or the top of a flagstaff, usually containing small holes for signal halyards (1).

VANG. A rope leading from the peak-end of the gaff of a fore-and-aft sail to the rail on each side of the ship in order to steady the gaff.

WAIST. The central part of a ship; that part of the deck between the forecastle and the quarterdeck.

WASHBOARD. A thin, broad plank fastened to and projecting above the side of a boat to keep out the spray and the sea.

WATCH. A division of time on board ship. Also, a certain portion of ship's company, appointed to "stand watch" (be on duty) a given length of time, usually four hours. In the merchant service all hands are divided into two watches, "port" and "starboard," with an officer to command each. First nightwatch, 2000–2400 hours; second night watch, 0001–0400 hours.

WATERLINE. Line of intersection of surface of water and hull of ship (2).

Wear ship. To bring a vessel on the other tack by swinging her around by means of the wind blowing from behind *into* the sails ("coming before the wind").

Weather. See windward.

Weigh. To lift up, as to "weigh" an anchor or a mast.

Wheel box. A small shelter erected around a steering wheel for the protection of the helmsman.

Windlass (as in "barrel of the windlass"). A machine used in merchant ships to heave up the anchor. The barrel is the main portion of the capstan, about which the rope winds (5).

Windward. In the direction from which the wind blows, as distinguished from leeward. The "weather" side of a ship is the windward side.

Wing transom. The uppermost cross-beam in the stern-frame.

Yard. A long piece of timber, tapering slightly toward the ends, and hung at the center to a mast, to spread the square sails upon (in square-rigged ships). To "trim the yards" is to adjust the yards with reference to the direction of the wind and the course of the ship (1).

Yardarm. Either end of a yard (1).

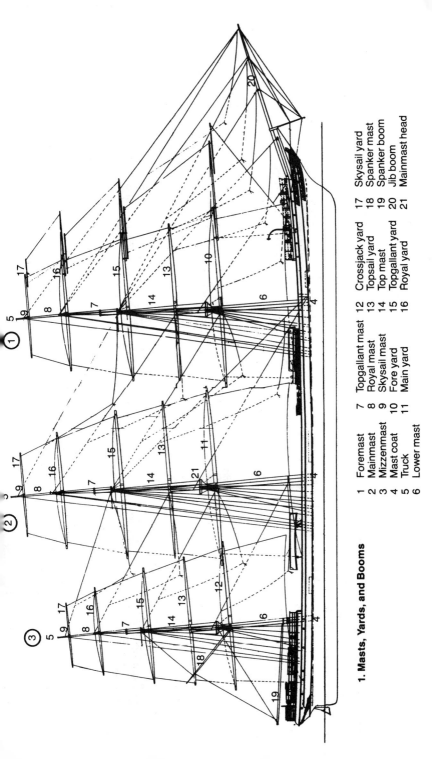

1. Masts, Yards, and Booms

1	Foremast	7	Topgallant mast	12	Crossjack yard	17	Skysail yard
2	Mainmast	8	Royal mast	13	Topsail yard	18	Spanker mast
3	Mizzenmast	9	Skysail mast	14	Top mast	19	Spanker boom
4	Mast coat	10	Fore yard	15	Topgallant yard	20	Jib boom
5	Truck	11	Main yard	16	Royal yard	21	Mainmast head
6	Lower mast						

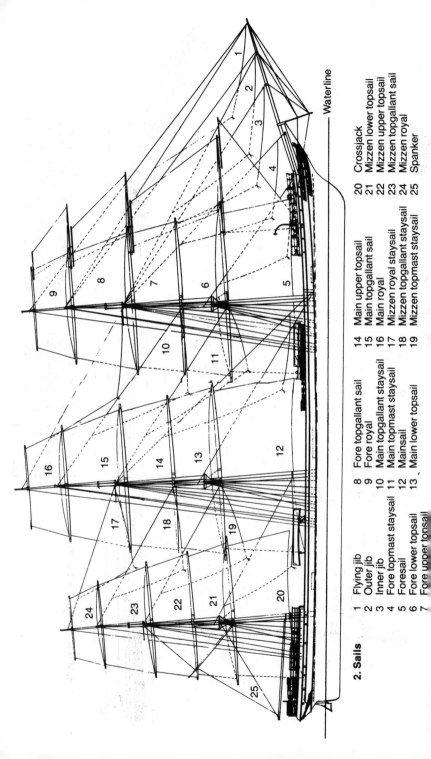

2. Sails

1	Flying jib	8	Fore topgallant sail	14	Main upper topsail
2	Outer jib	9	Fore royal	15	Main topgallant sail
3	Inner jib	10	Main topgallant staysail	16	Main royal
4	Fore topmast staysail	11	Main topmast staysail	17	Mizzen royal staysail
5	Foresail	12	Mainsail	18	Mizzen topgallant staysail
6	Fore lower topsail	13	Main lower topsail	19	Mizzen topmast staysail
7	Fore upper topsail				

20	Crossjack
21	Mizzen lower topsail
22	Mizzen upper topsail
23	Mizzen topgallant sail
24	Mizzen royal
25	Spanker

Waterline

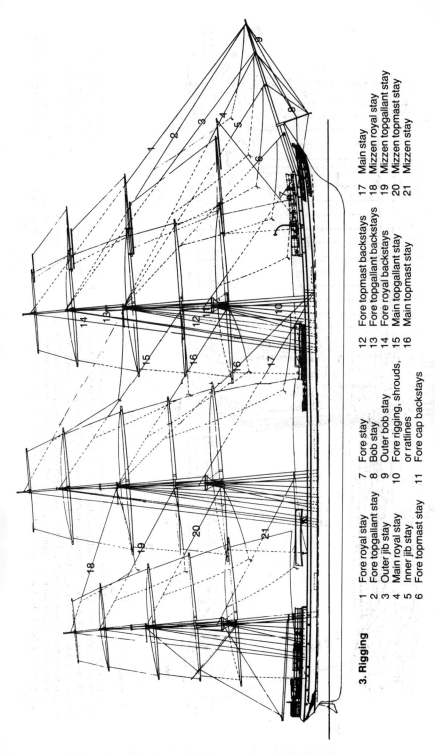

3. Rigging

1	Fore royal stay	7	Fore stay
2	Fore topgallant stay	8	Bob stay
3	Outer jib stay	9	Outer bob stay
4	Main royal stay	10	Fore rigging, shrouds,
5	Inner jib stay		or ratlines
6	Fore topmast stay	11	Fore cap backstays

12	Fore topmast backstays	17	Main stay
13	Fore topgallant backstays	18	Mizzen royal stay
14	Fore royal backstays	19	Mizzen topgallant stay
15	Main topgallant stay	20	Mizzen topmast stay
16	Main topmast stay	21	Mizzen stay

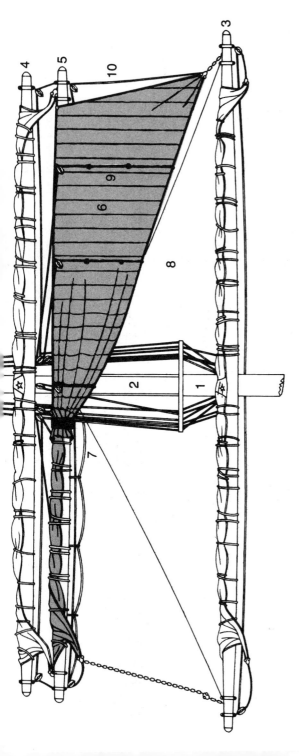

4. To Heave To

When a sailing ship was in a contrary gale of wind the order to heave to meant that most of the sails were taken in and the helm was put down. This kept the ship's head to the wind, and, with the sea on the bow, she would ride well enough as long as some sail could be carried. This full-rigged ship has the fore topmast staysail, the mizzen staysail, and the goose-winged main lower topsail set. To furl the weather half of a lower topsail was the last resource to shorten sail without having to furl all and drift under bare poles. The large-scale drawing shows a part of the main mast with the goose-winged lower topsail. The numbers indicate:

1 Mainmast
2 Heel of topmast
3 Mainyard with mainsail furled
4 Upper topsail yard with topsail furled
5 Lower topsail yard
6 Goose-winged lower topsail
7 Heavy lashing on sail, parcelled to protect sail from chafe
8 Size of lower topsail when set
9 Lower topsail buntlines
10 Lower topsail clewlines

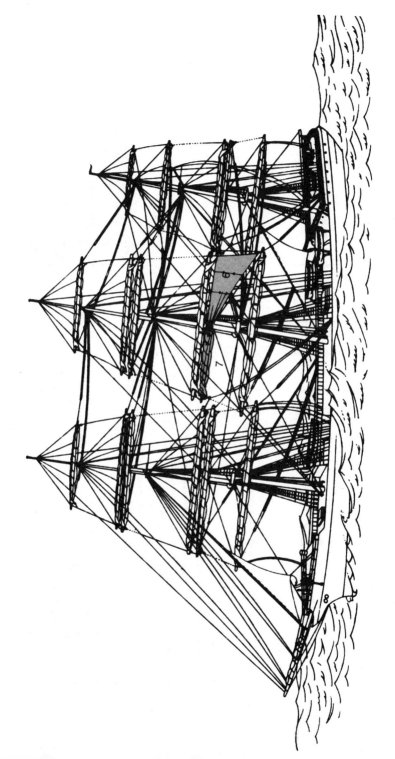

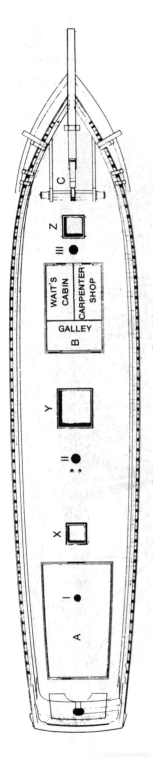

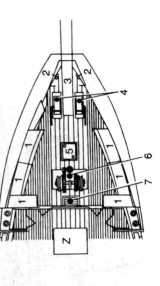

5. Deck Plan and Forecastle Layout

The deck plan, above, of the *Narcissus* shows three masts (I, II, III) coming out of the deck, three hatches (X, Y, Z) in the deck, the cabinhouse (A) for officers on the poop deck at the stern, the deckhouse (B) (with galley, carpenter's shop, and sail locker converted into a cabin for James Wait), and the forecastle (C) for the sailors below deck in the bow, from the fore hatch (Z) forward. The detail plan, to the right, shows the below-deck layout of the forecastle:

1 Upper and lower bunks
2 Hawse pipes
3 Bowsprit
4 Cable compressors
5 Fore peak hatch
6 Windlass
7 Hatch to chain locker
Z Fore hatch

DENIS MURPHY

Seamanship in Chapter Three of
The Nigger of the "Narcissus"†

In many of Joseph Conrad's novels, and specifically *The Nigger of the "Narcissus,"* we find ourselves intertwined within a mysterious web of lines and sails, innundated by a vocabulary rife with words such as "spars," "braces," and "yards."[1] For many modern readers an exact understanding of Conrad's precise language of the sea is tedious business; what concern is the distinction between a "mizzen-mast" or a "fore-mast" when the essential power of his descriptions communicates without such specific knowledge— enough that we have awesome, vivid accounts of nature's power and that the men are combating wind and wave as best they can— whether we specifically understand what they are doing or not. But do we understand? As they say in the Navy, a boat is not a "ship," and a "sheet" is most certainly not something you put on a bed.

What *is* happening in the crucial third chapter when the *Narcissus* appears to be in imminent danger of "foundering"? Why did the ship go over, and how far, and why couldn't it right itself for so long? Confronted with such speculations, students of literature experience a glazing of the eyes, an overdose of unwilling suspension of disbelief, and rapidly read to the nearest scene free from sailors' jargon. Yet the enduring strength of Conrad's vision, and the power of this chapter in particular, is so inextricably linked to the specific—whether it be the ocean's Janus face of succor and destruction, or the sailors' ability to confront the elements, and their own fear, by means of a tenuous and subtle manipulation of their vulnerable, stricken vessel. Without an awareness of the components which comprise this world, we strip Conrad's stage set of its elaborate rigging and reduce his magnificent three-masted *Narcissus* to an artificial prop, of no more mystery and grace than a modern super oil tanker running through a storm with a computer at the "helm" and the crew below decks watching a movie.

While weaving a pattern of human frailty pitted against the awesome force of the sea, Conrad never pauses to offer a course in basic seamanship. "Reefed sail" or a "starboard tack," "beating to wind" or "squaring the braces," were as common to him as retro-rockets, life-support systems, or reentry trajectory have become to us. Today

† Writtten especially for this edition.
1. See Glossary of Nautical Terms for definitions.

these terms are part of everyday speech; in Conrad's day a knowledge of sailing terminology was still common and hardly esoteric,
even though the great age of sail had already passed when the book
was published in 1897. Along with Melville and Dana, Conrad intimately understood the technology of sailing, and that knowledge
acts as a keel supporting the novel's other elements, including setting, narrative, and characterization. As extensive passages of military tactics and battle plans swell *War and Peace* or the beaded
necklace of side streets and pubs ground *Ulysses* in the actual, so,
too, does *The Nigger of the "Narcissus"* draw breath in its mundane. As in all great literature, though, the mundane is transformed;
Conrad did not write in order to impress us with his extensive lore
of the sea, but to illuminate a specific sector of the human family
—in this case the sailors before the mast who were already passing
into legend when the book was written. It may not be necessary to
paint in order to appreciate a Winslow Homer, but it is necessary
to translate, somewhat, the terminology of sailing ships if we wish
to comprehend and appreciate the artistry and power in the third
chapter of *The Nigger of the "Narcissus,"* one of literature's enduring descriptions of men trapped in a storm at sea.

The chapter opens with the *Narcissus* unable to find a steady
breeze: "She drifted slowly, swinging round and round, through a
few days of baffling light airs." In this lull before the storm, the
crew was hunting the wind from "brace to brace."[2] When the wind
stabilizes they sail on a southwest heading, passing Madagascar and
Mauritius without seeing land, drawing closer to the Cape of Good
Hope—also called the Cape of Storms. Preparations for heavy
weather are made: lashings are reinforced, heavier sails fastened,
and "washboards" installed. Fighting a headwind, the sea builds
and the ship begins to take waves over the bow: "Water tumbled in
cataracts over the forecastle doors. You had to dash through a waterfall to get to your damp bed." She rides the seas well, but the narrator injects a fearful warning: "We all watched her. She was beautiful and had a weakness. We loved her no less for that . . . and the
consciousness of her only fault we kept buried in the silence of our
profound affection."

The *Narcissus* demanded extreme care in the loading of her
cargo. "She was exacting." Since the "ballast" in these ships com-
prised its cargo, or comparable weight, and their draft was relatively
shallow in relation to their enormous superstructures, any shifting

2. A brace is a rope by which a yard is
turned about; a yard is a long piece of
timber, tapering slightly toward the ends,
and hung by the center to a mast to
spread the sails upon. Therefore, they
are swinging the yards back and forth
by the braces on either side of the yard
so as to catch the proper angle of the
wind. This action becomes extremely important later when the crew attempts to
right the overturned ship.

of the cargo in heavy seas could be fatal. (Modern sailboats have, proportionately, much deeper and heavier keels and a much lower center of gravity which, if knocked over by a heavy gust or wave, brings them back up in much the same way a child's weighted punching bag always pops back to the vertical.) Displacement of grain or cotton bales, for example, with the added weight of surface water entering through open hatches, could easily bring a ship over; or—more severe—pigs of iron suddenly dislodged could ram through the side and take her to the bottom immediately. Most ships lost for no known reason were probably casualties of improper loading. And even though this does not prove the undoing of the *Narcissus*, Podmore, the cook, well aware of the liability, fatalistically intones: "some voy'ge she will drown all hands! You'll see if she won't."[3]

"The thirty-second day out of Bombay began inauspiciously." As the wind and waves build, Captain Allistoun, anxious to gain lost time, refuses to "shorten sail"; *Narcissus* begins boring her way through the sea instead of rising to meet the oncoming waves. "Twice running, as though she had been blind or weary of life, she put her nose deliberately in a big wave and swept the decks from end to end." Sail is shortened soon after, and, in the face of a somber hail cloud, night closes in furiously: "Most seamen remember in their life one or two such nights of a culminating gale. Nothing seems left of the whole universe but darkness, clamour, fury— and the ship." The *Narcissus* absorbs the terrible pounding, rising steeply and, suspended, plunges back down into the void; occasionally, though, she would go over on her side, remaining there, "vibrating and still, with a stillness more appalling than the wildest motion." Taking in still more sail at midnight, the crew is transfixed by the "venomous violence" of the gale. At seven-thirty in the morning, having passed through the night, a gray light surrounds them: "The horizon seemed to have come on all sides within arm's length of the ship." With conditions worsening, they "goose-wing" the main topsail: they release one of the four points holding the rectangular sail to the yard, furl it back, and are left with a small triangle; this is the last and final rigging for storm conditions, and, in theory, this small amount of canvas should keep their bow into the waves.[4] With the masts vibrating from the pounding, even

3. The profile in Illustration 2 shows the relative shallowness of the hull beneath the waterline and the vast superstructure of sails and rigging which would tend to bring a ship over and keep her there, if not to capsize it completely. An interesting discourse on the proper loading of a ship is given by Edgar Allen Poe in *The Narrative of Arthur Gordon Pym*. Poe devotes the early pages of chapter 6 to a detailed description of the subject, with dire warnings and examples of improper ballast and shifting of cargo at sea.

4. Illustration 4 shows a ship rigged for storm conditions—"to heave to." The lower main topsail is goose-winged. The fore-topmast staysail is also set; it is precisely this sail which Captain Allistoun later orders raised when attempting to "wear ship."

threatening "to jump out" (popping out of their seating below decks and going overboard), a minimum number of men are allowed in the "rigging." Those manning the sails were flattened against the "ratlines," the gusts pinning "all up the shrouds the whole crawling line in attitudes of crucifixion." At eight o'clock half the crew scrambles forward across the flooded deck to the forecastle to get some rest, leaving the other "watch" clustered aft on the raised "mizzen-deck" (the "poop") with the officers and Singleton who is manning the wheel. The old mariner suddenly yells: "Look out for yourselves!"

"A big, foaming sea came out of the mist; it made for the ship, roaring wildly, and in its rush it looked as mischievous and discomposing as a madman with an axe." The ship rises to meet this monster, and, while some scramble up the rigging, most "held on where they stood," hypnotized with fear and unable to move:

> It towered close-to and high, like a wall of green glass topped with snow. The ship rose to it as though she had soared on wings, and for a moment rested poised upon the foaming crest as if she had been a great sea-bird. Before we could draw breath a heavy gust struck her, another roller took her unfairly under the weather bow, she gave a toppling lurch, and filled her decks.

The *Narcissus* goes over with the "lee" rail in the water up to the lower "deadeyes."[5] The men burst out of the forecastle door, which is up forward near the bow, and scramble "like vermin fleeing before a flood" back to the mizzen deck and the relative safety of its raised height. Once there, they watch helplessly as their gear and bedding comes floating out of the forecastle into the sea. A cry goes up to cut the masts, since the enormous weight of the rigging is keeping the ship pressed down: "A black squall howled low over the ship, that lay on her side with the weather yard-arms pointing to the clouds [and the lee yardarms deep into the water]; while the tall masts, inclined nearly to the horizon, seemed to be of an immeasurable length." Held down at an angle of what must be seventy or eighty degrees off the perpendicular (ninety degrees would put the masts flush in the water, while zero degrees is the true vertical pointing straight up), the deck has become a steeply inclined wall which they clutch wherever possible to keep from sliding down toward the submerged lee rail from where the waves are foaming and grabbing at them.

With the exception of the final page where she breaks loose, the *Narcissus* remains in this position for the remainder of the chapter. The force of the wind and waves pressing against the increased bulk of the exposed lower hull now riding high out of the water on the

5. Illustration 4 shows where the lower deadeyes connect the railing to the rat-lines which were used by the sailors as a ladder to go "aloft."

"starboard" (weather) side, and the added weight of the water which has entered the ship both conspire to keep her over—but not to turn her over completely. The ship, in a sense, has reached a point of precarious equilibrium—neither able to straighten up nor to roll further over. It is unlikely that the cargo has shifted; however, the added weight of the water within the ship has altered the center of gravity to the "port" side. Nearly broadside to the enormous sea, her hull on the weather side acting as a wall against breaking waves, the *Narcissus* has lost all headway and is being pummeled by the combined force of the elements. Given these outrageous conditions, the cry of the men to cut the masts free from the hull seems the very soul of sense; Captain Allistoun, however, wagering the ship will not capsize, refuses to turn his ship into a free-floating derelict. His simple no, without explanation, suffices: "They waited for the ship to turn over altogether, and shake them out into the sea; and upon the terrific noise of wind and sea not a murmur of remonstrance came out from these men, who each would have given ever so many years of life to see 'them damned sticks go overboard'!" Once a blow has silenced the mutinous Donkin who screeches for the masts to be cut, "In all that crowd of cold and hungry men, waiting wearily for a violent death, not a voice was heard; they were mute, and in sombre thoughtfulness listened to the horrible imprecations of the gale." Hours passed.

Even though the skies clear and the sun comes out, the wind and waves persist as before; the *Narcissus* remains over on her side. The men, though, begin to think she is "wonderfully buoyant." After the fresh water is painstakingly retrieved from the galley, someone discovers that James Wait is missing. Belfast organizes a rescue party which inches forward "swinging from belaying pin to cleat above the seas that beat the half-submerged deck." They reach the forward deckhouse, pass by the galley, and enter the carpenter's shop on the starboard (high) side. "All the doors had become trapdoors, of course." Wait had previously been moved from the forecastle below up to the room adjacent to the carpenter's shop. This topside space in the forward deckhouse was often used for storing sails (see illustration 5). Discovering that he is not only alive, but hysterical, they clear the rubble from the wall (now the deck) which separates the carpenter's shop from the sail locker; they manage to break through, pull out Wait, and get him on deck. "Streaming with perspiration, we swarmed up the rope, and, coming into the blast of cold wind, gasped like men plunged into icy water. With burning faces we shivered to the very marrow of our bones. Never before had the gale seemed to us more furious, the sea more mad, the sunshine more merciless and mocking, and the position of the ship more hopeless and appalling." With no help from the pathetic, maddening Wait—"like a bladder full of gas"—they manage to form a human chain and pass him back to the mizzen deck. "We literally passed him from hand to hand. Now and then we had to hang him on a handy belaying-pin, to draw a breath and reform the line." The success of this rescue rekindles their spirit and hope for survival, even though "the secret and ardent desire of our hearts was the desire to beat him viciously with our fists about the head; and we handled him as tenderly as though he had been made of glass." Securing Wait in a safe place, they watch the setting sun; as another night of turmoil looms—but this evening with the ship almost on her side. "A crested roller broke with a loud hissing roar, and the sun, as if put out, disappeared."

With the ship holding steady through the night, the men suffer the freezing weather, some losing sensation and even hallucinating that a block of ice was pressing on their chests. Mr. Baker, the first mate, senses that the wind has eased somewhat, although the sea remains as high as before: "The waves foamed viciously, and the lee side of the deck disappeared under a hissing whiteness as of boiling milk." Baker reminds the complainers that they are there to take care of the ship, not for Captain Allistoun to care for them. Belfast and Wait argue. The cook disappears "forward" in an heroic attempt to make coffee. The night passes, and "they could not spare a moment or a thought from the great mental occupation of wishing to live." After some hours, Podmore returns miraculously with the coffee—"it seemed incredible"; sustained by its warmth, they wait through the final, bleak hours before the dawn. As the sunlight passes across their faces, they see Singleton hanging "on by the wheel, with open and lifeless eyes. Captain Allistoun, unblinking, faced the rising sun. His lips stirred, opened for the first time in twenty-four hours, and with a fresh firm voice he cried, 'Wear ship'!"

To "wear ship" means to bring a vessel on the other "tack" by swinging it around before the wind. Since the wind has been coming from the starboard side, they must maneuver the stern into the wind (to get the wind "abaft the beam," as Conrad says) so that it is behind them, and then continue coming about so that the wind will be off the stern on the port side. The change in direction will be approximately one hundred and eighty degrees. Remember, though, that there have been no sails flying since the moment of the capsizing when "the topsail sheet [had] parted, the end of the heavy chain racketed aloft, and sparks of red fire streamed down through the flying spray." In order to wear ship Captain Allistoun wants the fore-topmast staysail (see illustrations 2 and 4) run up, and, as he says, "if you can't manage it standing up you must do it lying down—that's all." As soon as this sail is up they cast "the lee main braces off the pins" (the restraining lines securing the yards in place, and they try to "square the yard"). Swinging the yards across the wind, even though the sails are furled, will help bring the ship about more; along with raising the fore-topmast staysail it is an attempt to swing around so as to gain headway and, hence, steerage. All this takes place on a deck pitched over seventy degrees with the lower (lee) portion of the yards being dragged turning through the water. "The yards moved, came slowly square against the wind, that hummed loudly on the yard-arms." With her submerged side still dragging in the water, the *Narcissus* gains headway as soon as the wind is off the starboard rear quarter, gains steerage when it is directly behind them, struggles to raise herself, and does so when she has spun enough so that the wind is on the port quarter. Almost as if a great suction cup breaks loose, the pressure of the wind, previously pressing them down, now exerts a force to free the overturned ship:

> The ship trembled, trying to lift her side, lurched back, seemed to give up with a nerveless dip, and suddenly with an unexpected jerk swung violently to windward, as though she had torn herself out from a deadly grasp. The whole immense volume of water, lifted by her deck, was thrown bodily across to starboard. Loud cracks were heard. Iron ports breaking open thundered with ringing blows. The water topped over the starboard rail with the rush of a river falling over a dam. The sea on deck, and the seas on every side of her, mingled together in a deafening roar. She rolled violently . . . Lifted by a towering sea she ran along with it for a moment, spouting thick streams of water through every opening of her wounded sides.

The crew, now "amidships," attempts to secure the braces, as the yards whirl madly above their heads, and as "torn canvas and the ends of broken gear streamed in the wind like wisps of hair." With only the small staysail set, the *Narcissus*, now upright but rolling wildly, plunges downwind under "bare poles," pursued by the wind and a following sea. Conrad brings the chapter to a close with one final magnificent image: old Singleton with his white beard tucked beneath the top button of his coat, alone at the helm and guiding the ship through the swells. "He steered with care."

Backgrounds and Sources

JOSEPH CONRAD

Preface to *The Nigger of the "Narcissus"*†

A work that aspires, however humbly, to the condition of art should carry its justification in every line. And art itself may be defined as a single-minded attempt to render the highest kind of justice to the visible universe, by bringing to light the truth, manifold and one, underlying its every aspect. It is an attempt to find in its forms, in its colours, in its light, in its shadows, in the aspects of matter and in the facts of life, what of each is fundamental, what is enduring and essential—their one illuminating and convincing quality—the very truth of their existence. The artist, then, like the thinker or the scientist, seeks the truth and makes his appeal. Impressed by the aspect of the world the thinker plunges into ideas, the scientist into facts—whence, presently emerging, they make their appeal to those qualities of our being that fit us best for the hazardous enterprise of living. They speak authoritatively to our common sense, to our intelligence, to our desire of peace, or to our desire of unrest; not seldom to our prejudices, sometimes to our fears, often to our egoism—but always to our credulity. And their words are heard with reverence, for their concern is with weighty matters; with the cultivation of our minds and the proper care of our bodies; with the attainment of our ambitions; with the perfection of the means and the glorification of our precious aims.

It is otherwise with the artist.

Confronted by the same enigmatical spectacle the artist descends within himself, and in that lonely region of stress and strife, if he be deserving and fortunate, he finds the terms of his appeal. His appeal is made to our less obvious capacities; to that part of our nature which, because of the warlike conditions of existence, is necessarily kept out of sight within the more resisting and hard qualities—like the vulnerable body within a steel armour. His appeal is less loud, more profound, less distinct, more stirring—and sooner forgotten. Yet its effect endures for ever. The changing wisdom of successive generations discards ideas, questions facts, demolishes theories. But the artist appeals to that part of our being which is not dependent on wisdom; to that in us which is a gift and not an acquisition—and, therefore, more permanently enduring. He speaks to our capacity for delight and wonder, to the sense of mystery surrounding our lives; to our sense of pity, and beauty, and pain; to the latent feeling of fellowship with all creation; and to the subtle but

† See Preface to this edition, above p. x.

invincible conviction of solidarity that knits together the loneliness of innumerable hearts: to that solidarity in dreams, in joy, in sorrow, in aspirations, in illusions, in hope, in fear, which binds men to each other, which binds together all humanity—the dead to the living, and the living to the unborn.

It is only some such train of thought, or rather of feeling, that can in a measure explain the aim of the attempt made in the tale which follows, to present an unrestful episode in the obscure lives of a few individuals out of all the disregarded multitude of the bewildered, the simple, and the voiceless. For, if there is any part of truth in the belief confessed above, it becomes evident that there is not a place of splendour or a dark corner of the earth that does not deserve, if only a passing glance of wonder and pity. The motive, then, may be held to justify the matter of the work; but this preface, which is simply an avowal of endeavour, cannot end here—for the avowal is not yet complete.

Fiction—if it at all aspires to be art—appeals to temperament. And in truth it must be, like painting, like music, like all art, the appeal of one temperament to all the other innumerable temperaments whose subtle and resistless power endows passing events with their true meaning, and creates the moral, the emotional atmosphere of the place and time. Such an appeal, to be effective, must be an impression conveyed through the senses; and, in fact, it cannot be made in any other way, because temperament, whether individual or collective, is not amenable to persuasion. All art, therefore, appeals primarily to the senses, and the artistic aim when expressing itself in written words must also make its appeal through the senses, if its high desire is to reach the secret spring of responsive emotions. It must strenuously aspire to the plasticity of sculpture, to the colour of painting, and to the magic suggestiveness of music—which is the art of arts. And it is only through complete, unswerving devotion to the perfect blending of form and substance; it is only through an unremitting, never-discouraged care for the shape and ring of sentences, that an approach can be made to plasticity, to colour; and the light of magic suggestiveness may be brought to play for an evanescent instant over the commonplace surface of words: of the old, old words, worn thin, defaced by ages of careless usage.

The sincere endeavour to accomplish that creative task, to go as far on that road as his strength will carry him, to go undeterred by faltering, weariness, or reproach, is the only valid justification for the worker in prose. And if his conscience is clear, his answer to those who, in the fulness of a wisdom which looks for immediate profit, demand specifically to be edified, consoled, amused; who demand to be promptly improved, or encouraged, or frightened, or shocked, or charmed, must run thus: My task which I am trying to achieve is, by the power of the written word, to make you hear, to make you feel—it is, before all, to make you *see*! That—and no more: and it is everything! If I succceed, you shall find there according to your deserts: encouragement, consolation, fear, charm —all you demand; and, perhaps, also that glimpse of truth for which you have forgotten to ask.

To snatch in a moment of courage, from the remorseless rush of time, a passing phase of life, is only the beginning of the task. The task approached in tenderness and faith is to hold up unquestioningly, without choice and without fear, the rescued fragment before all eyes and in the light of a sincere mood. It is to show its vibration, its colour, its form; and through its movement, its form, and its colour, reveal the substance of its truth—disclose its inspiring secret: the stress and passion within the core of each convincing moment. In a single-minded attempt of that kind, if one be deserving and fortunate, one may perchance attain to such clearness of sincerity that at last the presented vision of regret or pity, of terror or mirth, shall awaken in the hearts of the beholders that feeling of unavoidable solidarity; of the solidarity in mysterious origin, in toil, in joy, in hope, in uncertain fate—which binds men to each other and all mankind to the visible world.

It is evident that he who, rightly or wrongly, holds by the convictions expressed above cannot be faithful to any one of the temporary formulas of his craft. The enduring part of them—the truth which each only imperfectly veils—should abide with him as the most precious of his possessions, but they all: Realism, Romanticism, Naturalism; even the unofficial sentimentalism (which, like the poor, is exceedingly difficult to get rid of); all these gods must, after a short period of fellowship, abandon him—even on the very threshold of the temple—to the stammerings of his conscience and to the outspoken consciousness of the difficulties of his work. In that uneasy solitude the cry of Art for Art itself, loses the exciting ring of its apparent immorality. It sounds far off. It has ceased to be a cry, and is heard only as a whisper, often incomprehensible, but at times, and faintly, encouraging.

———

Sometimes, stretched at ease in the shade of a roadside tree, we watch the motions of a labourer in a distant field, and, after a time, begin to wonder languidly as to what the fellow may be at. We watch the movements of his body, the waving of his arms; we see him bend down, stand up, hesitate, begin again. It may add to the charm of an idle hour to be told the purpose of his exertions. If we know he is trying to lift a stone, to dig a ditch, to uproot a stump, we look with a more real interest at his efforts; we are disposed to condone the jar of his agitation upon the restfulness of the landscape; and even, if in a brotherly frame of mind, we may bring ourselves to forgive his failure. We understood his object, and, after all, the fellow has tried, and perhaps he had not the strength—and perhaps he had not the knowledge. We forgive, go on our way—and forget.

And so it is with the workman of art. Art is long and life is short, and success is very far off. And thus, doubtful of strength to travel so far, we talk a little about the aim—the aim of art, which, like life itself, is inspiring, difficult—obscured by mists. It is not in the clear logic of a triumphant conclusion; it is not in the unveiling of one of those heartless secrets which are called the Laws of Nature. It is not less great, but only more difficult!

To arrest, for the space of a breath, the hands busy about the work of the earth, and compel men entranced by the sight of distant goals to glance for a moment at the surrounding vision of form and colour, of sunshine and shadows; to make them pause for a look, for a sigh, for a smile—such is the aim, difficult and evanescent, and reserved only for a very few to achieve. But sometimes, by the deserving and the fortunate, even that task is accomplished. And when it is accomplished—behold! all the truth of life is there: a moment of vision, a sigh, a smile—and the return to an eternal rest.

J. C.

1897

THOMAS LAVOIE

Textual History and Textual Notes: The "Preface"†

The copy text for the "Preface" to *The Nigger of the "Narcissus"* comes from the same text used for the novel itself, the 1921 Heinemann edition. The first version of the "Preface" is the manuscript (M) itself, presently housed in the Rosenbach Library in Philadelphia. It has been reproduced and transcribed by David R. Smith in *Conrad's Manifesto: Preface to a Career* (Philadelphia: Gehenna Press, 1966), whose transcriptions were used in the present collation. The manuscript version of the "Preface" is the only one which contains the suppressed paragraph Conrad dropped on Edward Garnett's advice. This paragraph does not appear in the Colgate University typescript (T), which, except for minor punctuation changes, resembles the copy text. The "Preface" was first published as an "Author's Note" to the periodical version of the novel (P)

† Written especially for this edition.

in the *New Review*, XVII (December 1897), 628–31. The periodical version was subjected to numerous editorial changes, including
the deletion of the fourth paragraph and the incorporation of the
second paragraph into the third.

The first appearance of the "Preface" largely as intended was in
a pamphlet which Conrad had printed by J. Lovick, High Street,
Hythe and Cherion (1902). One hundred copies were published for
private distribution, forty of which were accidentally destroyed. The
pamphlet ends with the line, "From the *New Review*, December,
1897," but differs considerably from the periodical version. The
next appearance of the "Preface" was in America as "The Art of
Fiction," published in *Harper's Weekly*, XLIV (May 13, 1905).
Except for some editorial changes it follows P (the *New Review*,
1897). In April 1914, the "Preface" was published as part of
another pamphlet, *Joseph Conrad on the Art of Writing* (Garden
City, N.Y.: Doubleday, Page and Co., 1914), and, except for minor
punctuation changes, follows the "Hythe" pamphlet (1902). This
second pamphlet also contains the first printing of the novel's second preface, "To My Readers in America," which was written by
Conrad at the request of Doubleday for a new edition of the novel
which they were soon to publish. The second preface follows the
manuscript version reproduced and transcribed in Smith (and reprinted below, pp. 167–68). At the top of the manuscript Conrad
wrote: "No time to have this typed if I am to catch the mail. Sorry."

The first appearance of the two prefaces with the novel itself was
in the 1914 Doubleday, Page and Co., "Deep Sea" edition of
Conrad's works. The "Preface" is the same as that printed in the
1902 pamphlet version except for minor punctuation changes. In
order to eliminate unnecessary repetitions, only the M, T, P, and
1902 variants are reproduced here.

145.2 itself may be defined as a M itself is a

145.8 essential—their M essential—that which makes them what they are —their

145.10 the scientist P the man of science

145.13 appeal to M appeal to what of us is on the surface, to

145.21 aims. M ends.

145.22 It is otherwise with the artist. [separate paragraph] M It is otherwise with the artist. Confronted

145.23 by M with

145.24 himself, and M himself. And

145.29 a steel 1902 the steel

145.34 is not dependent on M is independent of

145.35 He speaks M P He appeals to temperament, and he speaks

146.3 aspirations, M memories,

146.4 binds together all M P binds all

146.6 It is only * * * complete. P [whole paragraph absent]

146.7 aim of the attempt made in the tale which follows, to present an unrestful M aim and may perhaps obtain forgiveness for the imperfect and audacious attempt made here to present as an object of possible interest an unrestful

146.14 this preface, which is simply an avowal of endeavor, M the preface (which is only an avowal of endeavor),

146.15 end here—for the avowal is not yet complete. M stop here—and for this reason.

146.17 Fiction— P Thus, fiction—

146.23 it cannot M cannot

146.28 high M highest

146.43 amused; who demand to P amused, to

147.2 you hear, to M you touch, to

147.3 see! M see! P 1902 *see*.

147.4 everything! P 1902 everything.

147.5 to your deserts: P to the need of your hearts:

147.13 through its movement, its form, and its colour, M through movement form and colour

147.16 attempt M effort

147.18 vision of regret or pity, of terror or mirth, shall awaken in M vision shall awaken, through pity, through terror, through regret, through mirth, in

147.22 world. M world. And that is the end—and the reward.

147.24 expressed M set down

147.26 should abide M abides

147.29 these gods must M the gods have

147.30 of fellowship, abandon him— even on M of languid fellowship, abandoned him sadly, on

147.31 and to the M and the

147.33 cry P supreme cry

147.33 Art itself, loses the M Art, even, has lost the

147.35 and is heard only M P and when it is heard it is only

147.36 encouraging. ¶ Sometimes M encouraging. ¶ It may seem strange if not downright suspicious that so much should be said in introduction to the unimportant tale of the sea which follows. It may also appear the height of conceit or folly since every word of the preface may be brought in judgment against the work it is meant to introduce. But a preface—if anything—is spoken in perfect good faith, as one speaks to friends, and in the hope that the unprovoked confidence shall be treated with scrupulous fairness. And, after all, everyone desires to be understood; We all with mutual indulgence give way to the press- ing need of explaining ourselves— the politician, the prophet, the fool, the bricklayer they all do it: and if so then why not the writer of tales who is, as far as I know, no greater criminal than any of these. It is true that the disclosure of the aim otherwise than by the effective effort towards it is a confession of weakness. Yet in the reign of art such an avowal is not so fatal as it would be elsewhere. For in art alone of all the enterprises of men there is meaning in endeavor disassociated from success and merit—if any merit there be —is not wholly centered in achievement but may be faintly discerned in the aim. ¶ Sometimes

147.37 Sometimes P When

147.38 watch the motions of a labourer in a distant field, and, after a time, begin to M watch across a field the motions of a labourer and after a time begin to P watch in a field the motions of a labourer, we begin, after a time, to

147.40 movements M contortions

147.43 stone, to dig a ditch, to uproot M stone or dig a ditch, or uproot

148.8 which, like life itself, is inspiring, difficult—obscured by mists. M which is like life itself—inspiring— immense—obscured by drifting mists.

148.11 which M that

148.11 Laws of Nature M laws of nature

148.12 difficult! [emended from "difficult."] T difficult!

148.14 and compel M to compel

148.18 sometimes, M some times—

148.20 all M All

148.23 J. C. T J. C. 1897 **1902** From the *New Review*, December, 1897

IAN WATT

Conrad's Preface to *The Nigger of the "Narcissus"*†

Scores of anthologists and critics have given it their most bated breath, or intoned "To make you *see*" as a sovereign charm against blindness. Sacred cows invite bull, but are not served; at least until some contumelious infidel arrives. As he now has in the apologetic person of David Goldknopf, who, after a couple of pages of shrewd thrusts, despatches Conrad's Preface as a whole with: "I cannot make coherent sense of it. I do find repeated statements of faith in visualization, embodied in a hodgepodge of platonic, positivistic, and romantic sentiments. And when those are shaken out, there remains, I suppose, a credo of impressionistic realism—in Henry James's phrase, solidity of specification—qualified by the somewhat obsessive emphasis on the optical process."[1]

Doubts about the Preface actually began very early; indeed, with Conrad himself. The first reference occurs in a letter which he wrote to Edward Garnett on August 24, 1897. Conrad enclosed "a short preface to the *Nigger*," and begged Garnett, with more than usual trepidation, "not to be impatient with it and if you think it at all possible to give it a chance to get printed. That rests entirely with you . . . you knew very well I daren't make any move without your leave. I've no more judgment of what is fitting in the way of literature than a cow."[2]

Another letter from Conrad, written four days later, shows that Garnett had suggested the deletion of one paragraph.[3] Garnett does not seem to have been enthusiastic about the Preface; and later Conrad's editor at Heinemann's, Sidney Pawling, rejected it for the book form of *The Nigger of the "Narcissus."* W. E. Henley, however, who had accepted the novel for serialisation in *The New*

† From *Novel: A Forum on Fiction*, 8 (Winter 1974, 101–15) [Passages from the manuscript of the Preface and from an unpublished letter to Rollo Walter Brown are quoted by permission of the Philip H. and A. S. W. Rosenbach Foundation, the Harvard College Library, and the trustees of the Joseph Conrad Estate.—*Author's note.*]

1. David Goldknopf, *The Life of the Novel* (Chicago and London, 1972), p. 83. Later page references will be incorporated in the text. Goldknopf's chapter on Conrad appeared earlier under the ominous tautotes of "What's Wrong with Conrad: Conrad on Conrad," in *Criticism*, X (1968), 54–64.

2. *Letters from Conrad: 1895–1924*, ed.

Edward Garnett (London, 1928), p. 87.

3. This, along with other cuts and alterations by Conrad, can be seen in the manuscript of the Preface, which is now in the Philip H. and A. S. W. Rosenbach Foundation collection, and of which a fine facsimile edition has been published: *Conrad's Manifesto: Preface to a Career. The History of the Preface to The Nigger of the "Narcissus" with Facsimiles of the Manuscripts*, edited by David R. Smith (Philadelphia, 1966). Quotations from the Preface in its earlier versions, and any facts about it not otherwise documented, are drawn from Smith's edition, or from his thorough essay on its composition, argument, and later history.

Review, published the Preface as an "Afterword" to the last instalment, in December 1897. The Preface did not appear again with
the novel until the 1914 Doubleday, Page edition, although Conrad
arranged for a small private English printing in 1902, and also
pushed its appearance in the United States, where it was twice published to promote interest in Conrad's writings: first as "The Art of
Fiction" in *Harper's Weekly* (May 1905); and later as *Joseph
Conrad on the Art of Writing* in a 1914 publicity pamphlet by
Doubleday.

In general, Conrad was dubious about his capacity for writing literary citicism. "Criticism is poor work," Conrad wrote to William
Blackwood in 1899,[4] and most of the critical pieces reprinted in
Conrad's *Notes on Life and Letters* and in the posthumously collected *Last Essays* were originally written on request; Conrad desperately needed the money, and found he could turn out casual literary essays with little effort and without affecting his other work.
At their best these essays are eloquent and perceptive; but Conrad's
aim is merely to convey a personal train of thought provoked by a
few random recollections—"Critical wandering . . . is all I am capable of," he wrote to Garnett in 1901.[5] Conrad was also sceptical
about the critical enterprise in general: and one can surmise that it
was without any particular sense of pain that he gradually came to
the conclusion that "the form of writing consisting in literary appreciation of other men's work, implying analysis and an exposition of
ethical and aesthetic values . . . is not in my way."[6]

Samuel Hynes has argued that Conrad was "intellectually
simple," and that "he didn't theorize . . . because his mind was not
equipped to do so."[7] Possibly; yet Conrad's casual literary comments, and his letters to friends about their current manuscripts—
those to Galsworthy, Garnett, and Clifford, for example—reveal an
impressive ease in going to the essence of critical problems. One is
tempted to say that Conrad was a good literary critic who was bad
at writing literary criticism; the reverse phenomenon, of course, is
much more current.

In 1914 Richard Curle proposed including the Preface to *The
Nigger of the "Narcissus,"* which was still unavailable to the British
public, in his forthcoming study of Conrad. Conrad was reluctant.
He probably feared it would make the study sound like an author's
puff; but the excuse he gave Curle was that "I would sound declam-
atory, even windy, against your pages."[8] Conrad had by then

4. *Joseph Conrad: Letters to William
Blackwood and David S. Meldrum,* ed.
William Blackburn (Durham, N. Carolina, 1958), p. 71.
5. *Letters from Conrad,* p. 179.
6. Dale B. J. Randall, *Joseph Conrad
and Warrington Dawson: The Record of
a Friendship* (Durham, N. Carolina,

1968), p. 206.
7. Samuel Hynes, "Two Rye Revolutionaries," *Sewanee Review,* 73 (1965), p.
152.
8. *Conrad to a Friend: 150 Selected Letters from Joseph Conrad to Richard
Curle* (London, 1928), p. 19.

become more sensitive to the overblown quality of his earlier rhetoric, although he was never to reform it altogether. Nevertheless, as he wrote in a later letter, Conrad's reservations about the Preface bore "only on expression. My convictions in the main remain the same."[9] They remained the same for reasons which Conrad suggested in his note "To My Readers in America," for the 1914 edition of *The Nigger of the "Narcissus"*: "After writing the last words of that book . . . I understood that I had done with the sea, and that henceforth I had to be a writer. And almost without laying down the pen I wrote a preface, trying to express the spirit in which I was entering on the task of my new life." Conrad's notoriously unreliable and subjective memory seems to have betrayed him on one fact here—the Preface was probably not written immediately after finishing the novel, but some six months later, in July or August of 1897, just after Conrad had revised the proofs. However, there is no reason to doubt that the Preface does "express the spirit" in which Conrad committed himself to his new career.

Goldknopf's objections to the Preface are largely justified if we try to read it as an analytic exposition of a theory of fiction; in any rigorous sense of the word, Conrad had no such theory, and did not want to have. But since as Conrad wrote no other equally inward account of his creative aspiration, the Preface to *The Nigger of the "Narcissus"* remains by default the most reliable, and the most voluntary, single statement of Conrad's general approach to writing;[1] and it also, incidentally, demonstrates that, in his own eclectic and undoctrinaire way, Conrad was from the beginning quite aware of where he stood among the various critical traditions of his century.

I

The basic terms of Conrad's position were set by the Romantic tradition, and they derive from the substantially new ontological problems about literature with which history had confronted poets and critics at the end of the eighteenth century. The thought of Newton and Locke had made it necessary to face the question of what kind of truth was embodied in literature; the social tendencies represented by such movements as the French revolution and Utilitarianism had made it necessary to justify the usefulness of literature to mankind at large; and the various mechanistic models of the mind, notably that of associationist psychology, had raised the most difficult issue of all—what mental process could account for the creation and understanding of literature.

Such, in the very broadest terms, was the nature of the challenge to poetry as Wordsworth, Coleridge and Shelley conceived it; and,

9. Letter to Rollo Walter Brown, September 9, 1919 (Houghton Library).
1. This estimate is that of Samuel Hynes (p. 153), and of Frederick R. Karl in the most sustained study of "Joseph Conrad's Literary Theory" (*Criticism*, 2 [1960], 317–335).

equally broadly, their responses took similar forms. Literature embodied kinds of humanly necessary truths or values which were not attainable elsewhere; it therefore had a higher kind of utility than the material and the quantitative; and it was produced by, and communicated to, constituents of the human personality, usually described as the imagination or the sensibility, which were not available to scientific psychological study but were nevertheless necessary to explain not only man's aesthetic impulse but the grounds of his religious, moral, and social life. Conrad's Preface is centered on these three large Romantic issues, and it offers answers which are recognisably similar, although his formulations and emphases naturally reflect later critical and intellectual attitudes, as well as his own particular creative concerns.

Conrad's first three paragraphs[2] differentiate the kind of truth sought by the artist from that sought by the scientist or the philosopher. The general argument is close to Wordsworth's in the Preface to the *Lyrical Ballads*, where he asserts that the more philosophical antithesis of poetry is not prose but "matter of Fact, or Science."[3] Conrad assumes that all three modes of thought seek the truth, and seek it in "the visible universe"; but then their methods diverge: "The thinker plunges into ideas, the scientist into facts"; and since they both appeal to man's intelligence and his daily concerns, "their words are heard with reverence." The artist, on the other hand "descends within himself" to find the truth, and seeks "the terms of his appeal" to his audience in "that lonely region of stress and strife."

These opening paragraphs are open to two objections: that Conrad avoids crucial difficulties, and that he silently changes his theme from the kind of truth which art seeks to the nature of its appeal.

The most obvious difficulty which Conrad avoids occurs in his definition of art as "a single-minded attempt to render the highest kind of justice to the visible universe, by bringing to light the truth, manifold and one, underlying its every aspect." Here Goldknopf condemns Conrad's failure to recognise "the most vexing epistemological problem of the Western world since the time of the Milesian philosophers, namely, *how* do we go from the ephemeral and notoriously fallible evidence of the senses to the truth which is assumed, wishfully or not, to underlie that evidence?" (p. 82). As professional philosophers we are justly affronted by Conrad's cavalier circumvention of so illustrious a metaphysical problem. Yet actually the Preface does offer, in very general terms, a view of "how we go" from the irreducible pluralism of sense-perceptions to

2. To avoid excessive repetition, I assume the reader to have a copy of the Preface for consultation, and suggest he number the paragraphs.

3. *Poetical Works of William Wordsworth*, ed. E. de Selincourt (Oxford, 1944), p. 392. Later references will be incorporated in the text.

"the very truth of their existence": unlike philosophers, artists seek truth, Conrad asserts, in "that part of our being which is not dependent on wisdom," a part which presumably includes what the Romantics had called the imagination or the sensibility. Conrad's phrases "the highest kind of justice," and "the very truth of their existence," also make it clear that he is dealing with a hierarchy of values, in which the artist is concerned with the fundamental and enduring, as opposed to the practical and contingent truths sought by the scientist or the discursive thinker.

Conrad begins with a fairly simple correspondence theory of art. He was convinced that everything began with the sense-impressions made by external reality on the individual; but he had to avoid the idea of artistic communication as a simple circuit which transferred the artist's immediate sensory impression to his reader, like a photograph being developed in words and handed over to the recipient. For this physiological reductionism was too close to Realist or Naturalist theory; what Conrad needed was some intermediate psychological center which remembers, compares and combines all the impressions made by the external world, and seeks to ascertain their meaning and importance. The essential logic of the third paragraph, therefore, is to equate the "lonely region of stress and strife" inside the artist, with a parallel intermediate faculty in the audience which is capable of responding to his appeal. This "part of our nature," Conrad goes on to say, "is necessarily kept out of sight" while we are engaged in the "warlike conditions" of ordinary existence. It is to this "part of our being" that the artist makes his appeal; and that appeal is described in the famous words about how the artist: "speaks to our capacity for delight and wonder, to the sense of mystery surrounding our lives; to our sense of pity, and beauty, and pain; to the latent feeling of fellowship with all creation—and to the subtle but invincible conviction of solidarity that knits together the loneliness of innumerable hearts, to the solidarity in dreams, in joy, in sorrow, in aspirations, in illusions, in hope, in fear, which binds men to each other, which binds together all humanity—the dead to the living and the living to the unborn."

Conrad's expository method, like his syntax, tends to be additive; and this makes his thought in some respects refractory to conceptual analysis. Nevertheless, the passage is so central that it requires further consideration.

Wordsworth had found it necessary to distinguish between the way the mind responds to art and the way it responds to science: whereas scientific knowledge, he wrote, is "slow to come to us . . . by no habitual and direct sympathy connecting us with our fellow-beings"; but the knowledge of the poet, on the contrary, "cleaves to us as a necessary part of our existence, our natural and unalienable inheritance . . ." (p. 396). The substantial uniformity of human nature in this respect provided the necessary basis of Wordsworth's universalist claims for poetry. The poet was "a man speaking to men" (p. 393); he spoke of their "general passions and thought and feelings" (p. 397); and these in turn were connected with interests very similar to those which Conrad itemised for solidarity: they were connected, Wordsworth wrote, "with the operations of the elements, and the appearances of the visible universe; with storm and sunshine, with the revolutions of the seasons, with cold and heat, with loss of friends and kindred, with injuries asd resentments, gratitude and hope, with fear and sorrow" (p. 397).

Conrad represents the same central tradition of Romanticism of which Wordsworth is perhaps the most representative figure. Both men were by nature antipathetic to the more extreme forms of romantic individualism; and Conrad's theory in the Preface implicitly denies the basic division between the artist and the general public which such writers as Byron, Baudelaire, or later the Symbolists and Decadents, had made essential to their theory and practice. Indeed, in reasserting the ancient tradition of the supreme importance of art in civilisation, Conrad used terms very similar to the tradition's more democratic reformulation by Wordsworth: "In spite of difference of soil and climate, of language and manners, of laws and customs: in spite of things silently gone out of mind, and things violently destroyed: the Poet binds together by passion and knowledge the vast empire of human society, as it is spread over the whole earth; and over all time" (p. 396).

History has remorselessly apprised us of the objections to these high claims: that literature does not in fact do these things; and that any writer who thinks so is deceiving himself. In so far as both Wordsworth and Conrad write as if the binding together of human society by the poet and artist were a fact, they are obviously open to these objections; whatever their language may say, however, we must surely interpret their views as mainly orectic or conative in nature: orectic because their view of the social effects of literature is a matter of wish rather than fact: conative because they are really talking about what they themselves aspire to bring about through their writings.

The word which Conrad uses to denote this mode of human community within which art operates, "solidarity," is equally equivocal with regard to its ontological status. The term came into English from France in 1848, meaning "the fact or quality, on the part of communities, etc., of being perfectly united or at one in some respect, especially in interests, sympathies, or aspirations" (*OED*). Here the definition, like many uses of "solidarity" as political slogan, glosses over whether the identity of orientation is conscious or not on the part of the assertedly solidary individuals. When Conrad says that the "feeling of fellowship with all creation" is "latent", he is making solidarity often unconscious and even at times inoperative. This would imply a conative attitude for the artist, since, as Conrad later writes in the seventh paragraph, his task is to "awaken" solidarity "in the hearts of the beholders."

There is another problem in Conrad's use of "solidarity." The word is normally used for collective human activities, but Conrad uses it in a much wider sense to denote man's common experience in general; and this in relation to the natural, as well as the human, world. In paragraph three, it is true, the early phrase "the latent feeling of fellowship with all creation" is syntactically a parallel idea to "solidarity" rather than an element in it; but when Conrad returns to the idea at the end of the seventh paragraph he makes it bind "all mankind to the visible world." It would take a very intransigent sceptic to deny that the yeomen farmers of the Lake District did not, in some latent subliminal sense at least, share Wordsworth's responses to the lesser celandine, or that the crew of the *Narcissus* did not experience elation when they sailed into the purer air and light and water of the open sea. But we can more easily concede that men are conscious of sharing the same physical universe —the time of day and its weather are rarely divisive issues—than that they are united by common human experiences, whether of a collective kind or not. We can certainly agree that throughout history mankind has experienced many of the same individual experiences—birth and death, joy and sorrow, youth and age, and so on; but it is obviously very doubtful that they are conscious of being bound together by these common experiences, or that it much affects their behaviour.

The question of how far mankind "feels perfectly united" in its collective interests is, of course, an even more dubious matter. No one knew better than Conrad that actual human behaviour reveals solidarities that are at best irresolute, intermittent, and only occasionally conscious; and indeed this was one of the central conflicts of *The Nigger of the "Narcissus."* Conrad, however, made the most minimal and indirect concessions to these realities in the Preface. When he writes of "the invincible conviction of solidarity that knits together the loneliness of innumerable hearts," the word "invincible" no doubt implies that solidarity exists under the threat of defeat. But although in general one must see the popularity of the Preface, and particularly of what it says about solidarity, as the result of its telling people what they want to hear, it can hardly be accepted as a statement of a universal existential truth; and so its view of solidarity must be interpreted mainly as conative, as Conrad's explanation of what he was trying to achieve. This, indeed, is what Conrad goes on to say in the succeeding paragraph, "It is only some such train of thought, or rather of feeling, that can in a measure explain the aim of the attempt, made in the tale which follows . . ."

Conrad's uncertainty about the logical status of solidarity in the Preface is symptomatic. It largely derives from the difficulty of combining a general view of the basis of the artist's appeal to the reader, with a more personal apologia for his own distinctive subject-matter. Behind its more positive assertions we can detect Conrad's exhilaration at having discovered an aim as a writer which was to prove decisive, and which was first attempted in *The Nigger of the "Narcissus"*; the aim to discover and promote all those mutualities of human experience which Conrad calls solidarity.

II

Conrad's Preface has three main sections; and they all have a structure which may be described as partly expository and partly musical. The first three paragraphs sound Conrad's main themes, and the fourth gives them a personal modulation. Paragraphs five to eight are essentially variations on the original themes from a different point of view, and like the first section they also conclude with an application to Conrad's particular case. The last three paragraphs of the Preface constitute an extended coda which intermixes personal apologia with a recapitulation of the main critical themes.

The fifth paragraph is typical of the way in which Conrad almost conceals how his structure follows conventional expository order. Conrad begins: "Fiction . . . must be . . . like all art, the appeal of one temperament to all the other innumerable temperaments whose subtle and resistless power endows passing events with their true meaning, and creates the moral, the emotional atmosphere of the place and the time." This is essentially a transitional summary of what has gone before; but is not immediately recognisable as such because Conrad had not previously named the faculty in the individual where the artist sought truth, the reader responded, and solidarity had its latent being. In calling this center "temperament" Conrad made what was in some ways an unfortunate choice, because the word tends to have a pejorative connotation in English. Conrad certainly did not intend this connotation;[4] he used "temperament" in its original English meaning, which it retains in French, merely to denote the idiosyncratic mixture of elements in the total personality which controls its response to sensory, emotional, intellectual and aesthetic experience.

Conrad's use of the term may have been influenced by Maupas-

4. By 1902, at least, Conrad was aware of this more trivial sense of the word, writing of "the haphazard business of a mere temperament" (*Letters to Blackwood,* p. 155).

sant. In his Preface, "Le Roman", to *Pierre et Jean* (1888), which Conrad is known to have read, and which has been argued to have influenced his Preface,[5] Maupassant uses "temperament" as roughly equivalent to the "sensibility" and the "soul"; and he assumes that not only novels, but critical theories, and ultimately even reality itself, can only be the product of the individual temperament.[6]

Conrad's use of temperament is largely similar to Maupassant's, but there are two significant differences. Conrad does not give it Maupassant's Naturalist emphasis on the physiological elements which differentiate one individual temperament from another; and secondly, whereas Maupassant confines his attention to the temperament of the artist, Conrad gives it a more universal importance by attributing parallel functions to the temperament in the artist, and in "all the other innumerable temperaments" of mankind at large. Each individual temperament is different; but Conrad assumes that they are at least similar in the way they all convert immediate sense-impressions into meanings and values, and also that these meanings and values, being based on the common experiences which are listed in his description of solidarity, are sufficiently alike to afford a basis for the artist's appeal. One may object that Conrad does not fully clarify or explain how this happens; but his basic idea of the strategic role of the temperament is entirely consistent with what we have since learned about all those varied human tendencies —unconscious, symbolic, or social— which make its behaviour more than an automatic response to stimuli. It is in any case somewhat unfair to single out Conrad, as we have seen Goldknopf does, for not specifying "*how* the visible universe mediates" truth (p. 82); after all, three-quarters of a century and many foundation grants later, we still await reliable information.

The Preface then turns to the other stages of the circuit of communication. Since temperament is "not amenable to persuasion," Conrad argues, all art "appeals primarily to the senses"; and this sensory appeal must be transmitted by the written word if it is "to reach the secret spring of responsive emotions." Conrad has now reached the literary work, the specific point of intersection between the senses of the artist and those of his reader, as both are mediated through their individual temperaments. It is "only through complete, unswerving devotion to the perfect blending of form and substance," Conrad writes, that the artist can hope to achieve his aim; and Conrad carries through his idea of a direct appeal to the senses

5. George J. Worth, "Conrad's Debt to Maupassant in the Preface to *The Nigger of the 'Narcissus,'*" *JEGP*, 54 (1955), 700–704. Paul Kirschner, in the most extensive treatment of the influence of Maupassant on Conrad, does not ac-cept the argument (*Conrad: The Psychologist as Artist* [Edinburgh, 1968], pp. 272–273).

6. *Oeuvres complètes de Guy de Maupassant* (Paris, 1909), pp. ix–xvi.

by calling for a prose which will "aspire to the plasticity of sculpture, to the colour of painting, and to the magic suggestiveness of music—which is the art of arts."

The sixth paragraph draws the deduction that the artist must be single-minded in the pursuit of these aims, to the exclusion of any other possible demands of his readers; as Conrad puts it in the much-quoted words; "My task . . . is, by the power of the written word to make you hear, to make you feel—it is, before all, to make you *see*."

The force of the word "make" is worth noting; one of the characteristics of Conrad's fiction is the sense we get of a steady narrative pressure to make us look at the situation from a particular point of view. The later renown of Conrad's formula, however, probably resides mainly in the note of resonant finality which arises from the cumulated connotations of the word "see"; these obviously include the perception not only of visual impressions, but of ideas, as in "to see the point," and even of spiritual truths, as in "a seer." Even so, Conrad's formula is not to be taken either as a clinching revelation of ultimate fictional truth, or even as a full statement of Conrad's aims as a novelist.

"To make you *see*" has also been interpreted as implying an impressionistic doctrine. This is doubtful. Ford only wrote that Conrad "avowed himself impressionist,"[7] after Conrad's death, and it is unlikely that Conrad thought of himself as an exponent of that or any other specific literary doctrine. The Preface is certainly impressionist in one important, though limited, sense, because it places such emphasis on the translation of the artist's sense-perceptions into vivid and evocative language; and Conrad used the term in this sense when he wrote of a sailor's asking "in impressionistic phrase: 'How does the cable grow?' "[8] It may also be useful to call Conrad an impressionist in the more general sense that, like Henry James, for instance, he is primarily interested in presenting the subjective aspects of individual experience. But Conrad felt the doctrine of impressionism to be much too limited; of Stephen Crane's story "The Open Boat," for instance, he wrote: "He is *the only* impressionist and *only* an impressionist."[9] The main reason for this reservation is evident in the Preface where Conrad makes clear that his art's appeal is through, but not essentially to, the senses; his ultimate aim, as he says at the end of paragraph six, is to make us see "that glimpse of truth for which you have forgotten to ask"; and this involves the temperament rather than the eyes.

7. Ford Madox Ford, *Joseph Conrad: A Personal Remembrance* (London, 1924), p. 6. Ford tended to give a rather restricted view of Impressionism as a conscious concern to "render rightly the appearance of things."
8. *The Mirror of the Sea* (London: Dent, 1946), p. 21.
9. Letter to Garnett, December 5, 1897 (*Letters from Conrad*, p. 107).

In the seventh paragraph Conrad expands his earlier idea that art is "more enduring" than scientific or discursive thought. What the artist has to make us see is "a passing phase of life" before time consigns it to oblivion; and Conrad proceeds to deal with two aspects of the process whose logical connection is not immediately apparent. "To snatch . . . the rescued fragment . . . from the remorseless rush of time," he writes, is "only the beginning"; it must then be held up "before all eyes in the light of a sincere mood." Here Conrad is again invoking the mediating function of temperament, since "mood" is presumably its condition when it is most deeply responsive to "the moral, the emotional atmosphere of the place and time." This passing moment must be made to yield "the substance of its truth." To put it in other terms, the artist rescues the universal meaning from the evanescent concrete particular; and if he is successful his "presented vision" will find an echo in that collective repertoire of experiences and values in other temperaments which is the matrix of what Conrad calls solidarity.

The second temporal aspect of the artistic process is dealt with in the eighth paragraph. It follows from what Conrad has said both about the direct relation of the artist to the visible universe, and about how the course of time "demolishes theories," that the artist "cannot be faithful to any one of the temporary formulas of his craft"; these formulas—"Realism, Romanticism, Naturalism, even the unofficial sentimentalism"—all contain an "enduring part" which is true; but once the artist has learned from them, he still has a long way to go, and on his own. In that "uneasy solitude," Conrad continues, "the supreme cry of Art for Art . . . loses the exciting ring of its apparent immorality . . . and is heard only as a whisper, often incomprehensible, but at times and faintly encouraging."

This deft puncturing of the excessive claims made by both the supporters and the opponents of the Aesthetic movement, had originally provided Conrad with a graceful modulation into the cancelled paragraph of personal apology, which began: "It may seem strange if not downright suspicious that so much should be said in introduction to the unimportant tale of the sea which follows. . . ."[1] And Conrad's plea there that "in art alone of all the enterprises of men there is meaning in endeavour dissociated from success,"[2] in turn made a nice transition to the present paragraph nine about the

1. *Conrad's Manifesto,* pp. 38–39. Conrad's cancellations and revisions are more widely available in John Dozier Gordan, *Joseph Conrad: The Making of a Novelist* (Cambridge, Mass., 1940). The original draft of this paragraph was an awkward plea for "forgiveness." The change was part of Conrad's general aim in the revision to be less embarrass-ingly personal—"apology" was changed to "preface," and "confession of weakness" became "avowal of endeavour" (*Conrad's Manifesto,* pp. 62–64).

2. *Conrad's Manifesto,* p. 39. Conrad told Garnett that he did not "care a fraction of a damn" about any of the proposed deletions except for this idea (*Letters from Conrad,* p. 88).

labourer in the distant field. As it now stands, the logical connection between this and the faintly encouraging whisper of art for art's sake which now immediately precedes it, is very remote: the connection presumably lies in the lonely difficulty faced by both agricultural and literary workers. If we understand what either is trying to do, we will find more interest in their actions and look more kindly on their possible failures. It is a charming exemplum; the serene metaphorical distance of Conrad's plea for indulgence in having fallen short of his aim in The Nigger of the "Narcissus" makes it much more effective than direct personal apology of the original, and affords an effective preparation for the more abstract concerns of the last two paragraphs of the Preface.

In the tenth, Conrad restates the difference between the aim of art on the one hand, and of science and philosophy on the other, which was the subject of the first section of the Preface: art offers neither "the clear logic of a triumphant conclusion," nor "the unveiling of one of those heartless secrets which are called the Laws of Nature." The last paragraph then states what art does offer in positive terms which are related both to the temporal process which was discussed at the end of the second section, and to the image of the labourer in the field. The aim of art, Conrad writes is "To arrest, for the space of a breath, the hands busy about the work of the earth, and compel men entranced by the sight of distant goals to glance for a moment at the surrounding vision of form and colour, of sunshine and shadows; to make them pause for a look, for a sigh, for a smile—such is the aim, difficult and evanescent, and reserved only for a very few to achieve. . . . And when it is accomplished—behold!—all the truth of life is there: a moment of vision, a sigh, a smile—and the return to an eternal rest."

It would be nice to be able to respond to Goldknopf's sardonic challenge to Conrad's concluding phrase: "What returns to eternal rest I must leave to an abler intuition than my own" (p. 83). The answer would be easy enough if it were merely a question of Conrad's intention; he presumably meant that all of them—the artist, his work, and the reader with his momentary vision of the "rescued fragment"—are destined to return eventually to stasis, oblivion, or death.

But that, unfortunately, is not what Conrad's syntax means—there is no wholly acceptable grammatical subject for "the return." If we look closely we see that Conrad's referent has been slipping; in the first sentence of the paragraph the person spoken of is the reader, who is made to pause; the referent of "it is accomplished" can only be the successful work (actually called "the task" in a sentence which I omitted); by the time we get to the middle of Conrad's last sentence, however, we are back to the reader again, since he must be the recipient of the "moment of vision." This, however, won't do either; after all, we are naturally led to expect that, after finishing the book, the reader will get back on the job, and certainly not, as the text seems to say, find that its contact is lethal.

Conrad wanted to end the Preface with the theme of time, and with a characteristically sceptical qualification of the immemorial commonplace that only art can immortalise life. His earlier contrast between art and other modes of discourse had included the paradox that although the appeal of art is "sooner forgotten" than man's concerns with mundane means and ends, "its effect endures for ever." This contrast implies that two time-scales were at work. In the short run, art can at most "arrest" the work of the earth "for the space of a breath," just as all that Conrad can expect for *The Nigger of the "Narcissus"* is the reader's "passing glance of wonder and pity." In the long run, however, art endures in the sense that it plays its part in expressing that aspect of solidarity which "binds" the "dead to the living and the living to the unborn." The last paragraph, however, does not mention this longer time-scale; perhaps because a stress on the difficulty of achieving even a momentary arrest of the reader's attention was what Conrad needed at the end of the Preface; and a concluding phrase which enacted the brevity of the reader's attention may have seemed to Conrad an appropriately humble final rhetorical gesture, whose note of closure would also be sounded by ending the whole Preface with the word "rest." Conrad may have thought that adding the word "eternal" would recall the longer time-scale of the truism "Art is long and life is short," which he had invoked in the previous paragraph; unfortunately the implication of "eternal rest" conflicted with what had been said about the reader and the work of art, and this confusing conflation of grammatical subjects made the essay end in a logical blind alley.

III

The Preface is a highly personal and in many ways anomalous contribution to the criticism of fiction. It says nothing about plot or character; neither word, indeed, is even mentioned, and nor is "novel" or "novelist." Conrad's essential concern is with the subjective processes whereby the creation and the appreciation of *The Nigger of the "Narcissus"* can be understood in the larger perspective of other human activities.

That perspective, as it is presented in the first three paragraphs, is similar in its main lines to the early and more empirical aspects of English Romantic theory, especially as regards the psychology of creation and the social function of art. Wordsworth's Preface seemed a useful text to use for establishing the parallel, but of course Conrad is very different in his attitude to nature and in much else; and there are many important respects in which Conrad is either distinctly closer to later modes of thought, or is to a large extent original. Of these positions, four seem especially important: Conrad's treatment of the means of expression, of visual impressions, of time, and solidarity.

When Conrad begins the Preface by proclaiming that the work of art should "carry its justification in every line," he is making a demand for a concentrated perfection in the means of expression which is closer to Flaubert's reiterated insistence on verbal craftsmanship than to anything in Wordsworth, or in any other Romantic poet. Conrad's admiration for Flaubert and Maupassant is undoubted, but the Preface is not a very good text for studying its consequences, mainly because most of what Conrad says there need not come from any particular source, and could have come from many. Thus his phrase "the magic suggestiveness of music" sounds much closer to Symbolist doctrine or Pater, than it does to the French Realists; and throughout the Preface Conrad makes his independence from Realist doctrine very clear. Even in the passage that is verbally closest to Maupassant, Conrad is actually much closer to Pater or Impressionist theory. In "Le Roman", Maupassant complains that the public is composed of numerous groups who cry to the novelist: "Console me. Amuse me. Make me sad. Move me to pity. Make me dream. Make me laugh. Frighten me. Make me cry. Make me think."[3] Conrad similarly talks of how the public ask "to be promptly improved, or encouraged, or frightened, or shocked, or charmed." But whereas Maupassant says that the only legitimate demand which can be made of the artist is to ask, "Make me something beautiful, in the form which best accords with your temperament," Conrad does not talk about beauty; the only aim which he accepts is: "to make you hear, to make you feel —it is, before all, to make you *see*."

As to Pater, there is no specific evidence of borrowing; but we can say, as we cannot about Wordsworth, for example, that some influence on the Preface is quite likely. Conrad admired Pater, and seems to have read *Marius the Epicurean* a month or so before writing the Preface;[4] and in any case Pater's ideas were very much in the air during the nineties. On the other hand, the resemblance concerns a few points for which Pater was very widely known. Thus Conrad's words about "the magic suggestiveness of music—which is the art of arts," would probably have been taken by his original readers as an echo of Pater's famous dictum *"All art constantly*

3. p. ix.
4. See *Letters from Conrad*, pp. 56, 83. Conrad acknowledges receipt of *Marius* on May 26, 1897, and says he is "licking

[his] chops in anticipation." I have seen no evidence ⸱ Conrad had read Wordsworth's ⸱ but he was probably aware of its ⸱l position.

aspires to the condition of music";[5] while Conrad's insistence on the artist's fidelity to his own sensations uncontaminated by an intellectual prejudgment is echoed in Marius, who has to empty his consciousness of "such abstractions as are but the ghosts of bygone impressions," in order to be "absolutely virgin towards . . . the impressions of an experience, concrete and direct."[6] Pater's doctrine, like Conrad's, also allots time a role of crucial importance, since it gives supreme value to individual aesthetic experience, which, like other experience, can only be momentary. Thus Marius believes that "what is secure in our existence is but the sharp apex of the present moment between two hypothetical eternities, and all that is real in our experience is but a series of fleeting impressions."[7]

On the other hand, if there is one generalization which can safely be hazarded about Conrad it is that, unlike Pater, he was in no sense a hedonist; and Conrad could equally well have derived most of the parallels between the Preface and Pater either from Schopenhauer directly, or from his many admirers, who incidentally included both Maupassant[8] and Pater.[9]

Conrad also admired Schopenhauer,[1] and there is a general resemblance on many points between their thought. Schopenhauer had been very influential in giving music supreme status among the arts, and also in seeking the artistic genius as deriving from the capacity to achieve "pure perception." More generally he thought that the best available remedy, short of death or suicide, from the immersion of the will in the ceaseless flux of the illusions of temporal experience was to cultivate the attitude of aesthetic contemplation.[2] In effect Schopenhauer had already done to philosophy what Pater did to religion—undermined its claims to be man's supreme source of truth, and put those of art in its place.

Both here and elsewhere, however, Conrad's formulation and combination of similar ideas is personal and undoctrinal. Even the emphasis on time in the later part of the Preface seems not to much a reflection of the dominating role of time in late nineteenth-century thought[3] as of Conrad's own characteristic concerns:

5. "The School of Giorgione," *The Renaissance* (London, 1890), p. 140.
6. *Marius the Epicurean*, rev. ed. 1892 (London, 1939), p. 106.
7. *Marius*, p. 110. On Arthur Symons as a representative of this idea in the nineties, see Barbara Charlesworth, *Dark Passages: The Decadent Consciousness in Victorian Literature* (Madison and Milwaukee, 1965), especially p. 113.
8. A. Baillot, *Influence de la philosophie de Schopenhauer en France: 1860–1900* (Paris, 1927), pp. 228–230.
9. The connection between their aesthetics is analysed in William K. Wimsatt and Cleanth Brooks, *Literary Criticism: A Short History* (New York, 1962), pp. 487–488.
1. See Kirshner, *Conrad: The Psychologist as Artist*, pp. 266–277.
2. In sections 36 and 52 of *The World as Will and Representation* (trans. E. F. J. Payne [New York, 1958], I, 185, 255–267).
3. Which is the subject of J. H. Buckley, *The Triumph of Time* (Cambridge, Mass., 1966).

his works in general are pervasively retrospective; and *The Nigger of the "Narcissus"* in particular is avowedly an attempt to commemorate a vanishing phase in the history of the sea. J. Hillis Miller, indeed, sees this concern in larger terms. For him the closing paragraph of the Preface is "the most somber moment of all in Conrad's long dialogue with darkness"; and he interprets the return to an eternal rest as "a double return, the return of the darkness to its uninterrupted repose in the flux at the heart of things, and the return of man, after his evanescent glimpse of truth, to the forgetful sleep of everyday life."[4] Hillis Miller takes no account of how this is qualified by what Conrad has said earlier about art as mankind's most enduring record, a theme restated in his essay on Henry James which describes the novel as "rescue work" in which "vanishing phases of turbulence"[5] may be "endowed with the only possible form of permanence in this world of relative values—the permanence of memory."

The conclusion of the Preface, therefore, is probably less pessimistic and metaphysical in its implications than Hillis Miller assumes, and more personal and apologetic. It is also an expression of one of the two main personal motives behind Conrad's writing in general, the motive which he attributes to Decoud in *Nostromo*: "a desire to leave a correct impression of the feelings, like a light by which the action may be seen when personality is gone, gone where no light of investigation can ever reach the truth which every death takes out of the world."[6]

If Conrad sees fiction as impressions recollected in maturity, he finds its permanent value as a memorial record in the long chain of human solidarity. This persistent concern is where Conrad most radically diverges not only from Pater and Schopenhauer, but from the French Realists and Symbolists. There are, it is true, two possible doubts about the importance of solidarity in the Preface, quite apart from the objections already made. First, that Conrad does not return directly to the theme of solidarity in his concluding paragraphs; and secondly, that his earlier treatment of the idea is partly aimed merely at establishing a common psychological and moral basis of experience in men which makes it possible for the artist to communicate. But the urgency of Conrad's rhetoric strongly suggests that his deepest interest in the Preface was to communicate his hope that his presented vision would "awaken in the hearts of the beholders [the] feeling of unavoidable solidarity." Indeed there is much to support the view that the other most powerful motive in Conrad's writing in general was for an art that would

4. *Poets of Reality* (New York, 1969), p. 39.
5. *Notes on Life and Letters* (London: Dent, 1949), p. 13.
6. London: Dent, 1947, p. 230.

make real the yearning of the orphan, the exile and the sceptic for some special kind of human brotherhood.

There is nothing in the Preface which is contradicted in Conrad's later criticism, and he frequently returned to its main ideas. Nor did Conrad later take a clearer stand on the general literary issues which the Preface raises; his scepticism about intellectual formulae continued, and with it a disinclination either to endorse or reject most critical theories. In this the Preface remains characteristic. Conrad refuses to accept the aesthetic and symbolist doctrines of the separation of art from life, and maintains his own version of a correspondence theory of literature; yet the conclusion of the Preface is entirely consistent with the Art for Art's sake attitude of detached aesthetic contemplation. Similarly, although Conrad stresses the importance and the difficulties of the expressive and formal problems of writing, he was not a formalist and rejected, if indeed he ever considered, the idea of the autonomy of the literary work. Conrad's treatment of the issues raised by Naturalism, Symbolism and Impressionism is equally eclectic; he sees the point, but sidesteps controversy and goes his own way.

Conrad's Preface is written in a language much more elevated than that to which we have become accustomed in literary criticism; and we must go elsewhere for critical techniques that will help us to analyse fiction, just as we must go elsewhere in Conrad for what little he is willing to disclose about his own methods as a novelist. Conrad's main effort in the Preface is not in the ordinary sense critical at all; it is, rather to set his own personal feelings about writing within the general context of other human activities in the ordinary world. It is probably because Conrad confronts this vital but largely unexamined problem of the wider context of literature, and because he at least convinces most of us that we are genuinely sharing in his own anxious and unrigorous but committed and eloquent response to it, that Conrad's Preface has achieved, and deserves, its fame.

JOSEPH CONRAD

To My Readers in America†

From that evening when James Wait joined the ship—late for the muster of the crew—to the moment when he left us in the open sea, shrouded in sailcloth, through the open port I had much

† From David R. Smith, *Conrad's Manifesto: Preface to a Career* (Philadelphia: Gehenna Press, 1966), pp. 41–42.

to do with him. He was in my watch. A negro in a British forecastle is a lonely being. He has no chums. Yet James Wait afraid of death and making Her his accomplice was an imposter of some character —mastering our compassion, scornful of our sentimentalism, triumphing over our suspicions.

But in the book he is nothing; he is merely the centre of the ship's collective psychology and the pivot of the action. Yet he who in the family circle and amongst my friends is familiarly referred to as The Nigger, remains very precious to me. For the book written round him is not the sort of thing that can be attempted more than once in a life-time. It is the book by which, not as a novelist perhaps, but as an artist striving for the utmost sincerity of expression, I am willing to stand or fall. Its pages are the tribute of my unalterable and profound affection for the ship, the seamen, the winds and the great sea—the moulders of my youth, the companions of the best years of my life.

After writing the last words of that book, in the revulsion of feeling before the accomplished task, I understood that I had done with the sea, and that henceforth I had to be a writer. And almost without laying down the pen I wrote a preface, trying to express the spirit in which I was entering on the task of my new life. That preface on advice (which I now think was wrong) was never published with the book. But the late W. E. Henley, who had the courage at that time (1897) to seralise my "Nigger" in the New Review judged it worthy to be printed as an Afterward at the end of the last installment of the tale.

I am glad that this book which means so much to me is coming out again, under its proper title of ["]The Nigger of the Narcissus" and under the auspices of my good friends and publishers Messers Doubleday Page & Co., into the light of publicity.

Half the span of a generation has passed since W. E. Henley, after reading two chapters, sent me a verbal message: "Tell Conrad that if the rest is up to sample it shall certainly come out in the New Review." The most gratifying recollections of my writer's life! And here is the Suppressed Preface.

EDWARD GARNETT

Letters from Joseph Conrad†

Of this volume, *Letters from Joseph Conrad*, thirty-one have been selected by Monsieur G. Jean-Aubry and published in *The Life and Letters of Joseph Conrad*. The others are new. Apart from

† From Introduction, *Letters from Joseph Conrad, 1895–1924*, by Edward Garnett (Indianapolis: Bobbs-Merrill, 1928), pp. 1–10, 21–23.

other points of interest it may be said that this series supplies at first hand fuller and closer information about the first four years of Conrad's work, after he had turned author, than can be gathered from his letters to others. I met Conrad first as the "publisher's reader" who had recommended *Almayer's Folly*, and as the earliest of his literary friends he turned to me first for criticism and advice. He showed me the manuscript of everything he wrote up to November, 1898. I thus saw and commented on in turn *An Outcast of the Islands*, *Tales of Unrest*, *The Nigger of the Narcissus*, *The Rescue* first draft, and the tentative chapters of *The Sisters*. The first hundred letters, chiefly filled with Conrad's literary development and his difficulties in composition, show in detail his struggles, his hopes and fears, his dejections and exultations from month to month. More than twenty years later when Conrad wrote the Preface to the Collected Edition (1920), his memory naturally failed to recall many facts and details preserved by these letters, *e.g.*, his chronology of the composition of *Tales of Unrest* is wrong. My own memory certainly did not retain a tithe of the details which the letters set down. They fill out my general recollection that as regards Conrad's work, ninety-five was a leisurely year, ninety-six was a strenuous, prolific year, while ninety-seven and ninety-eight were years of struggling anxiety, years largely wasted by his unavailing labor over *The Rescue*, till with *The Heart of Darkness*, begun in December, 1898, Conrad suddenly found the channel clear and forged ahead.

I

As I have said I first met Conrad in November 1894, some months after I, as Mr. Fisher Unwin's "reader," had written one of my hasty, perfunctory "reports" and had advised the acceptance of *Almayer's Folly*. My friend, Mr. W. H. Chesson, whose duty it was to take charge of the manuscripts, tells me that he called my particular attention to the manuscript. My wife recollects that I showed her the manuscript, told her it was the work of a foreigner and asked her opinion of his style. What particularly captivated me in the novel was the figure of Babalatchi, the aged one-eyed statesman and the night scene at the river's edge between Mrs. Almayer and her daughter. The strangeness of the tropical atmosphere, and the poetic "realism" of this romantic narrative excited my curiosity about the author, who I fancied might have Eastern blood in his veins. I was told however that he was a Pole, and this increased my interest since my Nihilist friends, Stepniak and Volkhovsky, had always subtly decried the Poles when one sympathized with their position as "under dogs." Since I spent the greater part of every week in the country I rarely made the acquaintance of authors whose manuscripts I had read. But on this occasion Mr. Fisher Unwin arranged a meeting between Conrad and me at the National

Liberal Club. On the last Christmas before his death, Conrad described to Mrs. Gertrude Bone his recollection of this first meeting, and I quote from the account she has sent me.[1] My memory is of seeing a dark-haired man, short but extremely graceful in his nervous gestures, with brilliant eyes, now narrowed and penetrating, now soft and warm, with a manner alert yet caressing, whose speech was ingratiating, guarded, or brusk turn by turn. I had never seen before a man so masculinely keen yet so femininely sensitive. The conversation between our host and Conrad for some time was halting and jerky. Mr. Unwin's efforts to interest his guest in some political personages, and in literary figures such as John Oliver Hobbes and S. R. Crockett were as successful as an attempt to thread an eyeless needle. Conrad, extremely polite, grew nervously brusk in his responses, and kept shifting his feet one over the other, so that one became fascinated in watching the flash of his pointed, patent leather shoes. The climax came unexpectedly when in answer to Mr. Unwin's casual but significant reference to "your next book," Conrad threw himself back on the broad leather lounge and in a tone that put a clear cold space between himself and his hearers, said, "I don't expect to write again. It is likely that I shall soon be going to sea." A silence fell. With one sharp snick he had cut the rope between us, and we were left holding the loose end. I felt disappointed and cheated. Mr. Unwin expressed some deprecatory ambiguities and then, after turning his falcon-like glance down the long smoking-room, apologized for having to greet some friends in a far corner.

Directly he had left Conrad and me alone speech came to me in a rush. I may have been as diplomatic as Conrad has recorded.[2] What I then said to him with the fervency of youth would seem to me a little bizarre now, had I not caught myself the other day, thirty years later, addressing a young author with much the same accents and convictions. But I spoke then with youth's ardent assurance. My thesis was that the life Conrad had witnessed on sea and land must vanish away into the mist and fade utterly from memory, did he not set himself to record it in literature. And *Almayer's Folly* showed that he had the power. Conrad listened attentively, searching my face, and demurring a little. It seemed to me afterward that

1. "The first time I saw Edward," he went on, "I dare not open my mouth. I had gone to meet him to hear what he thought of *Almayer's Folly*. I saw a young man enter the room. That can not be Edward so young as that, I thought. He began to talk. Oh yes! It was Edward. I had no longer doubt. But I was too frightened to speak. But this is what I want to tell you, how he made me go on writing. If he had said to me, 'Why not go on writing?' I should have been paralyzed. I could not have done it. But he said to me, 'You have written one book. It is very good. Why not *write another?*' Do you see what a difference that made? Another? Yes, I would do that. *I* could do that. Many others I could not. Another I could. That is how Edward made me go on writing. That is what made me an author."

2. Author's Note to *An Outcast of the Islands*, Collected Edition, 1919: "A phrase of Edward Garnett's is, as a matter of fact, responsible for this book." Conrad has, however, misdated the conversation which took place at our first meeting.

he had come to meet me that night partly out of curiosity and partly as an author who deep down desires to be encouraged to write. And the *credo* he heard matched his conviction that it was the thing that one could do that mattered. This *credo* about artists in general, and Conrad in particular the curious will find set forth in a paper written in 1897 in *The Academy*.[3] It was no doubt partly my curiosity about Conrad's life as a sailor in the Eastern Seas that winged my words, and curiously the heavy, middle class atmosphere of the National Liberal Club with its yellow encaustic tiles, cigar-smoke, provincial members, political gossip from the "lobbies," and business news "on the tape," jarred less and less in the presence of this stranger who charmed one by something polished and fastidious in the inflections of his manner. Yes, he had "the temperament." After Mr. Unwin's return the talk naturally fell to an ordinary level and shortly afterward we bade our host good night and Conrad strolled some way with me on my way past the brilliantly lighted Strand. Our relations had been settled for good by this first contact.

We did not meet again for some weeks, when Conrad invited me to spend the evening with him at 17 Gillingham Street. After dining in a private room at a Wilton Street restaurant where an obsequious Italian waiter dashed up- and down-stairs all wreathed in smiles, I was introduced to Conrad's snug bachelor quarters where, having placed me in an easy chair, Conrad retired behind a mysterious screen and left me to study the coziness of the small firelit room, a row of French novels, the framed photograph of an aristocratic lady and an engraving of a benevolent imposing man on the mantel-shelf. On a little table by the screen lay a pile of neat manuscript sheets. I remained conscious of these manuscript sheets when Conrad reappeared and plunged into talk which ranged over things as far removed as the aspects of Malay rivers and the ways of publishers. Conrad's talk that night was a romance, free and swift; it implied in ironical flashes that though we hailed from different planets the same tastes animated us. To no one was the art of harmonizing differences so instinctive when he wished to draw near. To no one was the desire of emphasizing them more emphatic, when he did not. There was a blend of caressing, almost feminine intimacy with masculine incisiveness in his talk; it was that which gave it its special character. Conrad's courtesy was part of his being, bred in the bone, and serving him as a foil in a master's hand, ready for attack or defense. That first evening he took from the mantel-shelf and showed me the portrait of his mother with her sweet commanding eyes, and told me that both she and her father, a poet and translator of Shakespeare, had been arrested at the time of the Polish rising of 1862, and had afterward been sent into exile. Of himself Conrad spoke as a man lying under a slight stigma among

3. An *Appreciation of Mr. Joseph Conrad* reprinted in *Friday Nights*, 1922.

his contemporaries for having expatriated himself. The subject of Poland was then visibly painful to him, and in those early years he would speak of it unwillingly, his attitude being designed to warn off acquaintances from pressing on a painful nerve. Later he grew less sensitive and in a letter in 1901, he sketched at length his family history and connections.

In response to this first confidence about his family, thrown out with diffidence, I gave him some idea of my own position, which, at that time, as indeed later, was peculiarly isolated. A stranger to editors and to literary cliques I had no influence outside the publishing firm I worked for; but I could and did give new authors encouragement and practical advice about placing their work. My few literary friends were struggling young men, such as W. B. Yeats, men abler than myself and not so unskilled in the methods of success. My six years' work as a publisher's reader had taught me fully the anxieties and the hazards of the literary life, but youth believes instinctively that luck is on its side, and I had been lucky in finding authors for Mr. T. Fisher Unwin. However, to Conrad, ten years my senior, and incomparably more versed in worldly affairs, the ways of publishers, reviewers and editors were then an uncharted land, and his first view of New Grub Street, as he put it later to me was "as inviting as a peep into a brigand's cave and a good deal less reassuring." When later that evening, I had recurred to the subject of *Almayer's Folly*, Conrad suddenly picked up the pile of manuscript sheets from the little table and told me that he had embarked on a second book, and that I should live to regret my responsibility for inciting him. This charming flattery was very characteristic of Conrad. Placing the manuscript in my hands he retired behind the screen and left me to glance through the pages. By the time he had reappeared with a bottle of Benedictine I had been captivated by the brilliant opening of *An Outcast of the Islands*. I exclaimed with delight at the passage:

> They were a half-caste, lazy lot, and he saw them as they were—
> ragged, lean, unwashed, undersized men of various ages, shuffling
> about aimlessly in slippers; motionless old women who looked
> like monstrous bags of pink calico stuffed with shapeless lumps of
> fat, and deposited askew upon decaying rattan chairs in shady
> corners of dusty verandas; young women, slim and yellow, big-
> eyed, long haired, moving languidly amongst the dirt and rubbish
> of their dwellings as if every step they took was going to be their
> very last.

Conrad, exhilarated by my praise, then described his idea of the down-hill path of Willems and foreshadowed Aissa's part in the drama. The plot had already taken shape in Conrad's mind, but most of the action was still in a state of flux. Conrad's attitude to *An Outcast* was from the first a strange blend of creative ardor and skepticism. He spoke deprecatingly of his knowledge of Malay life, but all the same the figures of Willems, Joanna and Aissa captivated his imagination. His sardonic interest in Willems' disintegration reflected, I believe, his own disillusionment over the Congo. I agree with Monsieur Jean-Aubry that Conrad's Congo experiences were the turning-point in his mental life and that their effects on him determined his transformation from a sailor to a writer. According to his emphatic declaration to me, in his early years at sea he had "not a thought in his head. . . . I was a perfect animal," he reiterated, meaning of course that he had reasoned and reflected hardly at all over all the varieties of life he had encountered. The sinister voice of the Congo with its murmuring undertone of human fatuity, baseness and greed had swept away the generous illusions of his youth, and had left him gazing into the heart of an immense darkness. But Willems' figure was not merely the vehicle for Conrad's sardonic irony, but through it Conrad had to express also his own "romantic feeling of reality," and so this character had to bear too great a burden both of feeling and commentary. I do not think that this criticism was ever formulated exactly by either Conrad or myself during the nine months in which *An Outcast* came to me in batches. He was too engrossed in wrestling with his characters to see precisely the effect of all the parts in relation to the whole, and I was too enthralled by the strange atmosphere and poetic vision, and too intent on encouraging him to criticize Willems till the end was at hand. I well remember penciling notes of admiration on the margins of certain pages, as on those poetical passages that conclude Part II. On the delivery of the final instalment, however, I criticized adversely the psychology of Willems' motives and behaviour just before his death at Aissa's hand; and Conrad agreed, with reservations, to my strictures and set to work to remodel various passages. I think now that my criticism was not so just as I imagined at the time. Probably no record exists now of the cancellations and emendations made by Conrad in the last chapter (*See* his letter, September 24, 1895).

However, to come back to that first evening at Gillingham Street, I recall that Conrad took alarm at some declaration of mine about the necessity for a writer to follow his own path and disregard the public's taste. His tone was emphatic. "But I *won't* live in an attic," he retorted. "I'm past that, you understand? I *won't* live in an attic!" I saw then that it was essential to reassure Conrad about the prospects of *Almayer's Folly*. And I cited the names of various authors who, whatever they may have been doing, were certainly then not living in attics, public favorites such as Stevenson and Kipling and Rider Haggard—the work of the last-named, I remember, Conrad stigmatized as being "too horrible for words." He objected specifically to the figure of Captain Goode, as well he might! As I look back at that evening and at our subsequent meetings in little Soho restaurants, in Newgate Street, St. Paul's Churchyard and in a Mecca café in Cheapside, I recall an atmosphere of humble conspiracy *à deux*, which enfolded us. Humble, since Conrad was then more obscure than any publisher's reader. At that time he was experiencing all the hot and cold fits and the exultations of literary creation, often thrown back and skeptical, but also boyishly eager while perfecting his strokes and broadening his efforts as the novel grew under his hands; and I was taking this development of his genius for granted and was enthusiastic over the romantic magic of his scenes. My part indeed was simple—to appreciate and criticize all that he wrote, and to ask for more, more.

* * *

Conrad's return from Brittany in September, 1896, came to me in the form of a message—"When are you coming up to London. . . . When? How? Will you see me? Are you well? Have you time? Have you the wish?" At our meeting I found him very concerned about his prospects. In his six months' stay in Brittany he had earned about seventy-five pounds for three short stories. *The Rescuer* was at a standstill, and he had written ten pages of *The Nigger of the Narcissus*. The loss of most of his little capital made it imperative that he should receive better payment for his work, but all that Mr. Fisher Unwin would offer him was fifty pounds on account of a ten per cent. royalty on the first two thousand copies —the same terms as for *An Outcast of the Islands*, and Conrad demanded one hundred pounds on account. On my advice Conrad held out for these terms, but Mr. Fisher Unwin refused to go beyond his original proposal. I do not blame Mr. Unwin: I am told that the sales of Conrad's three early books showed a loss, in the publisher's ledger, for many years. But it was imperative that Conrad should find another publisher with faith in his future, and I now suggested that he should negotiate with Messrs. Smith Elder & Co., who had sent him flattering inquiries about his next book. I did not know till twenty years later that it was Mr. Roger Ingpen who, impressed with *An Outcast of the Islands,* had urged Mr. Reginald Smith to make overtures to Conrad. Alas! Mr. Reginald Smith, that ex-lawyer, with his bland, mellifluous flow of compliments to authors (later I experienced them on Kropotkin's account), offered Conrad nothing more substantial than a fifty pounds immediate advance on a higher royalty; and he also advised him to put his book of short stories "away for a time." This would not do at all, and I then went to S. S. Pawling, of Heinemann's, and put the case frankly before him. Pawling, "a good sort," as authors said, of whom I will speak in another place, though overshadowed by his partner Heinemann, was alive to the opportunity of getting hold of Conrad, and he sent him reassuring messages, saying that he would show the portion of the manuscript of *The Nigger of the Narcissus* to Henley for publication, and that, anyway, Conrad might expect better terms than Mr. Unwin had offered him.

The six letters from Conrad to me, November twenty-fifth–January tenth, when he was struggling day and night to finish *The Nigger of the Narcissus*, show that those seven weeks were perhaps the most strenuous in the whole of his writing life. The story of the finish of *Nostromo*—as detailed in a letter of September 2, 1903, to John Galsworthy—has indeed an impressive epic quality, but Conrad's place as an author was then assured. And had Conrad failed to "bring off" *The Nigger*, or had the novel missed fire, in the reviewers' eyes, as many a masterpiece has done, nothing more disheartening for Conrad and ominous for his future could be imagined. The prospect, indeed, looked alarming for an almost penniless author. But Conrad, inspired by his devil, did not falter. His heart was in his work. After a reassuring message from Henley I brought Pawling and Conrad together in a dinner at the Hotel D'Italie and what I remember of the evening is that Pawling succumbed wholly to the charm and the talk of this strange seaman author. Conrad continued his desperate struggle for another month, and in his letter of January 10, 1897, is the cry of victory. "And the end! I can't eat. I dream—nightmares—and scare my wife. I wish it was over! But I think it will do! It will do!—Mind I only think—not sure. But if I didn't think so I would jump overboard." But the end did not come till January seventeenth when, after finishing *The Nigger*, Conrad, exhausted, took to his bed for two days. But, as he said, it was a cheap price for finishing that story. * * *

JOSEPH CONRAD

From His Correspondence†

TO T. FISHER UNWIN[1]

[October 19, 1896]

* * * Should you entertain my modifications I wish to tell you that I would like to try W. Henley with my "Nigger"—not so much for

† From Edward Garnett, *Letters from Joseph Conrad, 1895–1924* (Bobbs-Merrill, Indianapolis, 1928), pp. 72–118 passim; G. Jean-Aubry, *Joseph Conrad: Life and Letters*, 2 vols. (Doubleday: New York, 1927), I, 197, 200, 201, 204–5, 206; II, 352; *A Conrad Memorial Library: The Collection of George T. Keating* (Doubleday: New York, 1929), pp. 34, 35, 36, 43; John Dozier Gordon, *Joseph Conrad: The Making of a Novel-*ist (Harvard: Cambridge, 1940), p. 223; *The Bookman*, 69 (May 1929), 229; *Joseph Conrad's Letters to Cunninghame Graham*, ed. C. T. Watts (Cambridge: Cambridge, 1969), pp. 48, 49, 53–54, 56–57.

1. T. Fisher Unwin headed the publishing house which had published Conrad's first novel, *Almayer's Folly*, in 1895. William E. Henley was the editor of the prestigious magazine *The New Review*.

my own sake as to have a respectable shrine for the memory of men with whom I have, through many hard years, lived and worked. The story will contain 25,000 words *at least* and shall be ready very soon.
* * *

TO EDWARD GARNETT[2]

[October 25, 1896]

Dear Garnett,

* * * As far as the *Nigger* is concerned I shall try to place it for serial publication with Henley or elsewhere. * * * It will be about 30,000 words. I must enshrine my old chums in a decent edifice. Seriously, do you think it would be too long? There are so many touches necessary for such a picture! * * *

[November 1, 1896]

My dear Garnett,

* * * I am letting myself go with the *Nigger*. He grows and grows. I do not think it's wholly bad though. * * *

[November 13, 1896]

My Dear Garnett,

* * * Nothing would induce me to go back to F.U. * * *

[November 21, 1896]

Dearest Garnett,

You are worth ever so many bricks.

It is a lovely arrangement.[3] Remains to be seen whether the story is good enough—or effective enough.

That I doubt. I also remember days when I did not doubt. So I sit tight now; like a man with a lottery ticket; and hope for unheard-of fortunes. * * *

I shall make sail with the "Narcissus" and expect to make a quick passage. Weather fine, and wind fair.

TO EDWARD LANCELOT SANDERSON[4]

[November 21, 1896]

Dearest Ted,

* * * But one of the short stories (a pretty long one too,—about half the length of *Almayer*) is now under Henley's consideration for

2. Garnett (1865–1937), as a reader for T. Fisher Unwin, had "discovered" Conrad in 1894 and urged the publication of *Almayer's Folly*.

3. Mr. Reginald Smith's proposal appeared to be quite unsatisfactory. I went to S. S. Pawling of "Heinemann's" and interested him in Conrad's work. [*Garnett's note.*]

T. Fisher Unwin had experienced poor sales with Conrad's first two books, *Almayer's Folly* and *An Outcast of the Islands,* and would agree to only one-half of the advance against future royalties

which Conrad asked. Garnett advised trying Messrs. Smith Elder & Co., who offered the same as Fisher Unwin. S. S. Pawling was a senior partner at Heinemann.

4. Sanderson, accompanied by John Galsworthy, met Conrad in March 1893 on the *Torrens,* on which Conrad was chief mate while bound from Australia to England. His father was headmaster of Elstree, near London, where Conrad often stayed while finishing *Almayer's Folly.*

serial publication in the *New Review*. If accepted by Henley, then Heinemann will publish it afterwards in a small volume. I want £100 for serial and book rights and of course some percentage on the sales.

Still I will take any offer (not absurdly low) they may make, because I do wish to appear in the *New Review*.

TO EDWARD GARNETT

[November 25, 1896]

Dearest Garnett,

I am as you may imagine exceedingly pleased with what Pawling writes. My dear fellow you are the making of me! My only fear is that I will droop with the end of the "Narcissus." I am horribly dissatisfied with the ideas yet unwritten. Nothing effective suggests itself. It's ghastly. I shall, end by this week, send you on a good many pages—but the end is not yet. I think I could almost *pray* for inspiration if I only knew where to turn my face.

[November 29, 1896]

Dear Garnett,

I send you seventeen pages more—65–82 of my Beloved Nigger. Send them on to Mr. Pawling, but first look at them yourself. I am ashamed to think how much of my work you have not seen. It is as if I had broken with my conscience, quarreled with the inward voice. I do not feel very safe.

Of course nothing can alter the course of the "Nigger." Let it be unpopularity it *must* be. But it seems to me that the thing—precious as it is to me—is trivial enough on the surface to have some charm for the man in the street. As to lack of incident well—it's life. The incomplete joy, the incomplete sorrow, the incomplete rascality or heroism—the incomplete suffering. Events crowd and push and nothing happens. You know what I mean. The opportunities do not last long enough. Unless in a boy's book of adventures. Mine were never finished. They fizzled out before I had a chance to do more than another man would. Tell me what you think of what you see. I am going on. Another 20 pages of type—or even less—will see the end, such as it is. And won't I breathe! Till it's over there's no watch below for me. A sorry business this scribbling. Thanks.

[December 2, 1896]

Dearest Garnett,

I have turned to with a will. I do not think I can give the whole on Friday but a good piece off the end I can.

Will you lunch with me on Friday, 1.30, Ang-Am?[5] I shall be there to time and with a handful of paper in my pocket. Some of that must be in MS. for I won't let my wife sit up to type. There

5. Anglo-American Cafe.

will be enough to see the last headland anyhow. So I suppose Henley likes it.

Thanks my dear fellow.

TO T. FISHER UNWIN

[December 13, 1896]

I think I have conquered Henley. He has practically accepted my story for the N.R. and it will appear some time next year. * * *

It strikes me that—should that story prove more popular than my previous work—my other stories will become more valuable. * * * If my hopes are even partly realized it may become, perhaps, worth your while (in a year or so) to publish them—and in that case I should try by and by to write a couple more so as to form a vol. for which you shall give me what you think fit. This is only an idea and if it appears practicable to you so much the better. * * *

TO EDWARD GARNETT

[December 19, 1896]

Dear Garnett,

Ever since I left you in the rain and mud of Oxford Street I have been at work. I had some real bad days but since last Monday I am going on all right. I think the pages just written won't dishonour the book. Your book which you try to coax into bloom with such devotion and care. And the thing is dramatic enough. It will be done by the 7th Jan. Not before!

We are off to Cardiff on Monday. I take my MS with me. I shall not stop writing unless I am stumped by something, when the only remedy is to wait. * * *

[January 10, 1897]

Dearest Garnett,

Nigger died on the 7th at 6 p.m.; but the ship is not home yet. Expected to arrive tonight and be paid off tomorrow. And the end! I can't eat—I dream—nightmares—and scare my wife. I wish it was over! But I think it will do! It will do!—Mind I only think—not sure. But if I didn't think so I would jump overboard.

[January 19, 1897]

Dear Garnett,

* * * I have been in bed two days. A cheap price for finishing that story. * * *

[January 21, 1897]

Dear Garnett,

* * *—I can't send the *Nigger*. It's too illegible! I haven't heard yet from S. P.[6] but suppose it's all right anyhow. He seemed so pos-

6. Sidney Pawling (see note 3, above).

itive when I saw him. I've sent him a suggestion for a title. What do you think of it?

THE FORECASTLE

A Tale of Ship and Men

———

How [will] this do? It's rather late to ask your opinion for I've already sent a slip to P. I really daren't inflict on you my MS. * * *

TO HELEN WATSON[7]

[January 27, 1897]

Dear Miss Watson,
* * * The story just finished is called *The Nigger: A Tale of Ships and Men.* Candidly, I think it has certain qualities of art that make it a thing apart. I tried to get through the veil of details at the essence of life. But it is a rough story—dealing with rough men and an immense background. I do not ask myself how much I have succeeded. I only dare to hope that it is not a shameful failure, that perhaps, here and there, may be found a few men and women who will see what I have tried for. It would be triumph enough for me.
* * *

TO EDWARD LANCELOT SANDERSON

[January 27, 1897]

Dearest Ted,
* * * Henley likes my story, but there is some hitch about the *Review.* What I do not know, but expect to hear soon. * * *

TO EDWARD GARNETT

[February 4, 1897]

Dear Garnett,
I have made the MS. just a little clearer and send it to you—the last fifty pages. It is still ghastly but I haven't energy enough to copy them for you. If too difficult do not read. I had a letter from Pawling. It appears from it that the final decision as to serial publication would be taken at some meeting (of directors I suppose) on Monday (yesterday). I haven't heard any more and am anxious. I do nothing yet. Take it easy and so on. But am collapsed for a time. I will let you know as soon as I know my fate.

7. Helen Watson was engaged to Edward Lancelot Sanderson (see note 4, above).

[March 12, 1897]

My dear Garnett,

* * * I must say, though, I don't exactly understand my position vis-a-vis of the N. R. Is it a question of "to be or not to be" or the more gross question of time only? To tell you the truth, now Henley has accepted me I don't care much whether I appear or not in the N. R. Or at least care only for the additional cash it may bring. Otherwise I would like to appear at once in book form and be done with it. It would settle doubts and if it kills hope it would also kill incertitude. * * *

TO EDWARD LANCELOT SANDERSON

[May 19, 1897]

My dearest Ted,

I send you on the *Nigger*. Galsworthy[8] had seen a couple of sheets when he was here last, so I let him have the lot first. He returned it today and I dispatch it at once to you.

I address it rather to you than to your dear Mother because I want you to see it first. I know, my dear fellow, that *you* will never suspect me of ingrained coarseness of thought and language. But I want you to read and judge before you hand it over to Mrs. Sanderson. Not that I mistrust her comprehension and indulgence, but I want to spare to her (even at the cost of my self-love) any unpleasant experience. Not, perhaps, because I think that the thing is not worth it. I am conceited enough about it,—God knows,—but He also knows the spirit in which I approached the undertaking to present faithfully some of His benighted and suffering creatures; the humble, the obscure, the sinful, the erring upon whom rests His Gaze of Ineffable Pity. My conscience is at peace in that matter, and it is with confidence and love that I send the work to you,—to read and to judge.

TO EDWARD GARNETT

[May 26, 1897]

My dear Garnett,

I do not know how to thank you for your letter about the *Nigger*. It has made me happy and very proud. And I am glad that your name shall be inscribed on something you like. * * *

[June 2, 1897]

Dear Garnett,

* * * The Nigger is bought in the States by the Batchelor Syndicate for serial and by Appleton for book. I begin in the August Number of the *New* R. (26th July).

8. John Galsworthy (1867–1933), friend, *Forsyte Saga.*
neighbor, fellow-novelist. Wrote *The*

TO HELEN WATSON

[June 27, 1897]

My dear Miss Watson,

* * * It is very good of you,—at this anxious time,—to think and speak of my book. The pleasure of your appreciation,—which I prize so highly,—is overshadowed by the news you send. I must however assure you that there was no intention of levity in my treatment of the cook. I did not try to,—and I trust I did not make —him ridiculous. Nothing was further from my thoughts than irreverence. It would have been untrue to my convictions. The worst that can be charged against me is artistic failure,—failure to express the mixed sentiments the men (whom I knew) awakened in me. * * *

TO R. B. CUNNINGHAME GRAHAM[9]

[August 9, 1897]

* * * I want to ask you a favor. There is a thing of mine coming out in the *New Review*. Being, as you inform me, my "Prophète en titre" I am afraid you must consider it your sacred duty to read everything over my signature. Now in this special case *please don't*. In November I shall send you the book—if you allow me—and then you shall see the whole. I am conceited about that thing and very much in love with it, and I want it to appear before you at its best. The instalment plan ruins it. I wouldn't make that fuss if I didn't care for your opinion. * * *

TO EDWARD GARNETT

[August 24, 1897]

Dearest Garnett,

* * * I send you * * * a short preface to the "Nigger."

I want you not to be impatient with it and if you think it at all possible to give it a chance to get printed. That rests entirely with you—the Nigger is *your* book and besides you know very well I daren't make any move without your leave. I've no more judgment of what is fitting in the way of literature than a cow. And you must be the Lord of that one head of cattle (Ain't I rural in my images? The farm tells. Eh?)

And let me hear the decree soon to ease my mind. On my eyes be it—I shall not draw one breath till your sublime Highness has spoken to the least of his slaves. We demand mercy. * * *

---

9. R. B. Cunninghame Graham (1852–1936), Scottish writer, aristocrat, and socialist, wrote Conrad an enthusiastic letter in the summer of 1897 when *An Outpost of Progress* first appeared. The two quickly became close friends, and remained so.

[August 28, 1897]

Dearest Garnett,

* * * As you may imagine I do not care a fraction of a damn for the passage you have struck out[1]—that is, the personal part. But I think that the eight lines at the end (of the paragraph struck out) conveying the opinion that in "art alone there is a meaning in endeavour as apart from success" should be worked in somehow. And whether your wisdom lets me keep them in or not I tell you plainly—fangs or no fangs—that there is the saving truth—the truth that saves most of us from eternal damnation. There!

I shall promptly patch the hole you have made and show you the thing with the infamous taint out of it.—If then, there is the slightest chance of it doing some good to the Nigger it shall *not* go to the Saturday or any other Review. Hang the filthy lucre. I would do any mortal thing for Jimmy—you know. * * *

[September 24, 1897]

Dear Garnett,

* * * I've asked Pawling to send me a copy of the *Nigger* in paper cover—of the copyright issue—you know. They aren't for sale. I thought I would ask you whether you would offer it to your mother who has so kindly consented to be misguided into enthusiasm—by her undutiful son. It would not be the common edition at any rate—and I shall not have any copies "de luxe" to distribute. * * *

[September 27, 1897]

My dear Garnett,

* * * The N. *of the* "N" comes out in November sure. P. wrote a personal letter to Scribner offering the N *of the* "N". The book is being set up. I've sent him a fair copy of the preface with the personal paragraph taken out as marked by you. It is quite long enough without it. It is certainly much better as expurgated by you. I told P. you said it would do no harm to the book; I also asked him to read it and give me his opinion—from the Public point of view. In the same letter I asked him for the second time to send me the copyright vol. Had no reply yet—of course. * * *

—When I parted with Unwin I said:—you shan't have the *Nigger*—but as you've copyrighted in America for me you shall have other stories to make up a vol. I won't touch the American rights—whatever they are. Otherwise you shall have the stories on your own terms.— * * *

I fancy, if the *Nigger* hits, he will make a good thing out of the vol: on such terms. If the *Nigger don't hit* then nothing matters

---

1. The passage is printed in Thomas La-voie's "Textual History and Textual Notes: The 'Preface,' " above, p. 150.

much to me and he would pull a long face at anything—at a gift—
at a premium—anything! * * *

[October 11, 1897]

It did me good to hear that the *Nigger* works miracles. You are a
dear fellow to send such news. Pawling after proposing me a paper
copy now says he hasn't one. I am horribly disappointed at not
being able to carry out my idea of offering it to your Mother.

Heinemann objects to the *bloody's* in the book. That Israelite is
afraid of women. I didn't trust myself to say much in Pawling's
room. Moreover Pawling is a good fellow whom I like more every
time I see him; and it seemed to me he wanted me to give way. So
I struck 3 or 4 *bloody's* out. I am sure there is a couple left yet, but,
damn it, I am not going to hunt 'em up. I've sent away the last
batch of proofs today. Now the Nigger is cast adrift from me. The
book strikes me as good; but I quite foresee it will have no sale.

[November 5, 1897]

* * * I have also a paper copy of the *Nigger*. I shall correct it this
evening. Do you think it would be breach of etiquette if I send it
direct to the Museum. Hadn't I better send it through you? I am
immensely relieved. I hope I've done with the *selling* business for
life.

[November 6, 1897]

* * * I send you a copy of the *N* for your mother. Present it
from me—if you think it isn't too cheeky of me. I've written a few
lines there. * * *

TO MRS. RICHARD GARNETT[2]

Madam,

Your son & my friend whose sympathy, criticism & counsel have
encouraged & guided me ever since I took pen in hand has told me
that you like this tale. I wish I could have expressed my sense of
your commendation by offering you a unique vellum copy. But
since that is impossible—then the other extreme would be better
than the middle course. I venture therefore to beg your acceptance
of this plain paper copy of the Copyright impression—which,
simple as it is, cannot at any rate be obtained for money. I am,
Madam,

Your most obedient humble servant,
The Author.

4th Nov., 1897

2. Garnett's mother, whose maiden name
was Singleton. Her gift from Conrad of
a deposit, or copyright, copy is now
owned by Colgate University, where the
present text was transcribed.

TO STEPHEN CRANE

[November 16, 1897]

I must write to you before I write a single word for a living to-day. I was anxious to know what you would think of the end. If I've hit *you* with the death of Jimmy I don't care if I don't hit another man. I think however that artistically the end of the book is somewhat lame. I mean after the death. All that rigmarole about the burial and the ship's coming home seems to run away into a rat's tail—thin at the end. Well! It's too late now to bite my thumbs and tear my hair. When I feel depressed about it I say to myself "Crane likes the damned thing"—and am greatly consoled. What your appreciation is to me I renounce to explain. The world looks different to me now, since our long powwow. It was good. The memory of it is good. And now and then (human nature *is* a vile thing) I ask myself whether you meant half of what you said! You must forgive me. The mistrust is not of you—it is of myself: the drop of poison in the cup of life. I am no more vile than my neighbors but this disbelief in one's self is like a taint that spreads on everything one comes in contact with: on men—on things—on the very air one breathes. That's why one sometimes wishes to be a stone breaker. There's no doubt about breaking a stone. But there's doubt, fear—a black horror, in every page one writes. You at any rate will understand and therefore I write to you as though we had been born together before the beginning of things. For what you have done and intend to do I won't even attempt to thank you. I certainly don't know what to say, tho' I am perfectly certain as to what I feel.

TO EDWARD GARNETT

[December 5, 1897]

My Dear Garnett,

The *Nigger* came out to date I believe but is not advertised in the *Sat. Review.* * * *

The *Nigger* is ended and the N.R. stops. I suppose you've heard already. Henley printed the preface at the end as an Author's note. It does not shine very much, but I am glad to see it in type. * * *

TO R. B. CUNNINGHAME GRAHAM

[December 6, 1897]

* * * But this is morbid—and I sat down intending to produce a good impression! I take it all back and declare my belief in lilies, gold harps—and brimstone, like my Podmore in the "Narcissus".

And à-propos of Podmore—I am afraid the 'Nigger' will bore you. C'est vécu—et c'est bête. There are twenty years of life, six months of scribbling in that book—and not a shadow of a story. As the critic in to-day's Dly Mail puts it tersely: "the tale is no tale at all". The man complains of lack of heroism! and is, I fancy, shocked at the bad language. I confess reluctantly there is a swear here and there. I grovel in the waste-paper basket, I beat my breast. May I hope you at least! won't withdraw your esteem from a repentant sinner? * * *

[December 14, 1897]

* * * I've been thinking over the letter you have written me about the *Nigger*. I am glad you like the book. Sincerely glad. It is clear gain to me. I don't know what the respectable (hats off) part of the population will think of it. Probably nothing. They never think. It isn't respectable. But I can quite see that, without thinking, they may feel an instinctive disgust. So be it. In my mind I picture the book as a stone falling in the water. It's gone and not a trace shall remain. But the words of commendation you and a few other men have said shall be treasured by me as a proof that the book has not beeen written in vain—as the clearest of my reward.

So You may rest assured that the time you have given to reading the tale and to writing to me has not been thrown away—since, I presume, You do not believe that doing good to a human being is throwing away effort and one's own life. And You have done me good. Whatever may be the worth of my gratitude You have it all; and such is the power of men to show feelings that "helas! Vous ne vous en apercevrez même pas!"

But as I said I've been meditating over your letter. You say: "Singleton with an education". Well—yes. Everything is possible, and most things come to pass (when you don't want them). However I think Singleton with an education is impossible. But first of all—what education? If it is the knowledge how to live my man essentially possessed it. He was in perfect accord with his life. If by education you mean scientific knowledge then the question arises— what knowledge, how much of it—in what direction? Is it to stop at plane trigonometry or at conic sections? Or is he to study Platonism or Pyrrhonism or the philosophy of the gentle Emerson? Or do you mean the kind of knowledge which would enable him to scheme, and lie, and intrigue his way to the forefront of a crowd no better than himself? Would you seriously, of malice prepense cultivate in that unconscious man the power to think. Then he would become conscious—and much smaller—and very unhappy. Now he is simple and great like an elemental force. Nothing can touch him but the curse of decay—the eternal decree that will extinguish the sun, the stars one by one, and in another instant shall spread a frozen darkness over the whole universe. Nothing else can touch him—he does not think.

Would you seriously wish to tell such a man: "Know thyself". Understand that thou art nothing, less than a shadow, more insignificant than a drop of water in the ocean, more fleeting than the illusion of a dream. Would you? * * *

[December 20, 1897]

Your letter reached me just as I was preparing to write to you. What I said in my incoherent missive of last week was *not* for the purpose of arguing really. I did not seek controversy with you—for this reason: I think that we do agree. If I've read you aright (and I have been reading You for some years now) You are a most hopeless idealist—your aspirations are irrealisable. You want from men faith, honour, fidelity to truth in themselves and others. You want them to have all this, to show it every day, to make out of these words their rule of life. The respectable classes which suspect you of such pernicious longings lock you up and would just as soon have you shot—because your personality counts and you can not deny that you are a dangerous man. What makes you dangerous is your unwarrantable belief that your desire may be realized. This is the only point of difference between us. I do not believe. And if I desire the very same things no one cares. Consequently I am not likely to be locked up or shot. Therein is another difference—this time to your manifest advantage.

There is a—let us say—a machine. It evolved itself (I am severely scientific) out of a chaos of scraps of iron and behold!—it knits. I am horrified at the horrible work and stand appalled. I feel it ought to embroider—but it goes on knitting. You come and say: "this is all right; it's only a question of the right kind of oil. Let us use this—for instance—celestial oil and the machine shall embroider a most beautiful design in purple and gold." Will it? Alas no. You cannot by any special lubrication make embroidery with a knitting machine. And the most withering thought is that the infamous thing has made itself; made itself without thought, without conscience, without foresight, without eyes, without heart. It is a tragic accident—and it has happened. You can't interfere with it. The last drop of bitterness is in the suspicion that you can't even smash it. In virtue of that truth one and immortal which lurks in the force that made it spring into existence it is what it is—and it is indestructible!

It knits us in and it knits us out. It has knitted time space, pain, death, corruption, despair and all the illusions—and nothing matters. I'll admit however that to look at the remorseless process is sometimes amusing. * * *

FROM W. H. CHESSON[3]

[January 13, 1898]

Dear Mr. Conrad:

I cannot delay telling you how good I find "The Nigger of the Narcissus." The psychology of the poltroon is traced with a hand so cunning and relentless that there are those who will think it inhuman. And words will not contain my contempt for those who deprecate the lack of story or plot in a novel that is alive with all the horrible antics of fear accompanied with the noise and tumult of the sea. I dismiss too, cheerfully, the argument that a seaman,—a "shell-back" maybe—is not to write with fervid orchestral style against which the colloquial speech of his comrades sounds with double futility and increased clearness.

As a work of art, the thing seems to me well-nigh faultless. There is no illegitimate interruption of the ironic spectacle at the end of which you cleverly inveigle the reader into sharing the superstition of the devoted mariners. I expected the breeze to come and I expected an impediment up to the last. The crawly way of Jimmy's obscene malady of mind dominated the accompaniment of ineffectual wind in order that all who serve him should be deeply involved in his uncanny night. Seldom have I talked with sailors, but I have sought to observe them and have been impressed with a curious childishness,—a chronic state of wonder and submission which intemperance and bad temper scarcely seem to disturb. You have caught that childishness.

One can't but congratulate you on the romantic force which you apply as a scheme so scientific in its loving inclusion of symptoms. The Captain's splendid patience and authority,—Singleton's indomitable fidelity, flash at me even now when the book is closed. Fine sentences like the first of Chapter IV march through my mind. The storm; the extrication of Jimmy (wonderful realist to have thought of those nails!); his death; (the extinguishing of his eyes); his funeral; the reluctance of the precipitated corpse; the throwing of the word of God upon the unlistening sea; I am in a percipience of it all. And lastly, though I repeat myself in saying so, it takes *shape*,—there is a beautiful anatomy, dexterously contrived, under all this display of imagination. "The Nigger" is not an episode of

3. Chesson was a reader at T. Fisher Unwin with Garnett, who credits Chesson for first having spotted the quality of *Almayer's Folly* in 1894. The passage referred to in the postscript is Podmore's "vision" while attending Jimmy, pp. 69–73.

the sea; it is a final expression of the pathology of Fear. At least you made your villainous oaf Donkin pull it out into an unbearable horror of countenance like a gutta percha mask. Is it, I wonder, some shrinking from an Irony made colder and for a moment less polished than steel that makes me almost regret Donkin being one of the crew?

One last word, and I know you will forgive me, why, O friend, will you encourage the asinine critics to prick up their ears by employing "like" when you ought to use "as"? You are sure to have a second edition and I therefore remark that "like" appearing for "as" on pp. 144, 170, 187, 214 and 222. It is used on page 187 in a conversation where I admit it may be natural enough, as slipshod chitchat.

With my warmest wishes for a very remarkable and powerfully written book, believe me,
Yours always,

W. H. CHESSON

What a lovely vision is that on pp. 170–171!

TO W. H. CHESSON

[January 16, 1898]

Dear Mr. Chesson:

Your unexpected and delightful letter reached me yesterday morning. I would have answered it at once had it not beeen that the house was in a state of disorganization on account of the arrival of an infant of the male persuasion. However this fuss is over thank God.

Your letter shows such a comprehension of the state of mind which produced the story, that had you given blame instead of generous praise it would still have been a rare pleasure to be thus understood—seized in the act of thinking, so to speak. Of all that has been said about the book this what you say gives the most intimate satisfaction, because you not only see what the book is but what it might have been. When you say, "One almost regrets Donkin being one of the crew," I take it as the very highest praise I have received—inconceivably different in its insight within those dark and inarticulate recesses of mind where so many thoughts die at the moment of birth, for want of personal strength—or of moral rectitude—or of inspired expression.

One would like to write a book for your reading.

This is what touched me most. The other words of commendation I take as your recognition of a tendency of mind repulsive to many, understood by few, clearly seen by you—and which I cannot help thinking of as not wholly without merit. But a tendency of mind is nothing without expression and that the expression should please you is in my opinion my very great fortune. It is to your letter (now incorporated with my copy of "The Nigger") that in moments of doubt and weariness I shall turn with the greatest confidence as to an infallible remedy for the black disease of writers. I've read it several times since yesterday.

I have also corrected all the "like" into "as" in my copy. One is so strangely blind to one's own prose: and the more I write the less sure I am of my English.

Thanks for going to the trouble of pointing out to me the passages. I don't think the N will have a second edition, but if—in years to come—it ever has, the corrections shall be made.

Believe me very gratefully and faithfully yours

JOSEPH CONRAD

P.S. I trust you haven't bought the book. I haven't forgotten I have the privilege to owe you a copy. But I am coming to Town soon and the precious debt shall be discharged.

TO HENRY SEIDEL CANBY[4]

[April 7, 1924]

* * * In the *Nigger* I give the psychology of a group of men and render certain aspects of nature. But the problem that faces them is not a problem of the sea, it is merely a problem that has arisen on board a ship where the conditions of complete isolation from all land entanglements make it stand out with a particular force and colouring. * * *

JOSEPH CONRAD

Stephen Crane†

My acquaintance with Stephen Crane was brought about by Mr. Pawling, partner in the publishing firm of Mr. William Heinemann.

One day Mr. Pawling said to me: "Stephen Crane has arrived in England. I asked him if there was anybody he wanted to meet and he mentioned two names. One of them was yours." I had then just been reading, like the rest of the world, Crane's *Red Badge of Courage*. The subject of that story was war, from the point of view

---

4. Canby (1878–1961), distinguished American man of letters, founded the *Saturday Review* in 1924.
† From two essays, both titled "Stephen Crane": the first selection being from Conrad's *Notes on Life and Letters* (Doubleday: New York, 1921), p. 49, and the second from his *Last Essays* (London: Dent, 1926), pp. 136–39.

of an individual soldier's emotions. That individual (he remains nameless throughout) was interesting enough in himself, but on turning over the pages of that little book which had for the moment secured such a noisy recognition I had been even more interested in the personality of the writer. The picture of a simple and untried youth becoming through the needs of his country part of a great fighting machine was presented with an earnestness of purpose, a sense of tragic issues, and an imaginative force of expression which struck me as quite uncommon and altogether worthy of admiration.

Apparently Stephen Crane had received a favourable impression from the reading of *The Nigger of the "Narcissus,"* a book of mine which had also been published lately. I was truly pleased to hear this.

* * *
———
* * *

* * * My wife's recollection is that Crane and I met in London in October 1897, and that he came to see us for the first time in our Essex home in the following November.

I have mentioned * * * that it was Mr. S. S. Pawling, partner in the publishing firm of Mr. Heinemann, who brought us together. It was done at Stephen Crane's own desire.

I was told by Mr. Pawling that when asked whom he wanted to meet, Crane mentioned two names, of which one was of a notable journalist (who had written some novels) whom he knew in America, I believe, and the other was mine. At that time the only facts we knew about each other were that we both had the same publisher in England. The only other fact I knew about Stephen Crane was that he was quite a young man. I had, of course, read his *Red Badge of Courage,* of which people were writing and talking at that time. I certainly did not know that he had the slightest notion of my existence, or that he had seen a single line (there were not many of them then) of my writing. I can safely say that I earned this precious friendship by something like ten months of strenuous work with my pen. It took me just that time to write *The Nigger of the Narcissus,* working at what I always considered a very high pressure. It was on the ground of the authorship of that book that Crane wanted to meet me. Nothing could have been more flattering than to discover that the author of *The Red Badge of Courage* appreciated my effort to present a group of men held together by a common loyalty, and a common perplexity in a struggle not with human enemies, but with the hostile conditions testing their faithfulness to the conditions of their own calling.

Apart from the imaginative analysis of his own temperament

tried by the emotions of a battlefield, Stephen Crane dealt in his book with the psychology of the mass—the army; while I—in mine —had been dealing with the same subject on a much smaller scale and in more specialised conditions—the crew of a merchant ship, brought to the test of what I may venture to call the moral problem of conduct. This may be thought a very remote connection between these two works, and the idea may seem too far-fetched to be mentioned here; but that was my undoubted feeling at the time. It is a fact that I considered Crane, by virtue of his creative experience with *The Red Badge of Courage*, as eminently fit to pronounce a judgment on my first consciously-planned attempt to render the truth of a phase of life in the terms of my own temperament with all the sincerity of which I was capable.

I had, of course, my own opinion as to what I had done; but I doubted whether anything of my ambitiously comprehensive aim would be understood. I was wrong there, but my doubt was excusable, since I myself would have been hard put to it if requested to give my complex intentions the form of a concise and definite statement. In that period of misgivings which so often follows an accomplished task I would often ask myself, who in the world could be interested in such a thing? It was after reading *The Red Badge*, which came into my hands directly after its publication in England, that I said to myself: "Here's a man who may understand—if he ever sees the book; though, of course, that would not mean that he would like it." I do not mean to say that I looked towards the author of *The Red Badge* as the only man in the world. It would have been stupid and ungrateful. I had the moral support of one or two intimate friends and the solid fact of Mr. W. E. Henley's acceptance of my tale for serial publication in the *New Review* to give me confidence, while I awaited the larger verdict.

* * *

JOSEPH CONRAD

[The Ship and the Sea]†

* * *

In such marine shore-talk as this is the name of a ship slowly established, her fame made for her, the tale of her qualities and of her defects kept, her idiosyncrasies commented upon with the zest of personal gossip, her achievements made much of, her faults

† From Joseph Conrad, *The Mirror of the Sea* (1906) (London: Dent, 1923, 1946), pp. 134–37.

glossed over as things that, being without remedy in our imperfect world, should not be dwelt upon too much by men who, with the help of ships, wrest out a bitter living from the rough grasp of the sea. All that talk makes up her "name," which is handed over from one crew to another without bitterness, without animosity, with the indulgence of mutual dependence, and with the feeling of close association in the exercise of her perfections and in the danger of her defects.

This feeling explains men's pride in ships. "Ships are all right," as my middle-aged, respectable quartermaster said with much conviction and some irony; but they are not exactly what men make them. They have their own nature; they can of themselves minister to our self-esteem by the demand their qualities make upon our skill and their shortcomings upon our hardiness and endurance. Which is the more flattering exaction it is hard to say; but there is the fact that in listening for upwards of twenty years to the sea-talk that goes on afloat and ashore I have never detected the true note of animosity. I won't deny that at sea, sometimes, the note of profanity was audible enough in those chiding interpellations a wet, cold, weary seaman addresses to his ship, and in moments of exasperation is disposed to extend to all ships that ever were launched—to the whole everlastingly exacting brood that swims in deep waters. And I have heard curses launched at the unstable element itself, whose fascination, outlasting the accumulated experience of ages, had captured him as it had captured the generations of his forbears.

For all that has been said of the love that certain natures (on shore) have professed to feel for it, for all the celebrations it had been the object of in prose and song, the sea has never been friendly to man. At most it has been the accomplice of human restlessness, and playing the part of dangerous abettor of world-wide ambitions. Faithful to no race after the manner of the kindly earth, receiving no impress from valour and toil and self-sacrifice, recognizing no finality of dominion, the sea has never adopted the cause of its masters like those lands where the victorious nations of mankind have taken root, rocking their cradles and setting up their gravestones. He—man or people—who, putting his trust in the friendship of the sea, neglects the strength and cunning of his right hand, is a fool! As if it were too great, too mighty for common virtues, the ocean has no compassion, no faith, no law, no memory. Its fickleness is to be held true to men's purposes only by an undaunted resolution and by sleepless, armed, jealous vigilance, in which, perhaps, there has always been more hate than love. *Odi et amo* may well be the confession of those who consciously or blindly have surrendered their existence to the fascination of the sea. All the tempestuous passions of mankind's young days, the love of loot and the love of glory, the love of adventure and the love of danger, with the great love of the unknown and vast dreams of dominion and power, have passed like images reflected from a mirror, leaving no record upon the mysterious face of the sea. Impenetrable and heartless, the sea has given nothing of itself to the suitors for its precarious favours. Unlike the earth, it cannot be subjugated at any cost of patience and toil. For all its fascination that has lured so many to a violent death, its immensity has never been loved as the mountains, the plains, the desert itself, have been loved. Indeed, I suspect that, leaving aside the protestations and tributes of writers who, one is safe in saying, care for little else in the world than the rhythm of their lines and the cadence of their phrase, the love of the sea, to which some men and nations confess so readily, is a complex senti-ment wherein pride enters for much, necessity for not a little, and the love of ships—the untiring servants of our hopes and our self-esteem—for the best and most genuine part. For the hundreds who have reviled the sea, beginning with Shakespeare in the line

"More fell than hunger, anguish, or the sea."

down to the last obscure sea-dog of the "old model," having but few words and still fewer thoughts, there could not be found, I believe, one sailor who has ever coupled a curse with the good or bad name of a ship. If ever his profanity, provoked by the hardships of the sea, went so far as to touch his ship, it would be lightly, as a hand may, without sin, be laid in the way of kindness on a woman.

The love that is given to ships is profoundly different from the love men feel for every other work of their hands—the love they bear to their houses, for instance—because it is untainted by the pride of possession. The pride of skill, the pride of responsibility, the pride of endurance there may be, but otherwise it is a disinterested sentiment. No seaman ever cherished a ship, even if she belonged to him, merely because of the profit she put in his pocket. No one, I think, ever did; for a ship-owner, even of the best, has always been outside the pale of that sentiment embracing in a feeling of inti-mate, equal fellowship the ship and the man, backing each other against the implacable, if sometimes dissembled, hostility of their world of waters. The sea—this truth must be confessed—has no generosity. No display of manly qualities—courage, hardihood, endurance, faithfulness—has ever been known to touch its irrespon-sible consciousness of power. The ocean has the conscienceless temper of a savage autocrat spoiled by much adulation. He cannot brook the slightest appearance of defiance, and has remained the irreconcilable enemy of ships and men ever since ships and men had the unheard-of audacity to go afloat together in the face of his frown. From that day he has gone on swallowing up fleets and men without his resentment being glutted by the number of victims—by so many wrecked ships and wrecked lives. To-day, as ever, he is ready to beguile and betray, to smash and to drown the incorrigible optimism of men who, backed by the fidelity of ships, are trying to wrest from him the fortune of their house, the dominion of their world, or only a dole of food for their hunger. If not always in the hot mood to smash he is always stealthily ready for a drowning. The most amazing wonder of the deep is its unfathomable cruelty.

* * *
•

JOSEPH CONRAD

A Familiar Preface†

* * *

* * * Once before, some three years ago, when I published *The Mirror of the Sea*,[1] a volume of impressions and memories, * * * I wanted to pay my tribute to the sea, its ships and its men, to whom I remain indebted for so much which has gone to make me what I am. That seemed to me the only shape in which I could offer it to their shades. There could not be a question in my mind of anything else. It is quite possible that I am a bad economist; but it is certain that I am incorrigible.

Having matured in the surroundings and under the special conditions of sea life, I have a special piety toward that form of my past; for its impressions were vivid, its appeal direct, its demands such as could be responded to with the natural elation of youth and strength equal to the call. There was nothing in them to perplex a young conscience. Having broken away from my origins under a storm of blame from every quarter which had the merest shadow of right to voice an opinion, removed by great distances from such natural affections as were still left to me, and even estranged, in a measure, from them by the totally unintelligible character of the life which had seduced me so mysteriously from my allegiance, I may safely say that through the blind force of circumstances the sea was to be all my world and the merchant service my only home for a long succession of years. No wonder, then, that in my two exclusively sea books—*The Nigger of the "Narcissus,"* and *The Mirror of the Sea* (and in the few short sea stories like "Youth" and "Typhoon")—I have tried with an almost filial regard to render the vibration of life in the great world of waters, in the hearts of the

† From Joseph Conrad, *A Personal Record* (1912) (London: Dent, 1923, 1946), pp. xiv–xxi.
1. Actually, 1906. [*Editor.*]

simple men who have for ages traversed its solitudes, and also that something sentient which seems to dwell in ships—the creature of their hands and the objects of their care.

One's literary life must turn frequently for sustenance to memories and seek discourse with the shades, unless one has made up one's mind to write only in order to reprove mankind for what it is, or praise it for what it is not, or—generally—to teach it how to behave. Being neither quarrelsome, nor a flatterer, nor a sage, I have done none of these things, and I am prepared to put up serenely with the insignificance which attaches to persons who are not meddlesome in some way or other. But resignation is not indifference. I would not like to be left standing as a mere spectator on the bank of the great stream carrying onward so many lives. I would fain claim for myself the faculty of so much insight as can be expressed in a voice of sympathy and compassion.

It seems to me that in one, at least, authoritative quarter of criticism I am suspected of a certain unemotional, grim acceptance of facts—of what the French would call *sécheresse du cœur*. Fifteen years of unbroken silence before praise or blame testify sufficiently to my respect for criticism, that fine flower of personal expression in the garden of letters. But this is more of a personal matter, reaching the man behind the work, and therefore it may be alluded to in a volume which is a personal note in the margin of the public page. Not that I feel hurt in the least. The charge—if it amounted to a charge at all—was made in the most considerate terms; in a tone of regret.

My answer is that if it be true that every novel contains an element of autobiography—and this can hardly be denied, since the creator can only express himself in his creation—then there are some of us to whom an open display of sentiment is repugnant. I would not unduly praise the virtue of restraint. It is often merely temperamental. But it is not always a sign of coldness. It may be pride. There can be nothing more humiliating then to see the shaft of one's emotion miss the mark of either laughter or tears. Nothing more humiliating! And this for the reason that should the mark be missed, should the open display of emotion fail to move, then it must perish unavoidably in disgust or contempt. No artist can be reproached for shrinking from a risk which only fools run to meet and only genius dare confront with impunity. In a task which mainly consists in laying one's soul more or less bare to the world, a regard for decency, even at the cost of success, is but the regard for one's own dignity which is inseparably united with the dignity of one's work.

And then—it is very difficult to be wholly joyous or wholly sad on this earth. The comic, when it is human, soon takes upon itself a face of pain; and some of our griefs (some only, not all, for it is the capacity for suffering which makes man august in the eyes of men) have their source in weaknesses which must be recognized with smiling compassion as the common inheritance of us all. Joy and sorrow in this world pass into each other, mingling their forms and their murmurs in the twilight of life as mysterious as an overshadowed ocean, while the dazzling brightness of supreme hopes lies far off, fascinating and still, on the distant edge of the horizon.

Yes! I, too, would like to hold the magic wand giving that command over laughter and tears which is declared to be the highest achievement of imaginative literature. Only, to be a great magician one must surrender oneself to occult and irresponsible powers, either outside or within one's breast. We have all heard of simple men selling their souls for love or power to some grotesque devil. The most ordinary intelligence can perceive without much reflection that anything of the sort is bound to be a fool's bargain. I don't lay claim to particular wisdom because of my dislike and distrust of such transactions. It may be my sea training acting upon a natural disposition to keep good hold on the one thing really mine, but the fact is that I have a positive horror of losing even for one moving moment that full possession of myself which is the first condition of good service. And I have carried my notion of good service from my earlier into my later existence. I, who have never sought in the written word anything else but a form of the Beautiful—I have carried over that article of creed from the decks of ships to the more circumscribed space of my desk, and by that act, I suppose, I have become permanently imperfect in the eyes of the ineffable company of pure esthetes.

As in political so in literary action a man wins friends for himself mostly by the passion of his prejudices and by the consistent narrowness of his outlook. But I have never been able to love what was not lovable or hate what was not hateful out of deference for some general principle. Whether there be any courage in making this admission I know not. After the middle turn of life's way we consider dangers and joys with a tranquil mind. So I proceed in peace to declare that I have always suspected in the effort to bring into play the extremities of emotions the debasing touch of insincerity. In order to move others deeply we must deliberately allow ourselves to be carried away beyond the bounds of our normal sensibility—innocently enough, perhaps, and of necessity, like an actor who raises his voice on the stage above the pitch of natural conversation—but still we have to do that. And surely this is no great sin. But the danger lies in the writer becoming the victim of his own exaggeration, losing the exact notion of sincerity, and in the end coming to despise truth itself as something too cold, too blunt for his purpose —as, in fact, not good enough for his insistent emotion. From laughter and tears the descent is easy to snivelling and giggles.

These may seem selfish considerations; but you can't, in sound morals, condemn a man for taking care of his own integrity. It is his clear duty. And least of all can you condemn an artist pursuing, however humbly and imperfectly, a creative aim. In that interior world where his thought and his emotions go seeking for the experience of imagined adventures, there are no policemen, no law, no pressure of circumstance or dread of opinion to keep him within bounds. Who then is going to say Nay to his temptations if not his conscience?

And besides—this, remember, is the place and the moment of perfectly open talk—I think that all ambitions are lawful except those which climb upward on the miseries or credulities of mankind. All intellectual and artistic ambitions are permissible, up to and even beyond the limit of prudent sanity. They can hurt no one. If they are mad, then so much the worse for the artist. Indeed, as virtue is said to be, such ambitions are their own reward. Is it such a very mad presumption to believe in the sovereign power of one's art, to try for other means, for other ways of affirming this belief in the deeper appeal of one's work? To try to go deeper is not to be insensible. An historian of hearts is not an historian of emotions, yet he penetrates further, restrained as he may be, since his aim is to reach the very fount of laughter and tears. The sight of human affairs deserves admiration and pity. They are worthy of respect, too. And he is not insensible who pays them the undemonstrative tribute of a sigh which is not a sob, and of a smile which is not a grin. Resignation, not mystic, not detached, but resignation open-eyed, conscious, and informed by love, is the only one of our feelings for which it is impossible to become a sham.

Not that I think resignation the last word of wisdom. I am too much the creature of my time for that. But I think that the proper wisdom is to will what the gods will without, perhaps, being certain what their will is—or even if they have a will of their own. And in this matter of life and art it is not the Why that matters so much to our happiness as the How. As the Frenchman said, "*Il y a toujours la manière.*" Very true. Yes. There is the manner. The manner in laughter, in tears, in irony, in indignations and enthusiasms, in judgments—and even in love. The manner in which, as in the features and character of a human face, the inner truth is foreshadowed for those who know how to look at their kind.

Those who read me know my conviction that the world, the temporal world, rests on a few very simple ideas; so simple that they must be as old as the hills. It rests notably, among others, on the idea of Fidelity. At a time when nothing which is not revolutionary in some way or other can expect to attract much attention I have not been revolutionary in my writings. The revolutionary spirit is mighty convenient in this, that it frees one from all scruples as regards ideas. Its hard, absolute optimism is repulsive to my mind by the menace of fanaticsm and intolerance it contains. No doubt one should smile at these things; but, imperfect Esthete, I am no better Philosopher. All claim to special righteousness awakens in me that scorn and anger from which a philosophical mind should be free. . . .

I fear that trying to be conversational I have only managed to be unduly discursive. I have never been very well acquainted with the art of conversation—that art which, I understand, is supposed to be lost now. My young days, the days when one's habits and character are formed, have been rather familiar with long silences. Such voices as broke into them were anything but conversational. No. I haven't got the habit. Yet this discursiveness is not so irrelevant to the handful of pages which follow. They, too, have been charged with discursiveness, with disregard of chronological order (which is in itself a crime) with unconventionality of form (which is an impropriety). I was told severely that the public would view with displeasure the informal character of my recollections. "Alas!" I protested, mildly. "Could I begin with the sacramental words, 'I was born on such a date in such a place?' The remoteness of the locality would have robbed the statement of all interest. I haven't lived through wonderful adventures to be related *seriatim*. I haven't known distinguished men on whom I could pass fatuous remarks. I haven't been mixed up with great or scandalous affairs. This is but a bit of psychological document, and even so, I haven't written it with a view to put forward any conclusion of my own."

But my objector was not placated. These were good reasons for not writing at all—not a defence of what stood written already, he said.

I admit that almost anything, anything in the world, would serve as a good reason for not writing at all. But since I have written them, all I want to say in their defence is that these memories put down without any regard for established conventions have not been thrown off without system and purpose. They have their hope and their aim. The hope that from the reading of these pages there may emerge at last the vision of a personality; the man behind the books so fundamentally dissimilar as, for instance, *Almayer's Folly* and *The Secret Agent*, and yet a coherent, justifiable personality both in its origin and in its action. This is the hope. The immediate aim, closely associated with the hope, is to give the record of personal memories by presenting faithfully the feelings and sensations connected with the writing of my first book and with my first contact with the sea.

In the purposely mingled resonance of this double strain a friend here and there will perhaps detect a subtle accord.

G. JEAN-AUBRY

[Conrad on the *Narcissus*]†

* * *

After his return from Marienbad and Dresden, he did not stay
long in London. On the 10th of September, 1883, he embarked as
second mate on board the sailing ship *Riversdale*, bound for
Madras. She was a ship of 1,500 tons, of the port of London. We
have no information about this voyage, but it seems to have suggested some scenes in the *Ferndale* episodes of *Chance*. It appears, however, that Conrad had a dispute with his captain, L. B.
McDonald,[1] in consequence of which he threw up his berth and
left the ship at Madras. From Madras he went to Bombay to look
for a new commission. He was first offered one on board a mail boat
of the British-India line, navigating in the Persian Gulf, but he was
reluctant to serve on board a steamer if he could possibly avoid it.
One evening he was sitting with other officers of the Mercantile
Marine on the veranda of the Sailors' Home in Bombay, which
overlooks the port, when he saw a lovely ship, with all the graces of
a yacht, come sailing into the harbour. She was the *Narcissus*, of
1,300 tons, built by a sugar refiner of Greenock nine years before.
Her owner had originally intended her for some undertaking in
connection with the Brazilian sugar trade. This had not come off,
and subsequently he had decided to employ her in the Indian
Ocean and the Far East.[2] Some days later, Joseph Conrad Korzeniowski became her second mate.

She left Bombay on April 28th, and was dismantled at Dunkirk
on the 17th of October following. Her name, the *Narcissus*, is, of
course, familiar to all who know the work of Joseph Conrad. It has
been immortalized in *The Nigger of the "Narcissus,"* one of his
indisputable masterpieces describing ships and the sea. The spirit
of that book is not only the creation of the writer's genius, it
also owes much to his memory. *The Nigger of the "Narcissus"* is
really a realistic and lyrical record of six months of Conrad's life
during the year 1884.

I obtained from Conrad himself some details as to the extent to
which the novel follows fact, and I write them down here just as he
gave them to me in conversation a little before his death:

† From G. Jean-Aubry, ed., *Joseph
Conrad: Life and Letters,* 2 vols. (New
York: Doubleday, 1927), Vol. I, pp.
76–78.
1. On the back of Conrad's certificate
of discharge from the *Riversdale* is written opposite "character for ability," in
the captain's hand, "Very good," while
"character for conduct" is annotated
in the same hand with the single word,
"Decline." This is the only example of
an unfavorable comment in the thirteen
certificates which were found among
Conrad's papers.
2. Information given me by Conrad
himself.

The voyage of the *Narcissus* was performed from Bombay to London in the manner I have described. As a matter of fact, the name of the Nigger of the *Narcissus* was not James Wait, which was the name of another nigger we had on board the *Duke of Sutherland*, and I was inspired with the first scene in the book by an episode in the embarkation of the crew at Gravesend on board the same *Duke of Sutherland*, one of the first ships the crew of which I joined. I have forgotten the name of the real Nigger of the *Narcissus*. As you know, I do not write history, but fiction, and I am therefore entitled to choose as I please what is most suitable in regard to characters and particulars to help me in the general impression I wish to produce. Most of the personages I have portrayed actually belonged to the crew of the real *Narcissus*, including the admirable Singleton (whose real same was Sullivan), Archie, Belfast, and Donkin. I got the two Scandinavians from associations with another ship. All this is now old, but it was quite present before my mind when I wrote this book. I remember, as if it had occurred but yesterday, the last occasion I saw the Nigger. That morning I was quarter officer, and about five o'clock I entered the double-bedded cabin where he was lying full length. On the lower bunk, ropes, fids and pieces of cloth had been deposited, so as not to have to take them down into the sail-room if they should be wanted at once. I asked him how he felt, but he hardly made me any answer. A little later a man brought him some coffee in a cup provided with a hook to suspend it on the edge of the bunk. At about six o'clock the officer-in-charge came to tell me that he was dead. We had just experienced an awful gale in the vicinity of the Needles, south of the cape, of which I have tried to give an impression in my book. . . .

As to the conclusion of the book, it is taken from other voyages which I made under similar circumstances. It was, in fact, at Dunkirk, where I had to unload part of her cargo, that I left the *Narcissus*.[3]

From this beautiful book and *The Mirror of the Sea* we know what Conrad's life was like, not only during the voyage of the *Narcissus*, but during the twenty years he spent on board sailing ships. The atmosphere, the dangers, the fatigues of that life, become real to us; also its arduous beauty, which appealed intimately to Conrad, brought up from childhood, as he was, to be familiar with the sentiment of the sublime and with struggle against odds.

He passed the winter of that year in London. On April 24, 1885, he left Hull as second mate on board the *Tilkhurst*, a London sailing ship of 1,500 tons. He disembarked at Cardiff on the 31st of May, but signed on again five days later, his destination being this time Singapore.

* * *

3. These notes were taken in June, 1924, at Oswald's, Bishopsbourne, Kent, after a conversation with Joseph Conrad about *The Nigger of the "Narcissus,"* apropos of a new edition of Robert d'Humières' translation of that book into French.

GERALD MORGAN

The Book of the Ship *Narcissus*†

The nineteenth century is remembered for the triumph of steam on the sea, which was contested and served by wind-ship marvels of swift grace. Among the throng of full-rigged ships launched from Clyde yards were those built for C. S. Caird in the 1870s and 1880s and known as "Caird's beauties." Lovely of line, they were named for legends of beauty and the sea: for Galatea, Nereus, Euphrosyne, Narcissus, Amphitrite, Poseidon.[1]

I: The Ship

The fleet began with *Narcissus*, though she was not the pride of Caird's shipyard at Greenock. She was launched instead from Robert Duncan's yard, a mile further upstream towards Saint Mungo's city; Duncans, one of eight Port Glasgow shipyards (their names now vanished) outpaced scores of others making a clangor on Clyde shores. The wonder of floating iron was still fresh; the expansion of steam was a matter beyond doubt, and builders for the world of those days might well tumble aside a granite kirk, a graveyard, a village, to raise up rows of keels, frames, iron-plated hulls; but the craft of sail still challenged a shipwright's art. Robert Duncan, having launched in 1873 one of the few steamers to measure 3,000 tons gross, still could not forbear from the iron sailing-ships of 2,000 tons or less. He built and sparred the three-masted full-rigged ship *Narcissus* under the shrewd survey of a Lloyd's man, who classified her in 1876.

She was 235 feet long (216 feet at the waterline), with short raised forecastle and poop and one deckhouse on the main deck; her beam amidships was 37 feet. She had two decks, her inside depth from upper (main) deck beams to keelson being 22 feet less 2 inches. Fully rigged, stored, loaded to a draft of 18 feet in salt water, her yachtlike form (about 0.63 coefficient of fineness) displaced some 2,590 tons. Lloyd's measured her space between beam and keel at 100 cubic feet per ton, and registered her underdeck tonnage as 1,200 tons. Added to this, the enclosed spaces above the main deck gave her a gross measure of 1,336 tons. Excluding space for living quarters, stoves, fresh water, and workshops, her measure was 1,270 tons net, on which she would be assessed for port fees,

---

† Written especially for this edition.
1. Details of ships, builders etc. are given in *Lloyd's Register* 1878 to 1892; histories in Basil Lubbock, *The Last of the Wind-jammers* (Glasgow, 1929) and *Sail* (New York, 1972). See also Harold Underhill, *Masting and Rigging* (Glasgow, 1946).

and lighthouse and other dues, throughout her life at sea. She became, for history: British ship *Narcissus*, 1,270 tons; thirty-eighth vessel registered at Greenock during 1876; official number 76149.

To this measured slim hull of *Narcissus*, Duncan's wrights gave a sweet sheer of the deck and an elegant S-curve cutwater for her stem. Having built her to float, when loaded, with her main deck 49 inches above the ocean, they shielded the deck with 5-foot iron bulwarks guarding 146 feet between forecastle and poop. They drew the lift of her lines far past the bow, with 70 feet of bowsprit and jib boom to spear the air 35 feet above a level sea and to stretch four headsails, leading with the outer jib on a foreroyal stay 142 feet long. They made her a tall ship. They gave her a mainmast growing 130 feet above the deck, with a foremast and mizzen to match. Six sails soared in a tapering tower along each mast, from the huge courses (70 feet wide and 30 feet deep at the bunt) aloft to the royals (as wide as the ship and 12 feet deep), 124 feet in the air.[2]

To man her aerial machinery of eighteen square sails, a spanker, and four headsails and nine staysails, with their lifts, halyards, downhauls, braces, buntlines, sheets, and tacks (led to the usual 135 belaying pins between knightheads forward and taffrail aft) *Narcissus* had her live components: her master and two mates, sail-maker, boatswain, carpenter, ten foremasthands and two boys, and a cook and steward. The captain and mates lived under the poop, the sailors in the forecastle; the cook, steward, and petty officers lived in a deckhouse 34 feet long (containing also the galley and the carpenter's shop) between the foremast and mainmast, 30 feet from the forecastle and 80 feet from the poop.

Narcissus was deemed fully manned with twenty hands all told, though she could accommodate fifty. She broke no speed records but she won the regard of seamen, and she made some good passages in the years 1882–84, while she was owned by Robert Paterson. During this time she made the voyage of the mad steward, followed by the voyage of the mad mate, the Georgia Negro, and the Polish second mate Joseph Conrad Korzeniowski, which last put her into a novel.[3]

Her master then was the forty-year-old Archibald Duncan of Campbellton: a confident and kindly man, thrifty on his owner's behalf. He had lately succeeded Captain McIntosh. Later in 1882 he sailed *Narcissus* from Liverpool and reached Calcutta in four months, having to replace only three men during two months on the Ganges. An ancient wooden barque, *Palestine,* which had left

2. Details of rig from *Narcissus* sail plan owned by Ugo Mursia and reproduced by Giuseppe Annovazzi in *Fifty Famous Italian Ships* (Milano, 1971), p. 108.

3. Voyages of British vessels are recorded in *Agreement and Account of Crew* for each voyage; records for 1878–94 are now held with Board of Trade papers at Public Record Office, London.

England within a week or two of *Narcissus*, had been crawling across the Indian Ocean, bound for Bangkok, almost till *Narcissus* was loaded for home. News reached Calcutta before Captain Duncan sailed, on March 24, 1883, that *Palestine* had been lost by explosion of her coal cargo ten days earlier in the Banka Strait. The fire in *Palestine* affected many other ships, including *Narcissus*, by prompting later government action to reduce peril; but Duncan at the time was probably more concerned with his steward. Duncan sailed *Narcissus* on a five-month passage to Dundee, where he had to pay the steward's wages to a government official because the steward was by now too mad to look after himself. When the rest of the crew was paid off and *Narcissus* unloaded her jute cargo, Duncan was less than pleased to learn that his own graceful ship had been chartered into the coal trade.

Other beauties had gone the same way. The hated and successful "steam kettles" forced more and more wind ships into earning their way as fuel carreiers. Coal paid a shady speculator who sent out decrepit *Palestine* to profit or perish (with a Polish second mate on board). Even the staunch John Willis had sent his China clipper *Cutty-Sark* away with coal in 1880 (for a voyage preserved in Conrad's *Lord Jim* and "Secret Sharer"). Coal paid the way for some of W. Price's fleet of hefty full-riggers with the Kentish names: *Tilkhurst*, *Falconhurst*, *Lyndhurst*. One of these, the 1500-ton iron *Tilkhurst*, lay discharging jute near *Narcissus* at Dundee, in September 1883. The two met again in October at Penarth, loading Welsh coal, and would enter the Indian Ocean again within days of each other. Each in turn, like *Falconhurst*, was to be sailed (and immortalized) by the Polish second mate of the sunken *Palestine*, who had left British waters that September 1883 as second mate of the 1,500-ton full-rigged *Riversdale* bound for Port Elizabeth.

Captain Duncan sailed *Narcissus* from Dundee to Wales with a fresh crew, of which he kept only three men back when paying off at Penarth: the Norwegian carpenter, the Canadian boatswain, and a Swedish able seaman. (The boatswain, John Evans of Kingston, had made the Calcutta voyage in *Narcissus* as able seaman; he was the only man on the Bombay voyage who could not write). For the ocean voyage Duncan signed on a Scottish mate and seventeen more hands, including four Welshmen and ten German and Scandinavian sailors. He also engaged a second mate older than himself, who then failed to join the ship, as did a German able seaman. Both were left ashore when Duncan sailed for Capetown on Sunday, November 3, 1883, without a second mate, after signing on another seaman at the last moment in his cabin.

Lacking a second mate, the ship was legally unseaworthy, and since there was no man he cared to promote, Captain Duncan had to stand watch and watch with his chief mate for seventy-five days.

They brought the ship from northern winter to southern summer without mishap, and came with some hope of relief into Table Bay on Thursday, January 17, 1884.

Next day the German steward was paid off in Capetown. After a week Captain Duncan signed on another cook, at a saving to the owner, and likewise engaged an ordinary seaman in place of an able seaman who had failed to join the ship at Penarth. Meanwhile two Scandinavians had deserted, while the last man to join at Penarth had found his way into Capetown jail. Captain Duncan was able to sign on three more British seamen, but on Monday, January 28, 1884, he set sail for Bombay with the second mate's berth still empty.

A few days later *Narcissus* passed the far-off Port Elizabeth, below the northern horizon, where *Riversdale* lay at the anchorage heavily moored against southeast gales (mentioned in Conrad's *Chance* and "The Partner"). *Tilkhurst* rounded the Cape a week later, to reach Port Elizabeth three days after *Riversdale* had sailed for Madras. By the end of February *Tilkhurst* had weighed anchor again for her voyage round the world, which brought her after fourteen months to Hull, where Conrad would join her for his second India voyage. Meanwhile *Riversdale* on a two-month passage to Madras overtook *Narcissus* on a three-month passage to Bombay, although the Liverpool ship was eleven years older than the Greenock beauty, which entered Bombay harbor on Sunday, April 27, 1884.

As she passed Colaba Point and glided by Cross Island, *Narcissus* stirred the admiration of Sunday loungers on the verandah of the Bombay Sailor's Home. Conrad was among them. Having quit *Riversdale* at Madras after bitter wrangling with her master (recalled in his novel *The Rescue*), and traveled overland to Bombay, he was now hoping to "give up the sea" and join a smart British India steamer (mayhap the *Patna*, launched in 1871?). Hearing that *Narcissus* wanted a second mate, he recanted instantly and hastened on board.[4] He had to show an adverse report of conduct from *Riversdale*; but this, when explained, weighed less with Captain Duncan than the recent 165 days at sea lacking a second mate. It would be rash to have blamed anyone for a quarrel in the hot, sticky weather, daily more oppressive, with the southwest monsoon about to break. Duncan engaged the young Polish officer at once, even before paying off three Capetown and two Penarth hands. Eight days later the Scottish chief mate left the ship; it seemed that his mates were to be the bane of Duncan, that voyage. Conrad took charge of ship and cargo for a week. Duncan then gave another sign of self-confidence (or desperation) by engaging a new mate, Hamilton Hart of Hull, who was not only older than Duncan (like the second mate

4. Early recall of Conrad's sea life is found in G. Jean-Aubry, ed., *Joseph* *Conrad: Life and Letters*, 2 vols. (New York, 1927).

missing at Penarth), but came from a mere "country" ship: the *Storm Queen* of Calcutta (of a kind, and a name, recalled in *Lord Jim*).

None of the Welshmen left *Narcissus*, though ten of her Penarth company had gone by now. Her complement was raised to twenty-four, by six fresh able seamen signed on by Duncan before sailing. These six came from three ships: a Cockney, an Irishman, and a Norwegian from the big Boston ship *Pharos*; a Scot and a Guernsey man from the Welsh vessel *County of Cardigan*; and a Georgia Negro from the Glasgow racer *County of Dumfries*.

At the end of May *Narcissus* mustered, for an epochal voyage, an Argyll captain, a Yorkshire mate, a Polish second mate; Norwegian carpenter, Canadian boatswain, Australian sailmaker; two English cooks, and sixteen foremast hands from seven countries. There was one Georgia Negro on board, and three Londoners: Youtton, the cook; Harry Powell, the ordinary seaman (both since Capetown); and Wild, the able seaman, who had come from *Pharos* with his friends, one of these the Belfast able seaman Craig. The solitary Finn was Lofstedt, aboard since Penarth. There were four Welshmen: Williams, Thomas, Morgan, Mathews. The Scandinavians numbered Nilsson (aged twenty-two), Jansson (aged twenty), and four others, including the carpenter. The one Scot, besides the captain, was Archie McLean, who had come from *County of Cardigan* with his friend John Williams of Guernsey.

For the second time, *Narcissus* sailed from India with news of disaster from one of Conrad's ships. *Riversdale* had been stranded at Masulipatam and declared a wreck on May 31. Captain Duncan, remembering *Palestine*, could reflect that he had survived a coal cargo with no second mate at all, which might be better than having a Jonah second mate on board; but he kept Conrad when sailing *Narcissus* from Bombay on Tuesday, June 3, 1884, into the rainy monsoon, and proved his luck.

Trouble came to the ship far at sea, when the new mate went mad[5] with melancholy (earning places for his name, and malady, in *The Shadow-Line*). Conrad, trained to "crack-on-sail" by Captain Stuart of *Loch Etive*, now had a chance to prove his worth as he drove *Narcissus* along for Captain Duncan.

This duty was his relief from the "dreadful boredom" of weeks without books. He liked the risky balancing of myriad stresses in the huge gear aloft, where seam, splice, sheave, shackle, and spar were stressed against each other by force of air and motion of the sea. From the mainyard (two feet thick at the slings) to the royals, to the slender studding booms run out with their sails in fair

5. John D. Gordon, *Joseph Conrad: The Making of a Novelist* (Cambridge, Mass., 1941), pp. 55, 349.

weather (lengthening the foreyard to 135 feet athwart ship and sea), all hung on his feel for *Narcissus* in her element; on his voice, giving commands in English; on the scarred hands of sailors.

Narcissus reached port with her masts and spars intact, but she lost a man. She went fairly fast, almost at clipper speeds, to the Dunkirk pilot in 136 days.

Weathering the Cape of Storms or edging through the doldrums, she may have been helped by having one seaman straight from a clipper, Jimmy Barron from *County of Dumfries*. The mate recovered after a while; the Negro died when the work was nearly done, with *Narcissus* near the Azores and eighteen days from Dunkirk. On Wednesday, September 24, 1884, Conrad took part in the first of his sea burials.

At Dunkirk (recalled in Conrad's tale "The Black Mate") Captain Duncan gave Conrad a good testimonial: Conrad could come back officially as mate if he passed the government examination he was leaving to write. Captain Duncan gave the dead Negro's wages and sea chest to the British consul, and paid off all the ship's company except one able seaman. When *Narcissus* was unloaded he sailed her, with a new mate and nine French seamen, back to Penarth for her next coal cargo.

This time at Penarth, *Narcissus* loaded shortly before Price's big 2,000-ton full-rigged *Falconhurst*. Here one of Conrad's recent shipmates anticipated Conrad's own fate. The able seaman, John Williams of Guernsey, having left *Narcissus* at Dunkirk, joined *Falconhurst* for another Eastern voyage which he ended in the Singapore hospital seven months later; no doubt he talked of the Polish second mate who had sailed *Narcissus*. Conrad meanwhile had joined *Tilkhurst* at Hull, home of the "mad" mate of *Narcissus*. In due course Conrad joined *Falconhurst* at London in December 1886, though he soon left her at Penarth; seven months later he was obliged to leave his next ship for the Singapore hospital. (*Falconhurst* is recalled in "The Brute," the hospital in *Lord Jim*.)

Narcissus maintained a shadowy presence in Conrad's subsequent seafaring. Thirty years after leaving her at Dunkirk he saw her for the last time—if indeed he noticed her. Escaping from Austrian occupied Poland during the first weeks of war in 1914, he took his family on board a Dutch mail boat homeward-bound from the East (so many of these had steamed through his tales!), at Genoa. Moored in the harbor of Genoa lay the hulk of *Narcissus*, owned by Italians.[6] Conrad himself had been idle, as sailor, for more than twenty years.

For the next two years, Conrad the author doubled as a private

6. Jerry Allen, *The Sea Years of Joseph Conrad* (New York, 1965), pp. 169, 321. It was Miss Allen who discovered that the Board of Trade papers (note 3 above) are still extant.

Polish diplomat. In 1916 he interviewed Sir George Clerk at the Foreign Office, concerning Poland's postwar existence. Clerk remarked, in parting:

> I never thought I would have this sort of conversation with the author of *The Nigger of the "Narcissus."*[7]

In the same year, 1916, Conrad returned to Dundee (last seen in *Tilkhurst*) as an important guest of the Admiralty. He was being "given the tour" in the hope that he would write naval propaganda of the kind that Kipling and others were turning out. Conrad did not oblige, just then. He used the occasion to make his last voyage under sail, in a forty-year old wooden brigantine of 110 tons, an armed decoy disguised with Norwegian name and flag, sent out to sink German submarines. The winter patrol along the Bergen route, when the cold sea swirled knee-deep in the cabin at times, revived the spirits of the fifty-nine-year old Conrad immensely.[8] It was in this year too that *Narcissus* went back to sea, rerigged as a barque, wearing the flag of Brazil and the name *Isis*. She was hulked for the last time in 1925, the year after Conrad's death.

II: *The Tale*

Often it seems that an author can set "life" aside. The force of steam is felt as fact, when Captain Conrad Korzeniowski becomes a steamer's second mate in 1894, and makes his last attempt to land a job as Suez Canal pilot. But the captain's choice does not mean that the values of life must change for Conrad the author, when he appears. Conrad champions the cause which, by his own actions, he has declared to be lost; he becomes the prose bard of the last great age of sail.

Within three years of the Suez attempt, Conrad is writing his first deep-sea novel. The work changes his perspective, while it interferes with his eighteen attempts to get a command at sea; he finds himself writing a valedictory to the ocean world. More specifically, it is his farewell tribute to life under sail. It is not about steamers, except as a caution. It is not the tale of his own achievement in command of the barque *Otago*. It is a selfless tribute to all his teachers, whether men or ships; it marks the lesson they teach; it names for the first and only time in Conrad's fiction, a deep-sea ship he has sailed: thus *The Nigger of the "Narcissus."*

The novel is the tale of a single voyage, from Bombay, in a ship as wanderer-symbol ("planet") of mankind. Yet the ship-symbol *Narcissus* is not the actual vessel Conrad drove through the gales; nor is her crew the same; nor is the famous Negro the same; nor is the doughty captain.

7. Conrad, letter of August 20, 1916; in Jean-Aubry, II, 174.

8. J. G. Sutherland, *At Sea with Joseph Conrad* (London, 1922).

As usual, Conradian time is a fictive dimension through which historical selves, and ships, are transposed across years and longitudes; but here the movement evolves as a pageant of honor, with figures chosen for reasons mostly unknown. The symbolic ship herself is formed of two ships, seven years apart in Conrad's sea life: of *Narcissus*, with a touch of "the beautiful *Torrens*" of the same size (praised in *Last Essays*). Her crew appear as if summoned by name, from these and three others of Conrad's ships, across various periods in thirteen years, to a journey more imagined than remembered. Her captain comes from the ship in which he has died, which yet cleaves the real sea (like *Narcissus*) while Conrad is writing his tribute.

The actual *Narcissus* had a short poop, extending 37 feet from the stern to the mizzenmast, and breaking at 63 feet abaft the mainmast. The ship in Conrad's novel has a long poop, from which the captain steps on deck close to the mainmast. This long poop is needed in passenger ships only, such as the famous *Torrens*, sailed by Conrad as chief officer from 1891 to 1893, she being 13 feet shorter than *Narcissus* and built with a poop 50 feet longer.

Where the boats are stowed, and whether they are washed away in the storm, we shall never know: the crew of *Narcissus* lives without them. Sharpness of detail has power to evoke a particular ship from an abstract idea of a ship; and it was Conrad's gift to discern, as Baudelaire could not, that symbolic value depends on concreteness of image. He renders magnificently the motion of the sea, though his skill is obscured by verbs in the preterite tense. But he omits the measure of masts and spars dragged through the water; also the ship's tonnage, port of registry, prospects, and present cargo. Gradually he reveals that the ship has made seven voyages since her launching on the Clyde; that she has a gray-painted iron hull, an open deck with a midship house and a pigsty; that she is rigged for studding-sails, and her shrouds are set up in the old way with deadeyes instead of bottle screws; that her poop cabins open directly onto the main deck, and that her foremast hands live under the forecastle instead of in a midship house, except for the "sick" Negro. The ship must be exceedingly well rigged, since she can lie capsized for twenty-four hours, with her yards and rigging awash and beaten by storm waves, without losing a single spar.

We hear the men speak to each other, but from a distance, or from a stage afloat, as if they were playing expected parts to themselves; their meanings are carried, tossed about, lost in the narrative stream. As a crew they are strangely muffled, even when free of a guilty care for Wait; though they are mostly English-speaking, they never sing a chantey for raising the anchor or for shifting or sweating-up or bunting a sail. This may be a tribute of realism to *Narcissus*, which actually had six Scandinavians aboard instead of the two of the novel. Few of the men belong, in memory, to the ship; they are brought together by Conrad's fusion of his most memorable voyages into one tale. The "crew of shades" for his symbolic *Narcissus* take their names, and some qualities, from his shipmates on four voyages between 1878 and 1893.

Three men, or five, belong to the actual *Narcissus*. "Young Nilsen" joined her at Dundee (as Nilsson) and stayed for the voyage; so did "Hansen" at Penarth, if he is Jansson the Swede and not the Johanson who made two voyages in *Torrens* with Conrad. "Archie" Maclean came on board at Bombay with his two ship-mates from *Pharos*; one of these was "Belfast" Craig, who, in the novel, has joined *Narcissus* so much earlier as to have made a friend of the cook. This conceited cook-hero, "Hallelujah Podmore," may represent the actual crazy steward who had been put ashore at Dundee after the previous voyage of *Narcissus*; in the novel he shares a surname with the original of Conrad's *Lord Jim*.[9]

Others on board the symbolic ship have displaced the actual crew of *Narcissus* as individuals rather than types, in Conrad's trans-mutation of the real. A Scottish captain, an English mate, a New World Negro, a solitary Finn—these did sail in *Narcissus* with sea-men from London and Wales, besides a Polish second mate who seems, at first, to be absent from the tale.

The *Narcissus* voyage is enclosed by memories of the *Duke of Sutherland* voyage (1878–79) and controlled by the *Loch Etive* voyage (1880–81), with some reminiscence from the *Riversdale* and *Tilkhurst* voyages mentioned above. The boarding scene at Bombay has been shifted from *Duke of Sutherland*, anchored at Gravesend in 1878, where Conrad began his first, and worst, deep-sea voyage in a British ship (he was "shanghaied" on a voyage round the world at a pay of one shilling a month). The docking scene has been shifted from Dunkirk to London, recalling Conrad's first arrival at the sooty metropolis from the open sea, in the same ship. Between these scenes, four people have appeared from the same voyage as the scenes. The gruff, kindly mate of the ship-symbol is not Hamil-ton Hart of *Narcissus* but Baker of *Duke of Sutherland*, a Norfolk man who took pity on the Polish ordinary seaman from the Lowes-toft schooner in 1878. From the same ship come "lame Knowles," one of Baker's favorites; and the Welshman "Taffy Davis," who relieves Singleton after the storm; and "Jimmy Wait" the Barbados Negro, who hails from Saint Kitt's in the novel.

Captain Duncan of *Narcissus* is displaced by the famous Captain Stuart of Peterhead, sometime whalerman, later champion of China Sea and Australia races. Master of *Loch Etive* from the day of her launching, he carried a Peterhead carpenter and a Peterhead sail-maker, John Alleston, under whose name the captain appears in the

9. Allen, pp. 120–22, 166.

novel. In 1880 Stuart promoted Alleston to second mate, when he also engaged a Polish third mate. Making, among this Peterhead group, his first voyage as officer, Conrad had learned from Captain Stuart the habit of "carrying on sail," which he still practiced thirteen years later in *Torrens* whenever the captain of that ship went below. Captain Stuart died aboard *Loch Etive* in 1894 at sea, after forty-six years of command without ever having lost a man or a mast overboard. Like an epitaph, the symbolic ship of Conrad's novel preserves his reputation; four years after his death, the will of "Captain Alleston" alone saves the masts of capsized *Narcissus* from the fear and prudence of her crew.

The actual Canadian boatswain of *Narcissus* is displaced by the Devon boatswain from *Loch Etive*, though the "authoritative drawl" may have been characteristic of both. The Finn of *Narcissus* gives way to the "Russian Finn," "Wamibo," whose name compounds Wamibo, the Norewegian of *Loch Etive's* outward voyage to Sydney, with Waraboi, the Finn of the same ship's homeward voyage. From the same tall ship comes the able seaman Smith to answer the *Duke of Sutherland* mate's roll call aboard *Narcissus*.

Another seaman, or two, at the roll call, sailed with Conrad in *Torrens* of the long poop, during his first voyage (1891–92) in a sailing passenger-ship: "Campbell," and possibly the "Hansen" already mentioned. The voyages in *Torrens* were memorable for the change of style, and shipboard company, afforded to Conrad after seventeen years in cargo vessels. One of Conrad's tasks had been to set up the new rigging in *Torrens*, which had been dismasted by a squall on her previous voyage; in his novel (perhaps with Captain Stuart in mind) Conrad spares *Narcissus* the havoc of a dismasting. Whatever mishaps befall them, the 400-odd ships in his other fictions are spared in the same way.

Three men aboard the symbolic *Narcissus*, besides the cook Podmore, have names which do not figure in the sixteen British lists of Conrad's shipmates. These are "old Singleton," "Donkin," and "Creighton" the second mate. "Singleton" is named for singularity, being drawn almost as caricature or as heraldic emblem (himself tattooed) of unconscious virtue. He is fifty-seven years old, uncorrupted by the land; in forty-five years at sea he has spent barely forty months ashore. As a vatic logician he dumbfounds the crew: Wait will die, all men will die. While his sententious folk wisdom serves Conrad's irony, he can pass judgment on the model captain: "It's no good bein' angry with the winds of heaven"; so that heaven in due course behaves like a lunatic, with *Narcissus* its toy, and the ancient sea pounds down Singleton's strength. Conrad has said that this persona belongs to fifty-four-year old Daniel Sullivan of County Kerry, who sailed from Penarth in *Tilkhurst* with Conrad (1885); he was singular then as the oldest man on board, the only man to quit the ship during her eight weeks at Calcutta. In the novel, the episode of the overloaded ship (discussed by the crew of *Narcissus*, all of them cynical about a Cardiff magistrate) may echo Conrad's memories of *Tilkhurst* or *Falconhurst* and Penarth, if not actual *Narcissus* gossip of that port.

Seldom can the same figure serve for two caricatures at once, be the ironies ever so mild. "Belfast" is the stock Irishman of the ship-symbol (Conrad had three Irish together for one voyage, when master of *Otago* in 1888); this being so, Sullivan the Irishman must change his name to "Singleton" as the oxlike extreme of sea-worthiness, the stock shellback of *Narcissus*. It is otherwise with "Donkin," who is drawn as a double caricature, both a loathsome Cockney and an extreme of shoreside evil, unconvincing antithesis of "Singleton." The function of "Donkin" is to negate all values ascribed to ship and sea; his actual source is untraceable, his rank in the *Narcissus* fiction obscure. He complains of working for a mere two pounds ten shillings a month, and no one argues with him, though he seems to do duty as able seaman, and should be earning three pounds a month; the sum he quotes is an ordinary seaman's pay (albeit Captain Duncan paid his two Welsh able seamen at the low rate of two pounds fifteen). He is one of the only two Cock-neys on board the ship-symbol, the other being "young Charlie," the ordinary seaman who is schooled by the crew. The actual *Narcissus* had two Cockneys: Powell, the ordinary seaman, joined at and stayed as far as Dunkirk; John Wild, the able seaman, joined at Bombay with his shipmates "Archie" and "Belfast" from *Pharos*. "Donkin" likewise comes on board at Bombay from a full-rigged Yankee ship, but he is a lone deserter from *Golden State* (named for an actual Yankee clipper which never sailed to India).[1] Being merely a symbol, he is named as a symbol. Donkin was the name of a London steamship owner who had interests in the Suez Canal,[2] being thereby doubly odious to any champions of sail.

Like "Donkin," the unnamed sailmaker of the ship-symbol, is of uncertain provenance. He is a naval reservist, having served in the frigate *Blanche* on the West Indian station (so as to be, histori-cally, more than 80 years old). Among Conrad's shipmates were only two known reservists: Captain Jones of *Falconhurst* and the able seaman Cummings, who walked overboard from *Tilkhurst* in the Malacca Strait. The actual sailmaker of *Narcissus* was fifty-three year-old W. G. Allen of Sydney, who would at least have known about the gunboat H.M.S. *Blanche* and her action to curb the Queensland slave trade from the islands (mentioned in *Lord Jim*) in 1871, eight years before Conrad first came to Sydney in *Duke of Sutherland*. (Conrad sets the frigate *Blanche* properly in the West Indies, in his Napoleonic tale "The Inn of the Two Witches.")

1. Details of *Pharos* and *Golden State* kindly provided by Mrs. Carole Bowker of the G. W. Blunt White Library, Mys- tic Seaport.
2. D. A. Farnie, *East and West of Suez* (Oxford, 1969), passim.

"Creighton," the second mate, is terse, competent, heedless of self—a model officer. His name, like "Singleton," "Donkin," "Podmore," does not belong in the crowd of Conrad's shipmates. But any second mate of *Narcissus*, with any name other than Conrad Korzeniowski, must be there only to take Conrad's place. No Polish sailor ever appears as such in Conrad's fictions (excepting the nameless narrator of "Prince Roman," far inland). There was no sea tradition for a Pole to represent. The function of a Pole in Conrad's tale is to be a patriot, open or secret, noble or peasant, faithful or false: to play, in a conquered land, exactly that role which Conrad declined when choosing the sea.

"Creighton" is one of Conrad's two representatives aboard *Narcissus*, insofar as his shipmates take him for a gentleman. He is injured during the storm, less severely than Conrad was in *Highland Forest* (1887, described in *Lord Jim*). He is not an author like Conrad's other, nameless substitute on board. Conrad at sea was doubly peculiar, as poetic foreigner, in French, British, Belgian ships; ashore he masked the fact through his nautical narrators. These are always English, usually captains. The peculiar Captain Marlowe serves for four tales, then a nameless captain reports the voyages of Conrad's nameless *Otago* (in "Falk," "The Secret Sharer," *The Shadow-Line*, "A Smile of Fortune"). In his first sea novel, however, beginning a trial of first-person narration, Conrad could not use a captain's voice in a tribute to Captain Stuart. He would not then, or ever (except in "The Brute"), use mainly a mate's voice; hence "Creighton."

The result is that Conrad's replacement for himself as narrator of the *Narcissus* voyage is a foremasthand, such as Conrad had been in *Duke of Sutherland*. This nameless, unselfed seaman, who alternates with the omniscient author of the tale, is the only one of his kind among Conrad's nautical narrators. His rank is unspecified. He speaks to us in language finer than the officers', but he uses the forecastle "we" rather than the poop deck "I." Thus he shows Conrad's structural and symbolical *tour de force*, for telling the ills of self-regard in a symbolic ship called *Narcissus*.

The lesson of the voyage is drawn by Conrad for the whole of life. Its exemplars are the "unconscious" Singleton, the self-disdaining captain and mates. Thus far the obvious. Veiled by time is the equally important fact that the lesson is played out by Conrad's own teachers on the sea: by a ship compounded of *Narcissus* and *Torrens*; by a crew whose names, for the most part, make an honor roll from Conrad's own ships; by a mate who treated Conrad kindly, and a great captain who taught him sea mastery under "the true peace of God—a thousand miles from the nearest land."

Reviews and Criticism

Contemporary Reviews

From the *Daily Mail* (London), December 7, 1897

[*"The tale is no tale . . ."*]

* * * The conspicuous ability which Mr. Joseph Conrad displayed in his East Indian novel, *Almayer's Folly* and in his novel of the Malay Archipelago, *An Outcast of the Islands*, led one to open with confident hope his new tale of the sea *The Nigger of the "Narcissus."* Possibly our expectation was too high; anyhow we must admit that in many respects this present work is a disappointment. Mr. Conrad, indeed, is in this instance in the position of the needy knifegrinder—'Story! Lord bless you, sir, I've none to tell.' The tale is no tale, but merely an account of the uneventful voyage of the *Narcissus* from Bombay to the Thames. One of the ship's crew is an intelligent negro named James Wait. He lies in his bunk most of the voyage, and at last he dies and is buried at sea. This is positively all the story in the book. There is no plot, no villainy, no heroism, and, apart from a storm and the death and burial, no incident. The only female in the book is the ship herself, which Mr. Conrad describes lovingly and with an intimate knowledge of seamanship. * * *

From the *Daily Telegraph* (London), December 8, 1897†

[*". . . the ugliest conceivable title . . ."*]

* * * Mr. Joseph Conrad does not shrink from the conditions involved in his literary art. He is an unflinching realist and, therefore, has no hesitation in giving to his singularly vivid and powerful tale of the sea the ugliest conceivable title. No one would say that *The Nigger of the "Narcissus"* was a pretty or attractive inscription to stand at the head of an exceedingly careful and minute study; but we know that aesthetic considerations are held to be of no value by those who are determined to paint with exact and merciless severity facts as they know them. * * * Hence it comes that the seamen of the *Narcissus*—very real, picturesque, and living personages—are heard talking as undoubtedly they ought to talk, and

† Written by W. L. Courtney.

would have talked, without any squeamishness on the part of the author in deference to our sensitive and refined nerves.

There is no doubt an advantage in this form of literal veracity; there is also a disadvantage. A man who is going to delineate an incident, a scene, or the cruise of a merchantship as it actually occurs, will not care for his story so much as for his technique. He is keen to give us the right atmosphere; he will surround his characters with elaborate descriptions of sky and sea, storm and calm; he will spend pages and pages prodigal in careful touches, and deliberate word-painting, so that at the end we may be under the illusion that we have listened to a tale, instead of being invited to a man's studio to see how he works. Mr. Conrad works like an artist—of that we are quite certain when we have finished his book; but we are left with only the vaguest idea of what the story has been all about.

* * *

Everyone will remember what a singular effect Mr. Stephen Crane produced some little time ago by his *Red Badge of Courage*. Mr. Joseph Conrad has chosen Mr. Stephen Crane for his example, and has determined to do for the sea and the sailor what his predecessor had done for war and warriors. The style, though a good deal better than Mr. Crane's, has the same jerky and spasmodic quality; while a spirit of faithful and minute description—even to the verge of the wearisome—is common to both. If we open any page of *The Nigger of the "Narcissus"* we are told with infinite detail what each one was doing, what the ship was doing, and what sky and sea were doing. * * *

From the *Glasgow Herald*, December 9, 1897

["...*plain, unvarnished realism* ..."]

A new novel by the author of *Almayer's Folly* and *An Outcast of the Islands* may well be welcomed by critics, for there is no novelist of the day who is more original in his methods than Mr. Conrad. He has chosen this time to turn from the steamy heat of the Far East to describe simply a voyage from Bombay to England. But how well he does it! * * * There is not a petticoat in all Mr. Conrad's pages. Nor is a burning ship descried on the horizon, nor do the crew land on an uninhabited island. Mr. Conrad is all for plain, unvarnished realism, but realism which only the hand of a master could make attractive. He looks at the crew of the *Narcissus* as if he had lived with them (which we cannot but believe he actually did), and he makes us know them, and if not exactly love them, at least respect them as only a shipmate could. The unfortunate Nigger is to the *Narcissus* even as was the man who shot the albatross to the companions of the Ancient Mariner. He is a hindrance, a curse, a reproach. Yet, he fascinates them, and an almost insane devotion to him, a hypnotic unaccountable pathos overcomes them when they try to deal with his harassing ways. On the voyage a storm is encountered. It takes very many pages to describe, but the reader follows the description breathlessly, and feels as if a storm had never been described before. We have nothing but the highest praise for this distinguished contribution to modern literature. * * *

From the *Daily Chronicle* (London), December 22, 1897

["... *an ordinary voyage* ..."]

* * * There may be better tales of the sea than this, but we have never read anything in the least like it. There is no pirate in it, no wreck, no desert island, no treasure trove. The story is simply an account of an ordinary voyage made by an ordinary sailing ship from Bombay round the Cape to the Thames. Nothing particular happens. There is a big storm, some dissatisfaction among the crew, which never ripens into anything like mutiny, and the least admirable of the men dies and is shot into the water. That is all. Yet there is in that story which sounds so simple a freshness, reality, and peculiar interest which raise the book far above the ordinary level of tales of the sea, and appear to us to leave it in a distinct place by itself. For it is written by a man who knows every phase of the sea, and has sailed as a seaman with varied crews. And (what we may be allowed to think at least as rare a qualification in an author) it is written by a man who can write.

* * *

The burial of Jimmy, the return to England, the passage up the Thames, and entrance into the docks—all are admirable. And in the mothers and one or two other women waiting on the quay we get the one touch of womanhood in the tale; for otherwise the book is entirely free of that eternal feminine.

From the *Spectator* (London), December 25, 1897

["... *vivid picture of life* ..."]

* * * Mr. Joseph Conrad, whose intimate knowledge of the Malay Archipelago was impressively illustrated in those two powerful but sombre novels, *Almayer's Folly* and *An Outcast of the*

Islands, has given us in *The Nigger of the "Narcissus"* an extraordinarily vivid picture of life on board of a sailing-vessel in the merchant marine. The incidents described all take place during a single cruise from Bombay to London; there is no heroine in the plot—for the excellent reason that there is no woman in the ship's company —no love interest, and practically no hero. The central figure is a negro, who ships as a new hand at Bombay, is soon invalided, but rather than admit the truth—for he is dying of consumption—accuses himself of malingering, and when the captain refuses to let him work, appeals so successfully to the feelings of his shipmates as nearly to stir up a mutiny. Eventually he dies in sight of land, having been robbed while in his death-agony by a villainous guttersnipe named Donkin; and at the very moment his body plunges into the sea the long spell of calm ends and a favouring breeze springs up. 'Jimmy Wait,' alternately the mascot and the Jonah of the *Narcissus,* is a type of West Indian negro—he comes from St. Kitt's—that we confess ourselves wholly unacquainted with, in or out of books, but Mr. Conrad's portraiture in every other instance is so convincing that we are content to admit its accuracy here also. As a picture of rough seafaring life, frank yet never offensively realistic, and illustrating with singular force the collective instincts of a ship's crew, as well as the strange and unlikely alliances that spring up on shipboard, this book is of extraordinary merit. * * *

Criticism

ALBERT GUERARD

The Nigger of the "Narcissus" †

The complexities of *Almayer's Folly* are those of a man learning —and with what a perverse instinct for the hardest way!—the language of the novelist. *The Nigger of the "Narcissus"* is the first of the books to carry deliberately and with care the burden of several major interests and various minor ones. The one interest which existed for most readers in 1897 remains a real one today: the faithful document of life and adventure at sea. The story is indeed the tribute to the "children of the sea" that Conrad wanted it to be: a memorial to a masculine society and the successful seizing of a "passing phase of life from the remorseless rush of time."[1] It is certainly a tribute to this particular ship on which (for her beauty) Conrad chose to sail in 1884. But it is also a study in collective psychology; and also, frankly, a symbolic comment on man's nature and destiny; and also, less openly, a prose-poem carrying overtones of myth. No small burden, and one which Conrad carried with more care than usual: one passage exists in as many as seven versions. "It is the book by which, not as a novelist perhaps, but as an artist striving for the utmost sincerity of expression, I am willing to stand or fall."[2]

A rich personal novel can hardly be overinterpreted, but it can be misinterpreted easily enough. The dangers of imbalance are suggested by three other masculine narratives which similarly combine

† From *Conrad the Novelist*, by Albert J. Guerard (Cambridge, Mass.: Harvard University Press, 1958), pp. 100–125 (chapter 3). Some of the footnotes have been omitted.

From Guerard's Preface: "The chapter on *The Nigger of the "Narcissus,"* while certainly as long meditated as the others, may seem very different in manner: more personal, and more elliptical in style. It reads in the assertive manner of an essay, and is 'impressionistic' in the sense that it returns (incrementally, I trust) to the same point three and four times. The fact is that this essay-chapter was written, substantially as it stands and before any of the others, for publication in the *Kenyon Review* (Spring 1957). This may explain why it occasionally makes a familiar assertion as for the first time. I considered rewriting this chapter from beginning to end to bring it more in accord with the tone of the rest, adding for instance more proof and more quotation. But in the end I decided to leave the chapter as it stands as a very direct yet considered expression of my affection for Conrad's work."
1. Preface. [*Editor.*]
2. American Preface. [*Editor.*] John D. Gordon, *Joseph Conrad: The Making of a Novelist* (Harvard: Cambridge, 1941), pp. 141–144.

faithful reporting and large symbolic suggestion. *The Red Badge of Courage* may well present a sacramental vision and still another of the ubiquitous Christ figures which bemuse criticism; the patterns of imagery are challenging. But it is also, importantly, a record of military life. So too I would allow that "The Bear" contains primitive pageant-rites, initiation ritual, the Jungian descent into the unconscious, perhaps even the Jungian mandala. These matters put the critic on his mettle. But he should acknowledge that some of the story's best pages concern hunting in the big woods and the vanishing of these woods before commercial encroachment. The dangers of imbalance are even more serious when provoked by a slighter work, such as *The Old Man and the Sea*. To say that the novel is about growing old, or about the aging artist's need to substitute skill for strength, is plausible. But can a critic be satisfied with so little? One has gone so far as to find a parable of the decline of the British Empire. This, I submit, takes us too far from the boat and the marlin attached to its side; from the small greatness of a story whose first strength lies in its faithful recording of sensations, of fishing and the sea.

The Nigger of the "Narcissus" (sixty years after the event) is peculiarly beset with dangers for the critic. For Conrad has become fashionable rather suddenly, and comment on this story has passed almost without pause from naive recapitulation to highly sophisticated analysis of "cabalistic intent." The older innocence is suggested by Arthur Symons' complaint that the story had no idea behind it, or by a journeyman reviewer's remark that James Wait had no place in this record of life at sea.[3] An example of recent sophistication is Vernon Young's important essay "Trial by Water," in the Spring 1952 issue of *Accent*. A single sentence will suggest its bias: "Fearful of overstressing the subaqueous world of the under-consciousness, the symbol-producing level of the psyche which, in fact, was the most dependable source of his inspiration, Conrad overloaded his mundane treatment of the crew." The comment is provacative; it leads us to wonder whether the crew isn't, for this fiction, too numerous. Yet we must rejoin that the crew is very important, and that many of the book's greatest pages have little to do with this subaqueous world. There remains the vulgar charge yet real menace that the critic may oversimplify a novel by oversubtilizing and overintellectualizing it—not merely by intruding beyond the author's conscious intention (which he is fully privileged to do) but by suggesting patterns of unconscious combination which do not *and cannot operate* for the reasonably alert common reader. Much of any serious story works on the fringes of the reader's consciousness: a darkness to be illumined by the critic's insight. But that insight remains irrelevant which can never become aesthetic

3. Gordon, *Joseph Conrad*, pp. 289, 286.

enjoyment, or which takes a story too far out of its own area of discourse. I say this with the uneasy conviction that criticism should expose itself to as many as possible of a novel's suasions, and that it is only too easy (above all with a Conrad or a Faulkner) to stress the abstract and symbolic at the expense of everything else. One might begin by saying that The Nigger of the "Narcissus" recasts the story of Jonah and anticipates "The Secret Sharer" 's drama of identification. This is a truth but a partial truth. And how many partial truths would be needed to render or even evoke such a mobile as this one. Touch one wire, merely breathe on the lovely thing and it wavers to a new form! In the pursuit of structured meaning—of obvious purpose and overtone of conviction and "cabalistic intent" and unconscious content; of stark symbol and subtle cluster of metaphor—one is tempted to ignore the obvious essentials of technique and style. One may even never get around to mentioning what are, irrespective of structure or concealed meaning, the best-written pages in the book. They are these: the arrival of James Wait on board, the onset of the storm, the overturning of the ship, the righting of the ship, old Singleton at the wheel, the quelling of the mutiny, the death of Wait and his burial, the docking of the ship, the dispersal of the crew.

It seems proper for once to begin with the end: with that large personal impression which an embarrassed criticism often omits altogether. The Nigger of the "Narcissus" is the most generalized of Conrad's novels in its cutting of a cross-section, though one of the least comprehensive. It is a version of our dark human pilgrimage, a vision of disaster illumined by grace. The microcosmic ship is defined early in the second chapter with an almost Victorian obviousness: "On her lived truth and audacious lies; and, like the earth, she was unconscious, fair to see—and condemned by men to an ignoble fate. The august loneliness of her path lent dignity to the sordid inspiration of her pilgrimage. She drove foaming to the south as if guided by the courage of a high endeavour." Or we can narrow the vision to a single sentence near the end: "The dark knot of seamen drifted in sunshine." The interplay of light and dark images throughout conveys the sense of a destiny both good and evil, heroic and foolish, blundered out under a soulless sky. If I were further to reduce the novel to a single key-word, as some critics like to do, I should choose the word grace. In thematic terms not the sea but life at sea is pure and life on earth sordid. Yet the pessimism of The Nigger of the "Narcissus" is (unlike that of The Secret Agent) a modified pessimism, and the gift of grace can circumvent thematic terms. Thus England herself is once imaged as a great ship. The convention of the novel is that the gift of grace may fall anywhere, or anywhere except on the Donkins. The story really ends with the men clinging for a last moment to their solidarity and standing near the Mint, that most representative object of the sordid earth:

> The sunshine of heaven fell like a gift of grace on the mud of the earth, on the remembering and mute stones, on greed, selfishness; on the anxious faces of forgetful men. And to the right of the dark group the stained front of the Mint, cleansed by the flood of light, stood out for a moment dazzling and white like a marble palace in a fairy tale. The crew of the *Narcissus* drifted out of sight.

So the novel's vision is one of man's dignity but also of his "irremediable littleness"—a conclusion reached, to be sure by most great works in the Christian tradition. In "Heart of Darkness," *Lord Jim*, and "The Secret Sharer" we have the initiatory or expiatory descents within the self of individual and almost lost souls; in *Nostromo* we shall see the vast proliferation of good and evil in history and political institution. But *The Nigger of the "Narcissus"* presents the classic human contradiction (and the archetypal descent into self) in collective terms, reduced to the simplicities of shipboard life. The storm tests and bring out the solidarity, courage, and endurance of men banded together in a desperate cause. And the Negro James Wait tests and brings out their egoism, solitude, laziness, anarchy, fear. The structural obligation of the story is to see to it that the two tests do not, for the reader, cancel out.

Presented so schematically, Conrad's vision may seem truly Christian. But this is indeed a soulless sky. In the restless life of symbols sunlight is converted, at one point, to that inhuman Nature which Man must oppose. The Norwegian sailor who chatters at the sun has lost his saving separateness from Nature, and when the sun sets his voice goes out "together with the light." The "completed wisdom" of old Singleton (one of the first Conrad extroverts to achieve some of his own skepticism) sees "an immensity tormented and blind, moaning and furious . . ." And in one of the novels central intellectual statements (the first paragraph of the fourth chapter) the indifferent sea is metaphorically equated with God, and the gift of grace is defined as labor, which prevents man from meditating "at ease upon the complicated and acrid savour of existence." The dignity of man lies in his vast silence and endurance: a dignity tainted by those who clamor for the reward of another life. The message is rather like Faulkner's, and these good seamen are like "good Negroes." But here too, as in other novels of Conrad, man's works and institutions must prepare him to profit from even such grace as this. From our human weakness and from the eternal indifference of things we may yet be saved . . . by authority, tradition, obedience. Thus the only true grace is purely human and even traditional. There are certain men (specifically

Donkin) who remain untouched. But such men exist outside: out-side our moral universe which is both dark and light but not inex-tricably both. And James Wait, as sailor and person rather than symbol? I am not sure. He seems to suffer from that "emptiness" which would be Kurtz's ruin: "only a cold black skin loosely stuffed with soft cotton wool . . . a doll that had lost half its sawdust."

This, speaking neither in terms of gross obvious intentions and themes nor of unconscious symbolic content but of generalized human meaning and ethical bias, is what *The Nigger of the "Nar-cissus"* says. This is its reading of life.

"My task which I am trying to acheive is, by the power of the written word, to make you hear, to make you feel—it is, before all, to make you *see!*" The sea story is beyond praise; there is no need to defend the amount of space and emphasis Conrad gives it. The long third chapter on the storm is one of the summits of Conrad, and the pages on the righting of the ship one of the summits of English prose. This is, as few others, a real ship. At the start the sol-idarity of the forecastle is built up gradually, presumably as on any ship, then disrupted by the foul Donkin and the lazy, narcissistic Wait. A sham fellowship first occurs when the seamen give clothing to Donkin, and is increased by their lazy sympathy for the malin-gering Negro. The true solidarity is created by the exigencies of the storm, and during the worst hours of crisis the good seamen are sig-nificantly separated from Wait, who is trapped in his cabin, buried. With the storm over the individuals again become Individuals, and by the same token capable of mutiny. In the Conrad universe we often have this sense of a few men banded together in desperate opposition to a cosmic indifference and to human nature itself. For this voyage ordinary men have come together, been isolated by their weaknesses, and have come together again. On land they separate once more; for one last poignant moment they are the dark knot of seamen drifting in sunshine. "Good-bye, brothers! You were a good crowd. As good a crowd as ever fisted with wild cries the beating canvas of a heavy foresail; or tossing aloft, invisible in the night, gave back yell for yell to a westerly gale." The novel is also about that solidarity Conrad admired but rarely dramatized.

In these last sentences of the novel Conrad himself is speaking, rather than the anonymous narrator. And this is perhaps the best place to consider the often-noted waywardness in point of view. The novel opens with objective reporting, and the first narrative voice we hear is stiff, impersonal, detached, a voice reading stage directions. But Conrad's natural impulse is to write in the first person, if possi-ble retrospectively; to suggest action and summarize large segments of time. His natural impulse is to meditative and often ironic with-drawal. (It is author not narrator who pauses to comment on the popularity of Bulwer-Lytton among seamen: an extreme with-drawal.) On the seventh page the narrator momentarily becomes a member of the crew, but we must wait unil the second chapter for this identification to be made frankly. Meanwhile we may detect in Conrad a restless impatience with the nominal objectivity adopted —a coolness of manner sharply broken through as he speaks out his admiration for Singleton, his contempt for Donkin. Passionate con-viction energized Conrad's visualizing power as nothing else in the chapter did; and we have immortally the Donkin of white eyelashes and red eyelids, with "rare hairs" about the jaws, and shoulders "peaked and drooped like the broken wings of a bird . . ."

With the second chapter, and the sailing of the ship, the prose takes on poetic qualities. A meditative observer outside and above the *Narcissus* sees her as "a high and lonely pyramid, gliding, all shining and white, through the sunlit mist." We return briefly to the deck for a paragraph of flat reporting, then have the developed and Victorian analogy of the ship and the earth with its human freight. The paragraph has the kind of obviousness an intentionalist would welcome, but I suspect its real purpose was tactical. By gener-alizing his ship in this gross fashion, Conrad freed himself from the present moment and from the obligation to report consecutively. "The days raced after one another, brilliant and quick like the flashes of a lighthouse, and the nights, eventful and short, resembled fleeting dreams." And now he can pursue his natural mode: to hover selectively over a large segment of time, dipping down for a closer view only when he chooses. On the next page (as though to achieve still further retrospective freedom) the narrator identifies himself as a member of the crew. Suddenly we are told that Mr. Baker "kept all our noses to the grindstone."

The subsequent waverings of point of view are the ones that have disturbed logicians. Vernon Young puts their case clearly: "Presumably an unspecified member of the deck crew has carried the narration; in this case the contents of the thoughts of Mr. Creighton and of the cook, and many of the conversations, between Allistoun and his officer or between Donkin and Wait, for example, are impossibly come by."[4] The classic answer to such logic is that all eggs come from the same basket. It may be given more lucidly thus: the best narrative technique is the one which, however imper-fect logically, enlists the author's creative energies and fully explores his subject. We need only demand that the changes in point of view not violate the reader's larger sustained vision of the drama-tized experience. Creighton's thoughts (since he is no more nor less than a deck officer) can violate nothing except logic. But serious violation does occur twice: when we are given Wait's broken inte-rior monologues. For we are approaching the mysterious Negro's

4. Vernon Young, "Trial by Water," *Accent* (Spring 1952), pp. 80–81.

death, and it has been the very convention of the novel that Wait must remain shadowy, vast, provocative of large speculation; in a word, symbolic. The very fact that he comes in some sense to represent our human "blackness" should exempt him from the banalities of everyday interior monologue. It would be as shocking to overhear such interior monologue of Melville's Babo or of Leggatt in "The Secret Sharer."

For the rest, the changes in point of view are made unobtrusively and with pleasing insouciance. What is more deadly than the ratiocinations of a narrator trying to explain his "authority," as the Marlow of *Chance* does? The movement of point of view through this novel admirably reflects the general movement from isolation to solidarity to poignant separation. So the detached observer of the first pages becomes an anonymous member of the crew using the word "we." He works with the others during the storm and joins them in the rescue of Wait; and he too, both actor and moralizing spectator, becomes prey to sentimentalism, laziness, fear. Then in the final pages the "we" become an "I," still a nameless member of the crew but about to become the historical Joseph Conrad who speaks in the last paragraph. "I disengaged myself gently." The act of meditative withdrawal at last becomes complete. Approach and withdrawal, the ebb and flow of a generalizing imagination which cannot leave mere primary experience alone—these are, in any event, the incorrigible necessities of the early Conrad, and they account for some of his loveliest effects.

So we have first of all, reported and mediated, the sea story and memorial realism suggested by the early American title, *The Children of the Sea*. But there is also (and almost from the beginning) the insufferable Negro James Wait. In his own right he is mildly interesting: as a lonely and proud man who is about to die, as an habitual malingerer whose canny deception becomes at last desperate self-deception. But his role in the novel is to provide the second test; or, as Conrad puts it in his American preface, "he is merely the centre of the ship's collective psychology and the pivot of the action." Merely! His role is to provoke that sympathetic identification which is the central chapter of Conrad's psychology, and through it to demonstrate Conrad's conviction that sentimental pity is a form of egoism. In their hidden laziness the members of the crew sympathize with Wait's malingering; later, seeing him die before their eyes, they identify their own chances of survival with his. The process of identification (dramatized with little explanation in *Lord Jim*) is defined explicitly here:

Falsehood triumphed. It triumphed through doubt, through stupidity, through pity, through sentimentalism . . . *The latent egoism of tenderness to suffering appeared in the developing anxiety not to see him die* . . . He was demoralising. Through him we were becoming highly humanised, tender, complex, excessively decadent: we understood the subtlety of his fear, sympathised with all his repulsions, shrinkings, evasions, delusions—as though we had been over-civilised, and rotten, and without any knowledge of the meaning of life.[5]

It could be argued that Conrad recapitulates too obviously, and reiterates rather too often, Wait's demoralizing influence. But the process of irrational identification was little understood by readers in 1897, or in fact by many readers since. It required explication. Thus the sentence I have italicized, almost the central statement of the novel, was omitted in Robert d'Humières' translation.[6] The "egoism of tenderness to suffering" must have struck him as meaningless.

Such, on the "mundane" or naturalistic level of psychology, is the function of Wait; and even the captain is finally corrupted by pity. He pretends to share in Wait's self-deception: "Sorry for him —as you would be for a sick brute . . . I thought I would let him go out in his own way. Kind of impulse." And this moment of pity causes the incipient mutiny. As for the crew, they cared nothing for Wait as a human being, hated him in fact, but had accepted him as a precious token. "We wanted to keep him alive till home—to the end of the voyage." But this is, of course, impossible. James Wait must die in sight of land, as Singleton said, and the *Narcissus* cannot finish her voyage until the body of Wait (like the living bodies of Leggatt and of Jonah) has been deposited into the sea. Then but only then the "ship rolled as if relieved of an unfair burden; the sails flapped." And the ship rushes north before a freshening gale. To the personal and psychological-naturalistic burden of Wait is added—almost "unfairly" for a story of little more than 50,000 words—the burden of an audacious symbolic pattern. In certain early pages Wait is A Death, and a test of responses to death. But ultimately he is written in larger terms: *as something the ship and the men must be rid of before they can complete their voyage.* What this something is—more specific than a "blackness" —is likely to vary with each new reader. But its presence as part of the wavering mobile, as a force the story must allow for, raises crucial questions of technique.

Conrad's task, briefly, was to respect both flesh ("A negro in a British forecastle is a lonely being") and symbol; to convey a vivid black human presence which could yet take on the largest meanings; which could become, as in Melville, "the Negro." Conrad faces the double challenge with the moment Wait steps on board, calling out that name which is mistaken for an impertinent com-

5. Italics added. [*Editor.*]
6. This was called to my attention by Mrs. Elizabeth Von Klemperer, who is preparing a dissertation on James and Conrad in France.

mand, "Wait!" Whether or not Vernon Young is right in detecting a play on the word (Wait: weight, burden), symbolic potentialities exist from the start. As we shall first see of Leggatt only a headless corpse floating in the water, so here we see only a body. "His head was away up in the shadows." And—cool, towering, superb—the Nigger speaks the words which, in a true morality, a symbolic force might speak: "I belong to the ship." But what saves the scene (what prevents the reader from detecting larger meanings too soon) is its concrete reality. The ambiguous arrival at once provokes action and talk, a dramatic interchange. And when it is over the magnitude of the Nigger is firmly established. We are able to accept that first "cough metallic, hollow, and tremendously loud," resounding "like two explosions in a vault."

I would insist, in other words, that Old Ben is also a real bear, and Babo a fleshly slave, and Moby Dick a real whale, and James Wait (though his name was "all a smudge" on the ship's list) a proud consumptive Negro. It is truly the critic's function to suggest potentialities and even whole areas of discourse that a hasty reading might overlook. But the natural impulse to find single meanings, and so convert symbolism into allegory, must be resisted. James's classic comment on "The Turn of the Screw" is relevant here: "Only make the reader's general vision of evil intense enough, I said to myself—and that already is a charming job—and his own experience, his own imagination, his own sympathy (with the children) and horror (of their false friends) will supply him quite sufficiently with all the particulars. Make him *think* the evil, make him think it for himself, and you are released from weak specifications."[7] Or, as Robert Penn Warren remarks, every man has shot his own special albatross. I am willing with Vernon Young to accept that Wait suggests the subconscious, the instinctual, the regressive; or, with Morton D. Zabel, to see him as the secret sharer and "man all men must finally know"; or, with Belfast more curtly, to know that Satan is abroad. This is neither evasion nor a defense of solipsism, I trust, but mere insistence that no rich work of art and no complex human experience has a single meaning. Wait is, let us say, a force; an X. But it is his role to elicit certain responses from the crew, and, through them, from the reader.

Thus our task is not to discover what Wait precisely "means" but to observe a human relationship. And the clue to any larger meanings must be found, I think, in the pattern of Wait's presences and absences. He is virtually forgotten (after the first dramatic appearance) while the men get to know each other and the voyage begins; he is something they are too busy to be concerned with. We return to him only when they have little work to do;

7. Henry James, Preface to *The Aspern Papers*.

when "the cleared decks had a reposeful aspect, resembling the autumn of the earth" and the soft breeze is "like an indulgent caress." And he is literally forgotten (by crew as well as reader) during the worst of the storm. After he is rescued, he is again neglected for some thirty pages, and returns only with the sinister calm of a hot night and beshrouded ocean. In the two major instances, the lazy Donkin is the agent who takes us back to him, the Mephistopheles for this Satan. The menace of Wait is greatest when men have time to meditate. Thus Conrad's practical ethic of a master-mariner (seamen must be kept busy) may not be so very different from the ethic of the stoic pessimist who wrote psychological novels. The soul left to its own devices scarcely bears examination, though examine it we must.

The pages of Wait's rescue are central, and manage brilliantly their double allegiance to the real and to the symbolic. Here more than anywhere else, even on a quite naturalistic level, the two sides of the seamen coexist, the heroic and the loathsome. "Indignation and doubt grappled within us in a scuffle that trampled upon our finest feelings." They risk their lives unquestioningly to rescue a trapped "chum." Yet these men scrambling in the carpenter's shop, tearing at the planks of the bulkhead "with the eagerness of men trying to get at a mortal enemy," are compulsive, crazed, and full of hatred for the man they are trying to save. "A rage to fling things overboard possessed us." The entire scene is written with vividness and intensity: the hazardous progress over the half-submerged deck, the descent into the shop with its layer of nails "more inabordable than a hedgehog," the smashing of the bulkhead and tearing out of Wait, the slow return to a relative safety. Everything is as real and as substantial as that sharp adze sticking up with a shining edge from the clutter of saws, chisels, wire rods, axes, crowbars. At a first experiencing the scene may seem merely to dramatize the novel's stated psychology: these men have irrationally identified their own survival with Wait's and are therefore compelled to rescue him. Ironically, they risk their lives to save a man who has already damaged their fellowship, and who will damage it again.

But the exciting real scene seems to say more than this. And in fact it is doing an important preparatory work, in those fringes of the reader's consciousness, for Wait's burial and for the immediate responding wind which at last defines him as "symbol." On later readings (and we must never forget that every complex novel becomes a different one on later readings) the resonance of these pages is deeper, more puzzling, more sinister. We observe that the men remember the trapped Wait only when the gale is ending, and they are free at last to return to their normal desires. Thereupon they rush to extricate what has been locked away. The actual rescue is presented as a difficult childbirth: the exploratory tappings and faint response; Wait crouched behind the bulkhead and beating with his fists; the head thrust at a tiny hole, then stuck between splitting planks; the "blooming short wool" that eludes Belfast's grasp, and at last the stuffed black doll emerging, "mute as a fish" before emitting its first reproach. At least we can say, roughly, that the men have assisted at the rebirth of evil on the ship.

It may well be that Conrad intended only this (and conceivably less), or to insist again that men are accomplices in their own ruin. But the larger terms and very geography of the scene suggest rather a compulsive effort to descend beneath full consciousness to something "lower." The men let themselves fall heavily and sprawl in a corridor where all doors have become trap doors; they look down into the carpenter's shop devastated as by an earthquake. And beyond its chaos (beneath all the tools, nails, and other instruments of human reason they *must* fling overboard) lies the solid bulkhead dividing them from Wait.[8] The imagery of this solid barrier between the conscious and the unconscious may seem rather Victorian. But the Jungians too tell us that the unconscious is not easily accessible. In such terms the carpenter's shop would suggest the messy preconscious, with Wait trapped in the deeper lying unconscious.

This is plausible enough, but does not account for the curious primitive figure of Wamibo glaring above them: "all shining eyes, gleaming fangs, tumbled hair; resembling an amazed and half-witted fiend gloating over the extraordinary agitation of the damned." Wamibo could, if we wished, take his obvious place in the Freudian triad (as savage super ego)—which would convert Wait into the id and the whole area (carpenter's shop and cabin) into all that lies below full consciousness. But such literalism of reading, of psychic geography, is not very rewarding. It could as usefully be argued that Wamibo is the primitive figure who must be present and involved in any attempt to reach a figure still more primitive, as the half-savage Sam Fathers and half-savage Lion must be present at the death of Old Ben. Is it not more profitable to say, very generally, that the scene powerfully dramatizes the compulsive psychic descent of "Heart of Darkness" and "The Secret Sharer"? In any event the men emerge as from such an experience. "The return on the poop was like the return of wanderers after many years amongst people marked by the desolation of time." (As for the rescued Wait, he presents the same contradictions as the rescued Kurtz.

8. "Then the mariners were afraid, and cried every man unto his god, and cast forth the wares that were in the ship into the sea, to lighten it of them. But Jonah was gone down into the sides of the ship; and he lay, and was fast asleep" (Jonah 1 : 5). It is Jonah who must be cast out. But he has *already* had an experience of descent: "The waters compassed me about, even to the soul: the depth closed me round about, the weeds were wrapped about my head. I went down to the bottom of the mountains; the earth was about me for ever: yet hast thou brought my life from corruption, O Lord my God" (2 : 5, 6).

Wait locked in his cabin and the Kurtz of unspeakable lusts and rites suggest evil as savage energy. But the rescued Wait and the rescued Kurtz are "hollow men," closer to the Thomist conception of evil as vacancy.) [9]

So the night journey into self is, I think, one of the experiences this scene is likely to evoke, even for readers who do not recognize it conceptually as such. But it may evoke further and different responses. It is so with any true rendering of any large human situation, be it outward or inward; life never means one thing. What I want to emphasize is not the scene's structuring of abstract or psychic meaning only, but its masterful interpenetration of the realistic and symbolist modes. Its strangeness and audacity (together with its actuality) prepare us for the symbolic burial which is the climax of the novel.

"We fastened up James Wait in a safe place." It is time to return to technical matters, and specifically to the art of modulation that was one of Conrad's strengths.

The ambiguous episode of a suspect heroism is over, Wait is again forgotten, and the chapter returns to its record of a genuine not specious courage. The impression left by the storm test must finally be affirmative, and we move toward that impression at once. Podmore madly offers to make hot coffee; and succeeds. "As long as she swims I will cook." And already the *Narcissus* herself has shown a tendency to stand up a little more. In the final pages of the third chapter the white virginal ship with her one known weakness is the human protagonist exerting a puny stubborn will; old Singleton is the indestructible machine. But the ship's heroism rubs off on the men. Captain Allistoun gives the command to "wear ship," the men do their work, but their eyes and ours are fixed on the wounded, still-living *Narcissus*. "Suddenly a small white piece of canvas fluttered amongst them, grew larger, beating." The ship makes several distinct attempts to stand up, goes off as though "weary and disheartened," but at last with an unexpected jerk and violent swing to windward throws off her immense load of water. And now she runs "disheveled" and "as if fleeing for her life," spouting streams of water through her wounds, her torn canvas and broken gear streaming "like wisps of hair." The chapter ends with

9. One is reminded of the surrealist disorder of the cuddy on the *San Domenick*, where Babo shaves Don Benito: the room an effective image of the unconscious, whatever Melville intended. And, more distantly, of Isaac McCaslin's discarding of gun, watch, compass (comparable to the tools thrown overboard) as he moves toward his archetypal confrontation of the unconscious and primitive. To the few intentionalists who may have consented to read this far: a great intuitive novelist is by definition capable of dramatizing the descent into the unconscious with some "geographical" accuracy, and even without realizing precisely what he is doing. If he is capable of dreaming powerfully he will dream what exists (the "furniture" of the mind) as he will dream archetypal stories. The more he realizes what he is doing, in fact, the greater becomes the temptation to mechanical explanation and rigid consistency to received theory.

old Singleton still at the wheel after thirty hours, his white beard tucked under his coat. "In front of his erect figure only the two arms moved crosswise with a swift and sudden readiness, to check or urge again the rapid stir of circling spokes. He steered with care."

This is the end of the first great test. But this is also and only, and almost exactly, the middle of the novel. These men united by crisis must return again to the egoism of their several lives, and hence face again that other test of their selfish allegiance to Wait. The return to Wait (i.e., to the Wait theme) posed one of the sharpest of the novel's many tactical problems: how to modulate downward from the heroic to the everyday, then upward again to the symbolic death and burial. Such "modulations" (for they are much more than transitions) take us close to Conrad's technical art at its best; they show an exceptional sense of how language can manipulate the reader's sensibility.

The end of the storm was grand enough to break such a novel in two. What sentence, to be precise, what particular level of language could succeed such a stroke as "He steered with care"? In *Typhoon* Conrad solves, with one laconic sentence, the whole problem of transition: "He was spared that annoyance." In *Lord Jim* we are told, a little more evasively, "These sleeping pilgrims were destined to accomplish their whole pilgrimage to the bitterness of some other end." The one fact to be communicated is that the ships did not sink; that these men were reprieved. But in *The Nigger of the "Narcissus"* the reader's feelings and beyond them his attitude toward the crew must be handled with extreme care.

Here is the way it is done. I submit the paragraph not as an example of supreme prose but rather to suggest that Conrad's evasiveness and difficulty, his grandiloquence even, may serve at times a dramatic end and solve a tactical problem:

> On men reprieved by its disdainful mercy, the immortal sea confers in its justice the full privilege of desired unrest. Through the perfect wisdom of its grace they are not permitted to meditate at ease upon the complicated and acrid savour of existence, *lest they should remember and, perchance, regret the reward of a cup of inspiriting bitterness, tasted so often, and so often withdrawn from before their stiffening but reluctant lips.* They must without pause justify their life to the eternal pity that commands toil to be hard and unceasing, from sunrise to sunset, from sunet to sunrise; till the weary succession of nights and days tainted by the obstinate clamour of sages, demanding bliss and an empty heaven, is redeemed at last by the vast silence of pain and labour, by the dumb fear and dumb courage of men obscure, forgetful, and enduring.[1]

1. Italics added. [*Editor.*]

The paragraph does tell us something; these men were reprieved, and had no chance to rest from their labors. Everything else might seem to belong to that rhythmed and global moralizing that enrages certain lovers of the plain style. And in fact the lines I have italicized do border on double talk. Is the "cup of inspiriting bitterness" life itself? And if so, how can it be withdrawn "so often"? We seem to have a passage as suspect, logically, as the famous one on the "destructive element." And even Conrad must have come to wonder what these lines meant, for he removed them from the definitive edition[1].

The rest of the paragraph offers, most obviously, its dignity of tone. We move from the elevation of Singleton steering with care to the austere elevation of a narrator's statement on man and destiny, before returning to the drenched decks and exhausted swearing crew. But the language is more highly charged than it might seem at a first glance. The double metaphor (*sea–indifferent justice–God*) is obvious enough, underlined as it is by so much irony: *reprieved, disdainful mercy, immortal, in its justice, the perfect wisdom, grace, justify, the eternal pity, commands toil to be hard, redeemed*. The paragraph expresses an ultimate skepticism; or, a conviction that man's dignity lies in his courage, labor and endurance. But the particular Conradian difficulty (or "tension") comes from the suddenness of the narrator's subversive intrusions. Thus the men desire life; it is the narrator who reminds us that life is unrest. And the sages who tarnish man's dignity by their references to an afterlife demand only the bliss of heaven. It is the narrator who remarks (a parenthesis within a parenthesis) that this heaven is empty. There is much more to say about the passage, and it would be interesting to know whether such flowing rhythms do not carry most readers, unnoticing, past these ironies. In general, however: not merely the austerity of tone and dignity of rhythm but the very difficulty of the language help to manipulate the reader's feelings, chill them even, in a way quite necessary at this point in the story.

This fine management of the reader through tone, style, and structure is the largest achievement, in 1897, of Conrad's technique. It would require a comment as long as Conrad's fourth chapter to describe and analyze the tact with which it leads us through the hard work of the storm's aftermath, through the desolation of the forecastle, through Singleton's physical collapse and also his collapse into skepticism, through Donkin's mutinous talk—back to Wait's cabin as the source of contagion. "The little place, repainted white, had, in the night, the brilliance of a silver shrine where a black idol, reclining stiffly under a blanket, blinked its weary eyes and received our homage. Donkin officiated." Only through many careful modulations (the gray human mixture a little darker after each) can we

---

1. Compare the quotation on p. 231 with the opening of Chapter Four on p. 55.

be made to accept the fact that such a brave crew would be capable of mutiny. The chapter is certainly more flawed than any of the others. But the transitional task it had to accomplish, and modulative task, was much the most difficult.

"A heavy atmosphere of oppressive quietude pervaded the ship." Thus begins the fifth and last chapter. The threat of mutiny has been broken; we are nearing the end of the voyage; ultimate meanings must be achieved now or not at all; and James Wait must die. Like Melville in *Benito Cereno* Conrad has prepared us early in the story for the themes of ambiguity and death by mortuary images:

> Over the white rims of berths stuck out heads with blinking eyes; but the bodies were lost in the gloom of those places, that resembled narrow niches for coffins in a whitewashed and lighted mortuary.

> The double row of berths yawned black, like graves tenanted by uneasy corpses.

> And alone in the dim emptiness of the sleeping forecastle he appeared bigger, colossal, very old; old as Father Time himself, who should have come there into this place as quiet as a sepulchre to contemplate with patient eyes the short victory of sleep, the consoler.

Beyond this Conrad has more than once asked us to regard the ship as a microcosm, and (in the rescue scene) has appealed darkly to the fringes of consciousness. But the hardest task remains, and this is to bring the symbolic possibilities of the ship and of Wait into full awareness. To put matters crudely: we must be directly prepared for the occult circumstance of a wind rising the moment Wait's body reaches the sea.

Singleton's prediction—his Ancient Mariner's knowledge that "Jimmy was the cause of the head winds" and must die in the first sight of land—accomplishes something. But the somber rhythms and Coleridgean distracted movement of the ship accomplish more. And there is at last the critical moment itself, a moment requiring audacity. How convince the reader that *anything* can happen on this more than ordinary ship? One way would be to use such words as "illusive," or frankly to say that nothing in the ship is "real." But more than flat statement is required to make us accept Coleridge's phantom ship. One could further suggest death through allusions to the moon, or *evoke a magic ship and transnatural night by imposing images of snow and cold and ice upon a hot night*. One could, indeed, appeal to the reader's recollection of *The Ancient Mariner*. And all this occurs, is done, in the last modulative paragraph:

> On clear evenings the silent ship, under the cold sheen of the dead moon, took on a false aspect of passionless repose, resembling the winter of the earth. Under her a long band of gold

barred the black disc of the sea. Footsteps echoed on her quiet decks. The moonlight clung to her like a frosted mist, and the white sails stood out in dazzling cones as of stainless snow. In the magnificence of the phantom rays the ship appeared pure like a vision of ideal beauty, illusive like a tender dream of serene peace. And nothing in her was real, nothing was distinct and solid but the heavy shadows that filled her decks with their unceasing and noiseless stir: the shadows darker than the night and more restless than the thoughts of men.

Donkin prowled spiteful and alone amongst the shadows, thinking that Jimmy too long delayed to die. That evening land had been reported from aloft . . .

These are matters of style: style as temperament, style as meaning, style as suasion and manipulation of the reader. And in *The Nigger of the "Narcissus"* we are watching the formation of a great style in which meditation becomes dramatic. We are dealing with a temperament chronically addicted to approach and withdrawal, and which can make the very ebb and flow of generalizing intellect an element of suspense. Thus a scene of action may be suddenly broken off and the reader alienated, *removed,* by the act of meditative withdrawal. And this removal intensifies the drama:

He shrieked in the deepening gloom, he blubbered and sobbed, screaming: " 'It 'im! 'It 'im!" *The rage and fear of his disregarded right to live tried the steadfastness of hearts more than the menacing shadows of the night that advanced through the unceasing clamour of the gale.* From aft Mr. Baker was heard:—"Is one of you men going to stop him—must I come along?" "Shut up!" . . . "Keep quiet!" cried various voices, exasperated, trembling with cold.[2]

This sudden deliberate distancing of narrator and reader will give *Lord Jim* and *Nostromo* some of their richest effects.

The writing of *The Nigger of the "Narcissus"* remains uneven, though vastly superior to that of the earlier stories. But the Conradian richness, it must be admitted again, is built out of initial excess. "The Lagoon" and its parody have shown us what Conradese could be, with its pervasive melodrama of language and landscape and its monotonies of sentence structure. The most monotonous paragraph in *The Nigger of the "Narcissus"* occurs in the first chapter, before the narrator has begun to speak in his own right and voice. We have instead a writer methodically blocking out and methodically enriching a static scene and mood. The passage suggests some of the indulgences which could, chastened, become strengths:

2. Italics added [*Editor.*]

Outside the glare of the steaming forecastle the serene purity of the night enveloped the seamen with its soothing breath, with its tepid breath flowing under the stars that hung countless above the mastheads in a thin cloud of luminous dust. On the town side the blackness of the water was streaked with trails of light which undulated gently on slight ripples, *similar to* filaments that float rooted to the shore. Rows of other lights stood away in straight lines *as if* drawn up on parade between towering buildings; but on the other side of the harbour sombre hills arched high their black spines, on which, here and there, the point of a star *resembled* a spark fallen from the sky. Far off, Byculla way, the electric lamps at the dock gates shone on the end of lofty standards with a glow blinding and frigid *like* captive ghosts of some evil moons. Scattered all over the dark polish of the roadstead, the ships at anchor floated in perfect stillness under the feeble gleam of their riding-lights, looming up, opaque and bulky, *like* strange and monumental structures abandoned by men to an everlasting repose.[3]

The paragraph is unmistakably Conradian, and has its genuine felicities; the rhythm of any one of the overextended periods is lovely. But the passage fails by attempting too many felicities; analogy becomes a weary obligation, to be met once or twice each sentence. And yet, the captive ghosts and monumental abandoned structures operate in a characteristic manner: taking the reader on far meditative journeys from their banal tenors, to "evil moons" and "everlasting repose." We are invited to dream and are being imposed upon by a temperament. A doubtful procedure, if the object is to clarify the tenor. But that is not Conrad's object, which is to create a tone and bemusing impression. Far more conducive to monotony are certain repetitions: the regular assignment of one adjective and one only to approximately half the nouns (the French "glow blinding and frigid" comes as a relief); the almost identical length of the first three flowing periods and of the second, fourth, and fifth sentences; and the predictable positioning of the subject in four sentences out of five. This is, one detects, the prose of a writer even more devoted to cadence than to evil moons; who must (for the moment) externalize rhythms rather than visions; who enjoys expending to its fullest each long drawn-in breath. The first sentence is in fact the most Conradian of all, since it pushes past no less than five natural stopping-places. The style (as in certain other novels the plot and over-all structure) refuses the reader's reasonable expectations, and hence—if it does not merely lull—excites a certain strain. This impulse to frustrate the reader's ear will presently, and even in this novel, produce great prose.

3. Italics added. [*Editor.*]

Another reader, less conscious of rhythms, would be irritated by the fact that the night's purity is "serene" and repose "everlasting." Let us acknowledge at once that Conrad, early or late, could stock a sizable dictionary of bromidic clichés. Another way to put it is that some of his best pages are built with exceedingly obvious blocks. Most readers would agree (unless they are compiling dictionaries) that the first five pages of the second chapter, the sailing of the *Narcissus* and its first days at sea, are successful. But if one is compiling a dictionary! The water sparkles *like* a floor of jewels, and is as empty *as* the sky; the upper canvas *resembles* small white clouds; the tug *resembles* a black beetle (this analogy extended for twelve lines); a ship on the horizon lingers and hovers *like* an illusion; stars people the emptiness of the sky, are *as if* alive, are *more intense than* the eyes of a staring crowd, and *as inscrutable as* the souls of men; the ship is a microcosm of the earth (extended for a full paragraph) and is a high and lonely pyramid; the days are *like* flashes of a lighthouse and the nights *resemble* fleeting dreams; the Captain is "such *as* a phantom above a grave," his nightshirt flutters *like* a flag; and his gray eyes are still and cold *like* the loom of ice. He seldom descends from the Olympian heights of his poop.

How does Conrad get away with so much obviousness, as by and large he does? For one thing, the elaborate rhythms are both more varied and more "spoken" than in the first chapter, and this emerging meditative voice gives us, along the way, a good deal of authenticating nautical detail. Further, some of these analogies work visually and morally at the same time. The high and lonely pyramid is also lovely: "gliding, all shining and white, through the sunlit mist." But the tug, stained by land and steam, leaves a memorable round black patch of soot on the water, "an unclean mark of the creature's rest." The analogies taken together have begun to establish two of the novel's secondary meanings: its contrast between life at sea and life on land, its contrast between sail and steam. And even the captain as a phantom above a grave has its place in a novel depending upon much mortuary imagery to prepare us for the occult death of Wait. As for the studied and Victorian analogy of the ship and the earth, it can well be argued that Conrad should have permitted the reader so to generalize his ship. But we would be the poorer if we censored all Conrad's deeply meant skeptic's comments on our human lot. "The august loneliness of her path lent dignity to the sordid inspiration of her pilgrimage." We would be the poorer without that sentence and its several considered judgments.

In the best pages of *The Nigger of the "Narcissus,"* the storm action in Chapter III, the elaborate prose conveys action, motion, as well as a trembling and menaced beauty of sound.[4] But some of the striking Conradian effects are based on insistences which turn out to be obvious, and on a certain lack of inhibition. In context the docking of the *Narcissus* is very moving. It sums up the differences of sea and land, high endeavor and commerce, the beautiful and the sordid; it is the violation of the virgin by the soiled and practical; it brings the great adventure to an end. Only by underlining our text do we discover how obvious the insistences have been, in this devaluation of the land: "the steaming brows of millions of men," "drifts of smoky vapours," "an immense and lamentable murmur," "the anxious earth," "the shadows deepened," "barges drifted stealthily on the murky stream," "begrimed walls," "a vision of disaster," "a mysterious and unholy spell," and—horror of horrors in this story of masculine integrity and weakness—"two bareheaded women." "The *Narcissus* came gently into her berth; the shadows of soulless walls fell upon her, the dust of all the continents leaped upon her deck, and a swarm of strange men, clambering up her sides, took possession of her in the name of the sordid earth. She had ceased to live."

"My Lord in his discourse discovered a great deal of love to this ship." Conrad began with the ship, and it is with the *Narcissus* that the critic is well advised to end. And not only because the sea story as sea story is one of the greatest in English fiction. For the ship reminds us of the novel's overall structural problem, which I have neglected to discuss. This structural problem, and even Conrad's solution of it, can be simply stated. It is only in the doing, only in the demands for sensitive modulation made by every paragraph, that such matters become truly difficult! The problem was simply to avoid writing two distinct short novels, one optimistic and the other pessimistic. The two tests and two impressions of human nature must not be allowed to cancel out; we must forget neither the men's sentimentality and egoism nor their heroic endurance; at the last, the dark knot of seamen must drift in sunshine.

Conrad's tact becomes evident once we conceive any other structure than the one he actually presents. Had the near-mutiny and Wait's death occurred before the storm, we would have had the two short novels, and been left with a more affirmative statement

4. Consider the imitative rhythms of these lines, and the dramatic change of the sentence from passive to active force, ending in a dying close: "The hard gust of wind came brutal like the blow of a fist. The ship relieved of her canvas in time received it pluckily: she yielded, reluctantly to the violent onset; then, coming up with a stately and irresistible motion, brought her spars to windward in the teeth of a screeching squall. Out of the abysmal darkness of the black cloud overhead white hail streamed on her, rattled on the rigging, leaped in handfuls off the yards, rebounded on the deck—round and gleaming in the murky turmoil like a shower of pearls. It passed away."

than Conrad wanted to make. Had Wait's demoralizing effect begun only after the storm, we would have been left with no affirmation at all. The first necessity, then, was to introduce the Wait-story (tentatively, on the whole realistically) before the storm, return to it briefly during the storm, but give it major symbolic import only afterward. We are introduced to dim potentialities of anarchy and fear before knowing, through much of the third chapter, a magnificent courage and endurance. So much is simple indeed, in the describing. But having the near-mutiny and symbolic death occur after the storm still threatened, of course, to leave an impression essentially negative and, it may be, excessively symbolic. What is to remind us, after Wait's burial, that these men were also, had also been, true extrovert children of the sea? How could the story redress its balance? The obvious answer would be to show them reacting heroically to another great storm. But this too would have left an imbalance, and invited further circular movements.

What Conrad does, instead, is to give up any close view of the men; to focus attention on the ship rather than on them; to make *her* swift homeward progress heroic; to distance the reader from human perils either outward or inward and so confer on the crew, by association, some of the ship's glamour. The individuals on board give way to the ship as microcosm and finally to the ship as ship. Thus the object that unifies the two stories is not really an object at all, but the white female ship, which had left the stained land and now returns to it. What connects nearly every page is the *Narcissus* herself. At the very end the seamen are revalued by our distaste for the children of commerce, who can dismiss Singleton as a disgusting old brute; and the *Narcissus* is consecrated by the land that stains her. Crew and ship become part of history:

> The dark knot of seamen drifted in sunshine. To the left of them the trees in Tower Gardens sighed, the stones of the Tower gleaming, seemed to stir in the play of light, as if remembering suddenly all the great joys and sorrows of the past, the fighting prototypes of these men; press-gangs; mutinous cries; the wailing of women by the riverside, and the shouts of men welcoming victories. The sunshine of heaven fell like a gift of grace on the mud of the earth, on the remembering and mute stones, on greed, selfishness; on the anxious faces of forgetful men. And to the right of the dark group the stained front of the Mint, cleansed by the flood of light, stood out for a moment dazzling and white like a marble palace in a fairy tale. The crew of the *Narcissus* drifted out of sight.

"I disengaged myself gently." And by the same token the reader disengages himself from an adventure both extraordinary and intimate. There are novels whose endings suggest a continuation of the lives we have watched. But *The Nigger of the "Narcissus"* is a completed experience, recorded of a dead time; the voyage becomes at last the book we have just read.

In mere outline the matter is as simple as that. But there are novelists who in all their calculating careers never achieve such a triumphant simplicity and rightness of structure.

IAN WATT

Conrad Criticism and *The Nigger of the "Narcissus"*†

> So our virtues
> Lie in the interpretation of the time
> —*Coriolanus*, IV, vii, 49–50

The increasing critical attention of the last decade brought forth in the centenary year of Conrad's birth a tolerably heated literary controversy: Marvin Mudrick's attack on the views of—among others—Robert W. Stallman, in his "Conrad and the Terms of Modern Criticism" (*Hudson Review*, Autumn, 1954), was answered in the Spring, 1957, issue of the *Kenyon Review* ("Fiction and Its Critics . . ."), an answer which provoked a pretty note of injured innocence from Mudrick in the subsequent issue. Their mutual acerbities may, I think, be welcomed, if only as a reminder that Billingsgate has an ancient title to not the least attractive among the foothills of Helicon; my present concern, however, is with the ultimate grounds of their disagreement and this because it involves several problems of some importance both for Conrad and for our literary criticism in general. It also happens that Mudrick amplified his case against Conrad in the March, 1957, issue of *Nineteenth Century Fiction* with an essay on *The Nigger of the "Narcissus,"* a book which was at the same time the subject of a full-scale essay in the *Kenyon Review* by another of the writers attacked by Mudrick, Albert J. Guerard; and since *The Nigger of the "Narcissus"* has also received considerable attention in the last few years from a representative variety of modern critics, it would seem that our discussion can conveniently be centered on the criticism of Conrad's first masterpiece.

I

In "The Artist's Conscience and *The Nigger of the "Narcissus"*" Mudrick grants Conrad's mastery of "sustained passages of description unsurpassed in English fiction"; the storm, for example, and the early presentation of Wait, are wholly successful, for there Conrad gives us "an extraordinarily close and convincing observation of the outside of things." But—alas!—our verbal photographer

† From *Nineteenth-Century Fiction*, 12 (March 1958), 257–83. Footnotes are omitted.

does not always "keep his introspection to a respectful minimum"; he has the gall to tell us "what to think about life, death, and the rest"; and there results "gross violation of the point of view" and "unctuous thrilling rhetoric . . . about man's work and the indifferent universe and of course the ubiquitous sea."

The sardonic irony of that last phrase may give one pause; on an ocean voyage the sea is rather ubiquitous—if you can't bear it *The Nigger of the "Narcissus"* and, indeed, a good deal of Conrad, is best left alone. True, Stallman can show how impatient Conrad was with being considered a writer of "sea stories," but this methodological strategy seems suspect—minimizing the importance of overt subject matter so as to ensure for the critic that amplitude of sea-room to which his proud craft has of late become accustomed. One may, indeed, find Mudrick's contrary assertion in his earlier essay that the sea is "Conrad's only element" less than final and yet salutary in emphasis; in any case his present jaded impatience seems ominously revelatory.

Mudrick's main charges, however, are not easily dismissed. A number of previous critics have drawn attention to the inconsistencies in the point of view of the narration in *The Nigger of the "Narcissus,"* and to the marked strain of somewhat portentous magniloquence in Conrad's work generally. Mudrick has only given old objections new force, partly by his enviable gift for the memorably damaging phrase, and partly by allotting them a much more decisive significance in his final critical assessment. In some form, I take it, the charges are incontrovertible; but a brief analysis of Conrad's practice and of its historical perspective (the book appeared in 1897) may lead both to a more lenient judgment on the technique of *The Nigger of the "Narcissus"* and to a clearer realization of some of the problematic implications of our current critical outlook.

Among the "gross violations of point of view" specified is that whereby the reader directly witnesses the final confrontation of Wait and Donkin, although no one else, of course, was present. Mudrick argues:

> . . . though the violation in itself compels no distressing conclusions, it is a more important fact . . . than it would be in other, more loosely organized fiction. From the outset, and through more than half of the novel, Conrad has made us almost nervously sensitive to the point of view as product and evidence of the stereoscopic accuracy of the account: I, a member of the crew, restricted in my opportunities but thoughtful and observant, tell you all that I see.

A brief historical reflection forces us to recognize that it is not really Conrad who has made us "almost nervously sensitive to the point of view," or, at least, not directly; it is a generation of critics who have developed, partly from Conrad's technique, partly from the theory and practice of Henry James, and even more from its formulation in Percy Lubbock's *The Craft of Fiction* (1921), a theory of point of view in narrative which has been tremendously influential in providing both the critic and novelist with an until-then largely unsuspected key to the technique of fiction. But there is a vast difference between welcoming a valuable refinement of formal awareness and accepting as a matter of prescription the rule that all works of fiction should be told from a single and clearly defined point of view. Yet in the last few years something like this seems to have happened, and one of Mudrick's phrases seems even to bestow on the dogma a quasi-ethical sanction: when he speaks of "illicit glimpses of the 'inside,'" doesn't that "illicit" attempt to convict Conrad of some kind of moral turpitude? To be fair we must at least admit that the charge only became criminal a generation after the fact. And, waiving the chronological defense, hasn't the time come to ask whether Dr. Johnson's point about an earlier formal prescription—the unities of time and place—isn't relevant here? "Delusion, if delusion be admitted, has no certain limitation": the reader knows that *The Nigger of the "Narcissus"* is just a story; and Conrad is surely at liberty to turn his pretended narrator into a veritable Pooh-Bah of perscrutation if it will serve his turn.

If it will serve his turn. Interestingly enough, Albert J. Guerard in his fine essay on *The Nigger of the "Narcissus"* can show very convincingly that the changes in point of view serve a number of turns, and yet there are signs of a lingering embarrassment. He writes, unexceptionably, that, in general, "the best narrative technique is the one which, however imperfect logically, enlists the author's creative energies and fully explores his subject"; in the present case he finds "the changes in point-of-view done unobtrusively and with pleasing insouciance," and shows how they mirror the story's "general movement from isolation to solidarity to poignant separation." However, when Guerard comes to another kind of change in Conrad's method of reporting—the shift from objective reporting to lofty generalization—he comments that it is one of the "incorrigible necessities of the early Conrad," and in that "incorrigible" concedes that such variations in narrative strategy are indisputably literary offenses, although he is prepared to be good-tempered about it.

But Guerard's earlier position is surely equally applicable here; for both kinds of change in Conrad's point of view, not only those concerning the identity of the presumed narrator but also those concerning his varying tone and attitude toward what he is narrating, are closely related responses to the rather complicated imperatives of Conrad's subject as it develops. If Conrad had wholly restricted himself to the mind of one individual narrator, he would have had to expend a great deal of mechanical artifice—the kind of dexterous literary engineering later exhibited in *Chance*—in arranging for them to be plausibly visible: but this particularization of the point of view could only have been achieved at the expense of what is probably Conrad's supreme objective in *The Nigger of the "Narcissus"*; the continual and immediate presence of an individualized narrator, sleeping in a certain bunk, member of a certain watch, caught up in a particular set of the past and present circumstances, could not but deflect our attention from the book's real protagonist —the ship and its crew. So protean a protagonist could be fully observed only from a shifting point of view: sometimes hovering above the deck, seeing the ship as a whole; sometimes infinitely distant, setting one brief human effort against the widest vistas of time and space, of sea and history; occasionally engaging us in a supreme act of immediate participation, as when the narrator becomes identified with one of the five "we's" who rescue Wait; and finally involving us in the pathos of separation, when the narrator becomes an "I" to pronounce the book's closing valediction to the crew as they disperse.

The terms of this valediction, indeed, seem to emphasize how well advised Conrad was not to make his narrator too immediate a person to the reader. In general, as soon as we feel that the author's reflections are issuing from an individual character we naturally expect them to be expressed in an appropriate personal vernacular; and this either sets severe limits on the range of reflection, or creates an almost insoluble stylistic problem. Both difficulties, and especially the second, obtrude in the last paragraph of *The Nigger of the "Narcissus"*; for example when Conrad writes: "Haven't we, together and upon the immortal sea, wrung out a meaning from our sinful lives?" The particularized individual cannot—in prose, at least, and since the rise of realism—be both microcosm and macrocosm without some kind of apparent inflation; such was the problem which the Irish dramatists, trying to escape from the "joyless and pallid words" of Ibsen and Zola, had to face; and in this momentary anticipation of the very note of Synge, Conrad surely reveals how inappropriate such quasicolloquial elevation was for his purposes.

The intrusiveness of the "I" narrator, who only becomes evident in the last two paragraphs of *The Nigger of the "Narcissus,"* thus underlines the book's need for a variable narrative angle easily adjustable to different kinds of vision and comment. Until then, I think, we can find many logical contradictions in Conrad's manipulations of point of view, but not, unless our critical preconceptions are allowed to dominate our literary perceptions, any consequent failure in narrative command; and we should perhaps conclude that E. M. Forster was in the main right, when he insisted, in *Aspects of the Novel*, that "the whole intricate question . . . resolves itself . . .

into the power of the writer to bounce the reader into accepting what he says."

The shifting point of view in *The Nigger of the "Narcissus,"* then, enacts the varying aspects of its subject; in a wider sense, it may be said to enact the reasons for Conrad's greatness: the fact that he was a seaman but not only a seaman, that he was able to convey, not only the immediacies of his subject, but their perspective in the whole tradition of civilization. The actual prose in which some of the loftier elements of this perspective are conveyed, however, is a good deal more grandiloquent than we can today happily stomach. As an example, we may take a well-known passage which Mudrick quotes as his clinching specimen of Conrad's "unctuous thrilling rhetoric," the opening of the fourth chapter:

> On men reprieved by its disdainful mercy, the immortal sea confers in its justice the full privilege of desired unrest. Through the perfect wisdom of its grace they are not permitted to meditate at ease upon the complicated and acrid savour of existence [, lest they should remember and, perchance, regret the reward of a cup of inspiring bitterness, tasted so often, and so often withdrawn from before their stiffening but reluctant lips]. They must without pause justify their life to the eternal pity that commands toil to be hard and unceasing, from sunrise to sunset, from sunset to sunrise; till the weary succession of nights and days tainted by the obstinate clamour of sages, demanding bliss and an empty heaven, is redeemed at last by the vast silence of pain and labour, by the dumb fear and the dumb courage of men obscure, forgetful, and enduring.

Conrad himself, apparently, was uneasy about some of this, and deleted the passage in brackets when revising for the collected edition some twenty years after. He had no doubt become more aware, and more critical, of the influence of the stylistic aims of French romanticism, the only specific literary influence on his work which he admitted. The passage is, in part, an attempt to write "la belle page"—to achieve the grandiose richness of verbal and rhythmic suggestion found, for example, in Victor Hugo's *Les Travailleurs de la Mer*; and it can, therefore, if we wish, be explained away in terms of a literary indebtedness which Conrad later outgrew.

But there are other, perhaps more interesting, certainly more contemporary, issues raised by historical perspective of the passage.

We have today an unprecedented distrust of the purple passage; the color has been banned from the literary spectrum, and "poetic prose" has become a term of abuse in the general critical vocabulary, including Mudrick's. Since T. E. Hulme, at least, we have demanded in poetry—and, *a fortiori*, in prose—tautness of rhythm, hardness of outline, exactness of diction; we have insisted that every word, every rhythmical inflection, every rhetorical device, shall contribute to the organic unity of the whole work, shall not exist for its local effect. Mudrick takes comment on the passage to be super-fluous, but the grounds of his objection are, I take it, somewhat along these lines. So, indeed are mine, I suppose. At least I can-hardly read the passage, or others in Conrad like it, without momentary qualms ("Should I let myself go and enjoy it? No, in real life relaxing's fine, but in literature? . . . Think of Leavis. . . ."); and yet, if we consider the Hulmean principle seriously, isn't the cost more than we are prepared to pay?

To begin with, a rather large series of literary rejections may be involved; not only Hugo and Pater and much of Flaubert but also a good deal of Proust and Joyce—not only the *Portrait* but much of *Ulysses*—Molly Bloom's reverie, for example. There are countless passages in the greatest literature which, though no doubt related by subject and theme to the rest of the narrative, are essentially set-pieces, developed largely as autonomous rhetorical units; and in a good many of them every device of sound and sense is, as in Conrad, being used mainly to induce feelings of rather vague exalta-tion. Nor is it only a matter of the illustriousness of the precedents; they may have valid literary justification. For, although we are no doubt right to reject de Musset's romantic certitude that our most beautiful feelings are our saddest, is there any more justification for the antiromantic prescription that our deepest or most complicated feelings—so often vague and penumbral—can and should be expressed through clear images? And why in images at all? How can we reconcile the symbolist rejection of logic and conceptualization with the fact that our minds often work by partial and groping movements toward conceptualization and logical ordering? More specifically, isn't it carrying the demand for imagistic particularity too far to assert that in literature every part of the picture must be in clear focus? Can we not, on the contrary, assert that Conrad, a preeminently pictorial writer, requires, on occasion, a chiaroscuro effect between one series of concretely detailed presentations and another? Such certainly is the way this passage—and many others of a similar kind—are disposed in *The Nigger of the "Narcissus"*: we get a relief from the immediate image, from the particularities of time and space, and this, by contrast, both brings out these particu-larities more clearly and at the same time reminds us that there are other less definite and yet equally real dimensions of existence.

It is probably because these less definite dimensions cannot be made real visually that Conrad's style changes abruptly and at once evokes analogies that are musical rather than pictorial. In the Pref-ace to *The Nigger of the "Narcissus"* he wrote that one of his aims was to approach "the magic suggestiveness of music"; and though nowadays we are very suspicious of "word music," there may in this case at least be something in Coleridge's apparently outrageous assertion that "a sentence which sounds pleasing always has a meaning which is deep and good." Conrad's particular sentences here certainly suggested a meaning not lacking in depth or goodness to one of the greatest practitioners of the prose poem; for this is one of the passages by which Virginia Woolf, in "Mr. Conrad: A Conversation" (*The Captain's Death Bed*), exemplifies her assertion that in Conrad's prose "the beauty of surface has always a fibre of morality within." She goes on, "I seem to see each of the sentences . . . advancing with resolute bearing and a calm which they have won in strenuous conflict, against the forces of falsehood, sentimentality, and slovenliness"; and so brings us, at long last, away from this rather inconclusive review of some of the theoretical issues raised by the passage by forcing us to ask whether the relation of form and content in the passage is as she suggests.

To make full sense of its content we must, of course, grant Conrad the benefit of the kind of flexible and cooperative interpretation we are accustomed to give poetry, allow him his steady reliance on ironic, elliptical, and paradoxical, personification. We must accept, for example, the dependence of the paradox of "desired unrest" upon an implicit assertion by the narrator that "life," which is what men literally "desire," is in fact always "unrest"; we must also accept the personifications of the sea's "mercy" and "grace" as necessary to prepare for the final modulation of "the eternal pity," where the sea's order is equated with God's; and we must excuse the somewhat obscure quality of the irony at God's supposedly merciful attributes and at the "empty heaven" because it is evident that Conrad wants to achieve his juxtaposition of religious illusions against the only redemptive power which he acknowledges, "the vast silence of pain and labour," without undermining the traditional sort of literary theism on which the passage's elevation of tone in part depends.

The gnomic compression, the largeness of reference, the latent irony, all suggest a familiar literary analogue, the Greek chorus: and the formal qualities of the passage offer striking confirmation. The Greek chorus's lofty and impersonal assertion of the general dramatic theme depends for its distinctive effect on the impact, at a point of rest in the action, of a plurality of voices and an intensified musicality: a plurality of voices, not an individualized narrator, because the function of a chorus in general, as of Conrad's in particular, is to achieve what Yeats called "emotion of multitude," which is difficult to achieve through a wholly naturalist technique for the presentation of reality; an intensified musicality because it emphasizes the requisite impersonal urgency, as in the present case Conrad's tired and yet hieratic emphasis on repetition and balance of sound and rhythm is itself the formal expression of his controlled exaltation at the prospect of the laborious but triumphant monotony offered by the endless tradition of human effort. The placing and the assertion of the passage are equally choric in nature, for Conrad seizes a moment of rest between two contrasted phases of the crew's exertion to remind us that, contrary to their longings and to what any sentimental view of existence would lead us to hope, man's greatness, such as it is, has no reward in this life or the next, and is a product only of the unending confrontation of their environment by the successive human generations, a confrontation that is unsought and yet obligatory, although "the forces of falsehood, sentimentality, and slovenliness" seek perpetually to confuse, defer, or evade its claims.

II

Mudrick's denigration of *The Nigger of the "Narcissus"* on the grounds of Conrad's rhetorical attitudinizing and of his use of point of view follows two of the major emphases of our modern criticism of fiction; and as we shall see his operative premises are typical in much else. But we must not overlook the fact that Mudrick, who has cast himself as the spectral Mr. Jones interrupting the feast celebrating Conrad's victory over the critics, is also possessed of a marked cannibalistic trait: he cannot abide the enthusiasm of his confreres for the "modish clues of myth, metaphor, symbol, etc." In his earlier essay on Conrad, Stallman's reading of "The Secret Sharer" was his main target; but he now finds *The Nigger of the "Narcissus"* subject to the same general charge: a heavy overemphasis on "catch-all" and "clap-trap" symbolism which only a naive predisposition for that sort of thing could possibly render acceptable.

That many critics have found a clue to *The Nigger of the "Narcissus"* in a unifying symbolic structure is certainly true. James E. Miller, for example, in his "*The Nigger of the 'Narcissus'*: A Reexamination" (*PLMA*, December, 1951), sees "James Wait and the sea as symbols of death and life; Singleton and Donkin as symbols of opposed attitudes toward death and life"; the other members of the crew hesitate whether to follow the true knowledge of Singleton or the deceptions offered by Donkin; and the conflict is only concluded when they unanimously reject Donkin's offer of a drink after being paid-off—"the crew has passed from a diversity based on ignorance through a false unity based on a lie perpetrated by Donkin, to, finally, the true 'knot' of solidarity based on genuine insight into the meaning of life and death."

Miller's analysis is, of course, presented as a confessedly simplified paradigm and I have had to simplify it further; his scheme certainly has the merit of drawing our attention to a certain number of important interrelationships which we might not have noticed: but the whole conception of a neat allegorical drama surely does violence to the patent diversity of Conrad's narrative; this may be the figure in one of the carpets but what of the many other richly furnished floors? Surely no one would have seized upon this particular pattern if he had not, in the first place, felt sure that there must be some such neat symbolic plot waiting to be discovered, and in the second, felt justified in giving decisive interpretative priority to a few selected details of character and incident which could be made to support it?

Essentially the same method—*reductio ad symbolum*—appears in Robert F. Haugh's "Death and Consequences: Joseph Conrad's Attitude Toward Fate" (*University of Kansas City Review*, Spring, 1952). Briefly, from the muster, in which they each challenge the order of the ship, both Donkin and Wait are seen as "emissaries of darkness and disorder, Conrad's synonyms for evil." Donkin's level is the overt, the social, while Wait's is the religious; the book as a whole dramatizes "all of the elements in the human solidarity of Conrad's world, arrayed against those forces which would destroy them," with Wait the deeper menace since he "somehow" comes to stand for the crew's "own darker natures." This analysis seems a good deal closer to our sense of the book's chief concerns, and in the main Haugh applies it convincingly; but as soon as the stress shifts from interpretative analytic summary to the attribution of specifically symbolic meanings to characters and incidents doubts begin to arise. Wait may be "a moral catalyst . . . who brings death aboard ship in many ways," but is he himself evil? And isn't it forcing the facts to say that when, after rescuing Wait, the crew return to the deck and find that "never before had the gale seemed to us more furious," this is somehow related to Wait's influence which has "undone . . . their courage," rather than to the material fact that, being on deck again, they are more exposed to the weather?

Vernon Young's "Trial by Water: Joseph Conrad's *The Nigger of the 'Narcissus'*" (*Accent*, Spring, 1952) reveals a very Galahad of the symbol. If the ship plunges "on to her *port* side," a parenthetic gloss at once nautical and symbolic reminds us that this is "the left, or sinister, side"; and if Conrad compares the *Narcissus* and her tug to a white pyramid and an aquatic beetle, "the antithesis . . . is unquestionably a sidelong glance at the Egyptian figure of the pyramid, prime-symbol of direction and sun-worship, and of the scarab, symbol of creative energy." It will serve us nothing to protest, for example, that this last image is patently visual, for we are in the presence of a Faith. In Young—as in many other of the more symbolically inclined critics—that faith is of the Jungian persuasion; and if I mention that I believe Jung to be a latter-day example of the same arrogant credulity which has given us astrology, the British Israelites, and the Baconian fringe, it is only because it seems to me that the kind of thinking exhibited there is exactly analogous to that in some kinds of literary symbol hunting: everything "proves x" because "proves" and "x" are defined with such accommodating tolerance—the terms of argument do not of their nature admit either of proof or of disproof.

Most of Young's essay, I must in fairness add, is concerned with elucidating a symbolic structure of a much less sectarian tendency. In its general view it is fairly similar to that of Haugh, though somewhat more schematically presented: Wait, for example, is defined as "serv[ing] a purpose comparable to that of El Negro in Melville's *Benito Cereno*: he is the spirit of blackness, archetype of unknown forces from the depths," and the mysterious adjuration of his presence "all but deprives the crew of their will to live." Allistoun and Singleton, on the other hand, stand for the superego, and they, together with Podmore, "discover, behind the mask of a dying shirker, the infrahuman visage of the Satanic."

Wait's portentous first appearance, and the way he later becomes the chief protagonist round whom the actions and the attitudes of the crew revolve, these certainly justify our impulse to look for some hidden significance in him. Some early readers no doubt thought the same, for in the 1914 note "To My Readers in America" Conrad wrote the very explicit denial: "But in the book [Wait] is nothing; he is merely the centre of the ship's collective psychology and the pivot of the action." If we set aside this disclaimer, as Young specifically (and scornfully) does, it should surely be only for the most imperative reasons; and those offered seem to be based upon the loosest kind of metaphorical extension.

Both Vernon Young and Albert Guerard make Wait's blackness their starting point, and this leads them to parallels in *Benito Cereno* and *Heart of Darkness*. Yet is is hardly necessary to adduce Conrad's antipathy to Melville to cast doubts on the former analogy: Conrad does not, in Melville's sense, believe in any absolute or transcendental "evil," and his Negro has not done any. As for the *Heart of Darkness* parallel, it is surely suspicious that Young should apply the color metaphor literally, and thus find his analogy in the "barbarous and superb woman," while Guerard, more metaphorical, plumps for Kurtz: in any case the native woman, quite unlike Wait, is conspicuous for her heroic resolution, while there seems to be little in common between Wait and Kurtz except that they are tall, proud, have African associations, are rescued with difficulty, and die painfully. Nor is the general metaphorical implication— Guerard's statement that Wait "comes in some sense to represent our human 'blackness' "—particularly convincing. Wait, we know, was based on an actual Negro, and his color offered Conrad a whole series of valuable dramatic oppositions. These are made full use of in Wait's first appearance, where his color at once establishes his difference, his mystery, his threat: yet later in the book the color issue becomes relatively unimportant; the crew assimilates him to their group with the jocular nickname of "Snowball"; only Donkin makes a serious issue of Wait's color, calling him "a black-faced swine," and if the narrator's own first description ends with the phrase "the tragic, the mysterious, the repulsive mask of a nigger's soul" we must remember that he is here only the spokesman of the first general and primarily visual reaction, that the color is after all "a mask," and that there is no suggestion later that the soul behind it is black.

Deferring the question of what James Wait's secret is—if any—we must surely ask why, in the absence of any convincing internal evidence or of any problem so intractable as to make recourse to extravagant hypothesis obligatory, critics capable of the perceptive felicities of Young and Guerard, to name only two, should try so hard (though not, as my present concern may inadvertently have led me to suggest, all or even most of the time) to discover some sort of occult purport in what is, on the face of it, a rich and complex but by no means equivocal narrative? More generally, why have the critics of the last decade or so, put such emphasis on finding esoteric symbols? In the phrase which the hero of Kingsley Amis's *That Uncertain Feeling* uses in another connection, I can see why the critics like them, but why should they like them *so much?*

The superstitition and obscurantism of our time, reflected, for example, in Young's indignation at Conrad's "fear of wholesale commitment to the irrational," will no doubt explain something, as I have already suggested; but what is perhaps more decisive is the prestige with which literary criticism is now invested. It is no longer the poet, but the critic who typically functions as the romantic seer; and a seer, of course, is someone who sees what isn't there, or at least has never been seen before. This role seems to enforce a no-doubt unconscious operative strategy along the following lines: a little like the bibliophile who is too proud to deal with anything but first editions, the critic feels his status as seer jeopardized unless he can demonstrate that he saw the book first, or at least that his reading of it is the first *real* one; his version must therefore be noticeably different from any likely previous one; and since certain kinds of symbolic interpretation, unlike the emperor's clothes, are incapable of empirical proof or disproof, they are laid under contribution as offering the easiest—and safest—means toward achieving the desired novelty of insight.

This is no doubt an unfair way of putting it; and in any case such pressures would probably have insufficient force were they not complemented by the obvious fact that the novel's length makes it impossible for the critic's anlaysis to approach the relative completeness which that of some short poems can attain. Given the impossibility of a full account, and the somewhat pedestrian tendency of the traditional summarizing of plot and character, the discovery of some inclusive symbolic configuration appears as the readiest way to combine the imposed brevity and the solicited originality.

In the case of Conrad, it is true, such interpretations seem to find some warrant from Conrad's own statement that "All the great creations of literature have been symbolic." The question, obviously, is "Symbolic in what sense?" and since the word "symbol" can be properly used in too many ways, it may clarify the discussion to suggest a set of rather ugly neologisms for the different kinds of literary symbolism that are involved in the present discussion.

The basic problem is to determine the kind of relationship between the literary symbol and its referent, between the narrative vehicle and its imputed larger tenor; most important, perhaps, are the distances between them and the basis on which the mutual rapport is ascribed. In the kind of symbolic interpretation I have been discussing, the distrance between the literary object and the symbolic meaning ascribed to it is rather great: and so I would describe making Wait a symbol of evil, darkness or Satan, an example of *heterophoric* interpreation; that is, it carries us to *another* meaning, it takes us *beyond* any demonstrable connection between the literary object and the symbolic meaning given it.

Many examples of symbolic interpretation differ from this, however, in that not only is the distance between literary object and imputed meaning relatively great, but the rapport is established, not through taking a particular quality in the literary object very far, but through referring the literary object to some other system of knowledge which it would not normally be thought to invoke. Young's interpretation of the pyramid and the scarab would be of this kind, and since it depends upon an allusion to a specific body of mythical, religious or literary knowledge, it could be called a *mythophor*; *mythophor* would be a variety of *heterophor*, since it makes the literary object stand for something very distant from it, but the correlation would depend upon a reference to a certain story or, in the Greek sense myth; another example of this would be Guerard's drawing the parallel between Wait and the legend of Jonah.

One particular case of *mythophor* seems to require some special term because it is common and raises peculiar problems—that case in which the body of knowledge invoked is one of the depth-psychologies: this subdivision of *mythophor* could be called *cryptophor*, since it depends upon analogies which Freud and Jung agree to be hidden and unconscious; one example would be when Guerard equates the rescuing of Wait from his confinement during the storm with a "compulsive psychic descent," or when he toys briefly with the scene's "psychic geography," proposing that the Finn Wamibo figures as the "savage *superego*" to Wait's *id*.

Heterophor in general tends toward allegory. Guerard, for example, although he jests at the fashion for "analysis of 'cabalistic
intent' " and cautions us against reading Conrad as an allegorical
writer, insisting that the overt subject is also the real subject, nevertheless argues for a series of superimposed *heterophoric* signifi-
cances which are essentially of the same allegorical kind as may
justly be imputed to the Negro in Meville's *Benito Cereno*. I do not
think that Conrad's work is symbolic in this way; even less is it
mythophoric or *cryptophoric*. To make it so, indeed, is surely to
emphasize novelty at the expense of truth; and the literary effect of
such interpretation is to reduce what Conrad actually created to a
mere illustration—something both secondary and—as Mudrick
would argue—second-rate. For all kinds of *heterophoric* interpretation inevitably disregard the great bulk of the concrete details of
character and incident in a literary work: just as T. S. Eliot's allegorical concern in *The Family Reunion*, for example, prevents us from
inspecting the psychology and the dynamics of Harry's wife's death
—did she fall or was she pushed?—so a *heterophoric* interpreter of
Wait will be disinclined to scrutinize the manifest developing pattern of his character and actions. The details of these latter, indeed,
will seem otiose compared to the few elements which, on *a priori*
grounds, have been selected as of primary importance; and so
Young can write, "Fearful of overstressing the subaqueous world of
the underconsciousness, the symbol-producing level of the psyche
which, in fact, was the most dependable source of his inspiration,
Conrad overloaded his mundane treatment of the crew."

To demur from Guerard's statement that, on top of the various
more obvious levels of narrative statement, Conrad imposed "an
audacious symbolic pattern," is not to deny that *The Nigger of the
"Narcissus"* is in many ways symbolic. Its symbolism, however,
seems to me to be of another kind. It works, characteristically, by
natural extension of the implications of the narrative content, and
retains a consistent closeness to it; for this the term *homeophor*
seems appropriate, suggesting as it does, "carrying *something similar*" rather than, as with *heterophor*, "carrying *something else.*"
When Guerard makes the parallel of the journey of the *Narcissus*
and the age-old theme of the pilgrimage, his interpretation, if
allowed, and at some level of generality it surely must be, would be
homeophoric because ships and pilgrimages, to those who know
anything of them, must suggest small human communities united
for the purpose of a single journey.

The terms proposed are no doubt grotesque; the distinctions on
which they are based would no doubt often prove difficult to apply;
and considered against the complexity of the problem and the richness of its literature, the brevity of their exposition may appear
unpardonable; but if they have made more manageable the problem

of what kind of symbolic writer Conrad is, and, perhaps, suggested the need for further discriminations in this general area, they will have served their turn. It only remains now to show, very briefly, how Conrad's method in *The Nigger of the "Narcissus"* is symbolic in a *homeophoric* way, working through a very accessible extension of the implications of character and event. This task, however, is complicated by the need to meet the charges against Conrad's use of symbolism made by Mudrick; for, believing that, for the novelist as well as for the critic, emphasis on symbolism tends to be at the expense of character and action which, surely rightly, he takes to be the essential components of fiction, Mudrick proceeds to argue that, in *The Nigger of the "Narcissus,"* Conrad did not "aim at elaborating or examining character and incident beyond the static, repetitive point of illustration and symbol." We must therefore attempt to show, not only that Conrad's symbolism is of a very exoteric kind, but that it does not have these damaging consequences for his presentation of character and incident.

III

Mudrick gives Conrad's early presentation of Wait two eloquent and appreciative paragraphs, but he finds the later treatment of him disappointing. It is true that the first commanding air of mystery slowly evaporates as we see Wait more closely: his curious pride, it appears, is merely the defense of an alien who is aboard only because, as he tells Baker, "I must live till I die—mustn't I?"; and his climactic confrontations with Donkin, Podmore, and Allistoun give increasingly clear illumination to the ordinariness of his secret, his unacknowledged terror of approaching death. These later developments undoubtedly have a deflating effect, and if we see Wait as an emissary from some spiritual chamber of horrors, they must seem mistaken; but the cumulative anticlimax can also be seen as an essential part of the book's meaning; it reveals that the influence Wait exercises on the crew is an irrational projection of their own dangerous fears and weaknesses; to put it in our terms, it asserts, eventually, that contrary to possible earlier expectation, Wait is not a *heterophor*; order and disorder on the *Narcissus* are temporary, contingent, man-made; behind the mysterious and menacing authority of a St. Kitts' Negro there is only a common human predicament; Wait is a symbol, not of death but of the fear of death, and therefore, more widely, of the universal human reluctance to face those most universal agents of anticlimax, the facts; and the facts, as always, find him out.

Mudrick, perhaps, mistook Wait for a *heterophor* and then found, as in that case I think one must, that Conrad didn't come through; but his disappointment has other grounds, notably that "there is no development and nothing mobile or unexpected" in the novel. This charge seems, specifically, to overlook or to reject the actions which focus round Wait in the fourth chapter; for when Mudrick writes that "Only Donkin—the gutter creature—'sees through' Wait" he is implicitly denying the picture of the case that is presented there. Donkin is no doubt the only person who most consistently sees Wait as an infuriatingly successful "evader of responsibility"; but everyone else has some such supicions, and the matter is obviously not so simple. No malingerer is ever wholly well, even if at times he thinks so; Wait's own agonizing divisions and contradictions about his condition seem a psychologically convincing reaction to all the elements in his situation; and his puzzling gratification at Donkin's insults is surely an expression of the desperation of his wish to believe that Donkin really has "seen through" him.

Actually, of course, only one man—Allistoun—can be said to "see through" Wait, as we realize in the scene when, after Podmore has told Wait that he is "as good as dead already," and Wait, supported by the crew, has urged that he be allowed to return to duty, Allistoun mystifies and outrages everyone by his brusque refusal— "There's nothing the matter with you, but you chose to lie-up to please yourself—and now you shall lie-up to please me." As Allistoun explains later to the mates, it was a momentary impulse of sympathetic insight into Wait ". . . three parts dead and so scared" which urged him to enact a form of Ibsen's beneficent lie by shielding him from the deception of his own wishful illusions, and letting "him go out in his own way."

That it is the most total act of sympathy for Wait which precipitates the mutiny is surely a "development" both "mobile and unexpected," and it dramatizes one of the general themes in *The Nigger of the "Narcissus"* which is far from commonplace: pity, emotional identification with others, as an active danger to society. Nor is the treatment of the theme by any means banal; for Conrad shows that pity, though dangerous, is also a condition of human decency, by juxtaposing the Allistoun scene between two others where Wait is subjected to the cruelty of two kinds of extreme and therefore pitiless egoism: to complete the picture, we must bear in mind the qualifications implied both in the subsequent scene where Donkin brutally satisfies his malice and cupidity by tormenting Wait to his death with fiendish cruelty, and in the earlier interview where the pious Podmore, a "conceited saint unable to forget his glorious reward . . . prayerfully divests himself of his humanity" and terrifies Wait with visions of imminent hell-fire.

Symbolically, Conrad seems to be saying that although pitilessness is characteristic of the selfish, yet the increasing sensitiveness to the sufferings of others which civilization brings necessarily poses grave problems of control for the individual and for society; and by making Singleton not so much unsympathetic as unaware of Wait's suffering he may be thought to have reminded us that the older and less humanitarian order was not so easily deflected from its collective purpose. Such a reading can be advanced with considerable confidence, since, as is necessarily the case with *homeophoric* extension, it is arrived at merely by extracting a more generally applicable statement from the manifest implications of particular characters and actions; and the reading could easily be supported, both by showing how the juxtaposition of certain episodes implies such a meaning, and by pointing out various explicit comments on the softening, refining and corrupting effects of pity, comments which authorize the assumption that any events which raise such issues were designed to have representative significance.

This is not to say that Allistoun, Wait, and the rest are to be regarded primarily as symbols of these attitudes and values, and I do not think that Mudrick would regard them as "elementary emblems of what they are intended to demonstrate" unless his own criteria, both of literary character in general, and of what is desirable to demonstrate, were so contrary to Conrad's.

It is undeniable that Conrad does not give us here, nor, typically, anywhere, the kind of psychological exploration focused on the individual sensibility in the manner of James or Proust: but there is surely some middle ground between this and mere "elementary emblems." If one assumes that Conrad's main objective is the ship —its voyage and its society—it is evident that, in what is little more than a long short story, not all its complement—twenty-six individuals—can possibly be particularized; nor, on the other hand, can any two or three of them be fully treated without disturbing the emphasis, which must be on the social group rather than the individual. It is inevitable that some characters of marginal importance should be portrayed with something approaching caricature—Belfast with his hypertonic Irish sensibility, Wamibo with his inarticulate frenzies of participation; and it would obviously be very unsettling to introduce characters who were flagrantly untypical of their setting. Mudrick takes exceptions to the stereotyped banality of the gentlemanly Creighton's daydreams—"a girl in a clear dress, smiling under a sunshade . . . stepping out of the tender sky"; and one hastens to concede that Creighton would be a more interesting character if he spent all his time at sea counting the days until the could have another stab at Kierkegaard; but what would that do to the book?

Nowadays we can swallow everything except the obvious; and one of the reasons that Mudrick singles out this particular passage for reprobation is probably that he shares our terror of whatever may seem cliché. He finds cliché, for example, when Wait talks to Donkin about his "Canton Street girl . . . cooks oysters just as I like," commenting that "Wait provided with the white man's conventional notion of the black man's secret desires" is less convincing "personally and symbolically" than "Wait with no background" at all, as at the beginning. But the girl is mentioned in context which gives Wait just the right kind of tawdry and hopeless pathos: off the Azores, with the crew talking of the joys of London, Wait naturally thinks of the London girl he will never see; the sick man's notorious dream of food (and rations are short) explains the oysters; while the fact that the remark is addressed to Donkin makes it Wait's last—and of course unavailing—effort to achieve some sort of triumph over the one man on the ship he has been unable to soften or impress.

Mudrick, both here and elsewhere, seems to me to have imported the cliché, and for two reasons: there is the already noted demand for a degree of individualization which is impossible and undesirable in many cases, including the present; and there is exactly the same fastidious rejection of the commonplace which, under the direction of other predispositions, causes the critics he attacks to coax esoteric symbols into the text. Both Mudrick's tendencies, of course, are closely related to his earlier demand for the sharpest possible definition in prose and in point of view: all his literary criteria, in fact, have total individualization as their basic premise.

His discussion of the moral and social dimensions of *The Nigger of the "Narcissus"* is informed with the equivalent premise, expressed as ethical and political nonconformity, and it operates with the same rude vigor. Conrad's "metaphysical and moral scheme" is based on the exaltation of the "grim-jawed, nerveless, reticent men in charge"; they inhabit "a hand-me-down 'aristocratic' universe in which everybody in charge deserves to be and everybody else had better jump"; and if we examine them, "all we find beneath the gritty authoritative British exterior is a collection of soft-headed Anglophilic clichés." We have seen that Allistoun in one crucial episode, at least, is far from nerveless, and that there are some elements in the book which are neither soft-headed nor commonplace; yet to exemplify and analyze further, or to attempt to assess how severe a disablement is involved in being an Anglophile, would probably be little to the purpose. For we are in the presence of a total incompatibility: Conrad's social and political attitudes, and Mudrick's diametrically opposed convictions.

Conrad, of course, was conservative in many ways: yet surely one can be, like Donkin, Mudrick—or myself—, "a votary of change" and still find that Conrad's picture of society commands respect. Even his presentation of the class issue, for example, has considerable objectivity: the hardships and the miserable economic rewards of the crew are not minimized, and we are given their cynical discussion of "the characteristics of a gentleman"; among the officers, Allistoun, with his "old red muffler" and his "nightshirt fluttering like a flag" is not a hero but a prisoner of the class to which his command has brought him, as we see when his smart wife arrives to collect him at the dockside; and our last picture of the ship shows the first mate, Baker, reflecting that, unlike Creighton with his "swell friends," he will never get a command. In any case, we can hardly make Conrad responsible for the fact that no ship was ever successfully sailed democratically; and we must also admit that, with all its rigidities and injustices, the *Narcissus* is a community with a genuine and in some ways egalitarian set of reciprocities: for the most part everyone on it knows and sees and wants the same things; while the class antipathy is qualified by the crew's recognition, in Allistoun or Baker, that individuals who in themselves are no way special or even particularly likeable can be wholly admirable and necessary in the performance of their roles. This dichotomy, of course, is an essential condition of Conrad's presentation of his characters: with the significant exceptions of Donkin and Wait, their function in one sense usurps their individuality but in another it endows them with heroic stature.

All these connections and contradictions, operating within a very restricted setting, gave Conrad his opportunity for a compressed drama which could, in part, be representative of society at large. The general values which emerge are on the whole traditional, if not authoritarian; but at least they are real values, and they are really there. If George Orwell could detect in Conrad "a sort of grown-upness and political understanding which would have been almost impossible to a native English writer at that time," it is surely because, as a foreigner, Conrad could be more objective about a social order which, for all its many faults, was in some ways admirable and rewarding; while as an exile from Poland he had cause to be presciently responsive to the existence of any viable social order at all.

Mudrick's case against Conrad, then, is largely the result of the conjunction of two value systems, neither of which happens to favor *The Nigger of the "Narcissus."* On the one hand he takes to their logical conclusion a rather complete set of modern critical assumptions—the pieties of point of view, of prosy-prose, of authorial reticence about character and meaning, of extreme fastidiousness about permitted attitudes and endorsements; on the other he lets loose a teeming menagerie of personal *bêtes noires*, ranging from symbolism, the sea, and the stiff upper-lip to hierarchical authorities, parvenus, and Anglophiles. Mudrick had a very nice irony in "Conrad and the Terms of Modern Criticism" about how, in our too perceptive times, "nose to nose, critic confronts writer and, astonished, discovers himself"; one could find striking confirmation both of this thesis and of the *cryptophoric* significance of proper names by considering how vivid an image of Mudrick was reflected when he came nose to nose with Narcissus.

As for Conrad, we must conclude, I think, that Mudrick's impatient intransigence forces one to realize, both by its palpable hits and by what I have tried to chalk up as its misses, how *The Nigger of the "Narcissus"* is, in a number of ways, not at all the answer to our modern critical prayer. No amount of symbol-juggling will or should divert us from seeing that there is an important Romantic and Victorian element in his work; and, although Conrad was, of course, in many ways a precursor of the modern movement in fiction, his deepest originality and perhaps the chief unacknowledged cause of his popularity today, derives from an attitude to his society, both as subject and as audience, which has been shared by no other greater writer of our century. Many things in himself, his life and his times, gave him as deep a sense of the modern alienation as any other of our great exiled and isolated writers; and yet Conrad's most vigorous energies were turned away from the ever-increasing separateness of the individual and towards discovering values and attitudes and ways of living and writing which he could respect and yet which were, or could be, widely shared. Mudrick has more than reminded us of the occasional cost in emphasis, repetition, and cliché, but no criticism has yet adequately assessed what Conrad gave in exchange. His aim—"to make you see"—has often been quoted: but there has been less emphasis on how Conrad specified that the objects in the "presented vision" should be such as to "awaken in the hearts of the beholders that feeling of unavoidable solidarity; of the solidarity in mysterious origin, in toil, in joy, in hope, in uncertain fate, which binds men to each other and all mankind to the visible world." In the centrality of his ultimate purpose Conrad is akin to Wordsworth; and if he expresses it grandiloquently, he at least does not, in the Arnoldian phrase, give us the grand word without the grand thing.

The third chapter of *The Nigger of the "Narcissus,"* for example, is not merely a magnificent evocation of a storm at sea; it is a sequence of unequaled enactments of the theme of solidarity. It begins as we experience gratitude for the efforts of the crew to save Wait, or of Podmore, incredibly, to produce coffee; and it achieves its final resonance in the famous ending when, after long forgetting him, our eyes are turned to Singleton at the wheel, and we are told, simply, that, after thirty hours, "He steered with care." It is the climactic recognition of our utter and yet often forgotten dependence, night and day, by sea and by land, on the labors of others; and by the kind of cross reference of attitudes which is Conrad's most characteristic way of achieving a symbolic dimension, this supereme image is linked with three other scenes; that where we later see how Singleton's endurance at the wheel brings him face to face with death; that where he has previously told Wait: "Well, get on with your dying, don't raise a blamed fuss with us over the job"; and that soon after where Donkin taunts Wait with slackness on the rope—"You don't kill yourself, old man!"—and Wait retorts "Would you?"

Singleton does, and the heroic quality of his labors reminds us, not only that what has been most enduring about human society has been the mere continuity of its struggle against nature, which is, as we have seen, the tenor of the ensuing paragraph about the sea which opens the next chapter, but also that Conrad's greatest art, in *Typhoon* and *The Shadow Line* as in *The Nigger of the "Narcissus,"* is often reserved for making us, in Auden's words, "Give / Our gratitude to the Invisible College of the Humble, / Who through the ages have accomplished everything essential." There is perhaps a moral for the critic here: for, in making us look up, briefly, to Singleton at the wheel, Conrad gives us a moment of vision in which, from the height of our modish attachment to ever-developing discriminations, we are compelled to affirm our endless, intricate, and not inglorious kinship with those who cannot write and who read only Bulwer-Lytton.

NORRIS W. YATES

Social Comment in *The Nigger of the "Narcissus"*†

The Nigger of the "Narcissus" has been interpreted as an allegory about isolation vs. solidarity, and critics have noted that one of the conflicts which disrupts the solidarity of the ship's community is that between officers and crewmen. Marvin Mudrick even accuses Conrad of a pitiless, antihumanitarian approach that presents an idealized "upper class" of officers, and a "lower" class of seamen that is ignorant, brutalized, and fickle. Ian Watt implicitly admits the charge while denying its relevance as literary criticism: "Symbolically, Conrad seems to be saying that although pitilessness is characteristic of the selfish, yet the increasing sensitiveness to the sufferings of others which civilization brings necessarily poses grave problems of control for the individual and for society."[1] This note will suggest that in addition to its symbolism and allegory, Conrad's novel includes sociohistorical criticism of attempts made by reformers during the author's sea-going days to improve the working condi-

† From *PMLA*, 79 (March 1964), 183–85.

1. Marvin Mudrick, "The Artist's Conscience and *The Nigger of the 'Narcissus,'*" *NCF*, XII (March 1957), 294–95; Ian Watt, "Conrad Criticism and *The Nigger of the 'Narcissus,'*" *NCF*, XII (March 1958), 277. Cf. Christopher Morley, "*The Nigger of the 'Narcissus,'*" in *A Conrad Memorial-Library* (Garden City, N.Y., 1929), pp. 28–31, and Morton Dauwen Zabel, *Craft and Character in Modern Fiction* (New York, 1957), 168–86. Morley calls this novel a "cruel" book, and Zabel refers to the crew as "closer to brutes than to civilized beings" (p. 181). See also George Garrett, "Conrad's *The Nigger of the 'Narcissus,'*" *Adelphi*, 3rd ser., XII (June 1936), 150–55, and Albert J. Guerard, *Conrad the Novelist* (Cambridge, Mass., 1958), p. 104.

tions of British seamen. Emphasis on this neglected theme of pro-test against social protest shows that Conrad saw the social tensions on shipboard as more than a purely symbolic microcosm of those on shore; for him they were a literal result of reform agitation on land.

The occasion on which the word "mutiny" is first spoken among the men includes a direct slap at the most publicized agitator for maritime reform during Conrad's years at sea. The gale and the Cape of Good Hope have been weathered, and during a leisurely interval, Donkin sarcastically compliments James Wait on his success in shamming illness. Knowles, one of the less competent seamen, remarks that they cannot all follow Wait's example: "There's six weeks' hard for refoosing dooty." He tells of how a "fatherly old gentleman," hired by "some kind people" to look for overloaded ships, talked a crew into such a refusal—"Said as how it was crool hard to be drownded in winter just for the sake of a few pounds more for the owner." The crew, says Knowles, depended upon "that 'ere Pimsoll man to see 'em through the court. They thought to have a bloomin' lark and two or three days' spree." Instead they were punished, because the ship was not overloaded—"There wasn't one overloaded ship in Penarth dock at all."[2]

Samuel Pimsoll was a former coal merchant turned politician who sat as a Radical in the House of Commons from 1868 to 1880 and continued his efforts at reform thereafter. In speeches and pam-phlets he charged that shipowners and shipmasters eager for more profits per voyage commonly overloaded their vessels to the danger point. His attacks won him the nickname of the "Sailors' friend," and in 1876 the first of several bills enforcing a maximum "load line" or "Plimsoll mark" on all British vessels was passed. His prom-inence, his aggressive piety, his habit of hurling sensational charges at prominent persons,[3] and his lack of sea-going experience doubt-less induced Conrad to associate his name with one type of fanati-cal do-gooder who, like Donkin, brings disruption and misfortune into a ship's company.

2. The original *Narcissus* sailed from Penarth, near Cardiff, to Bombay where Conrad joined her, but the roster of the crew does not suggest any concerted re-fusal of duty during this voyage. See Jo-celyn Baines, *Joseph Conrad: A Critical Biography* (New York and London, 1960); the roster is reproduced between pp. 292-93. A refusal of duty would be indicated in the dates of discharge of some of the crew and in their replace-ment. However, Conrad's impatience with hands who refused to sail after signing up for a voyage is reflected in "Youth" in which Marlow praises the "Liverpool hard cases" who sail the *Judea* in ignor-ance of the refusal of two previous crews and who work the ship until the last

possible moment.
3. David Masters, *The Plimsoll Mark* (London, 1955), pp. 122–30; G. D. H. Cole, *A Short History of the British Working-Class Movement 1789–1947* (London, 1952), rev. ed., pp. 221–22, 239–40, 243–45, 259, and E. H. Phelps Brown, *The Growth of British Industrial Relations* (London and New York, 1959), p. 72. See also Samuel Plimsoll, *Our Seamen* (London, 1873) and *Cattle Ships* (London, 1890). The former pam-phlet involved the author in an action for criminal libel, and his charges against colleagues in the House of Com-mons caused Disraeli to ask that he be reprimanded by the House.

Conrad himself sailed in the British Merchant Service from 1878 to 1894, and later professed satisfaction with the protection offered him as a crewman and officer by Parliament during his sea career.[4] In this novel, his main attack on maritime reforms was conducted through his depiction of Donkin. The cockney is explicitly identified as a universal type of incompetent and malingerer: "They all knew him. Is there a spot on earth where such a man is unknown?" He is also a "votary of change," i.e., an agitator. In A *Personal Record*, Conrad implied that almost any social change was directly hostile to his basic "idea of Fidelity." He declared that "I have not been revolutionary in my writings," and added that revolutionary optimism was unscrupulous and contained "the menace of fanaticism and intolerance." Often he drew no line between revolution and reform; the strong showing of the Liberals in the elections of 1885 meant to him that "every disreputable ragamuffin in Europe feels that the day of universal brotherhood, despoliation and disorder is coming apace."[5] Donkin (unlike Long, the Marxist in Eugene O'Neill's *The Hairy Ape*) expounds no ideology beyond his vague talk of "rights." Thus he can represent any unscrupulous self-seeker who has a divisive effect.

One of Donkin's first divisive thrusts is his abuse of the Finn and his generalization that these "damned furriners" should be taught "their place." In this as in his other attempts at subversion, Donkin remains essentially a landsman. In the 1880's and 1890's, maritime trade unions played an increasing part in the agitation for reform at sea. Plimsoll himself served as first president of the National Amalgamated Seamen's and Firemen's Union (1887–92). Nevertheless, in *The Nigger of the "Narcissus"* Conrad criticizes this agitation as officious meddling by soft-hearted landlubbers. His attack thus constitutes a neglected aspect of the shore-vs-ship contrast that recurs in the novel—"you hear a lot on shore, don't you?" the captain storms at the would-be mutineers.[6] Although Donkin has served on at least one vessel prior to joining the "Narcissus"—an American ship from which he deserted—he remains untouched by the lessons of the sea, and on shore at the end of the voyage he blossoms out while the rest of the ship's company are shrinking in stature: "He had better clothes, had an easy air, appeared more at home than

4. *The Works of Joseph Conrad*, XIX (Edinburgh and London, 1925), 154, hereafter cited as *Works*. The "Merchant Shipping Act" which Conrad called "a father and mother to me" actually consisted of many separate Acts of Parliament regulating shipowners, shipmasters, and crews. These Acts were not consolidated until 1894, the year Conrad left the sea. See *Chitty's Statutes of Practical Utility*, XIII (London, 1913), 6th ed., 361–677, esp. 402–64.

5. *Works*, IX, xxi–xxii; also *Joseph Conrad: Life and Letters*, ed. G. Jean-Aubry, I (New York, 1927), 84. In *The Rover*, Conrad associated progress, piracy, and the French Revolution.

6. This contrast is discussed by Thomas Moser, *Joseph Conrad: Achievement and Decline* (Cambridge, Mass., 1957), p. 69, and Vernon Young, "Trial by Water: Joseph Conrad's *The Nigger of the 'Narcissus,'*" *Accent*, XII (Spring 1952), 69 f.

any of us." Moreover, in his future capacity as a labor agitator he is specifically consigned to the earth rather than to the sea.

Indeed, Conrad's dislike of shore-going reformers often spills over into direct commentary. Donkin is called "the pet of philanthropists and self-seeking landlubbers," and, by contrast, Singleton is held characteristic of a bygone race of stalwarts who had no need of reformers or reform: "Well-meaning people had tried to represent those men as whining over every mouthful of their food,[7] as going about their work in fear of their lives. . . . [They were] men hard to manage, but easy to inspire; voiceless men—but men enough to scorn in their hearts the sentimental voices that bewailed the hardness of their fate . . . if they [their successors] had learned how to speak they have also learned how to whine." Conrad minces no words in claiming that reformers with the tender-minded ethic of landsmen play into the hands of such as Donkin by luring the minds of these "big children" away from fidelity to what Marlow in *Lord Jim* calls the "craft of the sea." This fidelity includes involvement in the orderly routine of the ship, acknowledgment of the skipper's absolute authority, and (as Wright and Watt have observed) a mutual respect between crew and officers based on each man's knowledge of his job and "place."[8]

Other characters besides Donkin are from time to time criticized by association with the meddling of land-bound reformers. Wait is a much greater threat to solidarity than is Donkin, but part of the West Indian sailor's effectiveness arises from his softening up of the crew for trouble-makers like Donkin. Moreover, despite the collapse of the mutiny, the men continue to affirm Jimmy's wildest claims, "as though he had been a millionaire, a politician, or a reformer—and we a crowd of ambitious lubbers." Belfast, the most sentimental of the crew, is "as tenderly gay as an old philanthropist" toward Jimmy. The cook too reflects Conrad's distrust of reformers. This character was doubtless inspired by some crewman on the original "Narcissus" or elsewhere whom Conrad had known, or by one or more of the street preachers whom he could have seen in London and other ports, but his surname suggests that of Frank Podmore, a co-founder in 1883–84 of the Fabian Society who, like Plimsoll, combined piety with zeal in social agitation.[9] Whether Conrad's

7. Bad provisions for seamen were one of Plimsoll's targets (Masters, pp. 256–57).

8. "He who loves the sea loves also the ship's routine," Conrad wrote (*Works*, IX, 7; see also XIX, 190–91). On mutual respect, see Walter F. Wright, *Romance and Tragedy in Joseph Conrad* (Lincoln, Neb., 1949), p. 41, and Watt, p. 280.

9. Edith S. Hooper, *DNB*, 2nd Supplement, III, "Frank Podmore"; Anne Fremantle, *This Little Band of Prophets*,

Mentor (New York, 1960), pp. 13, 27–28, 49–50, 75. Podmore is said to have suggested the name of the society. He also wrote much on psychical research. The uncommonness of his surname is attested by its nonappearance elsewhere in the *DNB* or its supplements. True, Conrad sometimes forgot or altered the names of real persons depicted in his novels; e.g., Wait, Singleton, and Donkin do not bear the names of their prototypes on the "Narcissus." See Baines, pp. 76–77, 77 n.

choice of this rather unusual name was unconscious or not, he could hardly have been unaware that designations like "a conceited saint" and "the desire to meddle," and the statement that "like many benefactors of humanity, the cook took him self too seriously, and reaped the reward of irreverence" contained anti-Liberal barbs that readers of William Ernest Henley's conservative *New Review*, in which the novel was serialized, would appreciate.

Through the cook's behavior, Conrad suggests that the reformers' compassion is merely a sentimentality that masks an egoism more pitiless than the sternest regime at sea. Podmore brings tea and sugar to Jimmy, but has "prayerfully divested himself of the last vestige of his humanity" to preach irrelevantly at the dying man. In tempting a crew to risk punishment by disobeying orders, the "Plimsoll man" showed equal callousness.

Through direct statement and through character, Conrad has thus worked into his novel a social commentary on one phase of late Victorian reform agitation. His distrust of this agitation may be held responsible in part for the strength of his bias toward the officers and against certain crewmen, Donkin in particular. In addition, the social comment adds body to the over-all life-allegory. Proper attention to this social vein should discourage the tendency in critics to treat Conrad's sea tales as disconnected from their larger sociohistorical context.[1] *The Nigger of the "Narcissus"* is a tale of the land as well as of the sea.

GERALD MORGAN

Narcissus Afloat†

The sea, as a subject, has a way of vanishing behind the conventions of art or chronicle which spring to our minds. Trying to conceive, to represent this reality of ceaseless change of light and shape, we have recourse to fictions, to dubious notions of time and space: to pictures explaining—pictures. As with the sea, so with the universe; and so with ourselves. Reality is guessed and hinted at by analogy and symbol, within the limitations of language by which reality itself is unaffected. There are more things in Heaven and earth than we can name, with worn-out coinage.[1]

1. E.g., Moser, pp. 11–12, 134; Frederick R. Karl, *A Readers' Guide to Joseph Conrad* (London, 1960), p. 113; Leo Gurko, "Death Journey in *The Nigger of the 'Narcissus,'*" *NCF*, XV (March 1961), 301–11. Allegories of ship and crew as humanity, a prison, and a band of fallen angels respectively are stressed, to the deemphasis of more literal elements in the novel.
† From *Bulletin de l'Association cana-*

dienne des Humanités, 15 (Autumn 1964), 44–55.
1. This paper was read at a meeting of the Association of Canadian University Teachers of English, in Charlottetown, June 16, 1964.
2. "Typhoon", in *Typhoon & other stories*, Dent Collected Edition, pp. 15 and 9. Except as otherwise indicated, this edition is the source of Conrad quotations.

Conrad was explictly aware of this by the time he wrote his third completed novel, *The Nigger of the "Narcissus."* Nonetheless he declared in the Preface to this novel his intention of doing justice, not only to the visible aspects of the universe, but also to the truth underlying these. The visible aspects he had observed for twenty years as a seaman, in their most dramatic and mobile—and most obviously illusory—form. For months on end he had gazed at the sea horizon, the illusory straight line forever unattainable. He had for years charted the inconstant locus of his vessel in time and space, and known that his assumptions could be upset by the "eloquent facts" of the sea which "can speak for themselves with overwhelming precision"[2]

As with the sea, so with the self; for Conrad wavered constantly between an epic of the sea and an epic of the soul, and in the end wrote both by reflecting the one in the other. He averred that personality is an illusion, "an aimless mask of something hopelessly unknown".[3] His method was to descend within the unknown self and there find some truth of the universe; the result was symbolism, with a difference. Things become symbolic in Conrad's work by reason of the clarity, rather than the obscurity, of their perceptible aspect, which Conrad describes with as much precision as non-technical language allows.

He uses similes very often, and metaphors very seldom. More often than not his literal representation takes the propositional form: A (like x) = A (like y). When he shifts into the stronger analogy of metaphor, where A = B, the metaphor takes increased strength from its rarity. Thus a sudden metaphor of Karain, performing an Odyssey among illusion;[4] illusions elsewhere referred to as visions of remote unattainable truth dimly seen.[5] An example of Conrad's literal precision is the description, in *Typhoon*, of a vessel in the eye of a cyclone.[6] As the club-hauling manoeuvre in Marryat's *Peter Simple* became a standard recitation-piece for Royal Navy examinations in sail, so Conrad's *Typhoon* passage could serve for candidates in marine meterorology. Likewise the opening chapter of *Nostromo* could be equally a copy of or a model for a chapter of Admiralty Sailing Directions describing the seaward approach to Sulaco. But the whole chapter is part of an epic metaphor. The novel begins with pilotage and ends with a lighthouse; it is the converse of the metaphor in "Youth"; a voyage as "a symbol of existence".[7] Within the symbolic frame, Conrad's descriptions mean exactly what they say. Thus, a storm-sunset seen from the capsized *Narcissus*:

3. Letter of 29/3/96, in J. G. Aubry, *Joseph Conrad, Life and Letters* London, 1927) Vol. I, p. 186.
4. "Karain—A Memory", in *Tales of Unrest*, p. 40.
5. *Lord Jim*, p. 323.
6. *Typhoon & Other Stories*, p. 82.
7. "Youth", in *Youth etc.*, p. 4; cf. *Notes on Life and Letters*, 185–9.

On the edge of the horizon, black seas leaped up towards the glowing sun. It sank slowly, round and blazing, and the crests of waves splashed on the edge of the luminous circle . . . The big seas began to roll across the crimson disc; and over miles of turbulent waters the shadows of high waves swept with a running darkness the faces of men. A crested roller broke with a loud hissing roar, and the sun, as if put out, disappeared. The chattering voice faltered, went out together with the light.

This passage alone would suffice to demonstrate, not only the descriptive exactitude, but also the symbolical and mythic saturation of Conrad's art. There is the Narcissus-shell, overturned; there is a capsized planet of men; a voyage of existence abruptly checked; the inept voice chattering and silenced; the sun of life swallowed up by the devouring sea, as if it had been itself a sun-myth like Balder or Osiris, doomed to be submerged in a final darkness.

Conrad begins with visible fact, vividly described, assumed to be illusion; he descends to the inner selfhood of persons affected by their pictures of visible fact and of themselves; he emerges with a vision of man in the universe voyaging through the visible toward the inscrutable, while peering within his unknown depths through the barely expressible toward the unspeakable.

Thus *The Nigger of the "Narcissus."* The name of the ship is highly symbolic in Conrad, but is not invented by him. A shipowner chose to name his vessel *Narcissus*, and Conrad chose to sail in her. From this fact springs a novel more famous than the ship, and a symbol for the whole of Conrad's imaginative achievement; a symbol of our century. The description of visible aspects is impressive, and at first sight seems exhaustive. An early critic perceived, on reading it, that the pasteboard ocean was gone forever.[8] But Conrad himself, master mariner, made no claim to have shown the sea as reality. What the critic did not remark was that the pasteboard had been replaced by a mirror, and the saucy *Arethusa* by the dreaming *Narcissus*.

The symbolism in Conrad's art has been sketched out by Conrad himself, in the choice of titles and epigraphs for his works. Reading these, we can discard chronology as readily as Conrad did; as readily as Captain Brierley discarded his timepiece before leaping down from *Ossa* into the destructive element, as readily as Verloc prepared to blow up time, as casually as Marlow floated on the Thames to the Roman Empire and the Belgian Congo in the same turn of the tide. We can rearrange Conrad's titles as logicians and mathematicians reshuffle propositions, changing the sequence of these without altering their significance, the better to perceive some truth

8. E. V. Lucas, cited by John D. Gordon, *Joseph Conrad: the making of a* *novelist* (Cambridge, Mass., 1940), p. 291.

in what Ayer calls "Complex tautologies."[9] Conrad's works are complex tautologies, expressing always the same truth or illusion, variations on a constant theme. We can read his titles in the following order, the better to perceive their symbolism: "An Outpost of Progress", "The End of the Tether", "The Heart of Darkness", *The Nigger of the "Narcissus," The Mirror of the Sea*, "The Secret Sharer", "The Secret Agent", *The Shadow-Line, Victory.*

The titles signify a progression of the soul, an explorer's journey into the interior, into something like the dark night of the soul known to the Spanish mystic or "the devil's poncho" known to our man—Nostromo—in Sulaco; into the reflective self-awareness of Narcissus afloat on an immense mirror in the darkness, discovering in the mirror, and sometimes overcoming, the secret agent that shares his selfhood and universe.

The title of *Victory* invited some confusion in 1915, when public interest was centred upon a struggle between anonymous masses. Some might have found in the title a heartening echo of the name of the flagship of Lord Nelson, who was in Conrad's view the "seaman of seamen", a genius of "exalted soul" who enlarged "the very conception of victory itself".[1] So said Conrad in *The Mirror of the Sea*, of the parson's sailor son; he provided a clerical origin to Leggatt in "The Secret Sharer", to Kurtz's Russian friend in "Heart of Darkness", and to Lord Jim, all of them sailors concerned with a special conception of victory or defeat. The title of *Victory* surely derives from the speech of the Polish hero in Calderon's drama *Life is a Dream* who says: "It is a question now of acheiving the highest victory: the victory over the self".[2]

Conrad had already quoted the Spanish drama twenty years earlier, in the epigraph to his second novel *An Outcast of the Islands*: "The worst fault of a man is his having been born",[3] The words are spoken by Calderon's drugged hero in a moment of anguish, when he finds truth and illusion inextricably confused, before he goes on to a victory over the self. Calderon is a Baroque master of the equivocal tradition developed in the Renaissance and bequeathed to the Romantics, eventually to Conrad by his father: the convention of mirrors, dreams, dubious madness, self-portraits, optical illusions; the notion of the world as a stage, and the obverse notion of art as a mirror of nature; the taste for mingling all of these in a marriage of contraries, an equivocation between reflection and object, subject and painter, world and soul, illusion and truth,

9. A. J. Ayer, *Language, Truth and Logic* (London, 1955) p. 86.
1. *The Mirror of the Sea*, p. 187.
2. "Hoy ha de ser la mas alta/vencerme a mé." *La Vidas es Suéno*, Jornada Tercera, Escena XIV; ed. Angel del Rio,

Antologia General de la Litteratura Es-panola (New York, 1954), vol. I.
3. "El mayor delito del hombre es haber nacito". Ibid., Jornada Primera, Escena II.

wit and madness, dream and fact. The tradition rests on the ancient principle of the *coincidentia oppositorum*, which was revived in the XV century by Nicholas of Cusa with his doctrine of *Learned Unknowing*.[4] The doctrine is paralleled, with the *noche oscura* of the Spanish mystic St. John of the Cross, by Conrad's credo in the Preface to *The Nigger of the "Narcissus"*. The principle is best symbolized by the mirror, wherein an object reflected appears in reverse, its spatial form altered but not it significance.

The dream and the mirror are important components of Conrad's work. Both of them are equivocal. Both, it may be said, aid in the projection of a man's ideal conception of himself, which is the opening move in most of Conrad's tales. When a Conrad hero loses his ideal conception of himself, embodied in himself or in another character conceived as his "double," he is like Erasmus in Hoffmann's tale,[5] who lost his reflection and went about in secrecy and dismay. In this event Conrad's characters often commit suicide, or a moral harakiri. Thus Willems, Kurtz, Jim, Brierley, Falk, Nostromo, Decoud, Razumov and many others, exceptions being the young anonymous captain of the nameless barque in "Secret Sharer" and *The Shadow-Line*. A rare recovery occurs in the case of Lord Jim, figuratively buried alive and reborn, after the famous "Stein" chapter which positively gleams with mirrors, doubles and dreams, and which poses the main question of the self-questing Narcissus: "how to be?"[6] Jim is Everyman, or everyman's double. He is "one of us", he is "an enigma", to be fathomed only by an austere naval officer (in the aspect of a priest) and by a romantic entomologist, collector of things "perishable and defying destruction". Thus Marlow in *Lord Jim*:

(Stein) lit a two-branched candlestick and led the way. We passed through empty dark rooms, escorted by gleams . . . (which) glided along . . . sweeping here and there . . . leaped upon a fragmentary curve . . . or flashed perpendicularly in and out of distant mirrors, while the forms of two men and the flicker of two flames could be seen for a moment stealing silently across the depths of a crystalline void . . .

(Jim's) imperishable reality came to me . . . with an irresistible force! I saw it vividly, as though in our progress through the lofty silent rooms amongst fleeting gleams of light and the sudden revelations of human figures stealing with flickering flames within unfathomable and pellucid depths, we had approached nearer to absolute Truth, which, like Beauty itself, floats elusive, obscure, half-submerged, in the silent still waters of mystery.[7]

4. E. Gilson, *History of Christian Philosophy in the Middle Ages* (New York, 1955) pp. 534–540.
5. E. T. A. Hoffmann, "The Lost Reflection", in *Eight Tales of Hoffmann*, ed. and transl. J. M. Cohen (London, 1952).
6. *Lord Jim*, p. 214.
7. Ibid., p. 216.

Conrad had introduced the crystalline void in his second novel, which borrowed its epigraph from Calderon. Here we find the sea extending, for the first of a hundred glimpses, as "the restless mirror of the infinite."[8]

The sea is represented as a mirror both physically and metaphysically. Its surface, when calm, is represented as polished stone or metal, "an adamantine surface",[9] "the silvered plate-glass of a mirror",[1] or strewn with islets "like a handful of emeralds on a buckler of steel".[2] Various similes of metal and gems are employed, on one occasion extending the sea, as an image of light, over the whole world.

> The sea was polished, was blue, was pellucid, was sparkling like a precious stone, extending on all sides, all round to the horizon— as if the whole terrestrial globe had been one jewel, one colossal sapphire, a single gem fashioned into a planet.[3]

In "The Secret Sharer" the narrator's ship is first seen near islets "set in a blue sea that itself looked solid;"[4] at the crisis the ship is immobilized on "the glassy smoothness of the sleeping surface,"[5] as befits the vessel of a dreamer on the mirror. In *The Shadow-Line* the same ship, bewitched at the same place, is like "a model ship set on the gleams and shadows of polished marble."[6] The same condition affects Lingard's brig as *The Rescue* opens:

> On the unruffled surface of the straits the brig floated tranquil and upright as if bolted solidly, keel to keel, with its own image reflected in the unframed and immense mirror of the sea. To the south and east the double islands watched silently the double ship . . .[7]

But this imagery leads us to its own opposite, where the mirror itself becomes invisible and the sea, from being solid, becomes pure space. The same brig is later seen floating at night "between an invisible sky and an invisible sea, like a miraculous craft suspended in the air".[8] This optical phenomenon is described several times between Conrad's first work and his last. In "Karain" the light-image, which elsewhere has given the sea a universal extension as a global sapphire, is fused with the mirror-image so as to confound dimensions:

> The bay was a bottomless pit of intense light. The circular sheet of water reflected a luminous sky, and the shores enclosing it made an opaque ring of earth floating in an emptiness of transparent blue.[9]

8. *An Outcast of the Islands*, p. 12.
9. "The End of the Tether", *Youth etc.*, p. 165.
1. Ibid., p. 245.
2. "Karain", *Tales of Unrest*, p. 2.
3. "Youth", *Youth etc.*, p. 20.
4. "The Secret Sharer", *Twixt Land and Sea*, p. 91.
5. Ibid., p. 142.
6. *The Shadow-Line*, p. 78.
7. *The Rescue*, p. 5.
8. Ibid., p. 203.
9. "Karain", *Tales of Unrest*, p. 5.

This mirror-imagery, in which the reflected and the reflection cancel out each other, producing "emptiness", is usually associated with light, but not always with the brilliance of gem-light. We can see the different hours of the day and night casting different hues about the emptiness. Renouard's schooner, for instance, "lay white, and as if suspended, in the crepuscular atmosphere of sunset mingling with the ashy gleam,"[1] of the sea. At night we see Captain Whalley's *Sofala*:

> Under the clouded sky, through the still air that seemed to cling warm, with a seaweed smell, to her slim hull . . . the ship moved on an even keel, as if floating detached in empty space.[2]

The ship detached in empty transparent space is naturally comparable to a planet, and Conrad underlines the symbolic connection.

> My command might have been a planet flying vertiginously on its appointed path in a space of infinite silence. I clung to the rail as if my sense of balance were leaving me for good.[3]

The *Narcissus* in fair weather, sails "lonely and swift like a small planet . . . Round her the abysses of sea and sky met in an unattainable frontier." And again: "Our little world went on its curved and unswerving path carrying a discontented and aspiring population". Eventually we see a compounding of the images of light, mirror and flaming astral body, when the *Narcissus* is caught in lightning:

> the becalmed craft stood out with its masts and rigging, with every sail and every rope distinct and black in the centre of a fiery outburst, like a charred ship enclosed in a globe of fire.

Thus it is to be observed that the mirror of the calm sea dissolves two elements, sky and water, into each other, and removes altogether two dimensions out of three, leaving only a sensation of suspension in altitude or depth. This sensation is perfectly familiar to any seaman who has floated above the stars reflected in tropic seas. The length and breadth of the sea, already compounded as the diameter of a circular horizon, disappear together with the horizon, leaving the ship at the centre of an illimitable globe as if bound to voyage forever. Space, as a measurable quantity, has vanished; and time has vanished too.

Conrad has perfectly described the phenomenon, and furnished it with appropriate imagery. This spacelessness is to be remembered when Conrad transposes the mirror of the sea as a metaphor of human life, which he often does. In this manner Conrad

1. "The Planter of Malata", *Within the Tides*, p. 31.
2. "The End of the Tether", *Youth etc.*, p. 318.
3. *The Shadow-Line*, p. 74.

approaches the late-Renaissance poet Johannes Scheffler, who wrote:

A heart that time and place
suffice to satisfy
Knows nothing of its own
immeasurability[4]

It remains only for Conrad to remove time, which he does in his storm-scenes. The sea, he suggests, is not merely a light-filled mirror of space, but is also a mirror of a condition older than light; it is a revelation of Chaos, ancient and ageless. It is a vat of time; in storms it looks "as if the immemorial ages had been stirred up from the undisturbed bottom of ooze".[5]

If you would know the age of the earth look upon the sea in a storm. The greyness of the whole immense surface, the wind furrows on the faces of the waves, the great masses of foam, tossed about and waving, like matted white locks, give to the sea in a gale an appearance of hoary age, lustreless, dull, without gleams, as though it had been created before light itself.[6]

The sea, embodiment of Chaos, is shown as being prior to light, and able to extinguish "the last rays of sinister light between the hills of steep rolling waves". The end is as the beginning, time is turned backwards and extinguished. The moon is seen "rushing backwards with frightful speed over the sky", just as the sun is seen swallowed up by the sea which antedates it:

Black seas leaped up towards the glowing sun . . . A crested roller broke with a loud hissing roar, and the sun, as if put out, disappeared.

The ship becomes again a lonely planet through mirror-effect. In the black sky the stars gleam at a black sea that flashes back at them "the evanescent and pale light of a dazzling whiteness born from the black turmoil of the waves". But at moments on this wild mirror, even the stars and the foaming tumult are swallowed by darkness:

Nothing seems left of the whole universe but darkness, clamour, fury—and the ship. And like the last vestiges of a shattered creation she drifts, bearing an anguished remnant of sinful mankind, through the distress, tumult and pain of an avenging terror.

When darkness pervades a calm, so that "your ship floats unseen under your feet, her sails flutter invisible above your head,"[7] it defeats both the eye of God Himself and the malice of the devil; a ship, or a soul, is perfectly isolated, "lost in a vast universe of night

4. Angelus Silesius, *The Cherubinic Wanderer*, transl. W. R. Trask (New York, 1953) p. 50.

5. *The Mirror of the Sea*, p. 71.
6. Loc. cit.
7. *Nostromo*, p. 7.

and silence".[8] This is a kind of passive annihilation, which merely disorients the soul:

> He had the strangest sensation of his soul having just returned into his body from the circumambient darkness in which land, sea, sky . . . were as if they had not been.[9]

But in a storm, the seaman faces annihilation by the active embodiment of chaos, where his ship becomes the last vestige of a shattered creation, itself about to be shattered by a maniac victor over space and time:

> A big, foaming sea . . . made for the ship, roaring wildly, . . . as mischievous and discomposing as a madman with an axe.

> It wasn't a heavy sea—it was a sea gone mad! I suppose the end of the world will be something like that.[1]

Thus the storm shows the beginning of time, "before light itself", and the ending of time, "the end of the world" and "shattered creation"; the "restless mirror of the Infinite" exerts its power before and after time, its roar sounding "like an indistinct noise from another world".

The mirror of the sea abolishes the meaning of up and down, of before and after, which it makes the same by reflecting, so to speak, one against the other until time and space are fused into a single dimension, an un-named condition of existence. In this condition, human experience is limited to that of elementary sight and sound; the eye perceives light delusively reflected, or else nothingness in the dark, while the ear is strained either by the silence of almost perfect isolation of the spirit from the senses. It is analogous to a moral isolation of a man from his fellows, and, like this latter condition, is best appreciated in solitude.

> Solitude from mere outward condition of existence becomes very swiftly a state of soul . . . (which) takes possession of the mind, and drives forth the thought into the exile of utter unbelief.[2]

The epigraph of *The Shadow-Line* is from Baudelaire's poem "La Musique":

> . . . D'autres fois, calme plat, grand-miroir
> de mon désespoir.[3]

Another poem by Baudelaire, "L'Homme et la Mer",[4] prefigures in 16 lines the whole Conradian symbolism, elaborated in 29 volumes, of the seafaring Narcissus and the double in the infinite mirror. It is never quoted by Conrad. Nor is the reference to Narcis-

8. Loc. cit.
9. *Nostromo*, p. 262.
1. "The Secret Sharer", *Twixt Land and Sea*, p. 124.
2. *Nostromo*, p. 497.
3. Baudelaire, *Oeuvres*, ed. Y-G, Le

Dantec (Paris, 1954), p. 141.
4. Ibid., p. 94. See also Gide's symbolist *Traité du Narcisse* (1892) and *Voyage d'Urien* (1893); in *Oeuvres Complètes*, ed. L. Martin-Chauffier (Paris, n.d.) Vol. I, pp. 207–220, 281–365.

sus in Milton's *Comus*, which, 30 lines earlier, provides the epigraph to Conrad's *Victory*.[5]

In a word, one might say that the Conrad *oeuvre* is simply the development, or tautological transformation, of symbolic formulas worked out by Calderon and Baudelaire. To the extent that Conrad is concerned with "the truth, manifold and one"[6] underlying every aspect of the visible universe, one might say that Conrad, inspired by these two masters, has dreamed his way to a Swedenborgian Narcissism particularly apt for our time. This would explain his present wide appeal.

Selfhood is the modern Sant-Graal, leading men to choose a flag, vote a new constitution, change their psychiatrist, by uncertain acts of a will to "be themselves." But selfhood is not readily identified. No common measure of identity is to be found in modern Western literature, except as provided in the Pythagorean utopias which Huxley, Zamiatin and Orwell described with the aim of prevention rather than promotion, though with a prospect of failure steadily before them. Selfhood in modern culture is something of an unknown soldier, giving and receiving multiple death, and symbolized by machine-cut granite blocks of sizes proportional to the density of population living or dead. Asserting selfhood nonetheless, the artist tends to waver between bravado and flight; between satire of a kind soon to be written by computers to amuse each other, and a headlong flight into irrationality—to the dark knowledge acquired in the gamekeeper's shed.

"All art is narcissistic", says a critic.[7] But how an artist may succeed as Narcissus cannot be told, in the absence of a definition of selfhood. "Man must invent himself", says Sartre.[8] But this means to cultivate the absurd, to apply Orwell's doublethink, not merely to a regimented cypher but to an individual believing himself intensely self-aware. "To thine own self be true", said Shakespeare, setting the stage for generations of walking shadows, full of sound and fury; for characters of diminishing import retreating from the throne-room to the parlour, to the bedroom, to the ashcan.

When mythology filled the place vacated by drama, as a ritual of collective identity, suffering became the measure of selfhood. Prometheus suffers with immense self-satisfaction, having invented a bird to devour him. Though in truth it would seem that it is the fire, not the bird, which punishes Prometheus; he is a 'noble savage', like Caliban, who stole language in order to abuse it. Thus the Promethean and Byronic heroes, bloody but unbowed, secure in their rebellious suffering. Yet the Satanic *non serviam* does not

5. *Comus*, lines 235–6; lines 206–8. H. F. Fletcher, ed., *The Complete Poetical Works of Milton* (Cambridge, Mass., 1941).
6. Preface. [*Editor.*]
7. J. G. Weightman, "High, Low, and Modern", *Encounter*, Vol. XV, No. 3 (1960) p. 69.
8. J. P. Sartre, "Existentialism is a Humanism", in W. Kaufmann, ed., *Existentialism from Dostoevsky to Sartre* (New York, 1957) pp. 287–311.

sufficiently define selfhood. The *poètes maudits* were obliged to go further, to spend a season in Hell without Vergil or Dante, to cultivate flowers of evil, and induce illuminations far removed from the madness of Hamlet or Don Quixote; alienation becomes the gauge of selfhood.

Here the creative genius in Conrad shows itself in the myth-maker. He is the first author to set Narcissus on the open sea, as a double of Aphrodite in Neptune's domain. Venus arises, he says, "not from the foam of the sea, but from a distant, still more form-less, mysterious and potent immensity of mankind".[9] Which reminds us of the Gnostic doctrine, that all gods and all men have their genesis in the ocean.[1] Conrad is the first modern author to identify Aphrodite's mirror with the sea itself, as a universal ana-logue resolving the dichotomy between world and soul, between reality and illusion. He is the first to double Narcissus with Odys-seus as a wanderer upon the mirror (Kazantzakis appears to be the second). He is the first to bring a *doppelganger* naked from the mirror of the sea, the first to launch an Ancient Mariner on long prose tales of communal introspection,. the first to set a Flying Dutchman in the China Sea. He is the first to transcribe the voy-ages of archaic myth as ventures in self-discovery:

> the voyage out of time (*The Nigger of the "Narcissus,"* Heart of Darkness)
> the voyage to the isle of death or transfiguration (*Outcast, Nar-cissus, Lord Jim, Nostromo, Secret Sharer, Shadow-Line,* Smile of Fortune, Planter of Malata, Freya, Vic-tory, The Rescue)
> the voyage to the underworld (*Narcissus,* Heart of Darkness, Falk)
> the voyage of atonement (*Narcissus, Shadow-Line, Alaska*[2])

All of these refashioned mythic voyages were refined by Conrad's imagination from the crude events of the maritime history of his day, with a brilliant nautical exactitude. It is illustrative of Conrad that, unlike Hardy and E. J. Pratt, he expressed only contempt for the whole episode of the *Titantic*.

The century of Prometheus the Titan ended symbolically with the *Titanic* rushing upon a mindless lump of ice, an "eloquent fact", a truth floating submerged, like that which Lord Jim's pil-grim-ship met on her course. The fire-stealer of our time is Andrew Undershaft, Shaw's precursor to Orwell's Big Brother. In our cen-tury, therefore, it is assumed that mythic selfhood must be sought in other damned heroes: in Oedipus, relic of the State founded on Kinship, for the Freudian mythology of lust; in Sisyphus, relic of

9. "The Planter of Malata", *Within the Tides*, p. 36.
1. V. Magnien, *Les Mystères d'Eleusis*
(Paris, 1950) p. 297.
2. *Last Essays*, p. 52.

Newtonian physics, for the Existentialist mythology of the absurd.

But it would seem that the proper mythical emblem for our time is Narcissus. The variety of emblems now used from mythology, in what is actually a quest for selfhood, suggests a Protean Narcissus, seeking the Procrustean couch for relief of his multiform aches and pains in murmured confessions of a fifty-minute hour, and seeing in a fluid sheet of time the shifting symbols of his mysterious identity: the Swedenborgian Narcissus. The "forest of symbols" of Baudelaire shelters a pool where Narcissus may, in constant danger of drowning, contemplate the riddle of selfhood and otherness, in what may be his own image or may be the Lady of the Lake.

(There is scant need at this point to enter into the erotic connotations of narcissism and its mirror-obverse, which are visible everywhere about us, thanks to the professional voyeur. Lewd or learned, Kinsey and the camera have caught us all.)

It is to be noted that Conrad's heroes are no good at loving. Lord Jim, Heyst, Gould, Nostromo, Kurtz, M. Georges, Captain Anthony and others, are far too concerned, each with his ideal conception of himself, to inspire anything but despairing self-sacrifice in women. In some cases the weakness is shared by women. One critic has written at some length on Conrad's failure in treating sexual themes.[3] The book may be termed an erotic fallacy. The failure seems to be less in Conrad than in his characters, since Conrad portrays faithfully the vagaries of Narcissus, in plots which are adequate comment on the failure of communication which is today the agonizing concern of authors and dramatists. The whole problem is very clearly stated in Conrad's short story "The Return", a domestic tale in which a mirror figures very prominently. In the ship *Narcissus*, where the *Heart of Darkness* theme is rehearsed on an immense mirror, there is no woman at all. Conrad's women, as a rule, don't take seriously the complicated masculine game of self-conception.

It can be shown, however, that the vessel *Narcissus*, traversing the crystalline void with a "crew of shades" to "the centre of the fatal circle",[4] the "very gate of Erebus",[5] means something more than self-absorption. The Narcissus-figures who flicker in and out of the Conradian mirror have also another quest, of solidarity and "fellowship with all creation". A mirror, like a Renaissance painting or a photograph, is optically extra-dimensional; in two dimensions it represents three. The Conradian mirror is polydimensional, absorbing time and space in shifting series of spatio-temporal points of $(n+1)$ dimensions, like the post-Einsteinian universe. On such a mirror the wandering Narcissus leaves Swedenborg behind: he is the nuclear Narcissus, a Ulysses of the interstices.

3. T. Moser, *Joseph Conrad: Achievement and Decline* (Cambridge, Mass., 1959).

4. *Shadow-Line*, p. 84.

5. "Secret Sharer", p. 140.

274 · *Gerald Morgan*

In *The Secret Agent*, a scheming diplomat meditates on the joy of dropping a bomb into pure mathematics. The event has come to pass. We are now deprived of universals, not only of selfhood, but also of a cosmos with a recognizable meaning. Our knowledge of the visible aspects of the universe has outrun our speech, as happened to Dante in Paradise. A new language is sought by mathematicians and philosophers, to represent conceptions of a cosmos in which the interstices are greater than the entities, and the entities are no more than systems of space-time points.[6] A statement of units of existential mystery conceived as having a certain order, is itself formulated as units of linguistic mystery accepted in a certain order.

What this means to literature has been demonstrated by three polyglot authors: by Hopkins, whose naming delves into the unique individuality of every thing for which he utters the inscape; by Joyce, whose Ulysses functions as a polyglot Narcissus; and by Conrad, whose Narcissus doubles Ulysses wandering among physical and psychic dimensions.

Conrad's celebrated time-shifts mean simply this: that time can be treated as a dimension. As a navigator can estimate his momentary position from points in space (and time) which he has already passed or not yet reached, so Conrad's narrator verifies the position, if not the entity, of his subject, by referring to events in time past or time to come. These events can be superimposed on the present, as points in space can be joined in a double image by the mariner's azimuth-mirror or by his sextant-mirror, and the relative angles verified. Thus in *Lord Jim* the narrator can take a hundred and seventy-five pages to discuss facts:

> visible, tangible, open to the senses, occupying their place in space and time, requiring for their existence a fourteen-hundred-ton steamer and twenty-seven minutes by the watch.[7]

The multiple point of view of Conrad's narrations, a device carried further in Durrell's *Alexandria Quartet* with explicit reference to the Einsteinian world,[8] is another way of taking bearings, to be drawn on a chart such as the Tudor seamen called a Mariner's Mirror.[9] This ranging on moving entities or personalities, like the juggling of antecedents and consequents, lends emphasis to Conrad's dictum that "the meaning of an event lies outside the event".[1]

It can be said that Conrad's is a navigator's art, a science of relativity, open to all the implications of a cosmology without abso-

6. See, e.g., R. Carnap, *Meaning and Necessity* (Chicago, 1956) pp. 205–221.
7. *Lord Jim*, p. 30.
8. L. Durrell, *Justine* (London, 1957) p. 248; *Balthazar* (London, 1958) p. 7;

Clea (London, 1960), p. 5.
9. L. Brown, *The Story of Maps* (Boston, 1950) p. 145.
1. "Heart of Darkness," *Youth, etc.*, p. 48.

lutes; a literature as well devised to represent our world as Narcissus is fit to symbolize it.

What the nuclear Narcissus may hereafter communicate, concerning the enigmas of selfhood or universe, depends on the language he is able to devise. A Conrad narrator says of one event:

> It had the power to drive me out of my conception of existence . . . I seemed to have lost all my words in the chaos of dark thoughts I had contemplated for a second or two beyond the pale. These came back . . . very soon, for words belong also to the sheltering conception of light and order which is our refuge.[2]

Narcissus is cut off from his refuge, and launched on what Conrad calls the "alien sea";[3] the otherness of which has lately been stressed in French literature by the *roman de l'objet*, including *Le Voyeur*.[4] But it is still, after all, none other than Dante's ocean of being.[5]

Conrad's conception of Narcissus as a vessel recalls that of the 12th century mystic Hugh of St. Victor, who compared the human soul to the Ark of Noah on the universal flood.[6] It was Hugh who said "To be oneself, one should enter into oneself, and transcend oneself, moving toward God.[7] Conrad will not go so far. An author is not a monk, he says, though literary activity is a religious rite.[8] What he does seem to suggest is that if, like the chastened crew of the *Narcissus*, one enters unselfconciously into one's voyage upon "the immortal sea", the "mirror of the infinite", one may possess at least the universe. Which brings him fairly close to what the existentialist Gabriel Marcel has said, in a book entitled *Reflection and Mystery*.[9]

DONALD T. TORCHIANA

The Nigger of the "Narcissus": Myth, Mirror, and Metropolis†

I

After all the attention devoted to Conrad's work generally, and to his early work in particular, one more reading of *The Nigger of the "Narcissus"* may well seem but one too many. Yet the recent publi-

2. *Lord Jim*, p. 313.
3. *Mirror of the Sea*, p. 101.
4. J. G. Weightman, "The Obssessive Object", *Encounter*, Vol. XIX, No. 1 (1962) pp. 67–71.
5. "onde si muovono a diversi porti / per lo gran mar dell' essere"— Paradiso I, 112–13; ed. L. Magugliani (Milano, 1949).
6. E. Gilson, *La Philosophie du Moyen Age* (Paris, 1947) p. 305.

7. Cited as epigraph to Gabriel Marcel's dissertation on Coleridge and Schelling; P. Colin, *Existentialisme Chrétien* (Paris, 1947) p. 15.
8. *A Personal Record*, pp. 99–109; cf. Letter of 6/10/08; in Aubry, op. cit., Vol. II, p. 89.
9. G. Marcel, *The Mystery of Being*, Vol. I: *Reflection and Mystery*, (London, 1950).
† From *Wascana Review*, 2 (1967), 29–41.

cation of three essays on the book shows, if nothing more, a restlessness with the standard interpretation offered by Albert Guerard or Maxine Green.[1] All three essays stress, in their different ways, Wait's association with death or his reflecting the separate entities of the crew or, finally, his being central to a crew that follows illusion in the mirror of the sea.[2] Now while none of these essays seems satisfactory to me in explaining the novel, each does point to the possibility of a radical re-interpretation, straining as the authors do towards an explication that has somehow eluded even the most sensitive readers of the story like Ian Watt.[3].

Let me then introduce what may be a beginning for such a new interpretation by offering the possibility that the organizing energy of *The Nigger of the "Narcissus"* is the Narcissus myth itself. Surprisingly, no one, so far as I know, has taken this cue. Let me go on to say that at the heart of that construct I shall maintain Jim Wait to be the black mirror that reflects the several selves, the selfish selves, of the crew. Further, I see his blackness connected with the foul soot, smear or smudge that Conrad arbitrarily allocates to the land, in this case, specifically to the metropolis of London.

At first glance, Ovid's central account of Narcissus and his fate might indeed seem irrelevant or even mistaken when applied to a novel where the ship, not the sailors, assumes his name. In one sense, the ship itself is quite properly thought to be an illusion—most of man's devotions are in Conrad, though there seem to be worthwhile *and* worthless illusions, as the commentators on *Heart of Darkness* never tire of telling us. Be that as it may, I choose to see the name Narcissus applying collectively to the entire crew, with the ship itself at certain crucial times assuming the role of the rejected female Echo. If we may think of the crew together as Narcissus, there appear to be many parts of the myth that point up their fate. In the first place, we recall that Narcissus was the product of the embraces of the river god Cephisus and the nymph Liriope. Tiresias, when asked by her if ever Narcissus should achieve longevity, is said to have replied cryptically, "*si ne non noverit*," if he never knows himself. However, upon scorning not only Echo but many another lover, Narcissus was condemned by Nemesis, who thus answered the prayer of one of the rejected that "so may he himself love, and not gain the thing he loves." Accordingly, Narcissus falls in love with an illusion, the image of himself, insubstantial, fascinating, binding, ultimately deadly. He becomes self-consumed,

1. See the introductions to the Dell and Collier Books editions.
2. Cecil Scrimgeour, "Jimmy Wait and the Dance of Death: Conrad's *Nigger of the Narcissus*," *Critical Quarterly*, VII (Winter 1965), pp. 339–52; Arthur F. Kinney, "Jimmy Wait: Joseph Conrad's Kaleidoscope," *College English*, XXVI

(March 1965), pp. 475–78; Gerald Morgan, "Narcissus Afloat," *Bulletin de l'Association Canadienne des Humanites*, XV, ii (1964), pp. 45–57.
3. Ian Watt, "Conrad Criticism and The Nigger of the Narcissus," *NCF*, XII (March 1958), pp. 257–83.

as is his image. Death is the basis of this love; wasting away is the prelude to union; self and its image will join in oblivion. The *memento mori* will be a flower, landbased. While one cannot ascertain how much of Ovid's account Conrad knew, certain obvious, general features can be more or less assumed: the rejection of Echo, the fatal love of the self-image, the attraction of a wasting death, and the metamorphosis to a flower—in some versions of the myth (Pausianus')—symbolic of entrance to the underworld.

James Wait draws around himself the crew—he is the cynosure of all eyes—and causes them to neglect the ship itself, which during the near-mutiny literally echoes their neglect. The storm that buffets the ship is echoed by the later near-abandonment of the crew. Moreoever, the black, malingering, dying image to whom they do obeisance reflects each man's sentimental concern with the possible extinction of his very precious self. This deification of the self, which every man performs differently, or rather sees differently in Wait—the name itself suggests a burden—is a sacrifice at the altar of death, on which rests the image of the imperiled self. At the same time, such worship is virtually a black mass for Conrad, deifying as it does the worst part of a heritage kept alive by Donkin from the lower depths of Cockney London.

Thus I also hope to show that the almost unrelieved pall that settles over the conclusion of the novel as the ship takes its way up the Thames had been, at least by suggestion, in the story from the moment Wait set foot aboard ship. In other words, the Negro Wait has been intentionally identified with smoke, mist, fog, shadow, darkness, or a veil of gloom from the very beginning to the end of his career on the *Narcissus*. He trails at sea, in a metaphorical sense, the clouds of what Conrad takes to be an inglorious, sentimental, philanthropic, liberally-oriented London. Perhaps, then, a review of the events of each of its five chapters may test my claim that a myth, a mirror, and a metropolis join to point the real drift of *The Nigger of the "Narcissus."*

II

Perhaps I need not bother to review the entire novel or even the chronological events of each chapter; all are well enough known. Most critics have noted the progression from the preparatory calm of the first and second chapters to the storm of the third; from the unrest of the fourth to Wait's death in the fifth; and then the ironic finale in the counting house and under the shadow of the Mint.

Yet a point that might best introduce my scheme in the first chapter is that Singleton, not Donkin or Wait, is the first of the powerful presences to be introduced. In him we are offered not the mirror or the metropolis identified with Wait and Donkin, but the opposite of the Narcissism to which the crew will fall prey. In most accounts Singleton is said to be the foil to Donkin, and so in part he is. Yet one might also be struck by the added possibility that in appearance, age, health, devotion to work, years at sea, and even in white beard, he is strongly contrasted with James Wait. To jump ahead for the moment, one recalls that the ultimate open confrontation will be between Captain Allistoun and Donkin. On the other hand, the covert opposition from beginning to end will be waged between Singleton and Wait, the one dying, doing nothing, and eliciting the fascination of the crew; the other thoroughly absorbed in his work and the life of the sea, very nearly disregarded by the rest of the crew yet given to unthinking but oracular truths about the destiny of the *Narcissus* and Jim Wait. Captain Allistoun and his officers may be said to administer a code or dogma of the sea personfied in Singleton, while Donkin serves an opposite faith at another altar where all sentimentally worship the dying image of themselves. Every reader may not agree with these alignments, yet I offer them to suggest, at the beginning, the virtual anagogic division of godheads aboard. Singleton himself in the middle of the chapter had hinted the division to come when he absolved the *Narcissus* herself of any blame and answered Wait's question "What kind of ship is this? Pretty fair? Eh?" with the words "Ship! . . . Ships are all right. It is the men in them!"

Thus when Wait makes his belated appearance in this first chapter, Conrad has already introduced a man wholly identified with the sea who will, like Tiresias, prophesy not only the end of Wait but, more important, a momentary end of Narcissism. Conrad leaves little doubt that Wait's face—tormented, misshapen, flattened, pathetic, brutal, tragic, mysterious, repulsive are the words that describe it—will serve as mirror for the savagery of selfishness at the heart of most men. After ambiguously intruding himself in announcing his name, Wait, the great Negro, adds tellingly, "I belong to the ship." Indeed he does belong to the *Narcissus*, especially to its human burden, as Singleton might have said, and as the name Wait implies in both its senses. Mr. Baker, the Mate, has already unwittingly signified that combination of weight and malingering in failing to distinguish Wait's name from a smudge: ". . . can't make out that last name. It's all a smudge." Thereupon, with the ring of Wait's sharp death cough, the love affair begins with the crew, and they help carry his chest and bag. Already their sentimentality has been roused in the benevolence and pity wasted in showering Donkin with cast-off clothes. Now, as Wait moves off in their midst to the forecastle, the cook puts the final seal on his presence by exclaiming that he had seen the devil.

But the final, and perhaps most difficult, piece of evidence to establish Wait's role as a mirror and his connection with the city is his curt settling of Donkin's ingratiating whine for tobacco with the answer, "Don't be familiar." This retort and the startled response from Donkin signal the strange relationship of master and man, mirror and attendant, where the rat-like Donkin, entirely selfish, will discover nothing he does not know in Wait, little to pity, no illusory image of a worse self, just his own naturally wretched being. Hence he will view Wait with tolerant disgust and disguised admiration as if viewing his own successful deceptions practiced on the crew's ever ready sympathy, despite their hatred for Wait.

At the end of the chapter we are left with Singleton, who knows nothing of the infamy of the land or Donkin's city, beyond the pleasing illusions of *Pelham* and strong drink. Singleton faces the light, his back to the crew, Wait, and darkness. His attention is on the sea and on his responsibility, here the hold of the anchor. His last words, in the last sentence of the chapter, are "You . . . hold!" So Conrad addresses us. Mischief is afoot. Yet we sense that Singleton will prevail. Like the tar pot that Belfast overturned on the white uniform of the second mate of a steamer—a tale with which he regaled the crew at the chapter's opening—the crew's near drowning in black, like their close call in the storm, will be but a temporary floundering in the treacherous seas of the self.

III

Chapter Two draws taut the lines already laid down in the first chapter. Wait moves almost unrelievedly to the center of the destroyed joy and sinister calm that will usher in the storms of the next two chapters. But this one gathers up into deadly concentration the reluctant and hostile fascination of the crew, the gloom that attends their enforced adoration, and the strong hint that the mirror of their concern may well be a dying man. As the last page of the chapter draws to an end, we feel that a spell has been cast on the ship; we are told quite literally that Jim Wait now "overshadows the ship."

First then to Wait's increasingly visible accomplice, death. Cleverly enough, Conrad places its portent on the disappearing land's horizon of the first page. The black tug that sets the *Narcissus* to windward is that ominous creature and contrasts starkly with the shiny, white sailing ship:

> She resembled an enormous and aquatic black beetle, surprised by the light, overwhelmed by the sunshine, trying to escape with ineffectual effort into the distant gloom of the land. She left a lingering smudge of smoke on the sky, and two vanishing trails of foam on the water. On the place where she had stopped a round black patch of soot remained, undulating on the swell—an unclean mark of the creature's rest.

The gloom, smudge, soot, and sunshine-avoiding insect clearly link the tug to the land and thus to blackness, uncleanness, and death. In virtually starring these connections at the opening of the chapter, Conrad maintains the significance of the vocabulary he has already settled on Wait from his first appearance. But now this Satanic presence—again the description offered by the religious cook—is more clearly demoralizing. Vacillation, cowardice, over-subtle self-inquisition on personal rights and status, feelings of unworthiness that alternate with flashes of vanity, all course through the crew.

The question becomes what should men's eyes focus upon—compass and sail or Wait? Should there be the hardened joy of prescriptive duties or the comforting sadness of contemplating black? In the midst of the joking and highjinks of the crew, finally immersed in the peaceful solitude of the sea, appears the mirror of their discontent, preceded by a groaning, rattling, murmurous cough:

> In the blackness of the doorway a pair of eyes glimmered white, and big, and staring. Then James Wait's head protruding, became visible, as if suspended between the two hands that grasped a doorpost on each side of the face. . . . He stepped out in a tottering stride. He looked powerful as ever, but showed a strange and affected unsteadiness in his gait; his face was perhaps a trifle thinner, and his eyes appeared rather startlingly prominent. He seemed to hasten the retreat of departing light by his very presence; the setting sun dipped sharply, as though fleeing before our nigger; a black mist emanated from him; a subtle and dismal influence; a something cold and gloomy that floated out and settled on all the faces like a mourning veil. The circle broke up. The joy of laughter died on stiffened lips. There was not a smile left among all the ship's company.

Thus, after the disappearance of the black tug, Wait takes up again the motifs of the land—gloom, sunlessness, and death. Halted before them like a mirror in its frame, he reduces the crew to silence. They await his words with fright. Sure enough, he announces to the crew, described as criminals and cowering slaves, his imminent death. Is he malingering? This doubt in their minds allows them to excite their own fears over the extinction of the self, and holds them fascinated just as did the doubts of the original Narcissus. Henceforth the taint of death keeps alive their sentimental hopes, expressed as their doubts. Only Singleton seems to be unfeeling as he puts the question to Wait, "Are you dying?" and, hearing his confused affirmation, suggests he get on with his dying. From there on, the crew, choosing the more pleasing possibility in Singleton's ambiguous retort "Why, of course he will die," loses hold of all the simple certainties of the sea:

> All our certitudes were going; we were on doubtful terms with our officers; the cook had given us up for lost; we had overheard the boatswain's opinion that "we were a crowd of softies." We

suspected Jimmy, one another, and even our very selves. We did not know what to do. At every insignificant turn of our humble life we met Jimmy overbearing and blocking the way, arm-in-arm with his awful and veiled familiar. It was a weird servitude.

So death and the image of the self prepare for the possible dissolution of the *Narcissus*.

A final consideration in the second chapter is this overwhelming reaction of the crew if only for the light it throws on their crazily complicated, troubled absorption in themselves. Belfast, whose emotional capacities bear out the extravagant mixture of Gael and evangelical Protestant usually fixed on the gloomy city of his name, is alternately bent on fighting Wait or weeping over him; he approximates beyond any other crew member the extremes of Narcissus' own reactions to his fateful love. Even the captain, it is rumored, had been baffled by Wait: " . . . no one could tell what was the meaning of that black man sitting apart in a meditative attitude and as motionless as a carving." He is of course the self that all so passionately watch, from Belfast on down the emotional scale. But it is Wait's *own* reaction to Donkin's singularly increasing hostility —he jeers the Negro and scorns him to his face—that again underlines his role as a mirror or reflector. For he not only uses his supposedly approaching death to malinger but, at the same time, fearing death greatly like the rest of the crew, he must also keep up *his* hopes. Donkin, slighted by the crew, put down physically by Mr. Baker, unsuccessful in his attempts to advance himself either by insolence or abasement, is maddened by Wait's apparently successful ruse, so much so in fact that before the others he calls him a "black fraud." However, Wait's own reaction is absolutely friendly, his looks brighten: "Jimmy positively seemed to revel in that abuse." Why? Because his hopes demand that there be at least one believer in his imminent death as wholly fictitious. On the other hand, in seeing himself in Wait as a total fraud, so to speak, Donkin ensures by his vision Wait's role as a mirror of the worst to be found in a group of otherwise average mortals—the crew. That is, of course, with the exception of Singleton, who in having no thought for himself resembles the crew at this point, we are told, only in his breathing.

IV

Chapter Three on the storm is longer than the two previous chapters of preparation combined. Yet it is the least relevant for my theory, except for the negative light it throws, since the crew is pictured at its best. Here they redeem themselves, though not entirely unmindful of Wait. As the storm grows, we are told outright, "We took no notice of him; we hardly gave a thought to Jimmy and his bosom friend." Through most of the chapter they, like their unde-viating captain, rivet their eyes on the ship. The captain himself views her "as a loving man watches the unselfish toil of a delicate woman upon the slender thread of whose existence is hung the whole meaning and joy of the world." The choice is then clear—re-peated by Baker and Singleton throughout the chapter—she, the ship, not the imperilled self must be their first concern. She has, of course, a weakness—"She was born in the thundering peal of ham-mers beating upon iron, in black eddies of smoke, under a grey sky, on the banks of the Clyde."

If this last is the extent of the humorous reach of the connec-tions I have tried to point out, the storm for all of its antics is sob-ering enough in that its threat of death is couched in the same terms that Conrad had originally pinned on Wait. At its height the roaring sea is constantly marked by sooty vapours, blind darkness, ghastly greyness, and black squalls. And in its way, the storm also exercises something of the same fascination on the crew as had Wait. For all of its deadly terror they are enthralled by it, crazily fixed as they often are in postures of crucifixion up and down the rigging. Its adversary—called "lifelong"—is, expectedly, Singleton, also the true opposite of Wait.

Unfortunately, a crew member suddenly recalls him. Belfast, true to form, leads the rescue and almost loses his life for his sentimen-tal impulse. Seemingly prematurely trapped in his own coffin, Wait, at a great expense of nails and blood, is literally torn from the bowels of the ship, reborn in all his sick potence. The crew itself is properly rewarded with a renewed feeling of hopelessness—never had the storm seemed to them more overwhelming. But now their reawakened hatred of Wait is alloyed with doubts again over his likely death, from which they have momentarily snatched him. There is a fine justice in their dilemma at the conclusion of the rescue: "The secret and ardent desire of our hearts was the desire to beat him viciously with our fists about the head; and we handled him as tenderly as though he had been made of glass. . . ." All quaking selves are refurbished in their secret mirror.

But the storm is weathered. The cook accomplishes the miracle of hot coffee; slowly the ship begins to right herself. In a swirl of white, shining, cascading foam she begins to respond to the crew's care, "as though she had torn herself out from a deadly grasp." We watch Singleton. From the famous phrase, "He steered with care," we know that the ship as a composite Narcissus indeed finally "clears herself." Just so, in the next chapter, must the crew tear themselves from just as deadly a grasp.

V

The greater storm, the tumult of the self, breaks in Chapter Four. The opening sentences point to man's restless self-concern as a sacrilege of unease and malaise that is mercifully terminated by painful struggle:

> On men reprieved by its disdainful mercy, the immortal sea confers in its justice the full privilege of desired unrest. Through the perfect wisdom of its grace they are not permitted to meditate at ease upon the complicated and acrid savour of existence. They must without pause justify their life to the eternal pity that commands toil to be hard and unceasing, from sunrise to sunset, from sunset to sunrise; till the weary succession of nights and days tainted by the obstinate clamour of sages, demanding bliss and an empty heaven, is redeemed at last by the vast silence of pain and labour. . . .

For perspective on this statement of permissive selfishness in this world, not to mention the philosophic rant of a Donkin and the subsequent restlessness of the crew huddled about their mirror in Wait's cabin, we ought to turn again to Singleton. Perhaps the key statement marking his distance from the Narcissism that will overtake the crew is this one: "He had never given a thought to his mortal self." This is made apropos of not only his thirty hours of steering but also his entire career as a seaman. Yet it is Donkin who metaphorically takes the wheel in this chapter, until the captain may be said finally to wrest it from him. The crew had in fact harshly demanded that Donkin take his turn at the wheel after Singleton literally collapsed, but he of course refused. Once the ship has turned North, homeward bound in sunshine, Conrad once more carefully distinguishes the degrees of mortal selfishness in this chapter: "She [the *Narcissus*] carried Singleton's completed wisdom, Donkin's delicate susceptibilities, and the conceited folly of us all." Although he will practically disappear from the mutinous scene ahead, towards the end of the chapter, when the storm of the crew's unrest is all about him, Singleton will step forward, once again "incomprehensible and exciting, like an oracle behind a veil," to foretell Jimmy's death and make the connection I have cited by timing that death with the first sight of land. Then the headwind will cease and presumably the spell will be lifted.

By contrast, the eye of the storm is Wait's cabin, where a languorous black mass is conducted by Donkin. The men

> . . . leaned on each side of the door peacefully interested, and with crossed legs; they stood astride the doorstep discoursing, or sat in silent couples on his sea-chest; while against the bulwark along the spare topmast, three or four in a row stared meditatively; with their simple faces lit up by the projected glare of Jimmy's lamp. The little place, repainted white, had, in the night, the brilliance of a silver shrine where a black idol, reclining

stiffly under a blanket, blinked its weary eyes and received our homage. Donkin officiated.

Donkin now urges Wait's malingering on the rest of the crew with some success and even goes on to hint that the ship be damned—let her drift. All are momentarily persuaded, confused, or tacitly sympathetic. The outstanding example is the cook Podmore, apparently forgotten in his heroic slogan "As long as she swims I will cook" of the previous chapter. Now his conceit is the crew's, his foggy incoherence their solicitous sentimentality, his vision of saving a soul the private good intention that proverbially paves the way to hell:

> There was a great stir in his brain; an addled vision of bright outlines; an exciting row of rousing songs and groans of pain. He suffered, enjoyed, admired, approved. He was delighted, frightened, exalted. . . . A tide of sudden feeling swept him clean out of his body. He soared. He contemplated the secret of the hereafter. It commended itself to him. It was excellent; he loved it, himself, all hands, and Jimmy. His heart overflowed with tenderness, with comprehension, with the desire to meddle, with anxiety for the soul of that black man, with the pride of possessed eternity, with the feeling of might.

Only the captain can rid the stifling cabin of Podmore. Yet even the captain reacts with pity to Jim and thereby incites the near-mutiny. As he ashamedly explains to Baker, "When I saw him standing there, three parts dead and so scared—black amongst that gaping lot—no grit to face what's coming to us all—the notion came to me all at once, before I could think. Sorry for him. . . . Kind of impulse." Captain Allistoun's cryptic explanation of his own brief Narcissism makes him too a fellow gaper at the mirror. Soon after, Donkin's wish is briefly fulfilled when the helmsman abandons the wheel to investigate the row. Only then are the men recalled "to the sense of reality, vigilance, and duty." The tide turns; the captain regains command; the living ship rights itself—after the physical example of the last chapter.

At the end, the master of the ship confronts Donkin, whom he resembles in size though in nothing else. The master expresses the need for a selflessness to be discerned at its purest in Singleton; Donkin had urged a selfishness that all had absorbed from gazing on Wait. And it is his absence, more than any other force, that settles for Donkin when he obeys the captain's command to return the belaying pin. In this absence of Wait, confined by express order to his cabin, the crew can no longer answer the captain's peremptory question, "What to you want?" It's Wait that they want, but their mortal concern for him, for themselves, has once again become vague, troubled, inarticulate, and imperfectly concealed. When one man manages to blurt out, "We don't want to

go shorthanded"—alluding to Wait's confinement despite his pro-
tests of renewed strength—and then adds, "and this 'ere black,"
Captain Allistoun silences him with the well advised command
"Enough!" Wait must await the appearance of the land.

VI

It appears in the form of the island Flores, meaning flower. But
before this metamorphosis in the myth, before Wait's soul and the
folly of the crew are absorbed into the land named flower, all
hands witness Singleton's one and only visit to Wait's cabin:

> There was a sense of a contest in the air. We felt the inward
> strain of men watching a wrestling bout. At last Jimmy with per-
> ceptible apprehension turned his head on the pillow. "Good eve-
> ning," he said in a conciliating tone. "H'm," answered the old
> seaman, grumpily. For a moment longer he looked at Jimmy with
> severe fixity, then suddenly went away.

In truth, the struggle is all but over, though Wait's spell will linger
even on shore in the maudlin grief of Belfast. Yet long before this
encounter, we read as part of the windless, becalmed atmosphere
that attends Wait's dying the following recapitulation of what I
have called the Narcissus theme:

> . . . Jimmy bobbed up upon the surface, compelling attention,
> like a black buoy chained to the bottom of a muddy stream.
> Falsehood triumphed. It triumphed through doubt, through stu-
> pidity, through pity, through sentimentalism. We set ourselves to
> bolster it up, from compassion, from recklessness, from a sense of
> fun. . . . The latent egoism of tenderness to suffering appeared in
> the developing anxiety not to see him die. . . . He was becoming
> immaterial like an apparition; the cheekbones rose, the forehead
> slanted more; the face was all hollows, patches of shade; and the
> fleshless head resembled a disinterred black skull. . . . He was
> demoralising. Through him we were becoming highly humanised,
> tender, complex, excessively decadent: we understood the sub-
> tlety of his fear, sympathised with all his repulsions, shrinkings,
> evasions, delusions—as though we had been over-civilised, and
> rotten, and without any knowledge of the meaning of life. . . .
> We watched him intently.

From six to eight in the evening his cabin overflows with well-wish-
ers. All stare at him. All wish him to live until the journey's end.
All maintain to his face the absurd comedy of his recovery. In other
words, the crew and ship reflect each other in a dead calm. The
realities are the heavy shadows by night that festoon the illusory
beauty of the listless ship and of the dying black to whom all look.
The conclusion to both storms, physical and human, has been the
same as their prelude.

Then Flores appears, "like a sombre ruin upon a vast and
deserted plain," a fitting repository for Wait's soul and the collec-

tive selfishness of the ship. For even in visiting Wait, each crewman, like Narcissus himself at the end, "seemed to leave behind a
little of his own vitality, surrender some of his own strength, renew
the assurance of life—the indestructible thing!" The dead calm of
ship and mirror does indeed sap them. They must tighten their
belts, almost as if in emulation of the wasted dying figure they gaze
at. Even Donkin is seen at his worst, if that is possible, during his
last visit, showing himself to be but a common thief, although with
the proper admixture of self-pity for his own inevitable death. Wait
dies at the moment of his departure. Yet the mirror of life as she
ought to be, the sea, appears to reject Donkin, the supreme egotist
and landsman of the crew, as he slinks off into the dawn.

And with the dawn, not only is Wait gone but also "a common
bond was gone; the strong, effective and respectable bond of a sentimental lie." In treacherously removing himself from life, Wait
had seemed to let down his fellows, for "in going he took away with
himself the gloomy and solemn shadow in which our folly had
posed, with humane satisfaction, as a tender arbiter of fate."
Then, after much seeming reluctance, the corpse finally slides
into the sea, the ship appears to be relieved of a burden, and of
course the breeze comes up, just as Singleton had predicted.

And now more than ever the link between Narcissism and the
metropolis of London is underscored. The prelude or key is the
paean to England as a mighty ship bejewelled in the sea, like the
Narcissus herself, filled with past and present potential for greatness
and meanness. Then, as the *Narcissus* enters the Thames and, obediently following the tug, re-enters the blackened surface of the
shore, the mirror of the confusion, folly, and complication that had
beset her at sea is held up to us:

> A low cloud hung before her—a great opalescent and tremulous
> cloud, that seemed to rise from the steaming brows of millions of
> men. Long drifts of smoky vapours soiled it with livid trails; it
> throbbed to the beat of millions of hearts, and from it came an
> immense and lamentable murmur—the murmur of millions of
> lips praying, cursing, sighing, jeering—the undying murmur of
> folly, regret, and hope exhaled by the crowds of the anxious
> earth. The *Narcissus* entered the cloud; the shadows deepened;
> on all sides there was the clang of iron, the sound of mighty
> blows, shrieks, yells. Black barges drifted stealthily on the murky
> stream. A mad jumble of begrimed walls loomed up vaguely in
> the smoke, bewildering and mournful, like a vision of disaster.

On shore, the normal course of events begins to reproduce the
abnormal events, fostered by Narcissism, that had brought near-
tragedy to the ship. The self that held sway in the black mirror of
James Wait on board ship is now the judge of the chastened crew.
This judgment seems to stare back from the miles of brick masonry

rising virtually out of the water's edge: ". . . soulless walls, staring through hundreds of windows as troubled and dull as the eyes of over-fed brutes." Entering into this atmosphere of precious filth, innundated with the foul dust of the world's trading center, and suddenly overwhelmed by numerous strangers, the *Narcissus*, we are told, dies and, I would add, Narcissism triumphs. For the judgment of the sea on Donkin and Singleton is now reversed by the judgment of the metropolis. The pale clerk who pays off the crew takes Singleton for little more than a beast, and Donkin as an intelligent creature like himself. Fittingly too, we last see the crew on its way to the Black Horse tavern where the actualities of the struggle with the sea will on land become illusions to be dispensed from a bottle: ". . . the illusions of strength, mirth, happiness; the illusion of splendour and poetry of life." The real possibilities of these have ostensibly died with the ship's coming to rest in her berth. We are told that the sound of the city compares with the sound of the sea, both cruel and ruthless. Yet the entire novel has asserted that the struggle with the sea, while ultimately illusory, in the sense that no passage or voyage is ever absolutely accomplished, has allowed men to forget the burden or weight of themselves. The metropolis does not.

Thus is the grace of heaven beamed upon them momentarily from the clouds—"the dark knot of seamen drifted in sunshine." Yet they are also flanked by the Tower and the Mint, reminders that on land the crimes of high ambition and the bonds of greed are the natural expressions of the admired self as it takes itself on its mortal journey over the earth's mud. But for a moment that sunshine, like the crew's camaraderie of the sea, can efface all thoughts of gain, anxiety, and dishonor:

> The sunshine of heaven fell like a gift of grace on the mud of the earth, on the remembering and mute stones, on greed, selfishness; on the anxious faces of forgetful men. And to the right of the dark group the stained front of the Mint, cleansed by the flood of light, stood out for a moment dazzling and white like a marble palace in a fairy tale.

So they have come to reside, temporarily, in the land of Wait's spirit. But their selfishness has been abated by selfless toil. So too the myth of Narcissus has lent not only a glimpse into possible disaster at sea, but, if we follow Conrad's vision of England as a mighty ship herself, a glimpse into the disaster that may well overtake a modern England at the height of its progressive, wealthy, and liberal 19th century. From a smudged name to a black mirror to a flowering land to a dark metropolis of Black Horses, dark Tower, and stained Mint: the living darkness she admires may well be England's dying culture, or so Conrad strongly warned in *The Nigger of the "Narcissus."*

JOHN E. SAVESON

Contemporary Psychology in
The Nigger of the "Narcissus"†

Psychological assumptions and their moral implications in Conrad's *The Nigger of the "Narcissus,"* the first of his works with a claim to high moral and psychological sophistication, must strike the reader as utilitarian in a general sense. Conrad's assumptions, I believe, are also utilitarian in an exact sense. They correspond to assumptions in late nineteenth-century Utilitarian psychologists such as Alexander Bain, James Sully, and especially the widely translated French writer Théodule Ribot. That Conrad had read their works or knew their theories is most likely, for they were well known to H. G. Wells, to whom Conrad was quite close at the time of the writing of *The Nigger of the "Narcissus."*[1]

The nature of a disharmony and the starting point of abnormal psychology for Utilitarian psychologists is perversion of the ordinary motives of pleasure and pain. Such disharmonies in Ribot occur notably in the "conservative instinct" or "self-feeling," which has two aspects: one, offensive; one, defensive. The self-feeling manifests itself in the primitive emotions of anger or fear and in the more complex emotions connected with personality and ego, namely, audacity or debility.[2] Pleasure in pain, in Ribot's descriptions, results often from the disharmony created by man's indisposition to disciplined labor. The excessive pain of work induces an excessive pleasure in the morbid refinement of the conservative instinct in its forms of fear and debility and is marked by an excess of self-pity and melancholia. A person suffering in this way dwells upon the contrast between his estimate of his own worth and the estimate of others. Melancholia, finally, according to Ribot, is a stage only on the way to self-destruction and suicide.[3]

In his Preface to the 1914 edition of *The Nigger of the "Narcissus,"* Conrad wrote: "But in the book he [Wait] is nothing; he is merely the centre of the ship's collective psychology and the pivot of the action."[4] If it is assumed that Conrad here uses "psychology" in an informed way—a logical assumption—he must intend that Wait should embody egoistic debility, an important principle of analysis in the dominant Utilitarian psychology at the turn of the century. The correspondence is exact. Wait shirks work. His weakness, giving the lie to his apparent strength, suggests a psychoso-

† From *Studies in Short Fiction*, 7 (Spring 1970), 219–31. Some of the author's footnotes have been omitted here.
1. Wells' knowledge is evident in his *Saturday Review* articles. See 8 December, 1894, pp. 617–618, and 29 December, 1894, p. 715.
2. *The Psychology of the Emotions* (London, 1897), pp. 13–15.
3. Ibid., p. 65.
4. See above. [*Editor.*]

matic condition as does his illness, which is mental rather than physical, a fact the crew sense in their suspicion that Wait is a sham. Wait complains at length that he is treated unjustly by the crew. And Conrad marks off for the reader the separate stages of melancholia and self-destruction at that point at which the Captain denies Wait the privilege of being on deck. The Captain's order is invested with a Ribot-like insight into the condition of Wait's mind: Wait is already "three parts dead," the Captain observes. "If ever creature was in a mortal funk to die . . . I thought I would let him go out in his own way."

To the identity of analytical points in Conrad's and Ribot's psychology, it may be added that Conrad's phrasing recalls Ribot's. For example, the crew, clinging for hours to the capsized ship, are "plunged in a hopeless resignation." As the Captain and Mate attempt to rouse them, "their thoughts floated vaguely between the desire of rest and the desire of life." And, further, the "longing to be done with it all gnawed their breasts, and the wish to do things well was a burning pain." The crew in these passages suffer more than physical exhaustion; they suffer a morbid debility like that reaction against the pain of labor Ribot describes.

Wait as the "centre of the ship's collective psychology," in Conrad's phrase, represents an extreme to which the crew are inclined but do not reach or an extreme in which the crew are not allowed to sustain themselves. The crew deteriorate not only toward debility. While the crew cling to the capsized ship, extreme debility alternates with extreme malevolence: "Then suddenly men who had been plunged in a hopeless resignation became as if possessed with a desire to hurt. They belaboured one another with fists." The center of psychological analysis in *The Nigger of the "Narcissus"* is this alternation between opposite emotions or between the two aspects of the conservative instinct. As Wait is an instrument for representing one aspect in its extreme form in the psychology of the crew, Donkin is an instrument for representing the other. One discerns in his characterization several analyses from Utilitarian psychology.

Donkin displays natural viciousness early on. Soon after the crew give him articles of clothing, Donkin picks a quarrel with Charley: "The filthy object of universal charity shook his fist at the youngster.—'I'll make you keep this 'ere fo'c'sle clean, young feller!' he snarled viciously." Donkin then pushes Wamibo out of his way. "He flung all his worldly possessions into the empty bedplace, gauged with another shrewd look the risks of the proceeding, then leaped up to the Finn, who stood pensive and dull.—'I'll plug your eyes for you, you blooming square-head.' " On this occasion Donkin displays fairly primitive emotion, emotion that forms in context an opposite to the uncomplicated emotion of sympathy displayed by the crew. The contrast Donkin and the crew furnish is recognizable as another contrast Utilitarian psychologists draw between two fundamental dispositions in the human mind significant for morality: man's capacity for sympathy and his equally natural disposition toward cruelty. Even as tenderness toward suffering is a refinement of sympathy, so malevolence is a refinement of brutal and predatory instincts.

The ruling passion of Donkin's mind, like Wait's, becomes more complex in the course of the novel. The stage in which he "glares harmfully" or "grins malevolently" precedes a stage in which he wears a far more vicious aspect and commits murderous acts. A dividing point is the disciplining given him by the Mate, to whom Donkin is systematically insolent. "From that day he became pitiless; told Jimmy that he was a 'black fraud'; hinted to us that we were an imbecile lot, daily taken in by a vulgar nigger." Donkin's exacerbated instinct at its height asserts itself in an attempt to murder the Captain with a belaying pin. The crew's disarming him ushers in a degree of hatred that can only be called *malevolence*. That night, as Donkin surveys the crew in their bunks, "His heart leaped wildly in his narrow chest. They slept! He wanted to wring necks, gouge eyes, spit on faces." In this part of Conrad's text Donkin is called a "sick vulture" even as Wait is called a "sick brute."

Donkin's frustrated instinct takes one further direction. Avoided by the crew, he becomes a familiar of the cook. Like Donkin, the cook is estranged from the crew. Donkin curses them and Podmore prophesies their damnation. "Donkin, who did not admit of any hereafter (except for purposes of blasphemy) listened, concentrated and angry, gloating fiercely over a called-up image of infinite torment—as men gloat over the accursed images of cruelty and revenge, of greed, and of power." During the extreme peril of the ship, exhausted and resigned, Podmore rouses himself to tell the Mate how on his last Sunday ashore he beat his son for falling into a pond on the way to church: "I whopped him, sir, till I couldn't lift my arm. . . .' His voice faltered. 'I whopped 'im!' he repeated, rattling his teeth; then, after a while, let out a mournful sound that was half a groan, half a snore." Both Donkin and Podmore are crazed and sick. The frustration of their wills stimulates imagination; and the impulse to cruelty spends itself in terrible visions.

Donkin's progress into malevolence, partially detailed in the examples above, like Wait's progress toward a denial of the will to live, is governed by certain psychological principles found in Ribot. Ribot and other Utilitarian psychologists hold that malevolence is a refinement of natural hunting and combative instincts through their coalescence with the lust for power.[5] Donkin desires power over the

5. See Ribot, *Psychology of the Emotions*, pp. 221–222.

crew to the extent of inciting them to mutiny. He seduces them with illusions: "they dreamed enthusiastically of the time when every lonely ship would travel over a serene sea, manned by a wealthy and well-fed crew of satisfied skippers." Similarly, Podmore's fanatic preaching and his abortive attempt to convert Wait aim at domination of the minds of the men.

Secondly, Sully describes the sentiment of power itself as a combination of self-exaltation and malignity.[6] The latter trait has been obvious in both pieces of characterization. Conrad emphasizes also Donkin and Podmore's supreme egoism. Podmore's religious convictions are a manifestation of a narrow egoism. Conrad summarizes Podmore's state of mind in his attempt to convert Wait as follows: " 'Jimmy!' he cried in an inspired tone. Then he hesitated. A spark of human pity glimmered yet through the infernal fog of his supreme conceit." Even though the net in which Donkin attempts to capture Wait's mind is not the net of religion but the net of nihilism, Donkin's attempt is an assertion of ego—like the cook's, an attempt on the member of the crew least able to defend himself. Conrad summarizes Donkin's motives on his last visit to Wait as follows: "He had a desire to assert his importance, to break, to crush; to be even with everybody for everything; to tear the veil, unmask, expose, leave no refuge—a perfidious desire of truthfulness!" And later in the episode there is reference to Donkin's "passionate sense of his own importance." Podmore's fanatic visions illustrate this additional observation in Ribot, that egoistic feelings have no check and often end in paranoic delusions.[7] Wait and Donkin, finally, in that juxtaposition the story establishes for them illustrate Ribot's observation that the self-feeling in its negative form reaches a culminating point in suicide and the self-feeling in its positive form reaches its culmination in megalomania.[8]

Thus far the contemporary pathology of the conservative instinct, especially as Ribot set it down, has been traced very fully in *The Nigger of the "Narcissus."* Further analytical points from contemporary abnormal psychology, namely, the close connection and rapid alternation of debility and malevolence can be detected in the *novella.* The mere fact of connection and relationship between Donkin and Wait suggests a close relationship between the two aspects of the self-feeling. The realistic psychology of the crew, from which the symbolic significance of Donkin and Wait has been taken, supplies the principle of alternation.

Ribot stresses the fact that the "fatal impulse to suicide is closely linked to the craving to kill."[9] He offers as an example of alternation of contrasting emotions the actions of Alfred de Musset, who

6. James Sully, *The Human Mind: A Text-Book of Psychology* (London, 1892), p. 99.
7. *Psychology of the Emotions*, pp. 242–243.
8. Ibid., pp. 244–245.
9. Ibid., pp. 244–245.

treated his mistress George Sand alternately as a divinity and as an object of contempt.[1] Instability between tenderness and a murderous impulse, according to Ribot, is familiar not only in genius, as in this example, but also in "grown-up children," a phrase which recalls Conrad's description of the crew as "children of the sea."[2] The psychology of instability, of "mobility of mood," further, is very frequent in the criminal pathology of this period.[3] Instability is described there as a result of degeneracy, degeneracy being thought of as a return to a primitive kind of egoism. The restraints of society fail to produce stability and to transform egoistic into social and altruistic emotions. Instead, the restraints of society exacerbate the conservative instincts. Conrad was familiar with the leading criminologist at the turn of the century, Cesare Lombroso, as is evident from references in *The Secret Agent*. In that novel the character of Stevie is drawn according to Lombroso's precepts and very obviously illustrates an extremely rapid fluctuation between the extremes of tenderness and murderous impulse. Stevie is a degenerate. In *The Nigger of the "Narcissus"* the psychology of the self-feeling is applied typically to men of primitive rather than to men of degenerate emotion.

Although Wait and Donkin are a dichotomy, Wait is still, in Conrad's words, "the centre of the ship's collective psychology and the pivot of the action." Resignation for Conrad is a malady peculiar to the sea, to judge from the fact that he described Donkin as the "independent offspring of the ignoble freedom of the slums." Donkin excites aversion, whereas Wait draws out the crew's most profound affinities. Perhaps Conrad associates resignation with sea life because it exemplifies, more than any other kind of life, Ribot's pathology. The sea imposes extreme hardship, the root cause of apathy in Ribot, and demands an excess of labor. Conrad's descriptions of the storm, of the capsized ship, of the effort of the crew to right it make these points in the most vivid way.

II

In extracting from *The Nigger of the "Narcissus"* its morality as distinct from its psychology, one needs to mark off with care those areas in which symbolism is and is not important thematically. Wait is an unusual character; his unusual quality results partly from the fact that the thing he symbolizes is an empirically detailed pathology of mind. Symbolic statement ordinarily substitutes for a more factual or more scientific utterance. Conrad's symbolism, in contrast, grows out of the analytical. Wait illustrates realistically, in the fashion I have described, Ribot's pathology of fear even though as

---

1. Ibid., p. 421.
2. Ibid., p. 422. *The Nigger of the Narcissus* was published in 1897 under the title *The Children of the Sea*.
3. Cf. Henry Maudsley, *The Pathology of Mind: A Study of its Distempers, Deformities, and Disorders* (London, 1895), pp. 339–340, and Cesare Lombroso, *Les Anarchistes* (Paris, 1896), p. 68.

an embodiment of *one* of the primitive emotions he has no real
dimension as a character and thus becomes a broad symbol of the
susceptibility of the seamen on the *Narcissus*, who less obviously or
in a lesser degree suffer his disharmony. Wait is at once a symbol of
the psychological danger inherent in extreme subjectivity and also
the realistic object that furthers that subjectivity. Distinctions of
this kind enable one to consider Wait's thematic significance first in
a realistic and, secondly in a symbolic context.

The crew degenerate toward resignation through the increasing
complexity of their compassion for Wait as object. Again, Conrad
marked out in stages the psychological progression in stages; principles found in Utilitarian psychology govern this progression. The
crew's charity toward Donkin when he first appears on the ship—
they offer shoes, trousers, a blanket—has been described as uncomplicated emotion, a conclusion from Conrad's phrasing. Donkin in
his pleas and complaints, it is said, knows how "to conquer the
naive instincts of that crowd." But there is a suggestion also of
incipient refinement. The novel comments that the "gust of their
benevolence sent a wave of sentimental pity through their doubting
hearts." *Sentimental* is pejorative and conveys the susceptibility, at
least, of a corrupt generation to false feeling that spreads itself over
the base of emotional life.

Wait, however, inspires the full complexity and false refinement
of that feeling. "Jimmy's hateful accomplice seemed to have blown
with his impure breath undreamt-of subtleties into our hearts. We
were disturbed and cowardly." Jimmy's accomplice is death, and
some part of the subtlety of the crew's emotion is the fear and the
fascination of death. But the crew's emotion more explictly is compounded of tenderness and hate, hate inspired by the crew's suspicion that Wait's illness is a sham: "We oscillated between the
desire of virtue and the fear of ridicule; we wished to save ourselves
from the pain of remorse, but did not want to made the contemptible dupes of our sentiment." Conrad describes one more
complexity. As Wait's impending death becomes evident to the
crew, they set about fortifying in themselves the deception of
Wait's own belief that he will not die. "Falsehood triumphed. It
triumphed through doubt, through stupidity, through pity, through
sentimentalism."

Conrad names at least two psychological principles at work in
the complication of feeling detailed above; and these principles are
found in Ribot and other Utilitarian psychologists. Spencer believed
that altruism arose out of imaginative sympathy; and in that sense
Sully and Ribot assert that altruism has always one root in egoism[4]
Ribot judges, further, that sympathy may exist without tender emo-

4. Ribot agrees with Spencer's designa-
tion of tender emotion as "ego-altruis-
tic." "It must be so, for altruism cannot
be innate." *Psychology of the Emotions*,
p. 237.

tion and tender emotion, in a degree, without egoistic sympathy. The statement is designed to distinguish simple from complex emotion, for Ribot offers as an example the fact that men often avoid the spectacle of suffering because of the pain it awakens sympathetically. In that sense tender and refined emotion may seem to exist or may exist in a degree without egoistic sympathy.[5] This kind of distinction, which reflects the influence upon Ribot of Eduard von Hartmann's principle of the pain of compassion,[6] is evident in Conrad in the difference he depicts between the emotion the crew feel toward Donkin and the emotion they feel toward Wait. Conrad acknowledges the distinction rather explicity in this observation concerning the crew's feeling for Wait at the height of its complexity: "The latent egoism of tenderness to suffering appeared in the developing anxiety not to see him die." Ribot does not claim that egoism is absent from sentimental pity but that, as here, it is submerged and minimal. In Conrad's example the base of feeling is uncovered, paradoxically, by a further complication. Egoism is evident, also, more obviously, in the crew's reluctance to be duped.

Falsehood is prominent in the complexities of the crew's emotion, falsehood in the sense of illusion. James Sully, the chief exponent of the psychology of illusion in the period, describes this causal chain: emotion, and generally egoistic emotion, affects ideation; and feeling and ideation affect and distort perception.[7] Conrad's analysis is similar. The magnitude of the distorting influence of sentimental pity upon ideation and perception is measured in the following passage: "In going he took away with himself the gloomy and solemn shadow in which our folly had posed, with humane satisfaction, as a tender arbiter of fate. And now we saw it was no such thing. It was just common foolishness; a silly and ineffectual medling with issues of majestic import." Ribot deplores the impoverishment of feeling caused by the growth of images and concepts; he would have agreed with Conrad's estimate of the harmfulness of false sentiment, namely, that it leads the crew into a foolish preoccupation, into a distortion of the truth of life, into an imperfect and cowardly morality.

One can discern some other Utilitarian principles in Conrad's text even though they are not phrased abstractly as are the two just cited. The crew's hatred for Wait is reminiscent of Bishop Butler's view, which is frequently repeated by nineteenth-century psychologists, that malevolence within limits has a social function.[8] In *The Nigger of the "Narcissus,"* as egoistic resentment, it is a balance to the weakness of pity and functions, although ineffectually, as a

5. See *The Psychology of the Emotions*, pp. 233–234.
6. See Eduard von Hartmann, *Philosophy of the Unconscious*, III, pp. 41 ff.
7. See, e.g., *Illusions: A Psychological Study* (New York, 1884), p. 39.
8. See, e.g., Henry Sidgwick, *The Methods of Ethics* (New York, 1890), p. 371.

curb to sentimental excess. The assumption of the weakness of pity is common to much late Utilitarian psychology. Sully observes of "pity arising out of sympathy" that the self-denial involved in virtue will readily pass into a full denial of the will to live,[9] a statement that actually summarizes the whole deterioration of the affective life of the crew as it is conveyed both realistically and symbolically. Such attitudes as well as the Utilitarian analysis of the origin of altruism in empathy, no doubt, are reflected in Conrad's remark in a letter to H. G. Wells that "enlightened egoism is at least as valid as enlightened altruism."[1]

Tracing Ribot-like principles in *The Nigger of the "Narcissus"* has revealed fully Wait's thematic significance. But one may add some discussion of old Singleton, whom the novel sets against Wait as protagonist against antagonist. Ribot's stress on simple emotion and his distrust of images and concepts result quite obviously from his attention to Hartmann's celebration of primitive mentality and Hartmann's theory that unhappiness results in the evolution of consciousness from conflict between the intellect and the will. Utilitarian psychologists at the turn of the century were influenced by Hartmann even though they were hostile to most of his theories. In a letter of December 14, 1897, Conrad discusses the suggestion made by R. B. Cunninghame Graham of "Singleton, with an education." Conrad's reply uses "consciousness" in Hartmann and Ribot's sense. "Would you seriously, of malice prepense, cultivate in that unconscious man the power to think? Then he would become conscious,—and much smaller,—and very unhappy. Now he is simple and great like an elemental force."[2] The description is interesting not only for its psychological analysis but also for the further insight it offers into Conrad's whole attitude toward sea-life. If the toil of the sea gives an impulse to a morbid development of character, it is also a restorative, chastening simple minds and inducing in them the quality of endurance. "Through the perfect wisdom of its grace they are not permitted to meditate at ease upon the complicated and acrid savour of existence. They must without pause justify their life to the eternal pity that commands toil to be hard and unceasing."

The subject of *The Nigger of the "Narcissus"* is morbid emotion belonging to an advanced stage in the history of the race. Conrad summarizes the crew's feeling for Wait as follows: "Through him we were becoming highly humanised, tender, complex, excessively decadent"; or, again, the crew in its sympathetic understanding of Wait's condition of mind is over-civilised, and rotten, and without any knowledge of the meaning of life." Set apart from other members of the crew, not susceptible to their emotions and insensitive to their affinities, old Singleton seems a "learned and savage patriarch,

9. *Pessimism* (London, 1877), p. 100.
1. G. Jean-Aubry, *Joseph Conrad: Life*

and Letters (New York, 1927), I, 329.
2. Ibid., p. 215.

the incarnation of barbarian wisdom serene in the blasphemous turmoil of the world." This contrast extending throughout the novel
dramatizes a Ribot-like demarcation of primitive from complex feeling, of the harmonies of savage from the disharmonies of civilized
life. Conrad's use of Singleton as a norm has the same effect as Ribot's admonition against intellectualized emotion, which he considers an "impoverishment" of feeling: "let the antagonistic action of
reflection, or of the intellectual state—whatever it may be—cease,
and hatred will once again become anger, resignation, grief, or
despair; mystical will change to sexual love, and the primitive form
appears under the ruins of the derivative.[3] The delicacy and precision of Conrad's time sense in his treatment of the character of
Wait may be thought of as an effect of Ribot's theories. Describing the morbid phenomenon of "being pleased with one's own suffering and tasting it like a pleasure," Ribot observes: "This disposition of the mind is not, as one might think, peculiar to *blasè* persons and to epochs of refined civilization; it seems inherent in
humanity the moment it emerges from barbarism."[4] Conrad's use
of a Negro seems to capture that historical moment.

The thematic significance of Wait considered in the symbolic
context of the novel must be estimated from dispositions of characters and events Conrad makes for symbolic suggestion. The text
itself often makes evident the meaning of the symbolism. During
the worst of the storm, Wait is shut up in his cabin and forgotten;
but once the crew are no longer preoccupied, they dig him out.
The episode is a symbolic figuring of the re-entry of morbid feeling
into the consciousness of the crew. "Never before had the gale
seemed to us more furious, the sea more mad, the sunshine more
hopeless and appalling." This episode illustrates what Conrad
means when he says that Wait is the center of the crew's "collective psychology" and a "pivot of the action."

Another meaningful example is the relationship that develops
between Donkin and Wait after the storm. The crew become
accustomed to congregate in the evening outside Wait's cabin.

> The little place, repainted white, had, in the night, the brilliance
> of a silver shrine where a black idol, reclining stiffly under a blan-
> ket, blinked its weary eyes and received our homage. Donkin
> officiated. He had the air of a demonstrator showing a phenome-
> non, a manifestation bizarre, simple, and meritorious that, to the
> beholders, should be a profound and an everlasting lesson.

The symbolic relationship between Donkin and Wait in this
description is something more than a relationship between the two
sides of the coin of the self-feeling. Donkin's position is subordinate; he has the aspect of a priest; he ministers to a deity. To

3. *The Psychology of the Emotions,* p. 267.   4. Ibid., p. 63.

understand this development of the symbolism in the novel's own terms, one must consider another attribute Donkin possesses.

As prominent as viciousness in Donkin's character is his antipathy to discipline and disciplined labor. The crew recognize him as a type: "He was the man that cannot steer, that cannot splice, that dodges the work on dark nights; that, aloft, holds on frantically with both arms and legs, and swears at the wind, the sleet, the darkness; the man who curses the sea while others work." He is not a phenomenon known only to the sea; his type is universal, a point the novel phrases in this way: Donkin is "an ominous survival testifying to the eternal fitness of lies and impudence." He represents the resurgence of the will and ego in a primitive form at a late stage in the evolution of the race. He is a survival nurtured by the "ignoble freedom of the slums."

Donkin as atavistic disharmony, to return to the earlier symbolism, ministers to the spirit of discontent (his own and Wait's); and that spirit leads to resignation before hardships and to a denial of duty. That meaning is made evident in the following passage. Donkin incites the crew by pointing to Wait's refusal of duty. Knowles raises this objection: "If we all went sick what would become of the ship?" Donkin answers, "Let 'er go to 'ell." But the stature of Wait allows the meaning of this symbolic relationship to be stated somewhat more philosophically, still in the novel's own terms. Wait's passivity is not simply a dodge to avoid work as Donkin supposes but ultimately a denial of the will to live. Wait's superiority, furthermore, is striking. When he first boards the ship he is "naturally scornful, unaffectedly condescending, as if from his height of six foot three he had surveyed all the vastness of human folly and had made up his mind not to be too hard on it." Donkin as priest conveys to the reader the conclusion that negation, denial of the will to live, and extreme pessimism have their origin in a critical disposition ultimately in an atavistic disharmony.

Donkin's symbolic relationship to Wait is a relationship to one of two aspects of the conservative instinct. Donkin himself is the other aspect. And so in a sense in the symbolic implications of the piece, Donkin as priest ministers also to himself. More intelligibly stated, the short novel conveys the point that a close connection exists between discontent generated by an atavistic disharmony and malevolence. The most encompassing symbolic dispositions of the novel thus say to the reader that atavistic disharmonies lead either to a pessimistic view of life and a negation of the will or to a savage desire to destroy those restraints that we find to be intolerable; lead, indeed, to nihilism. The statement rings true not only with respect to the content of *The Nigger of the "Narcissus"* but also with respect to the content of *The Secret Agent*.

The statement, also, is immediately recognizable as a generalization found in Ribot and in some other Utilitarian psychologists, who in their most important polemics, use associational and Spencerian principles to combat the pessimistic-nihilistic view of life articulated by the German philosophers Schopenhauer and Hartmann. Sully describes the temperament of the German Pessimists with some reference to atavistic disharmonies as a "carping, fault-finding disposition. This variety of temper," he continues, "involves, besides that fundamental irritability and quarrelsomeness of disposition already referred to, the co-operation of the sentiment of power."[5] This description summarizes accurately also the disposition of the contemptible Donkin. Needless to say, the debility of Wait must remind the reader of the Schopenhauerian doctrine of the negation of the will.

If we identify psychological assumptions and analyses in *The Nigger of the "Narcissus"* in the fashion attempted in this study, the subject matter is seen through a clear focus as "Schopenhauerian." That possibility is not remote when one considers that the *novella* was written in a period in which Conrad was intimate with H. G. Wells and that Wells was strongly attracted to Schopenhauer's philosophy.[6] To identify subject and theme in this way is to establish a connection between *The Nigger of the "Narcissus"* and a novel from the end of Conrad's career, namely, *Victory*, which reflects without championing a Schopenhauerian vision of life. I hope in this study to have contributed to understanding of the several kinds of continuity that exist among Conrad's quite dissimilar pieces of fiction.

SANFORD PINSKER

Selective Memory, Leisure, and the Language of Joseph Conrad's *The Nigger of the "Narcissus"*†

"On men reprieved by its disdainful mercy, the immortal sea confers in its justice the full privilege of desired unrest. Through the perfect wisdom of its grace they are not permitted to meditate at ease upon the complicated and acrid savour of existence . . . redeemed at last by the vast silence of pain and labour, by the dumb fear and the dumb courage of men obscure, forgetful and enduring."
—Chapter 4, *The Nigger of the "Narcissus"*

5. *Pessimism*, p. 423.
6. It is interesting to note that Wells lists Schopenhauer as one of the notable contemporary *psychologists* in his article "The Position of Psychology," *Saturday Review*, 29 December, 1894, p. 715.

Conrad's correspondence with Wells between 1896 and 1904 indicates that Conrad read almost everything Wells wrote in that period, both fiction and intellectual texts. It indicates that Wells criticized Conrad's writing. And it is

clear that Wells recommended authors. On October 30, 1903, for example, Conrad wrote: "Don't forget to send me Metchnikov's book. I am really curious to see that." No doubt Wells refers to the *Études sur la nature humaine*, published in Paris earlier that year. See *Life and Letters*, I, 321.

† From *Descant: Texas Christian University Literary Journal*, 15 (Summer 1971), 38–48.

As the son of a political prisoner exiled to northern Russia, the young Conrad had learned early the value of substituting a world of romance and adventure for the unhappy one he actually occupied. The sea stories of Marryat, Cooper, and Louis-Ambroise Garneray were his special favorites, along with more factual accounts of exploration. But the romances we read about are almost never the ones we get. The glamour Conrad had attributed to sailing ships—if, indeed, such a mystique *ever* existed—was in serious jeopardy by the time Conrad arrived at Marseilles in 1874. To be sure, the conversion to steam power had its effects on the traditions of the sea, but Conrad's persistent attempt to make the steam engine stand as a symbol of all that was corrupting about modernism probably contains more poetry than truth. And while critics like Gustav Morf and Wit Tarnawski view the decision to "jump" into the sea as a betrayal (conscious or otherwise) which continued to haunt Conrad throughout his career as a fiction writer, the tension between the assumptions of the reading room and the actualities on the forecastle were probably closer to Conrad's own experiences in the years between 1874 and 1894.[1] No doubt Conrad himself felt something of the despair which afflicted that ultimate sea-going romantic, Lord Jim, particularly where the matter of expectation and discovery were concerned.

> After two years of training he went to sea, and, entering the regions so well known to his imagination, found them strangely barren of adventure.
>
> Chapter 2, *Lord Jim*

On the few occasions when Conrad did try to reconstitute that world of boyhood adventure which had been such an important part of his early reading—one thinks of such late works as *The Rover* or the long delayed *The Rescue*—critics tend to invoke Thomas Moser's now-famous formula of "achievement and decline," feeling that Conrad had turned his back on the tensions which made his

---

1. In *The Living Conrad* (London, 1957), Wit Tarnawski suggests that "It is significant that the main theme of 'An Outcast of the Islands,' written just after Conrad has 'entered' the career of an English writer with 'Almayer's Folly,' is the hero's betrayal of his race and his subsequent punishment—an appalling solitude ending in death. The plot of the novel bears strong resemblance to Conrad's own situation at that particular time and, possibly, we may even see in it such developments as he might have feared for himself . . . the theme of betrayal—a theme which appears to haunt Conrad's mind in these first creative years" (p. 294). Gustav Morf's *The Polish Heritage of Joseph Conrad* (London, 1930) gives Conrad's betrayal-and-guilt a decidedly Freudian cast, suggesting that

Jim's story is little more than a "confession" and the novel itself little more than a thinly disguised allegory:

The sinking ship is Poland. The very names are similar. *Patna* is the name of the ship, and *Polska* the (Polish) name of Poland. *Poland* (i.e., Polonity) is doomed to disappear in a short time. There is, rationally speaking, no hope whatever for her . . . At this moment, Jim's superiors advise him to "jump," but Jim did not want to for a long moment. As a matter of fact, Conrad's uncle *urged him during more than seven years* to become a British subject. And finally, Jim yielded and jumped, i.e., Conrad became a British subject (p. 164).

other stories of the sea so impressive.[2] And yet, writers seldom develop in ways that their critics might wish for them and this is particularly true of Joseph Conrad. He was a creature fairly driven by ambiguous doubts and obsessed with a dark vision of human experience that became a constant, if only half understood, companion. His public posture seemed often to be that of the coldly formal aristocrat, but the private realities were more akin to the sort of whiner one often meets in, say, a Saul Bellow novel—a man who leaned on friends for advice, encouragement, criticism or praise and, sometimes, even an advance. A few characteristic lines from one of his many such letters to his editor Edward Garnett should make the point painfully clear:

> Is the thing tolerable? Is the thing readable? Is the damned thing altogether insupportable? Am I mindful enough of your teaching —of your expounding of the ways of the readers? Am I blessed? Or am I condemned? Or am I totally and utterly a hopeless driveller unworthy even of a curse?[3]

But when he was working at his best—which is to say, when he was closest to felt tensions, most deeply involved with what he called the "conversion of nervous energy into phrases"—he could mediate between the tested and the yet untried, between those who skim efficiently across the surface and those destined to descend into the terrible depths of Self, without making a final commitment to either view. Another of Conrad's Polish critics—Czeslaw Milosz —suggests that the source of such an ambivalent vision has its roots in the twin-poles of Conrad's parental figures—the poetically idealistic Korzeniowskis on the one hand and the more sedate Bobrowskis on the other:

> This clash between the two powerful personalities of uncle and father may help to elucidate the contradictions to be found in Conrad himself: what may be called his anti-romantic romanticism, his strange blend of polish patriotism and skepticism toward the 'Polish cause,' his love of adventure and his simultaneous cultivation of order and self-discipline.[4]

But Conrad is, finally, too Protean a creature to be held for very long by the nets of such speculation, particularly where matters of the creative process are involved. Critics wonder about his decision to leave Poland for an uncertain career at sea and then, after twenty years, to try his hand at the even more uncertain career of writing. Conrad's readers *wonder* because, in a very real sense, they must— whether the issues can ever be settled finally or not. As Professor

2. See particularly the concluding chapter of Professor Moser's impressive study, *Joseph Conrad: Achievement and Decline* (Cambridge, Mass., 1957).
3. Edward Garnett, ed., *Letters from Joseph Conrad* (New York, 1928), p. 49.
4. Czeslaw Milosz, "Joseph Conrad in Polish Eyes," *Atlantic Monthly*, CC, 5 (Anniversary Issue, 1957), 31.

Albert Guerard points out: ". . . Joseph Conrad was one of the most subjective and most personal of English novelists. And his best work makes its calculated appeal to the living sensibilities and commitments of readers; it is a deliberate invasion of our lives, and deliberately manipulates our responses."[5]

And it is this sense of a "manipulation of response"—although perhaps not in the way Professor Guerard intended—which marks his first, and possibly, greatest story of the sea, *The Nigger of the "Narcissus."* Here the non-verbal language of the sea most directly confronts the highly romanticized language of selective memory and here, too, the Donkins in Conrad's world—men who know "nothing of courage, of endurance, and of the unexpected faith, of the upspoken loyalty that knits together a ship's company"—meet the silent wisdom of Conrad's penultimate sailor, Singleton.

In Vernon Young's provocative and often brilliant essay "Trial By Water," he points out what appear to be failures in narrative technique, presumably because Conrad was "fearful of overstressing the subaqueous world of the underconsciousness" (which Young reminds us is "the most dependable source of his [Conrad's —or, perhaps, Young's?] inspiration"):

> Conrad overloaded his mundane treatment of the crew. As separate units of consciousness they are beautifully deployed for angles of relationships, but no one can deny that their professional virtues are overwritten, amost to the detriment of the narrative's aesthetic integrity. It is clear, in this direction, that Conrad had difficulty in serving myth and memory with equal justice. His narrator-perspective is awkwardly handled. The novel gets under way in the third person; in the middle of the second chapter it switches abruptly to the viewpoint of first person plural and remains there until the coda section, when it becomes first person singular . . . And, with this handicap, the gilded sermonizings on the crew's high endeavor are doubly hard to accept. If Conrad was solicitous for the phenomenal level of his narrative, he might at least have supplied a recorder to whose endowments his own opulent prose would have been more apt. However, this novel was an early trial in the marriage of subject with its coordinating agencies; Conrad's craft was not yet wholly adequate to sustain an unfailing integrity of means.[6]

But the narrative point-of-view—however much it may appear to vacillate between third person singular and first person plural—represents the collective sensibility of the *Narcissus'* crew, complete with all the ambivalences and initiations into complexity which make for the story's tightly balanced tone. For example, the initial description of Singleton—"stripped to the waist," and "tattooed like a cannibal chief all over his powerful chest"—suggests a spirit that is as central to Conrad's tale as the endless discussions about the light/dark imagery in sentences like "Mr. Baker, chief mate of the ship *Narcissus*, stepped in one stride out of his lighted cabin into the darkness of the quarter-deck." To be sure, the abundant use of light/dark imagery has rich connotations, although Conrad often throws his prose into a kind of symbolic overkill when such matters are involved. My point is, simply, that the unnamed figure who narrates the story cannot connect—or, of that matter, make *sense*—of mixtures like the following:

> With his spectacles, and a venerable white beard, he resembled a learned and savage patriarch, the incarnation of barbarian wisdom serene in the blasphemous turmoil of the world. He was intensely absorbed, and as he turned the pages, an expression of grave surprise would pass over his rugged features. He was reading *Pelham*.

The tableau excites the narrator's curiosity, but, more importantly, it unleashes a barrage of language which tends to falsify and romanticize the situation. And, while all the verbiage may tell us something about Singleton, I suspect it tells us a good deal more about the sensibility of the speaker—all of which is surely Conrad's point:

> What meaning can their rough, inexperienced souls find in the elegant verbiage of his pages? what excitement?—what forgetfulness?—what appeasement? Mystery! Is it the fascination of the incomprehensible? is it the charm of the impossible? Or are those beings who exist beyond the pale of life stirred by his tales as by an enigmatical disclosure of a resplendent world that exists within the frontier of infamy and filth, within that border of dirt and hunger, of misery and dissipation, that comes down on all sides to the water's edge of the incorruptible ocean, and is the only thing they know of life, the only thing they see of surrounding land—those lifelong prisoners of the sea? Mystery!

Singleton, of course, is framed by language—from the initial descriptions of his reading ("his lips, stained with tobacco-juice that trickled down the long beard, moved in inward whisper") to that final scene on shore when a pay clerk assumes the old sailor cannot sign his name. And, yet, Singleton himself is not defined so much by what he says, but, rather, by what he *does*. After all, it is Singleton who "steered with care," Singleton who is least affected by the rhetoric of Donkin or the symbolic potential of Wait. Apparently Conrad would have us believe that Singleton operates out of a kind of instinct born of discipline and long years of faithful service. Evidently Conrad had moments when the Singleton style and code must have looked terribly attractive. In fact, he wished such a life for his son Borys—as the following lines from a letter to Edward Garnett suggest:

He [Borys] is bigger every day. I would like to make a barge-man of him: strong, knowing his business and thinking of nothing. That is *the* life my dear fellow. Thinking of nothing! O bliss.[7]

However, Conrad's sentiment says more about hopes he held out for himself than they do about "wishes" he might have had for his son. To be sure, Conrad—as a young boy reading Cooper, as a master seaman lugging his five shilling Shakespeare from port to port and, finally, as a writer himself—cared about language, about *words* in ways that make it hard to see him as secret sharer of the mindless Singleton. After all, the novel's narrator tells us that Singleton was so unimaginative that "the thoughts of all his lifetime could have been expressed in six words." And yet, Conrad was obviously suspicious of the verbal machinations of a Donkin who comes, more and more, to stand for that Machiavellian manipulator of language who can corrupt a more simple-minded crew and, ultimately, threaten the harmony of the *Narcissus* herself. His introduction to the crew—and, subsequently, his first exploitation of sympathy—is at least partly, a matter of his language:

> . . . The ragged newcomer [Donkin] was indignant—"That's a fine way to welcome a chap into a fo'c'sle," he snarled. "Are you men or a lot of 'artless cannybals?"—"Don't take your shirt off *for a word*, shipmate," called out Belfast, jumping up in front, fiery, menacing, and friendly at the same time.—"Is that 'ere bloke blind?" asked the indomitable scarecrow, looking right and left with affected surprise. "Can't 'ee see I 'aven't got no shirt?"
>
> He held both his arms out crosswise and shook the rags that hung over his bones with dramatic effect.
>
> " 'Cos why?" he continued very loud. "The bloody Yankees been tryin' to jump my guts out 'cos I stood up for my rights like a good 'un. I am an Englishman, I am. They set upon me an' I 'ad to run. That's why. A'n't yet never seed a man 'ard up? Yah! What kind of blamed ship is this? I'm dead broke. I 'aven't got nothink. No bag, no bed, no blanket, no shirt—not a bloomin' rag but what I stand in. But I 'ad the 'art to stand up agin' them Yankees. 'As any of you 'art enough to spare a pair of old pants for a chum?"
>
> He knew *how to conquer the naive instincts of that crowd*. In a moment they gave him their compassion, jocularly, contemptuously, or surlily; and at first it took the shape of a blanket thrown at him as he stood there with the white skin of his limbs showing his human kinship through the black fantasy of his rags.
>
> (*Author's Italics*)

Donkin's rhetoric—like Wait's enigmatic symbolism—disorients the crew by forcing the essentially simple to confront the profoundly complex. He appeals to what David Daiches (in *The Novel*

7. Edward Garnett, ed., *Letters from Joseph Conrad* (New York, 1928), p. 136.

and the Modern World) calls that public sense of values which traditional novelists counted upon and Conrad treated with unrelent-
ing skepticism.[8] Donkin's "rights" as an Englishman; his abiding
sense of pride and personal principle; his obvious poverty—these are
the blocks upon which the rhetoric of his confidence game are
based. And, like any really good con man, he knows the value of a
good offense, particularly when the *terms* of his pitch are likely to
sound convincing on the first go.

Wait, on the other hand, relies upon mystery and understate-
ment, preferring to let others (including, I suspect, his critics—literary and otherwise) fill in the blanks. His very name on the ship's
roll is "all a smudge"—unreadable and, ultimately, unknowable. If
Donkin is introduced in terms of appeals to conscience and corrup-
tible sympathies, Wait boards the ship by a series of puns. As
Vernon Young has pointed out, Wait can mean "weight" as well as
"pause." To be sure, Wait's mystery is a combination of factors:
his blackness, his symbolic (?) character as life-in-death/death-in-
life, his very *presence* aboard the *Narcissus*. But, whatever the terms
of the particular mystery—whether it be Hamlet or Bartleby;
Keat's silent urn or Kurtz's cryptic "Horror!" we are driven to pluck
out its heart by giving the enigma a label, some "word" which will
allow us to control what, finally, cannot be controlled. In *Nigger*,
the mounting complexities are precariously balanced by an exaggerated romanticism about Singleton which gushes from the story's
narrative sensibility. Thus, Singleton—his very name suggesting his
status as the solitary one, the last of the old time sailors—comes,
more and more, to stand as a "lonely relic of a devoured and forgotten generation," a time (so goes the reactionary's vision of an unex-
perienced, re-structured past) when the moral fabric of sailors was
somehow stronger, the world somehow less complicated, the situations of life somehow less ambiguous:

> He stood, still strong, as ever unthinking; a ready man with a vast
> empty past and with no future, with his childlike impulses and
> his man's passions already dead within his tatooed breast. The
> men who could understand his silence were gone—those men
> who knew how to exist beyond the pale of life and within sight
> of eternity. They had been strong, as those are strong who know
> neither doubts nor hopes . . . voiceless men—but men enough to
> scorn in their hearts the sentimental voices that bewailed the
> hardness of their fate.

Critics have rightly identified the tensions which grow out of the
dramatic situation on the *Narcissus* but not, it seems to me, those
which are a necessary by-product of the narrator's waxing eloquence
about the value of silence. Very often, the narrator's highly selective

8. See particularly Mr. Daiches' discussion of the novel as "public instrument"
in his introductory chapter entitled
"Selection and Significance" (pp. 1–11).

memory plays an important role when the language-as-leisure and/or recollection is pitted against the silent character of Conrad's work ethic. Thus, the narrator can report that

> We remembered our danger, our toil—and conveniently forgot our horrible scare. We decried our officers—who had done nothing—and listened to the fascinating Donkin. His care for our rights, his disinterested concern for our dignity, were not discouraged by the invariable contumely of our words, by the disdain of our looks. Our contempt for him was unbounded—and we could not but listen with interest to that consummate artist.

For Conrad, the moment of action had a special majesty; here men disciplined in the exacting rigors demanded by an indifferent universe gripped the ropes of frail ships and, for a moment, became lost "in a vast universe of night and silence, where gentle sighs wandering here and there like forlorn souls, made the still sails flutter as in sudden fear, and the ripple of a beshrouded ocean whisper its compassion afar—in a voice mournful, immense and faint . . ." It is, by now, a critical commonplace to see Conrad's voyages as journeys of learning—usually through long dark nights of the Jungian soul —and *Nigger* has received more than its fair share of such readings. Yet, if the narrative point-of-view represents (at least loosely) the sensibility of the sailors, there is a real question as to what, if any, learning was achieved. For most of the voyage, the crew—always with the notable exception of Singleton—wallows in a vacillation that borders on total paralysis:

> Was he a reality—or was he a sham—this ever-expected visitor of Jimmy's? We hesitated between pity and mistrust, while, on the slightest provocation, he shook before our eyes the bones of his bothersome and infamous skeleton . . . It interfered daily with our occupations, with our leisure, with our amusements. We had no songs, and no music in the evening, because Jimmy (we all lovingly called him Jimmy, to conceal our hate of his accomplice) had managed, with that prospective decease of his, to disturb even Archie's mental balance . . . We served him in his bed with rage and humility, as though we had been the base courtiers of a hated prince; and he rewarded us by his unconciliating criticism. He had found the secret of keeping for ever on the run the fundamental imbecility of mankind; he had the secret of life, that confounded dying man, and he made himself master of every moment of our existence. We grew desperate, and remained submissive.

And, at a later point in the novel, Wait—by now more a "colossal enigma" than a fellow sailor—becomes the process by which the crew becomes thoroughly demoralized and

> . . . highly humanised, tender, complex, excessively decadent: we

understood the subtlety of his fear, sympathised with all his repulsions, shirkings, evasions, delusions—as though we had been over-civilised, and rotten, and without any knowledge of the meaning of life.

Conrad was more than a little suspicious where such attempts at understanding were concerned. Language—particularly in *Nigger*—tends to falsify experience; things seem to go better on the *Narcissus* when "very little was said" and problems of life ("too voluminous for the narrow limits of human speech") are

> abandoned to the great sea that had from the beginning enfolded it in its immense grip; to the sea that knew all, and would in time infallibly unveil the wisdom hidden in all the errors, the certitude that lurks in doubts, the realm of safety and peace beyond the frontiers of sorrow and fear.

In fact, the sea is one of the more dependable pockets of strength (another is the officers) which sustains the ship. At the very moment when Donkin's predictable brand of mutinous "talk" escalates into action (he has just thrown an iron-belaying pin at one of the officers),

> The ship trembled from trucks to keel; the sails kept on rattling like a discharge of musketry; the chain sheets and loose shackles jingled aloft in a thin peal; the gin blocks groaned. It was as if an invisible hand had given the ship an angry shake to recall the men that peopled her decks to the sense of reality, vigilance, and duty.

And, too, the sea holds secrets—myths—which Singleton has (presumably) known about all along. When the Jimmy who has wavered between sicknesses real and imagined actually dies, it "came as a tremendous surprise"—to everyone but Singleton. For the others,

> A common bond was gone; the strong, effective, and respectable bond of a sentimental lie.

But the moment gives Singleton all the triumphs of an "I-told-you-so" mentality:

> Singleton only was not surprised. "Dead—is he? Of course," he said, pointing at the island right abeam: for the calm still held the ship spell-bound within sight of Flores. Dead—of course. *He* wasn't surprised. Here was the land, and there, on the fore-hatch and waiting for the sailmaker—there was that corpse. Cause and effect. And for the first time that voyage, the old seaman became quite cheery and garrulous, explaining and illustrating from the stores of experience how, in sickness, the sight of an island (even a very small one) is generally more fatal than the view of a continent. But he couldn't explain why.

And, yet, one wonders if Wait's situation is *really* so enigmatic that the felt myths and half-understood superstitions of a Singleton are the only viable explanations? To be sure, where a Singleton can easily give himself to the irrational, the crew of the *Narcissus* prefers that "subtle association of ideas" which, predictably enough, leads to

> . . . violent quarrelling as to the exact moment of Jimmy's death. Was it before or after "that 'ere glass started down"? It was impossible to know, and it caused much contemptuous growling at one another.

And, yet, Singleton's much-celebrated "wisdom" is a distinctly limited commodity, evidently not portable enough to withstand the complexities and pressures of life on shore. The sailors of the *Narcissus* see Singleton from the perspective of the forecastle; the clerk must look at the aging sailor over a crowded pay-table:

> One by one they came up to the pay-table to get the wages of their glorious and obscure toil. They swept the money with care into broad palms, rammed it trustfully into trousers' pockets, or, turning their backs on the table, reckoned with difficulty in the hollow of their stiff hands.—"Money right? Sign the release. There—there," repeated the clerk impatiently. "How stupid these sailors are!" he thought. Singleton came up, venerable— and uncertain as to daylight; brown drops of tobacco juice hung in his white beard; his hands, that never hesitated in the great light of the open sea, could hardly find the small pile of gold in the profound darkness of the shore. "Can't write?" said the clerk, shocked. "Make a mark then." Singleton painfully sketched in a heavy cross, blotted the page. "What a disgusting old brute," muttered the clerk.

The shifting prespective is even more poignant if we remember that it was Singleton who had been reading Bulwer-Lytton's *Pelham* as the *Narcissus* began her voyage and the narrator who had (characteristically) turned that observation into a barrage of language about the curious habits of seamen.

With *Nigger* Conrad lays the ground work necessary to explore that relationship between raw experience and assimilated understanding which was to be a persistent feature of his sea stories. In a certain sense, *Nigger* is that encomium to the harmony of sailing men and the potential for learning aboard ship which Conrad's readers have insisted was the central meaning of the tale. Yet, the last lines are troubling nonetheless, particularly when they seem to chronically misrepresent and/or falsify what happened on the *Narcissus*:

> Haven't we, together and upon the immortal sea, wrung out a meaning from our sinful lives? Good-bye, brothers! You were a good crowd. As good a crowd as ever fisted with wild cries the

beating canvas of a heavy foresail; or tossing aloft, invisible in the night, gave back yell for yell to a westerly gale.

To be sure, the narrator's experiences aboard the *Narcissus* can only be recaptured through language—and, yet, his very *language* betrays the experience itself. In this sense his rhetorical question may not be rhetorical—and the crew of the *Narcissus* may have been something less than the "good crowd" with which he hails their memory. An inflated sense of romance and a highly selective memory account for some of the disparities, but Conrad implies that the roots of the problem may lie in the nature of language itself. Even his metaphors of a crew fisting "with wild cries the beating canvas of a heavy foresail" or giving back "yell for yell to a westerly gale" suggest that the juxtaposition of men and Nature is a function of sensibility rather than fact.

ROBERT FOULKE

Postures of Belief in *The Nigger of the "Narcissus"*[†]

Conrad's voyage fiction has always been praised for verisimilitude. Though critics have been preoccupied with other dimensions of the voyage tales during the past twenty-five years such as archetypal patterns, political analogues, and psychic autobiography, fidelity to the actual conditions of sea life has been assumed and valued. This assumption is much too simplistic to be useful as a start towards understanding either the mimetic base or the rhetorical strategies of the voyage tales. It may lead us to somewhat egregious mistakes of interpretation and to a generally inadequate conception of how mimesis operates in Conrad. The reflexive nature of the novel (as described by Professor Miller in his English Institute paper several years ago)[1] is fully exploited by Conrad's technical virtuosity. To understand how this is done, we need discriminations finer than those which the shopworn terms "mimesis," "verisimilitude," and "realism" can provide, at least in their present state of overlapping jurisdiction.

In its simplest form, the mimetic relationship describes that part of the meaning of words which used to be called their "reference" —i.e., their pointing or naming function, their capacity to call segments of the non-verbal universe to our attention. Among the many inadequacies of this approach to mimetic theory, one is crippling for the reader of fiction. The lack of any exact correspondence

[†] From *Modern Fiction Studies*, 17 (Summer 1971), 249–63. Some of the author's footnotes are not reproduced here.
1. J. Hillis Miller, "Three Problems of Fictional Form," *Experience in the Novel*, ed. Roy Harvey Pearce (New York: Columbia University Press, 1968), pp. 28–29.

between words and what they seem to be pointing to becomes over-whelming in many typical Conradian sentences. Consider the first sentence of Chapter Four in *The Nigger of the "Narcissus"*: "On men reprieved by its disdainful mercy, the immortal sea confers in its justice the full privilege of desired unrest." How can we possibly relate this sentence to the debilitating storm which the crew of the *Narcissus* has just survived in Chapter Three? All the key terms make sense only as metaphysical, moral, or psychological constructs. Abstractions are bundled together as properties of an anthropo-morphic "sea" which seems totally alien to the breaking waves and flying spume of the preceding chapter. Clearly, the word "sea" is functioning more as idea than as image in this sentence. When we put the two "seas" together, we are testing one of the many possi-ble correlations between structures of ideation and perception within the narrator's head. What mimesis and verisimilitude refer to is here internalized; the reader is never given an unmediated world of sensory imagery. As Professor Kermode suggests, we can imagine a world of absolute contingency coming to us through language rather than through immediate sense experience only as an ideal possibility.[2] Our problem comes in trying to determine what a mimetic base is, what its limits are, how and when it is being used.

If more readers had taken long voyages in sailing ships or if the story were told in one voice, we would have less difficulty in noticing how complex the mimetic relationships are in *The Nigger of the "Narcissus."* There are at least three modes of perception apparent in the language of the text. The first is most closely allied to ordi-nary notions of verisimilitude because it grows out of the narrator's direct observation. The only gap here, and it is sometimes a very wide one, is the reader's lack of information about sea life, which he needs to judge what is being changed or left out. He may miss the implied meaning of described or dramatized events where implication depends upon the way things happen on a sailing ship voyage; he may misconstrue characterization which is completed by historical knowledge of conditions in the British Merchant Service. In neither case is the text a total determinant of meaning because it cannot explain its own holes and distortions. The second mode of perception consists of abstract judgments about men and events in the narrator's voice, with obvious explicit meaning but no clear authority in events. The reader's problem is making connections, either to what is happening or to a narrator revealing himself in what he says, or to both simultaneously. Because this mode often occurs in generalizing passages about mental or emotional states, implied phenomena cannot be distinguished from the perception of them, and the result is blocks of text which contain untestable

2. Cf. Frank Kermode, *The Sense of an Ending* (Oxford: Oxford University Press, 1966), Ch. V, esp. pp. 150–.151.

assertions; their truth depends neither on the world being imitated in the first mode or on the known eidetic propensities of a fallible, placed character. The third mode of perception emerges from clusters of metaphor suggesting a mythic voyage complete with archetypal motifs and polarized characters. These constructs are located within the perceiving imagination but are not related to all the persons which the narrating presence assumes. They tend to be visualized rather than voiced, and they are clearly evoked by what can be seen by a man on board the *Narcissus* as the generalizations of the second mode are not. In quite different ways, all three modes of perception internalize parts of the mimetic base of the novel.

II

We can see why Conrad needed diverse rhetorical strategies by examining the connection between mimesis and point of view throughout the voyage stories. *The Nigger of the "Narcissus,"* *Typhoon*, and "The End of the Tether" convey perceptions which no character is capable of having on his own. The Singletons, MacWhirrs, and Whalleys of the voyage stories are often interesting to us because their relation to the sea world being imitated is complicated, not because they are intrinsically complex characters. Conrad's technical problem becomes one of catching the full reality of the lived moment at sea without having any intelligence on board ship subtle enough to see analogies between that moment and other experiences in the past, between an action and some abstract value inherent in it, or even between the simple facts of experience and some emotional response to them. Some of Conrad's seamen are perceptual incompetents. We remember that Captain MacWhirr, for example, has no conception of the typhoon beyond "dirty weather" and that he is incapable of human feelings about it until the cataclysm is reduced to disorder in his own cabin.

As Conrad's techniques evolved, he developed two increasingly sophisticated strategies for marrying perception and mimesis in voyage stories. The most obvious is Marlow. We can see a paradigm of Marlow's function, though a clumsy one, in his first appearance as the narrator of "Youth." All the perception is poured into the old Marlow telling the story, all the mimesis into the young Marlow acting—a young man naively unresponsive to the decrepit hulk which he sails on and half insane captain who commands her. Conrad uses this same cub, particularly in the closing scenes of the small boat voyage and first glimpse of the East, as a vehicle for reaching beyond ordinary human perception to a fantasy world, dreamlike and solipsistic. Reality is totally internalized, being merely triggered by what is happening to ship and crew. The young Marlow who thrills to the last supper on the poop of the burning ship, who sees the lifeboat as his first "command," and who trans-

forms an ordinary Javanese harbor into paradise prefigures the absolute innocence of the young Russian in "Heart of Darkness" and
the vulnerability of Lord Jim. Such characters cannot be said to
"live" in the mimetic world of their voyage any more than the
MacWhirrs and Whalleys do if we mean by living what old Marlow
represents: a man who can observe the minutiae of the visible and
audible world, who can entertain conceptions which unify parts of
this world into wholes, who can relate these wholes to human
values like honor, courage, work, craft, fidelity, and solidarity without falsifying his perceptions or abandoning the values. As a device
for simultaneously creating a solid mimetic world, an intelligence
for perceiving it, and a means of transforming it into the absolute
terms of archetypal quest, the old-young Marlow works surprisingly
well, not only in "Youth" but in "Heart of Darkness." In this
connection the elaborate frames surrounding old Marlow as he tells
the story remind us that the old man is as real as the young one,
and that neither is Conrad himself, an almost disappearing presence who is the totally silent crewman of the *Nellie*.

In *Lord Jim* the device is modified: old Marlow identifies with
young Jim, and the tensions between the experience of the teller
and the innocence of the actor become stronger and more explicit.
Marlow can vacillate between acceptance and rejection, and fragments of his perception of Jim become objective characters like the
French Lieutenant, Brierly, Chester, Robinson, and Gentleman
Brown, while Marlow himself has an ideal alter-ego in Stein. Ways
of being start in Marlow's head, then move inexorably towards the
cast and consequences which a recalcitrant mimetic world (as Kenneth Burke uses that term) might impose on any ideal conception
of self. If the derelict *Patna* is the reality principle in the first part
of the novel, one which is totally at odds with Jim's immature
dreams of a world acclimated to heroism, Patusan in a country both
imaginary and real, where a Hollywood scenario of the East mingles
with the muck of a river village in Borneo. A later version of the
same narrating device is the *Doppelgänger* of "The Secret Sharer"
and *The Shadow-Line*, where all the conflict of perception is built
into the schizophrenic young captains who tell their own stories.
Although the use of Legatt in "The Secret Sharer" and Captain
Giles in *The Shadow-Line* can be seen as remnants of the objectify-
ing technique of *Lord Jim*, it seems clear that only internal perception counts in these late fear-haunted voyages. The seascape is
almost totally a projection of the narrator's mood, and the tests
which the young captain passes are largely self-created since both
the approach to Koh-ring and putting to sea with an incomplete
and sickly crew are avoidable in the real world of seafaring. The
mimetic principle has been totally submerged in the dream world

which permeates these voyages, and the normative perception of old Marlow has disintegrated into the hollow principles of Captain Archbold of the *Sephora* and the talky platitudes of a senile harbor-master like Captain Giles.

This evolution of Conrad's narrative technique can also be construed as a movement away from mimesis towards fantasy. It is certainly true that a dream world saturates much of his later fiction— *Under Western Eyes*, *The Arrow of Gold*, "Freya of the Seven Isles," "The Planter of Malata," and "The Tale" as well as "The Secret Sharer" and *The Shadow-Line*. In the voyage stories which use a narrator, there is a shift in the way of relating external and internal reality. The early device of an older and more experienced man musing on what he did as a youth dichotomizes perception with a cleavage between act and understanding, dream and fact. The result is a process of disillusionment in a narrator who is unwilling to repudiate his former self and unable to connect what the world is like with inner visions of what it ought to be. Thus old Marlow in "Heart of Darkness" ends by telling a lie to the Intended because the truth which he has discovered has no human value. He is left with an absolute disrelation between what he has heard or seen and the civilizing constructs of his own imagination —work, restraint, even truth itself.

The second Marlow of *Lord Jim* (and *Chance*) is no longer narrating his own autobiography, but the gain in objectivity paradoxically allows him to be more subjective and hypothetical. As has already been suggested, he has the freedom of approach and withdrawal, sympathy and repudiation in his relations to Jim; he is no longer confined by the fundamental premise of a continuing self as he was in the earlier stories. His role as tale-teller is less restricted because he has no obligation to maintain the minimal illusion of verisimilitude built into autobiographical narration: completeness. He lacks the constraint of knowing the whole of Jim's life, as he would his own, and can, therefore, freely play with juxtapositions which have no effect on Jim's consciousness but illuminate his "case." In this sense Big Brierly is an imaginative projection of one of Marlow's ideas about Jim; his suicide, which has no etiology in the novel, sucks meaning from Jim's case through a metaphor of infection. Brierly's jump is connected to Jim's only through this intricate mental structure: the same act (abandoning ship) in Jim's case *is* his unadmitted failure whereas in Brierly's it prevents an imagined failure somehow caught at the court of inquiry by simple exposure to Jim, who is connected to Brierly only by the slim links of nationality and profession. Brierly is meaningful only as a figment of Marlow's imagination. Mimetically considered, his suicide could have been motivated by ennui or self-disgust or a bagful of other unprovided reasons more convincing than his tenuous link with Jim. But the controlling principle of Marlow's narration is not what he sees and hears so much as the structures of explanation being spun out of his own head as a web to catch events. This non-autobiographical Marlow succeeds as a perceiver, though somewhat erratically and clumsily, because he does unite internal vision with external fact. He has less hard truth than his predecessor in "Youth" and "Heart of Darkness," but more meaning.

The third stage of Conrad's technical evolution rejoins narrator and actor in one person without erecting impenetrable barriers between thought and act, but many of the later Marlow's perceptual gains are sacrificed. The hallucinatory quality of the world perceived by the captain-narrators of "The Secret Sharer" and *The Shadow-Line* leads to a new solipsism and continually threatens schizophrenia. Young Marlow in "Youth" had the power of transforming external fact into dream, whereas the somewhat paranoid young captains in the later voyages are menaced by nightmares which assimilate external sensations. The slightest deviation in nautical routine can unleash malevolent powers which must be ritually exorcised. Assuming the first watch (which is traditionally stood by the first mate) in "The Secret Sharer" and failing actually to taste the quinine powder in *The Shadow-Line* bring upon the young captains a disproportionate sense of guilt and fill their minds with traumatic visions of failure. Every sensation must be read for its occult significance. These young captains are enclosed in a self which screens out unanticipated signals from the outer world to such a degree that they invent second selves, Leggatt and the dead Captain, to anthropomorphize the threat of that outer world. Unlike the later Marlow, they are trapped by their own perceptions; they are unable to conceptualize a dichotomy between world and self. One key to this change is the lack of any stable orientation in space or time. The measurable progress of an ordinary voyage disappears, making navigation useless; even the comforting stability of sensory expectation—the heel of the ship, the curve of sails, the feel of wind coming from a constant direction, the regularity of waves, the straight wake stretching out astern —evaporates in the total immobility of a becalmed ship. The very fact that the external world does not change casts doubt upon its reality. The perspective of time also disappears. The mature narrator implied at the beginning and end of both tales loses his distance in the middle and is no longer able to evaluate an experience which he relives. What he knows about the world outside of his head cannot restrain the chaotic images filling his imagination.,

III

It has been convenient to describe the correlation between mimesis and point of view in terms of later voyage stories where the use of a narrator is explicit and relatively consistent. To speak of *the* narrator in *The Nigger of the "Narcissus"* is to create a fiction within a fiction, for there are many, each one performing some of the functions of the more clearly objectified narrators in later voyages. Conrad had not yet found Marlow when he wrote *The Nigger of the "Narcissus,"* though he does want to do what Marlow can do best—i.e., juxtapose abstract statement with fictional event, time of narration with time of action, explanation of cause with immediate perception. The result is a ghostly paradigm of Marlow, eyes and ears which cannot always be fixed in time or space combined with an unmistakable but often mistaken voice. And this is the dilemma for the reader: a human voice which cannot be held accountable for all of its pronouncements. The elusive narrator of *The Nigger of the "Narcissus"* resembles Kurtz more than Marlow, an insubstantial voice rather than a physical presence, and one which vacillates between the extremes of rhapsody and denunciation. Yet this unreliable, shifting voice has often been taken as Conrad's mouthpiece of theme in the novel. To do so is to overlook a number of important cues in the text. The three interlocked modes of perception distinguish the narrator from an omniscient, editorializing author.

Spatially, the narrator is versatile to the point of exasperation. This technique can be justified in terms of the novel's scope: individual seamen, the crew as a whole, officers, and the ship herself must be seen in ways which no firmly placed narrator could manage.[3] The reader's problem is clearly one of authority. Are the narrator's mutations an index of his reliability? Is he less fallible the higher he gets in the sky, the farther he is removed from the "we" who is presumably an ordinary seaman in the forecastle? The easiest answer to these questions attaches greater authority to the withdrawn narrator, less to the involved, but we cannot justify this weighting when we look closely at the generalizing passages of the text. They are charged with possible attitudes rather than simple truths. The narrator is just as susceptible to momentary impulses in the third person as he is in the first person. In his attempts to comprehend the chaotic experience of the crew, visions of order quickly fade into their opposites. Such inconsistency is most apparent when he tries to create a moral dichotomy between pure life at sea and sordid existence ashore: "The true peace of God begins at any spot a thousand miles from the nearest land; and when He sends there

3. Cf. Albert Guerard, *Conrad the Novelist* (Cambridge, Mass.: Harvard University Press, 1958), Ch. 3 and Ian Watt, "Conrad Criticism and *The Nigger of the 'Narcissus,' " Nineteenth Century Fiction*, 12 (March 1958), 260. For Guerard and Watt, see above, pp. 219–58.

the messengers of His might it is not in terrible wrath against crime, presumption, and folly, but paternally, to chasten simple hearts—ignorant hearts that know nothing of life, and beat undisturbed by envy or greed." Apart from our general suspicion of this passage—throughout the novels and letters, references to Christianity tend to be ironic—we recall its contradiction just two paragraphs earlier:"like that earth which had given her up to the sea, she [the *Narcissus*] had an intolerable load of regrets and hopes. On her lived timid truth and audacious lies, and, like the earth, she was unconscious, fair to see—and condemned by men to an ignoble fate."

Another example of the narrator's inability to hold his attitudes steady occurs in his distanced vision of the final stages of the voyage, balancing his struggle with the land/sea dichotomy of the beginning. At the end the land itself becomes a giant pure ship—"a vessel of fabulous dimensions . . . an indestructible craft riding motionless upon the immortal and unresting sea"—in the most notorious extended metaphor of the novel. Structurally, this metaphor which reduces the life of the earth to that of the ship is the inverse of the one which expanded the ship into "a small planet," "a fragment detached from the earth." The voyage begins and ends in macrocosm/microcosm figures which identify ship and earth. In both passages the narrator struggles for coherence by jamming opposites together, as though forcing them into the confines of a single sentence would automatically fuse them. The planet-ship of departure houses timidity and audaciousness, truth and lies, and is herself both beautiful and ignobly condemned. The ship-earth which the *Narcissus* approaches at the end of the voyage "towered up immense and strong, guarding priceless traditions and untold suffering, sheltering glorious memories and base forgetfulness, ignoble virtues and splendid transgressions." The double oxymoron at the end of this sentence prepares the narrator for his final plunge into apostrophe: "A great ship! . . . A ship mother of fleets and nations! The great flagship of the race; stronger than the storms! and anchored in the open sea." But the narrator does not even try to hold on to this apocalyptic (and chauvinistic) vision. By the end of the next paragraph the land is again sordid, and the city appears as the black cloud which opens and closes "Heart of Darkness." The narrator returns to the now familiar regret, hope, and folly of the initial planet-ship, applied to the city which is heard as "an immense and lamentable murmur—the murmur of millions of lips praying, cursing, sighing, jeering—the undying murmur of folly, regret, and hope exhaled by the crowds of the anxious earth." Summarizing these opposed sets of images applied to land, sea, ship, seamen, and city dweller shows us how unreliable the narrator is when he generalizes, but logical inconsistencies are beside the point. The intellectual content of these passages is minimal, a frame for metaphor more than prediction. Incantatory prose bolsters up the narrator's unsteady view of life.

Third-person narration closer to the immediate scene seems to be more reliable, but it is often undercut by minute observation (sometimes in the first person plural). The narrator wants to believe that human effort has some meaning. During the righting of the ship, which occurs as the storm subsides, we can believe in Captain Allistoun's determination: "The master's ardour, the cries of that silent man inspired us." In a scene which reminds us of Leggatt's crime in "The Secret Sharer," Allistoun threatens Donkin with a belaying pin and bullies the crew into risking their lives for the sake of the ship. But the same heroic pose earlier in the storm represents nothing but the narrator's wish fulfillment: "with living eyes he was still holding the ship up, heeding no one, as if lost in the unearthly effort of that endeavor." Quite literally, the captain has nothing to do at that point. The storm has dwarfed his authority and destroyed his power to control the small universe of the ship. Like the rest of the crew, the narrator wants to believe in the old hierarchy, the old routine, even though decks have become walls and rudders no longer steer.

A disoriented ship and a mad sea do not foster a sense of proportion, so what he reports often undercuts his illusions. Wait's rescue, the most heroic deed of the crew, is bracketed by two moments of total indifference to the value of saving human life. The first occurs when Belfast almost falls overboard: "We shouted all together with dismay; but with legs overboard he held and yelled for a rope. In our extremity nothing could be terrible; so we judged him funny kicking there, and with his scared face. Some one began to laugh, and, as if hysterically infected with screaming merriment, all those haggard men went off laughing, wild-eyed, like a lot of maniacs tied up on a wall." After the rescue, Podmore disappears on his heroic mission—making coffee: "An hour or more afterwards some one said distinctly: 'He's gone for good.'—'Very likely,' assented the boatswain; 'even in fine weather he was as smart about the deck as a milch-cow on her first voyage. We ought to go and see.' Nobody moved." A few paragraphs later the narrator spends a whole paragraph extolling the cook's heroism and berating his conceit; there is an unmistakable note of the mock heroic in this paragraph, just as there is open sarcasm in the narrator's later evaluation of the whole crew's behavior during the storm: "And we were conceited! We boasted of our pluck, of our capacity for work, of our energy. We remembered honourable episodes: our devotion, our indomitable perserverance—and were proud of them as though they had been the outcome of our unaided impulses. We remembered our danger, our toil—and conveniently forgot out horrible scare." Thus the total meaning of the storm cannot be reduced to themes of fidelity and solidarity; it remains hung between the poles of "indomitable perseverance" and "horrible scare." The narrator's insecurity makes us entertain Marlow's doubt in *Lord Jim*—"the doubt of the sovereign power enthroned in a fixed standard of conduct."[4]

There are also complications within the narrator's identified position, the "we" which represents an anonymous seaman in the forecastle. This "we" fluctuates between immediacy and retrospection. At some times he reports sensations as if they were happening; at others, he evaluates them in the perspective of what is to come. Questions of authority do not arise in "Youth" and "Heart of Darkness" because we can easily distinguish the old narrator's conceptualizing from the young seaman's naive response to the same experience. The *Nigger of the "Narcissus"* does not have this mechanism for projecting attitude and observation simultaneously, but the first person plural narrator vacillates between the same poles of foreknowledge and innocence. At a number of points in the text we catch him speaking as if the voyage had been completed. The second section of Chapter Four begins with a paragraph in which the "we" shapes the whole voyage conceptually as a journey in two parts, divided geographically and psychologically by the Cape of Good Hope; "Yet from that time our life seemed to start afresh as though we had died and had been resuscitated." Serial narration of the voyage makes this kind of retrospection unavoidable in the first person plural. The use of "we" establishes a double identification, linking the narrator with the crew (time of action) and with the reader (time of narration). Since this convention destroys any illusion that the two times are identical—that the narrator is having his experience as we read—we can never believe the narrator to be totally innocent. The "we" who tells us the beginning of the voyage has already experienced its end, so as wise speaker he can only pretend to be naïve by recalling his impressions at the time of action. The difficulties of this role are insurmountable when the narrator needs to back away in space (shifting from the first to the third person) or condense time (shifting from the definite past to the continuous past). The narrating "we" uses a syntax and vocabulary beyond the reach of an ordinary seaman, and the seaman expresses a gullibility which is impossible after the voyage has been completed. These are the clues telling us which "we" is speaking at any point in the text and reminding us that neither one can be taken at face value.

This split "we" gives us a double take which is essential if we are

4. *Lord Jim* (Dent Collected Edition), p. 50.

to believe in the crew's corruption by Wait. The naïve narrator, as spokesman for the emotions of the crew, is alternately attracted and repelled by Jimmy, remaining in doubt about his sickness until the end of Chapter Four. The wise narrator, on the other hand, knows that Jimmy is both shamming and dying. After expostulating "No man could be suspected of such a monstrous friendship!", the naïve narrator asks the question in his typical either/or form: "Was he a reality—or was he a sham—this ever-expected visitor of Jimmy's?" A few pages later he starts a sentence which the wise narrator finishes; "We were trying to be decent chaps, and found it jolly difficult; we oscillated between the desire of virtue and the fear of ridicule; we wished to save ourselves from the pain of remorse, but did not want to be made the contemptible dupes of our sentiment." The conjunction of simple and sophisticated attitudes towards Wait sometimes occurs in sentences which nearly match each other: "You couldn't see that there was anything wrong with him: a nigger does not show"; ". . . no one could tell what was the meaning of that black man sitting apart in a meditative attitude and as motionless as a carving." The style of the naïve narrator returns once more just after Jimmy's death: "In our hearts we thought that in the matter of his departure Jimmy had acted in a perverse and unfriendly manner. He didn't back us up, as a shipmate should." The wise narrator has the final word a few lines later: "Doubt survived Jimmy; and, like a band of criminals disintegrated by a touch of grace, we were profoundly scandalized with each other." It is easy to overlook the point of all this vacillation. The narrator who feels the doubts of the crew is looking for a simple truth which can be proved or disproved by the course of events, a certainty comparable to Singleton's superstition. The narrator who tells the story and looks back upon the whole voyage is not so easily satisfied. When he joins the crew in lying to Jimmy "with unshaken fidelity," the dichotomy between truth and falsehood collapses. The poles coalesce as he questions the relevance of *any* belief to the structure of reality, if there is a structure. His truth is partial, unstable, perhaps illusory, and always inadequate; his doubts cannot be allayed by the arrival of wind.

In all of his persons, the narrator gives us postures of belief, grasped hopes rather than absolute truths. This becomes obtrusively clear in the final switch to the first person singular. The "I" who describes the reunion of Charley with his mother is so maudlin that he seems to be parodying his former roles: "I was passing him at the time, and over the untidy head of the blubbering woman he gave me a humorous smile and a glance ironic, courageous and profound, that seemed to put all my knowledge of life to shame." The final phrase becomes absurd when it is lifted out of its original context ("We understood the subtlety of his [Jimmy's] fear, sympathised with all his repulsions, shrinkings, evasions, delusions—as though we had been overcivilised, and rotten, and without any knowledge of the meaning of life" and placed here. The same narrator avoids Belfast with a magazine cliché: " 'So long!' I said, and went on my way." And his concluding rhapsody reminds us of the crew's "sentimental lie": ". . . at times the springflood of memory sets with force up the dark River of the Nine Bends. Then on the waters of the forlorn stream drifts a ship—a shadowy ship manned by a crew of Shades. They pass and make a sign, in a shadowy hail. Haven't we, together and upon the immortal sea, wrung out a meaning from our sinful lives? Good-bye brothers! You were a good crowd. As good a crowd as ever fisted with wild cries the beating canvas of a heavy foresail; or tossing aloft, invisible in the night, gave back yell for yell to a westerly gale." Such passages are often ridiculed by associating them with a direct authorial voice, but the speaker here is really a distillation of the two "we's." One, like any sentimental old voyager, is bound to exaggerate the hardships which he has endured; the other has been reading "The Rime of the Ancient Mariner."

Thus the reader is left with two impulses at the end of the narrative. One leads him to doubt the celebration of a seaman narrator, to wonder whether the question buried in the middle of this last paragraph is in fact rhetorical. The other leads him to follow the narrating voice as it becomes excited to the pitch of high rhetoric —to share a vision appropriate to pure romance in which characters are noble and actions heroic within a surrealistic seascape. Both impulses are valid; to deny either distorts the text. One has its source in the naturalistic rendering of life at sea, the other in the hallucinatory world evoked by a fulness of metaphor.

IV

Although the voyage cannot be simplified into moral allegory, symbolic interpretation is unavoidable. The text is crammed with metaphoric structures. Just as what the narrator says is an attempt to establish belief—to fill the skies, or at least man's head, with the abstract principles of an unshakeable code of conduct—what he sees, or more precisely the way in which he sees, is often a compulsive matching of immediate and imagined experience, marked by a torrent of eidetic imagery and elaborate simile. The narrator continually propels us into a world of mysterious presences where wind becomes a "reminder of their [the crew's] dependence upon the invisible." The ship is "lost in a vast universe of night and silence where gentle sighs wandering here and there like forlorn souls, made the still sails flutter as in sudden fear, and the ripple of a beshrouded ocean whisper its compassion afar—in a voice mournful, immense, and faint. . . ." When the *Narcissus* docks a bridge

opens "as if by enchantment" and capstans turn "as though animated by a myterious and unholy spell." There is a frequent cross-
ing of the shadow-line between the seen and the unseen, the everyday and the extraordinary. During the struggle to rescue Wait from
the deckhouse, his body mysteriously ascends; during the burial
scene, the corpse refuses to descend until Belfast's ritual touch
sends it whizzing into the sea. Repeatedly, we get both a sense of
the actual voyage, with its scrupulously rendered detail, and suggestions of a world appropriate to pure romance.

The three major tests of the story—storm, mutiny, and death—
are associated with mysterious appearances from below. During the
rescue, we recall, Wait rises "like a bladder full of gas," and the
final corruption of the crew is accomplished when "Jimmy bobbed
up upon the surface, compelling attention, like a black buoy
chained to the bottom of a muddy stream." Similarly Donkin
appears before the captain in the final phase of the mutiny "as
though he had come up through the deck." The end of two tests is
marked by a wanderer's return from the wasteland. After the
rescue, "the return on the poop was like the return of wanderers
after many years amongst people marked by the desolation of
time." After Wait's death, Donkin is "perfectly astounded to find
the world outside as he had left it; there was the sea, the ship—
sleeping men; and he wondered absurdly at it; as though he had
expected to find the men dead, familiar things gone for ever: as
though, like a wanderer returning after many years, he had expected
to see bewildering changes." Bracketed between storm and death is
the other test of mutiny, which closes with the imagery of rejuvenation and treasure usually found at the end of romance:

> In the morning the ship, beginning another day of her wandering
> life, had an aspect of sumptuous freshness, like the spring-time of
> the earth. The washed decks glistened in a long clear stretch; the
> oblique sunlight struck the yellow brasses in dazzling splashes,
> darted over the polished rods in lines of gold, and the single drops
> of salt water forgotten here and there along the rail were as limpid
> as drops of dew, and sparkled more than scattered diamonds.

The ship herself is the treasure here—for a moment. In a manner
anticipating *Nostromo*, the treasure motif recurs in such images as
"jewels," "gold," "priceless," "splendid," and "prize" when the
Narcissus is transformed into the macrocosmic "vessel of fabulous
dimensions." And it returns again in a black-and-white cluster at
the end of the novel: "And to the right of the dark group the
stained front of the Mint, cleansed by the flood of light, stood out
for a moment dazzling and white like a marble palace in a fairy
tale."

As we respond to the imagery of wasteland, descent, and treasure, and to the religious imagery associated with it (e.g., the crew climbing the shrouds "in attitudes of crucifixion," the rescue party casting nails upon the sea, or the deckhouse appearing as "a silver shrine where a black idol . . . received our homage") the archetypal pattern of romance is clear and strong. The elements of initiation, three major tests, three descents to the underworld (deckhouse) in the rescue, Podmore's Hell, and the death scene, and three returns to the normal world of the ship after wandering are all there. But this whole structure is fabricated of similes, as the repetition of "like," "as," and "as though" reminds us, and the moment of rejuvenation occurs between the rage of the storm and the demoralization of death. At the end the ship dies in a filthy dock and the crew disintegrates in a sordid city. What one critic calls "the ultimate quality of sense experience"[5] is counterpoised against the narrator's dreams.

Taken together, the metaphoric structures do not support simplified readings of *The Nigger of the "Narcissus."* Polarities of vision are not aligned with the oppositions of a speaking narrator who tries to impose moral order on the world. There is really no a priori reason for holding that the novel should be a romantic affirmation of traditional values. Conrad's ironic tendencies are already strong in *Almayer's Folly* and *The Outcast of the Islands,* and they gain full force in "Heart of Darkness" and *Lord Jim,* both written just a few years after *The Nigger of the "Narcissus."* The image of men "lost, alone, forgetful, and doomed" at the end of the novel suggests one of Conrad's recurrent themes: "they were like castaways, like reckless and joyous castaways, like mad castaways making merry in the storm and upon an insecure ledge of a treacherous rock." Here, as elsewhere in Conrad's fiction, men cannot pretend that their truths offer anything but a choice of illusions, that their code of conduct is anything more than Lord Jim's "merciless dream."

WILLIAM W. BONNEY

Semantic and Structural Indeterminacy in *The Nigger of the "Narcissus"*: An Experiment in Reading

I

In recent years critics have been provided with a number of new and significant intellectual tools which bolster their efforts to determine the abstract nature of a literary text and to respond to it adequately as interpreters of specific passages and works. The criterion

5. J. Hillis Miller, *Poets of Realty* (Cambridge, Mass.: Harvard University Press, 1966), p. 24.

† From *ELH*, 40 (Winter 1973), 564–83.

of mimetic realism particularly has been assaulted and judged to be an unfortunate and misleading concept which has mistakenly been imposed upon artifacts that exist apart from such comforting epistemological assumptions. J. Hillis Miller has perhaps stated the problem most succinctly:

> One important aspect of current literary criticism is the disintegration of the paradigms of realism under the impact of structural linguistics and the renewal of rhetoric. If meaning in language rises not from the reference of signs to something outside words but from differential relations among the words themselves, if "referent" and "meaning" must always be distinguished, then the notion of a literary text which is validated by its one-to-one correspondence to some social, historical, or psychological reality can no longer be taken for granted.[1]

Although literary criticism has long dealt with intellectual constructs derived from metaphors that are founded upon the idea of mimesis, there is at present a tendency to reject as futile all attempts to validate a text through references to supposedly extralinguistic presences. And the growing awareness that one cannot evade forests of purely verbal relationships which threaten to engulf reassuring potential for correctness and truth has given rise to a body of theoretical criticism that emphasizes "indeterminancy" and "discontinuity" in literature as typical, if not necessary, aesthetic facts.[2]

Morse Peckham has suggested that ". . . as behavior language has two polarities, the exemplary and the explanatory"; he does not mean that there are two types of statements that can be made, but rather ". . . two opposite directions in which discourse moves. A statement is exemplary if it is explained by another statement; it is explanatory if it explains another statement."[3] Literary interpretation is in essence "nonexemplary or explanatory discourse" which is capable of "infinite regressions, a process which is halted . . . by satisfaction on the part of the interpreter."[4] In an effort to evade the accumulation of long sequences of interpretations, the validity of which must always remain tentative, some critics have begun to plead for an increase in pure research, asserting that "Interpretive

1. "The Fiction of Realism: *Sketches by Boz, Oliver Twist,* and Cruikshank's Illustrations," in *Dickens Centennial Essays,* ed. Ada Nisbet and Blake Nevius (Berkeley, 1971), p. 85.

2. See, e.g., Morse Peckham, *Man's Rage for Chaos: Biology, Behavior, and the Arts* (Philadelphia, 1965), *Art and Pornography* (New York, 1969), and *The Triumph of Romanticism: Collected Essays by Morse Peckham* (Columbia, S.C., 1970); *The Interpretation of Narra-*

tive, ed. Morton W. Bloomfield, Harvard English Studies, I (Cambridge, Mass., 1970); *Aspects of Narrative: Selected Papers from the English Institute,* ed. J. Hillis Miller (New York, 1971); Frank Kermode, *The Sense of an Ending: Studies in the Theory of Fiction* (Oxford, 1966).

3. "Order and Disorder in Fiction," in *The Triumph of Romanticism,* p. 300.

4. Ibid., pp. 301, 300.

critical commentary . . . cannot form the basis of sound scholarship, although serious scholarship can form the basis of sound interpretive commentary."[5] Such remarks suggest a desire to assemble a body of generative sources in order to make available a "sound" basis of knowledge which can redeem verbal behavior from the risk of a high level of uncertainty; a desire, that is (using Peckham's terminology), for achieving in a basically exemplary sort of discourse the security of referring ultimately to semantically inert things. The concomitant need, however, to devalue a response to literature which is predicated on the ". . . conception of a narrative as a fabric of language generating meaning from the reference of words to other, anterior words"[6] is unfortunate. Although a reassuring division of critical activity into the categories of "serious scholarship"[7] and "critical flying-by-the-seat-of-the-pants"[8] may be appealing, it is a simplistic escape from the haunting suggestions of current literary theory that "The pre-text of a given text is always another text open in its turn to interpretation."[9]

In the face of the tendency toward such reductive categorical divisions I wish to experiment with a kind of analysis which possibly may satisfy both those who wish that critical readings of literary works would acknowledge a serious scholarly basis, and those who, like J. Hillis Miller and Morse Peckham, recognize also that one can never penetrate to an epistemological plenum no matter how much one manipulates the language or the card catalogue. Rather than founding an analysis upon an edition of letters or new biography, I plan to take as my major body of "anterior words" only recent theoretical scholarship dealing with semantic indeterminacy and discontinuity and an isolated literary text; and I will try to demonstrate by means of a detailed reading that the chosen theoretical concepts are useful, thus at once attempting to fly seriously by the seat of my pants and reluctantly imposing the unpleasant situation upon several undeserving colleagues. The text I have chosen to examine is Conrad's *The Nigger of the "Narcissus."*

II

Most readers of Conrad's novels are aware that point of view in *The Nigger* is discontinuous, fluctuating between a first-person singular narrator (who at times makes use of the first-person plural) and a third-person omniscient narrative voice, and that the artistic quality of the work has repeatedly been questioned by reference to this

5. John Feaster, "Currents in Conrad Criticism: A Symposium," *Conradiana*, 4, no. 3 (1971), 5.
6. .J Hillis Miller, *Aspects of Narrative*, p. vii.
7. Feaster, loc. cit.

8. Bruce Johnson, "Currents in Conrad Criticism: A Symposium," *Conradiana*, 4, no. 3 (1971), 11.
9. J. Hillis Miller, *Thomas Hardy: Distance and Desire* (Oxford, 1970), p. vii.

device.[1] A careful consideration of the function of point of view in this novel, apart from conveniently limiting the scope of the discussion, will involve directly the problem of discontinuity in characterological presentation and in the overall structure of the book, as well as providing an opportunity to take Miller's advice and turn away ". . . from our traditional concern for 'point of view,' with its overt or covert commitment to certain representationalist assumptions."[2]

When an author creates a character, be it an anonymous persona or Tom Jones himself, what is accomplished quite simply is the presentation of "a proper name [or pronoun]" and then the verbal ascription of "a series of attributes to that name [or pronoun] while presenting it in an increasing range of verbally signified situations."[3] All one can possibly talk about in the case of a named character is "a term."[4] Mimetic criteria are of little significance, serving frequently only to pervert a properly aesthetic response into a debate as to whether a character is "believable" or not, leaving us intellectually "defenseless before the degree of our tolerance of violations of our expectations."[5]

Since the character of the persona dominates *The Nigger* throughout, a great many attributes are constellated around it. Consequently, one can expect a high degree of discontinuity in the novel, for, according to Morse Peckham, "In fiction, the prime source for . . . discontinuity is character."[6] An author achieves this quality

> . . . by continuously introducing characterological sentences (which . . . may also function simultaneously as situational and narrative sentences) in order to force the reader to abandon his effort to create a stable cognitive model whenever the presence of the character in question is indicated in the narrative sentences or even merely implied.[7]

In *The Nigger* a major source of attributional confusion is derived from the temporal involvement of the point of view. Using his excellent memory, the narrator tells his tale in retrospect; he has already passed through his initiatory experience in time and recalls the story from a timeless position—that is, he is no longer changing. The knowledge the narrator has gained as a result of his experiences on board the "Narcissus" conditions the attitude in terms of

1. See, e.g., Albert Guerard, *Conrad the Novelist* (Cambridge, Mass., 1958), pp. 107, 203–10; Vernon Young, "Trial by Water: Joseph Conrad's *The Nigger of the 'Narcissus'*," in *The Art of Joseph Conrad: A Critical Symposium*, ed. R. W. Stallman (East Lansing, 1960), p. 19.
2. *Aspects of Narrative*, p. vii.

3. Peckham, "Discontinuity in Fiction: Persona, Narrator, Scribe," in *The Triumph of Romanticism*, p. 327.
4. Ibid.
5. Ibid.
6. "Order and Disorder in Fiction," p. 311.
7. Peckham, *Art and Pornography*, pp. 105–06.

which he presents the tale, for his point of view involves futurity in the sense that only at the end of the novel is the reader finally led to (and thus able to comprehend) the state of mind which is embodied in the narrator throughout. The reader is presented the problem of learning from and about a person who has already attained a certain knowledge, yet who, by reliving the past from a point of view which the reader can only understand at the end of the novel, portrays himself as learning from the events he describes in a process paralleling the reader's second-hand learning experiences. The burden which these complex requirements place upon the artistic convention of a narrator is immense. Only with great difficulty, and never with certainty, can the reader decide at a given moment whether the assumptions underlying a particular descriptive mode are exclusively part of the past as the narrator conceives it or part of the narrator's completed wisdom and projected from his physically and temporally detached position; and, moreover, the reader can properly accomplish this only after multiple experiences of the novel.

The attitudinal shift which the narrator undergoes involves primarily his relationship with the concepts that he identifies with the person of James Wait. Elaborate metaphors and similes are a common intellectual device by means of which the narrator orients himself toward his perceptions. By observing carefully which qualities in the figures of speech alter and which remain unchanged one can tentatively distinguish between an awareness which is being dramatized as having been modified or newly gained during the voyage and a static attitude which the narrator imposes from the perspective of his final detachment (in which case one cannot tell whether the attitude was held even before the voyage, or acquired during or after the voyage).

James Wait's influence plainly discomposes the narrator. He at first seems only to be capable of understanding the great Nigger by recourse to often extreme subjective elaboration, in terms of which elaboration the very structure of the novel is developed. To the narrator the physical world seems to be morally neutral; the land is a place of "perfumes and dirt," at once both "precious and disgusting." The sea is likewise largely ambiguous and "inscrutable." Since the narrator's shocking initiation has been primarily a function of the confusing intellectual darkness consequent upon the ambivalent intellectual assaults of James Wait and the ocean, according to his implicit subjective logic, the narrator seems to conclude that these three ideas share a common essence; and he repeatedly applies the same descriptive mode to the night, James Wait, and the sea. Not only does Wait have black skin, and materialize out of the night at the beginning of the novel; his physical appearance, a disorienting muddle of darkness and sparks of light, is presented in a manner exactly parallel to the narrator's vision of the sea and the night. James Wait is seen in this way:

> He held his head up in the glare of the lamp—a head vigorously modelled into deep shadows and shining lights—a head powerful and misshapen with a tormented and flattened face—a face pathetic and brutal: the tragic, the mysterious, the repulsive mask of a nigger's soul.

It is clear that this huge black man, whose physical appearance is so enigmatic ("The whites of his eyes and his teeth gleamed distinctly, but the face was indistinguishable"), is beyond the literal understanding of the narrator. He is forced to rely upon an elaborate subjective fiction to cope with what he sees, talking about tragedy, mystery, and the particularly "repulsive mask" characteristic of "a nigger's soul"; thus, even before Wait's strange influence upon the crew begins, he is almost a supernatural manifestation to the narrator. In the following description of the night and the sea, the parallel with the intermingling of lights and darkness visible in Wait's face is readily apparent:

> On the town side the blackness of the water was streaked with trails of light which undulated gently on slight ripples, *similar to* filaments that float rooted to the shore. Rows of other lights stood away in straight lines *as if* drawn up on parade between towering buildings; but on the other side of the harbour sombre hills arched high their black spines, on which, here and there, the point of a star *resembled* a spark fallen from the sky. Far off . . . the electric lamps at the dock gates shone on the end of lofty standards with a glow blinding and frigid *like* captive ghosts of some evil moons. Scattered all over the dark polish of the roadstead, the ships at anchor floated in perfect stillness under the feeble gleam of their riding-lights, looming up, opaque and bulky, *like* strange and monumental structures abandoned by men to an everlasting repose.
>
> (italics mine)

Both James Wait and the night evade the narrator's ability to feel he can understand them directly; consequently, he resorts to the device of altering his perceptual mode through simile (note the italicized instances). The tenors of the narrator's figurative comparisons are of relatively slight importance; in the above passage the tenors all are founded upon one detail of the speaker's world—the confusing interpenetration of lights and reflections in the night. Incapable of comprehending these visual sensations, the narrator extends the vehicles of his similes ever farther subjectively from experientially validated sensory data. This epistemological desperation parallels significantly the way he reacts to his initial glimpse of

James Wait's face, when the description also culminates in subjective metaphoric vehicles, in a psychic imposition of concepts like tragedy, mystery, and the mask of "a nigger's soul." Like the night, the Nigger is essentially inaccessible, a strange, ambiguous interpenetration of light and dark, a tragic and mysterious mask, and thus always at least once removed from a physical appearance which can be accepted without subjective speculation and analogy on the part of the perceiver.

An important reason for the narrator's uncertainty as to how best to conceive of James Wait and the night can be derived from the comments he makes in the following seminal descriptive sequence. While the "Narcissus" is becalmed and Wait, with excruciating delays, approaches death, the narrator offers the following visualization of the ship's appearance on a moonlit night:

> On clear evenings the silent ship, under the cold sheen of the dead moon, took on a false aspect of passionless repose, resembling the winter of the earth. Under her a long band of gold barred the black disc of the sea. Footsteps echoed on her quiet decks. The moonlight clung to her like a frosted mist, and the white sails stood out in dazzling cones as of stainless snow. In the magnificence of the phantom rays the ship appeared pure like a vision of ideal beauty, illusive like a tender dream of serene peace. And nothing in her was real, nothing was distinct and solid but the heavy shadows that filled her decks with their unceasing and noiseless stir: the shadows darker than the night and more restless than the thoughts of men.

The narrator's use of diction derived from the winter season, emphasizing frigid withdrawal and death, in an effort to render the debilitating effects of suspension and stasis, is appropriate and obvious. More significant for the present discussion, however, is his figurative alignment of light itself with both the condition of motionlessness and ideas of inauthentic transcendence. Departing subjectively from the neutral fact of a celestial body, the narrator views the moon as a source of cold, lifeless illumination, which attaches itself to the ship almost parasitically, in a manner suggesting frost, snow, and mist, quiescent forms of water that stand removed from the flux of the sea and impede physical process; indeed, even the mighty blackness of the amniotic ocean is descecrated by illusory lunar gilding. In the face of this overwhelmingly inert glow the narrator seems orientationally distressed. He is aware that, because of its inertia, the scene he beholds warrants a negative response; and he delivers such judgment by resisting an aesthetic appeal and by interpreting the visible aspects of his surroundings as analogous to extreme yet insubstantial states of delusive subjective merit: "a vision of ideal beauty" and "a tender dream of serene peace." But, having drained value from the radiant and precisely discernible surfaces in his environs, the narrator has deprived himself of all visually concrete bases upon which he can establish the concept of actuality. Thus, like Goethe's Mephistopheles, he is intellectually compelled to stand opposed to what seems to be physical existence and assign validity only to darkness. In a climactic inversion of Platonic rhetoric, the speaker asserts that only "the heavy shadows" are substantial and reliable; moreover, his vocabulary and sentence structure imply that authenticity is derived only from the presence in the mental shadows of the qualities of apparent weight, excessive blackness, and movement; thus, they are antithetical to the illusory and deadly static radiance which assaults the narrator's eyes and tempts him to conceive of a comforting and motionless aesthetic transcendence. Only the "heavy shadows" are "real" and "solid" as they admirably fill the decks with "their unceasing and noiseless stir," being properly dark and restless, because only they partake of the attributes upon which the narrator has come to depend when he measures the reliability of an experience.

The narrator's assignation of delusive, negative values to light and glowing surfaces helps explain why the appearance of James Wait's face, as well as that of the reflecting but essentially dark waters, is so confusing. What he perceives is, in effect, a positive, reliable constellation of ideas (the darkness and its refreshing connotations of flux and authenticity) stultifying before his eyes under the imposition of light, and attempting to transform itself into an extension of humanly fabricated meaning as the act of perception takes place. The narrator is confident that he grasps the nature of the black, aqueous world surrounding the protective construct of the ship on which he sails. But when a human being appears who seems to partake of this darkness through his very physical essence, the narrator becomes disoriented, for he knows that human beings and human things tend to embody fictive "radiance," the projection of subjective models of perfection, due to man's enduring, tempting, yet debilitating, desire to envision the world as a source of fulfillment; in other words, the humanity of James Wait is at war with the connotations of his color in the narrator's mind.

III

At first the speaker aligns the Nigger with the "immense and hazy" ocean, implicitly focusing only upon the fact of his blackness in an effort to define his nature with satisfying rapidity. Consequently, descriptions are offered in which James Wait seems to function in a manner opposed to light according to the narrator's subjective interpretation. For instance, he extinguishes the sun as the sea does at sunset:

> He [Wait] seemed to hasten the retreat of departing light by his very presence; the setting sun dipped sharply, as though fleeing before our nigger; a black mist emanated from him; a subtle and dismal influence; a something cold and gloomy that floated out and settled on all the faces like a mourning veil.

Note the narrator's use above of figurative elaboration, and the presence of the reliable qualities of darkness and mortality ("a mourning veil"). The "black mist" emanating from the Nigger contrasts significantly with the illuminated "frosted mist" that was identified in a previously examined passage as a threatening propagation of delusive and static moonlight; "black mist," on the other hand, far from sustaining a luminous surface, can annul the sun as the watery horizon itself does at evening: "A crested roller broke with a loud hissing roar, and the sun, as if put out, disappeared."

As the novel progresses, however, James Wait's conduct efficiently works to cancel the narrator's initial complimentary response to him; the narrator's discovery of the Nigger's humanity, which effectively cuts Wait off from the authentication of the darkness regardless of the hue of his skin, alters radically the narrator's rhetorical values, and therefore functions as the major structural principle of the entire work. James Wait's willful eagerness to shirk active strife gradually aligns him with the quiescence which troubles the narrator so deeply when he witnesses it occurring haphazardly in the phenomenal world. Appropriately, "Jimmy's cabin" becomes a center for the sort of stagnant, idealized transcendence which the sailcloth's whiteness of "stainless snow" in the "sheen of the dead moon" suggests at another time to the narrator; and the darkness is temporarily banished by the "glare of Jimmy's lamp" in his quarters, which have significantly been "repainted white," and which flouresce "in the night [with] the brilliance of a silver shrine." Moreover, unlike the inky sea, which, as interpreted by Singleton, causes men to " 'Look out for yourselves!' " the Nigger, who is also, meaningfully, known as "Snowball", urges the crew to look out only for him in a grotesque perpetuation of infantile dependence.

The narrator's interpretational struggle with James Wait reaches a climax in the description of the rescue of the helpless Nigger from the cabin in which he is trapped underwater while the "Narcissus" is swamped. The rescue project itself imposes an unwelcome redemptive occasion, causing the crew to struggle actively and forcing them to deny their wishes to surrender to the temptation of reclining "back on the poop where we could wait passively for death in incomparable repose." The diction once again aligns ideal extremes with a vitiated quietude; and, fittingly, the wish for such a state is routed through a temporal perspective by use of the verb "wait," thus recalling ominously the parallel behavior in fact of

James Wait himself. While the narrator takes an active part in the deliverance of the Nigger he necessarily is acutely aware of the ontological significance of the suffering which he and his shipmates voluntarily bear, as the above description of their frustrated wishes for passive "repose" clearly implies, for this important word is echoed later in the narrator's visionary and thematically crucial elaboration of the "passionless repose" captivating the "Narcissus." Consequently, James Wait's cowardly passivity as the rescue progresses is particularly outstanding to the narrator, and he begins to grasp directly the weak and merely ˙mortal essence of the miserable "squeak[ing]" man whom up to now he had regarded as being aligned occultly with the omnipotent sea and validating darkness. The episode in which Wait is delivered from the cabin where he has been trapped due to the ship's having capsized is of vital significance, therefore, because it provides the narrator with an embarrassingly direct enactment of the Nigger's pathetic vulnerability as well as with a factual situation upon which he can handily found a metaphor that will enable him to alter his attitude toward the hitherto frighteningly powerful black man.

The sequence of events leading to the Nigger's rescue have commonly been regarded as a presentation of "a difficult childbirth";[8] what is usually overlooked, however, is the presence of equally stressed vocabulary related to mortality. As the narrator describes the rescue, that is, he undergoes the unpleasant experience of having his two major conflicting values brought into violent collision as they constellate themselves around James Wait. Measured against death, darkness, and the sea, the Nigger sheds his cryptic potency and appears shockingly mortal; and the narrator's mind, with its propensity to deal in figurative extremes, effects an emphatic revaluation by transforming the victim into a grotesque child. The very situation, the crew at the mercy of the storm and Wait trapped underwater in his cabin, is dominated by the threat and presence of death, and the imagery seems to support this idea: the crew hears Wait "screaming and knocking below us with the hurry of a man prematurely shut up in a coffin"; later, Wait becomes silent, "as quiet as a dead man inside a grave; and like men standing above a grave; we were on the verge of tears"; when the men finally succeed in penetrating the bulkhead, they almost kill Wait with the crowbar—"Suddenly the crowbar went halfway in through a splintered, oblong hole . . . miss[ing] Jimmy's head by less than an inch"; after the men got Wait out of his cabin they "Tottered all together with concealing, absurd gestures, like a lot of drunken men embarrassed with a stolen corpse." However, the narrator balances the death images with equally prominent images

8. See Guerard, *Conrad the Novelist*, p.112.

and suggestions of a trying childbirth: trapped in his cabin, Wait "screamed piercingly, without drawing breath, like a tortured woman"; the place of confinement is "deep as a well," and "Every movement of the ship was pain"; as the crew struggle to rescue Wait, they must contend with the sea splashing over their heads and penetrate a layer of nails barehanded—water and blood are both present in significant quantities at a birth; when Wait in terror tries to come through the small hole made by the crowbar, the imagery of a human being trying to pass headfirst through an opening described very much like the female genitalia is unmistakable—"he pressed his head to it, trying madly to get out through that opening one inch wide and three inches long"; Wait is finally rescued, but only after the men, despairing because they cannot pull him out by his short hair, see him emerge unaided—"suddenly Jimmy's head and shoulders appeared"; last of all, the men climb out of the confinement of the space above Wait's cabin and, overheated, come "into icy water"—the method of inducing breathing in new-born infants by dipping them into cold water is well known. The scene is further complicated by the fact that, in the last example cited above, the birth imagery applies to the crewmen, who have functioned primarily as midwives, as well as to James Wait; just as, when the Nigger "screamed . . . like a tortured woman," the distinction between parent and child is blurred. This ambiguity, apart from indicating clearly that a "real" analogical birth is not supposed to be occurring but rather a discontinuous figurative interpretation, indicates that in the narrator's mind the state of shrieking dependence aboard a capsized and crippled vessel is as inappropriate as a nativity scene. Although the men properly evade the seductive wish for "incomparable repose" by suffering to save James Wait, on another level they are only perpetuating and courting infantile parasitism, and are soon thereafter derided by Mr. Baker for being "worse than children."

The Nigger's metaphoric birth both from himself as "tortured woman" and the sea is quite important. The old James Wait, whose physical appearance and figurative effects resembled so closely the "immortal sea . . . with a glittering surface and lightless depths" which potently can extinguish the sun, is left behind with the sea itself; he now becomes a ridiculous and mortally ill "child" identified with the delusive, fictive light itself, dwelling in a cabin "repainted white" and shining with "the brilliance of a silver shrine"; no longer is he primeval and frightening to the narrator, almost an Anglo-Saxon *nicor*, but only incredibly inauthentic and "demoralizing" as he partakes directly of the essence of the "phantom rays," becoming "immaterial like an apparition." Furthermore, the descriptive mode in which his burial is presented clearly indicates that, far from being a source of "black mist" capable of swallowing up the sun like the waters themselves, James Wait is now, like the spectral radiance whose nature he shares, engulfed effortlessly by the sea. During the burial ceremony the narrator notes that "the whole vast semicircle of steely waters visible on that side seemed to come up with a rush to the edge of the port, as if impatient to get at our Jimmy." The sailmaker's comment, " '. . . you don't know where it[Wait] comes from. Got nobody. No use to nobody. Who will miss him?' ", and the facts that he simply disappears when he is returned to the sea ("Charley, who anxious to see Jimmy's last dive, leaped headlong to the rail, was too late to see anything but the faint circle of a vanishing ripple") and that he had "No papers of any kind—no relations—no trace," are all details which the narrator cites implicitly to reinforce the flickering insubstantiality of the human essence as manifested in James Wait, whose mortal remains continue to partake of the fictive light until they vanish physically into the sea. The corpse, significantly, is stashed in "a white blanket" and sewed into "gray sailcloth"—sailcloth previously was an important medium for the propagation of "the phantom rays" that threateningly connote delusive human ideals to the narrator. Moreover, as he encloses the body in canvas, the sailmaker mumbles of having "sewed in twenty men a week" and "Thought nothing of it" aboard a fittingly named vessel, the "Blanche"; and, at last, the corpse climatically departs the wooden chute "like a flash of lightning."

IV

The point may scarcely seem worth making that the narrator and James Wait are the most important characters in the novel; and, indeed, the prospect of critical debate over the relative significance of a figure is most uninviting. Such an inquiry here may be useful, however, for Morse Peckham relates interestingly the degree of a character's consequence to the amount of discontinuity that a reader can expect to experience in the presentation of that particular character. He suggests that the importance of a character ". . . is defined by the amount of discontinuity he displays. That is, we know that a character is unimportant precisely because he has a narrower range of responses than other characters and appears in a smaller variety of situations."[9] Certainly the number of attributes that *The Nigger* manages to assign to the persona and to James Wait, respectively, is extremely high; one can make many merely exemplary statements about each of them, for many specific situations and details are involved. This sort of detailed characterization would be regarded conventionally as a means of severely limiting the range of interpretational responses which could be elicited by

9. "Order and Disorder in Fiction," p.314.

each portrayal; and on one level of reading perhaps this is true. Nevertheless, Wolfgang Iser has recently observed that ". . . the more a text tries to be precise . . ." through the inclusion of many "representative aspect[s]," the greater will be the potential for indeterminacy in the reader's response, since ". . . between the 'schematized views' there is a no-man's-land of indeterminacy, which results precisely from the determinacy of the sequence of each individual view."[1] As Peckham puts it, "Characters are discontinuous according to their distance from the central character. Spear-bearers are always the same."[2]

The previously analyzed sequence of figurative interpretations of James Wait clearly reveals discontinuity in the narrator, and, consequently, in the presentation of the Nigger as well, since the latter is largely a function of the fluctuating attitudes manifested by the narrator. I say "largely" because James Wait is not entirely at the mercy of the speaker: the point of view of *The Nigger* is also discontinuous, as was mentioned earlier, and alternates first-person subjectivity with third-person omniscience in order, occasionally, to present James Wait from a significantly different perspective, and thus call into doubt the human view represented by the narrator. Only after many years has this device of narrative discontinuity been received positively and not labelled an artistic blunder on Conrad's part; for instance, a refreshing and recent critical response suggests that

> The evidence of textual investigation clearly shows that Conrad consistently, deliberately, and consciously labored to establish a dual perspective in the novel by these shifts from an omniscient to a crewman narrator and back again to the omniscient. And I do not believe that these shifts represent a structural weakness. They represent, instead, one of the strengths of the novel. . . .[3]

The interpretational problems posed by such narrative inconsistency are great. Not only must the reader cope with the set of attributes gathering around James Wait as he is seen through varying perspectives of the narrator, but also the details that accrue as the omniscient narrative voice presents him must be assembled, yet all kept separate and distinct. And, if Iser is correct, interpretational indeterminacy increases accordingly, for the dynamic narrative perspective causes a blurring of differentiations among the rhetorical devices employed by the narrator as crewman, the narrator as distinct from the crew and growing in awareness, the narrator as voice of futurity telling his tale in retrospect and employing his completed wisdom, and the omniscient narrative voice.

1. "Indeterminacy and the Reader's Response," in *Aspects of Narrative*, ed. Miller, pp. 10–11.
2. "Order and Disorder in Fiction," p. 313.
3. Marion Michael, "Currents in Conrad Criticism: A Symposium," *Conradiana*, 4, no. 3 (1971), 14.

The presence of the third-person omniscient narrative perspective distresses Albert Guerard, for example, who appears troubled by the tensions that develop due to the markedly differing view of James Wait which is thereby made available; he protests that

> . . . it has been the very convention of the novel that Wait must remain shadowy, vast, provocative of large speculation. . . . The very fact that he comes in some sense to represent our human 'blackness' should exempt him from the banalities of everyday interior monologue.[4]

Although Guerard's suggestion that Conrad violates his own aesthetic conventions is inadequate, it is clear that the multiple dimensions of James Wait generate an opposition, which it seems to me is precisely to the point. One of the major concerns of *The Nigger*, as well as of most of Conrad's fiction, is the dramatization of the necessary entrapment of the human psyche as it assigns meaning to the phenomenal world in the act of perception. This theme can be demonstrated most immediately by providing the reader with a point of view which, by virtue of the very definition of omniscience, is free of subjective coloring and also able to transcend human temporal and spatial limitations to make available information which serves to qualify or even negate the attitudes of the human subjects in the work. To be specific, the reader is permitted to enter the mind of James Wait on two occasions in order to explode both the narrator's and Singleton's preposterous interpretations of him. The lengthy fantasy of death and burial at sea that James Wait suffers logically results from his memory of previously having been trapped underwater while the ship was swamped; and, instead of a wierdly potent emblem, the reader discovers a mere man, terribly ill, and very much afraid to die. Similarly, somewhat later the reader learns that James Wait has been a ladies' man when ashore and that his dying fastasies concern getting back to land to see the "Canton Street girl" who chose him over "a third engineer of a Rennie boat." Here appears a weak, frightened human being who is reliving his past nostalgically, and desperately hoping for a comparably successful future. Singleton is ridiculously wrong in his opinion of Wamibo as a sorcerer who casts spells to delay the ship, and he has a similar conception of James Wait. He feels the Nigger is working with Wamibo to impede the ship's progress because Wait does not want to get home since he knows that the presence of land will mean his death. The Nigger's meditation clearly proves Singleton is wrong, for the sick man eagerly anticipates returning to shore.

Although I imply above that the omniscient narrative voice deserves a higher level of credibility than the narrator, it must be

4. *Conrad the Novelist*, p. 107.

remembered that the quality of reliability is solely a function of the conventions operant through an aesthetic device; Conrad as author never claims the same perceptual abilities for himself, never pretends to be free from delusive subjectivity. The perspectives presented through the third-person narrative voice were instilled in it by a human subject, and consequently have no more authenticity outside the aesthetic configuration than any other illusory specifications of the nature of human experience. Appropriately, the omniscient narrative voice is so thoroughly suppressed in *The Nigger* by the sheer sustained temporal dominance of the narrator's subjective struggles that until recently, if it was detected at all, critics could justify its presence only by chastizing the author for permitting an illegitimate intrusion.

And perhaps, after all, perceptive men like Guerard are also correct. An essay dealing with indeterminacy and discontinuity can scarcely afford to be dogmatic. As Martin Price has asserted,

> The full import of any detail remains a problem at best, just as does the structural form itself. We may easily force meanings by distortion of emphasis or failure of tact. The elements of a novel shift in function . . . as the work unfolds and as new linkages are revealed. For this reason we can never with confidence ascribe a single purpose or meaning to a detail nor can we give an exhaustive reading of the structure.[5]

Suitably, *The Nigger* is developed rhetorically in terms of only the narrator's subjectivity, and consequently the very structure of the novel, as well as the narrator's visionary elaborations, is brought into doubt by the qualifying function of the omniscient narrative voice. As we saw, after the rescue of James Wait from the sea and the recovery of the "Narcissus" a transformation occurs that reverses the associations built up around the Nigger in the early part of the novel. The change in rhetorical values was previously demonstrated by close textual analysis; it can here best be illustrated by the following columnar comparison:

Before Rebirth.	After Rebirth.
Wait's confusing influence is temporally paralleled with the perplexing "fair monsoon" and with the violent storm.	Wait's influence is still confusing, but is now supposedly (according to Singleton, whose intellectual pronouncements the narrator absurdly idolizes) the cause of calm weather, of headwinds and a high barometer.

5. "Irrelevant Detail and the Emergence of Form," in *Aspects of Narrative*, ed. Miller, p. 89.

Wait's "unmanly lie," which is seemingly told only to avoid work, is that he is sick when he really appears to be well; he uses the fact of death as a tool to shame the crew into treating him with deference.

Wait's "unmanly lie" now is that he is healthy and can work, when he obviously is dying; it is told in a pathetic attempt to deny the fact of death, whereas before he continuously told the crew that he was dying.

It is disconcerting to the crew to believe Wait ill and not be able to see any physical evidence: "He became the tormentor of all our moments; he was worse than a nightmare. You couldn't see that there was anything wrong with him: a nigger does not show."

It disturbs the crew to see Wait fail visibly while denying that he is at all sick: "The latent egoism of tenderness to suffering appeared in the developing anxiety not to see him die. His obstinate non-recognition of the only certitude whose approach we could watch from day to day was as disquieting as the failure of some law of nature."

Wait is a slick confidenceman, actively bullying and contemptuous of the entire crew, continually abusing them for his personal benefit.

Wait becomes inactive, physically declines, and gives up life (he makes no attempt to save himself even during the storm).

Plainly the transformations which form the major structural principle of the novel occur exclusively according to the perceptual contortions and distortions effected by the narrator's and Singleton's minds, and at the expense of the crucial information made accessible by the omniscient narrative voice as it gives the reader entry into James Wait's private thoughts.

The values of the third-person narrative voice never change; in its bleakly objective description it has no trouble comprehending what is presented, for it is not human. Similarly, Capt. Allistoun remains unperplexed by the Nigger, although he provides no psychological aid to the crew, for the accusation which he directs at James Wait before the ship's company is just the opposite of what he knows to be true:

> "You have been shamming sick. . . . Why, anybody can see that. There's nothing the matter with you, but you chose to lie-up to please yourself—and now you shall lie-up to please me. Mr. Baker, my orders are that this man is not allowed to be on deck to the end of this passage."

Only later does the Captain reveal to Mr. Baker, in secret, that he really understands Wait's problem; fittingly, this information is conveyed to the reader by the omniscient narrative voice, not from the subjective point of view of the narrator:

> "When I saw him standing there, three parts dead and so scared —black amongst that gaping lot—no grit to face what's coming to us all—the notion came to me all at once [to order Wait confined to quarters], before I could think. Sorry for him—like you would be for a sick brute. If ever creature was in a mortal funk to die! . . . I thought I would let him go out in his own way. Kind of impulse."

Although discontinuity is injected momentarily into Capt. Allistoun's personality when he admits to Mr. Baker that he is not sure about the efficacy of his techniques of dealing with the "row" on board and asks "Did you think I had gone wrong there . . . ?" and when he at the same time evasively reduces his problems with the crew to a meterological analogy, saying "head wind! all the rest is nothing," the Captain nevertheless maintains, like the omniscient narrative voice, a static conceptual relationship with James Wait. And if Peckham's ideas are valid these details conclusively indicate that the major characterological significance in the novel rests with the persona and James Wait, for, indeed, like the Captain and the omniscient narrative voice, "Spear bearers are always the same."

That the dominant characters of *The Nigger* should manifest a high degree of discontinuity, and the normative functions, the sources of valid perception according to aesthetic convention, should be relegated to a minor and implicitly qualified position, thus causing also structural indeterminacy, brings to light an important paradox inherent in Conrad's art. If, as J. Hillis Miller suggests, the "aim of all Conrad's fiction [is] to destroy in the reader his bondage to illusion . . . ,"[6] the works are also thereby involved in an impossible task; for the attainment of the goal of successful "demystification"[7] is not consistent with Conrad's ontology, since ". . . we, living, are out of life. . . . The mysteries of a universe made of drops of fire and clouds of mud do not concern us in the least."[8] Conrad feels, in other words, that human consciousness cannot begin to conceive validly of the phenomenal world; and he appropriately deprecates the very artistic device that provides him with the means to achieve his "demystification," the omniscient narrative perspective: Conrad growls "Why the reading public, which . . . has never laid upon a storyteller the command to be an artist, should demand from him this sham of Divine Omnipotence, is utterly incomprehensible."[9] Thus, when the definitive

6. *Poets of Reality* (Cambridge, Mass., 1965), pp. 18–19.
7. Ibid.
8. G. Jean-Aubry, *Joseph Conrad, Life and Letters* (New York, 1927), I, 222.
9. *Notes on Life and Letters*, p. 18.

attitudes toward James Wait presented by the omniscient narrative voice and by Capt. Allistoun are weakened tentatively due to the remote possibility that, somehow, Singleton's absurd prophecy has come true (that indeed "the barometer had begun to fall," though whether "it [was] before or after 'that 'ere glass started down' " that the Nigger died "was impossible to know"), Conrad is merely sustaining his own epistemological assumptions within the novel and insisting that a measure of indeterminacy limit subtly even the aesthetic convention of omniscience.

It is possible that the theoretical constructs of scholars like Miller and Peckham, who explore the ramifications of the presence of indeterminacy and discontinuity in verbal behavior, are most useful as tools of aesthetic response when applied only to comparatively recent works of art. As Wolfgang Iser attests, it is a "striking historical fact that since the eighteenth century indeterminacy in literature—or at least an awareness of it—has tended toward a continual increase."[1] Conrad, in any event, clearly operates in terms of an epistemology which makes his writing quite responsive to recent theoretical criticism that asserts ". . . literature is an instrument of knowledge with its own unique epistemological conventions . . . committed to forms and to a species of language which tend to hold opposites in suspension . . . [and] yield . . . a heightened sense of human dilemmas, and of Man's ultimately paradoxical relation to his universe."[2] If the theoretical foundations of this essay permit no final resolution of problems of specific aesthetic function and semantic content, they echo thereby the intellectual attitudes and thematic intention of many authors, whose works, when regarded in the light of unpretentious yet sophisticated constructs, may yield gracefully a level of unity seldom anticipated previously. More specifically, if Conrad criticism is indeed "at the end of the tether" as has recently been lamented,[3] possibly some careful application of current theoretical scholarship, exploring ". . . the reciprocal relation . . . between the story narrated and the question of what it means to narrate a story,"[4] treating a literary text properly as a "performative utterance"[5] that in fact generates its own object, may revitalize the situation and define a critical enterprise at once free from contextually empty "new readings" and from illusions of semantically redemptive "serious scholarship."

1. "Indeterminacy and the Reader's Response," p. 23.
2. John Palmer, *"Introduction"* to *Twentieth Century Interpretations of "The Nigger of the 'Narcissus' "* (Englewood Cliffs, N. J.: Spectrum Books, 1969), pp. 10–11.
3. John Feaster, "Conrad and Ford: Criticism at the End of the Tether," *Journal of Modern Literature*, 2 (1972), 417–21.
4. J. Hillis Miller, "The Fiction of Realism," p. 86.
5. See J. L. Austin, *How to Do Things with Words*, ed. J. O. Urmson (Cambridge, Mass., 1962), p. 1.

JOHN HOWARD WESTON

The Nigger of the "Narcissus" and Its Preface†

I

Conrad's composition of the Preface to *The Nigger of the "Nar-cissus"* followed with some urgency his completion of the novel: "almost without laying down the pen," he wrote in "To My Read-ers in America", "I wrote a preface." Despite its being so tightly hinged to the work it followed, this Preface has come by common consent to be considered "by default the most reliable, and the most voluntary, single statement of Conrad's general approach to writing."[1] As a result it is widely anthologized and very likely more widely read than the novel itself. As one looks at this odd state of affairs two questions obtrude: is the severing of Preface from novel fair to either? and, as a statement of Conrad's "general approach" is the Preface accurate?

Second things first. Unquestionably the crucial concept of the Preface is "solidarity," yet even so shrewd a critic as Ian Watt finds Conrad's use of the word equivocal.[2] If Watt is right, and I am convinced that he is, then the possibility arises that Conrad himself used the word with a less than complete grasp of what he meant by it. The claim that Conrad did not know what he was talking about in the Preface—for that is what I am saying—may seem singularly ill-chosen, but the deep differences between what the Preface asserts and what the fiction suggests encourage it. Conrad's stance in the Preface is clearly public; as Watt puts it, "in general one must see the popularity of the Preface, and particularly of what it says about solidarity, as the result of its telling people what they want to hear."[3] Indeed it does: its assertion that the truth of Conrad's art might lead us to glimpse "the stress and passion within the core of each convincing moment" and will "awaken in the hearts of the beholders that feeling of unavoidable solidarity"—this is a most comforting formulation.[4] Yet it is hardly adequate to the general pattern of Conrad's fiction, a pattern in which the perception of truth—in the Preface, "stress and passion"; in the fiction, exis-

† Written especially for this edition.
1. Ian Watt,"Conrad's Preface to *The Nig-ger of the 'Narcissus*,' " p. 153, above. As Watt nots, his opinion is shared by Samuel Hynes, "Two Rye Revolutionaries," *Se-wanee Review*, 73 (1965), 153, and Fred-erick Karl,"Joseph Conrad's Literary The-ory," *Criticism*, 2 (1960), 317 35).
2. Watt, p. 156, above.
3. Watt, p. 157, above.
4. References to the Preface will not be footnoted.

340 · John Howard Weston

tential meaninglessness—awakens feelings of anything but solidarity in the perceiving character. In the light of the discontinuity between the assertions of the Preface and the suggestions of the fiction, and in conjunction with one critic's well-documented argument that Conrad occasionally adopted an "official" version of himself for the purpose of dealing with his own complexities, the publicity of the Preface gains significance.[5] The fact of Conrad's designedly public and/or self-evasive stance there can give us some understanding of his emphatic yet elliptical use of "solidarity." For the Preface, in its easy and attractive resolution of perceived truth with solidarity, contains only about half of Conrad's conceptual universe—the public half.

Rather than by facile reconciliation, Conrad's fiction seems to be informed by a thoroughgoing conflict between two deeply felt ideas. The first, which Conrad fully expresses in the Preface with regard to art and the artist, is that for a man to have moral worth he must act to affirm solidarity, which in some way "binds men to each other and all mankind to the visible world." The second idea, however, is wholly absent from the Preface; it is that until a man comes to grips with the essential meaninglessness of existence he lives a life of illusion. Briefly put, the root conflict in Conrad's works is between *will*—the ability to affirm solidarity—and *perception*—the intuition which probes through the illusions of moral self, code, and universe to the truth of meaninglessness within and without.[6] The ideas of will and perception are, of course, utterly opposed: perception denies the value of what will strives to create. Yet throughout his career as a writer Conrad attempted to reconcile these ideas, to create a fictional character who might, despite his perception of existential meaninglessness, affirm solidarity. Such a reconciliation might be termed *courage*, and if in his work Conrad never created an image of it in which he could wholly believe, and few images of it at all, he was certainly courageous in his many attempts. Condemned to failure by his sincerity, Conrad could go no further than to create characters who will, not in spite of perception, but on the basis of imagination. Perception's opposite, imagination, creates images of an ordered self and world, a universe of "illusions" which denies meaninglessness. But because it creates illusions, imagination is always vulnerable to the disillusionments of perception.

Conrad's reconciliation in the Preface of will—the artist's task—and imagination—the vision of "unavoidable solidarity"—is a rec-

5. Edward Said, *Joseph Conrad and the Fiction of Autobiography* (Cambridge, Mass.: Harvard University Press, 1966), p. 62.
6. It should be clear that my use of "will" is not intended to echo Schopenhauer, Nietzsche, or other users of the term, and that none of my terms is intended to reflect Conrad's typical usage.

onciliation of the type many of his characters also achieve, to their later disillusionment. Nowhere in the Preface does Conrad intimate that the affirmation of solidarity may result in the denial of truth, that the perception of truth may entail the negation of solidarity, or that to arrest one's hand from the work of the world may be to open oneself to the perception of meaninglessness. Rather, Conrad here sees his art as an attempt to liberate the reader: "it arrest[s], for the space of a breath, the hands busy about the work of the earth, and compel[s] men entranced by the sight of distant goals to glance at the surrounding vision of form and colour, of sunshine and shadows. . . ." But in his fiction, Conrad sees the dangers of self-liberation as certainly as great as, and probably greater than, its advantages. What can be learned in "that glimpse of truth" might better be ignored for the sake of the ability to will. Pure perception —not the imaginative vision of "form and colour," but the perception of meaninglessness—rarely leads to a response affirmative of solidarity in Conrad's characters. Rather, self-liberation and consequent perception usually result in loss of self, and when the self is lost, so are all chances for the response which reinforces solidarity.

In the Preface, Conrad avoids the problem which forms the crux of his major fiction. By entirely ignoring perception, he denies meaninglessness, and is thereby able to present his art as affirmative in intent, rather than as about the difficulty, perhaps even the impossibility, of affirmation in the face of acknowledged meaninglessness. One reason for Conrad's awkward handling of "solidarity" is that his "inner" or private self—the self revealed in the fiction— knew the meaning of "solidarity" to be not only suspect but, in any practical sense, incomprehensible. The other reason is *The Nigger of the "Narcissus"* itself.

II

Readers who import the Preface's "solidarity" into their discussions of *The Nigger of the "Narcissus"* (and this includes almost all the novel's critics) are simply taking Conrad at his word: "It is only some such train of thought, or rather of feeling," he writes immediately after his first references to solidarity, "that can in a measure explain the aim of the attempt, made in the tale which follows. . . ." Perhaps we should go further than Conrad's word. The ticket he offers is only one-way: from the justifying Preface to the justified work. Why not take a return? To my knowledge no one has done so, yet the trip seems worthwhile. If the Preface explains the aim, then the tale in which the attempt was made may quite possibly explain the Preface. More specifically, it may lend some additional insight into Conrad's emphatic yet elliptical use of "solidarity."

A convenient point of departure is the value-structure of the novel. While several critics have argued that this structure is dichotomous, they are far from agreeing on its elements.[7] A cautionary note is sounded, however, by Bruce Johnson. Dismissing others' antitheses, Johnson finds "sympathy, and its culmination in some ideal of human solidarity, . . . the compelling mystery of [Conrad's] art." Because it avoids apparent oversimplification, Johnson's is an inviting argument, deserving expanded statement:

> Civilization demands we control self-love; but this is best accomplished through means other than an access of sympathy. Far from despising sympathy, however, Conrad has simply recognized its enormous potency and several forms of its decadence. Paradoxically, one of the great civilizing forces, man's ability to identify imaginatively with another (as the crew does with Wait), often serves only to intensify ego and to challenge the order which makes life more than a survival of the fittest.[8]

Although Johnson's argument has Conrad anticipating himself by a year or two, its implications are notable; not only does it suggest the nature of the difficult conceptual task which Conrad confronted in composing *The Nigger of the "Narcissus,"* but it also opens the way to an understanding of the mutual coherency of the Preface and the novel.

During the writing of the Preface and *The Nigger of the "Narcissus,"* Conrad seems to have been preoccupied with the topic Johnson discusses. Not having arrived at Johnson's neat analysis, Conrad was still in the midst of the attempt to discriminate between the concept of solidarity he emphasized so strongly but confusedly in the Preface, and what the narrator sees as the causes of falsehood's triumph on the *Narcissus:* "pity," "sentimentalism," and "compassion." In the world of the novel, sympathy (my generic term for the preceding series) and solidarity are differentiable by their practical effects: feelings of sympathy are detrimental to the common effort to survive, and the conviction of solidarity is

7. Marvin Mudrick formulates them as "authority, skill, responsibility, duty, courage *versus* anarchy, ineptness, panic, malingering, the touchy indocile solidarity of the mob" ("The Artist's conscience and *The Nigger of the 'Narcissus' ";* Paul Kirschner as authority *versus* sympathy (*Conrad: The Psychologist as Artist* [Edinburgh: Oliver and Boyd, 1968], pp. 102–9); Lawrence Graver as altruism *versus* egoism (*Conrad's Short Fiction* [Berkeley and Los Angeles: University of California Press, 1969], pp. 63–70). While Mudrick (*pace* his twisting of "solidarity") and Watt present supple readings, Kirschner is led by his categories to see Captain Allistoun as "a martinet far more interested in his own glory and prestige than in the welfare of the ship," and Graver (63–64) by his to proclaim that Singleton, whose "natural" egoism "is admirable because it exists as an instinctive response to a fundamental challenge" nevertheless "displays a touch of altruism." When one's categories turn so in one's hand, it comes time to drop them.

8. Bruce Johnson, *Conrad's Models of Mind* (Minneapolis: University of Minnesota Press, 1971), p. 34.

beneficial.[9] And in the terms of my first part, feelings of sympathy begin in imagination, specifically in imaginative identification, and may culminate in a shattering perception of the contingency of one's own and all existence, while the conviction of solidarity is wholly unimaginative and unperceptive, totally the cognitive equivalent of will.

If my formulation looks suspiciously like the dichotomies against which Johnson is an apparent antidote, it must nevertheless stand. Johnson's reading of *The Nigger* too much reflects his reading of the works which were soon to follow it; he describes not what Conrad achieved, but what he was working toward; what he was to achieve in *Lord Jim*, for instance, but had not in *The Nigger*. In 1896–97 Conrad's structure of values—the structure of sympathy *versus* solidarity—was still dichotomous. But Conrad's failure precisely to discriminate between these concepts, either in the novel alone or in the novel and its Preface together, implies what the succeeding works demonstrate. In his ongoing preoccupation with the problem, he would soon discover that imagination, which is active in *The Nigger* only as sympathy, is the source of all significance as well as of all decadence.

What I take to be the aim of Conrad's attempted discrimination between sympathy and solidarity may be clarified by rephrasing the problem interrogatively: how does my conviction that I share in the fate of all men differ from the self-serving effort to cannibalize the lives of others, to live for pure sensation, and to avoid the attempt to create significance and identity through action within a community? Nietzsche responded firmly: "No one can build the bridge on which you must cross the river of life, no one but you alone."[1] And in this century Gottfried Benn has responded with fewer heroics:

> Life is the building of bridges
> over rivers that seep away.[2]

Conrad, too, was at pains to drain away any possible romantic heroism from his bridge builders, as the anticlimax of the *Narcissus's* homecoming and the dark elegiac mood of the novel's last few pages testify. His concern was with "what *knits together* the loneliness of innumerable hearts" and with what meaning *"we, together"* may have "wrung out . . . from our sinful lives" (my ital-

9. Though "sympathy" does not appear in the novel, "sympathised" and, contextually less importantly, "sympathetic" do. "Solidarity" appears only in the Preface.

1. Friederich Nietzsche, *Schopenhauer as Educator*, trans. James W. Hillesheim and Malcolm R. Simpson (Chicago:

Henry Regnery Company, Gateway Editions, 1965), p. 4.

2. From Gottfried Benn, "Epilogue," trans. Michael Hamburger, in *Primal Vision: Selected Writings of Gottfried Benn*, ed. E. B. Ashton (New York: New Directions, 1971), p. 291.

ics), not with exalted individualism; with the meaning of the communal effort of building, not with the magnificence of the bridge. But whether Conrad fully understood the discrimination he attempted, and whether his novelistic technique enabled him to wring maximum meaning out of his work, are the problems which must now be addressed.

In composing *The Nigger of the "Narcissus"* Conrad set himself several new technical problems, all of which he had to confront before going on to "Youth," *Heart of Darkness*, and *Lord Jim* and, what is more to the point, all of which bear directly on his discrimination between sympathy and solidarity. First, he sought a more sophisticated and fruitfully simple union of setting and plot. While the Malayan settings of *Almayer's Folly* and *An Outcast of the Islands* offered Conrad an apparently ready-made mood, they did little else: characters had to be introduced into the setting and given motives. But in *The Nigger* the setting of the sea journey supplies the motive: to get from here to there; the characters: officers and seamen; and the complications with their accompanying moods: dissension and dodging, storm and calm. Only with such an achievement behind him could Conrad go on to the similarly unidirectional journey of "Youth," the approach-retreat movement of *Heart of Darkness*, and the elaborate complexities of *Lord Jim*. Second, Conrad sought a far more balanced array of characters in *The Nigger*; the almost schematic series of relationships provides increased resonance and provides, too, the necessary starting-point for the less tendentious schema of *Heart of Darkness* and *Lord Jim*.[3] The third problem Conrad set himself, first-person narration (the implications of which for his later work are, of course, enormous), has received voluminous critical attention. But because it, too, reveals Conrad's troubles with sympathy and solidarity, his narrative technique deserves yet another look.

In its plot and setting *The Nigger of the "Narcissus"* reveals how intent Conrad was on creating a structure of which sympathy and solidarity are the polar and defining values. Just as the microcosmic *Narcissus*, "a fragment detached from the earth . . . a small planet," must work her way through brutal storm and tense calm, so the crew must endure, without succumbing to them, the blandishments of the bombastic, violent Donkin and the passive, sinister James Wait. Like the ship, which capsizes in the storm and yaws about aimlessly in the calm, the crew became fragmented and disorderly in their succumbings. Only at their ordeal's conclusion are they a cohesive "dark knot of seamen." Thus the most basic structure of

3. David R. Smith (" 'One Word More' About *The Nigger of the 'Narcissus,' " Nineteenth Century Fiction*, 23 [1968], 212) writes: Conrad "had schematized his ideas and had found a way to make them the subject, even to make them the characters of his novel."

the novel is one in which solidarity means orderly survival, and sympathy means degeneration and death.

The schematic array of characters, too, shows how attentively Conrad structured *The Nigger of the "Narcissus"* to reflect the essential opposition of sympathy and solidarity. The major characters form a triad of pairs: Wait and Singleton, Donkin and Captain Allistoun, and the crew and the *Narcissus*.[4] The initial terms of each pair—Wait, Donkin, and the crew as individuals—constitute the negative pole of the novel; they elicit the crew's sympathy and lead them toward self-concern, dissolution, and death. The second terms—Singleton, Captain Allistoun, and the *Narcissus*—elicit the crew's sense of solidarity, their more or less inarticulate and unconscious recognition that the survival of each individual depends on the survival of the group, and that the group's survival depends on work, order, and devotion to the "visible world" of the novel: the *Narcissus* herself.

Wait and Singleton are most readily differentiable by their opposing attitudes toward death. Here is Wait's rebellious realization:

> James Wait rallied again. He lifted his head and turned bravely at Donkin, who saw a strange face, an unknown face, a fantastic and grimacing mask of despair and fury. Its lips moved rapidly; and hollow, moaning, whistling sounds filled the cabin with a vague mutter full of menace, complaint, and desolation, like the far-off murmur of a rising wind. Wait shook his head; rolled his eyes; he denied, cursed, threatened—and not a word had the strength to pass beyond the sorrowful pout of those black lips. It was incomprehensible and disturbing; a gibberish of emotions, a frantic dumb show of speech pleading for impossible things, promising a shadowy vengeance.

Wait dies four pages later, a near parody of the self-pity his presence does so much to stimulate in the crew. Singleton, on the other hand, tacitly accepts his approaching end. During his life aboard ship "He had never given a thought to his mortal self," but the power of the storm awakens him:

> And like a man bound treacherously while he sleeps, he woke up fettered by the long chain of disregarded years. He had to take up at once the burden of all his existence, and found it almost too heavy for his strength. Old! . . . Getting old . . . and then? He looked upon the immortal sea with the awakened and groping perception of its heartless might; he saw it unchanged, black and foaming under the eternal scrutiny of the stars; he heard its impa-

4. In this scheme I follow Donald T. Torchiana ("The Nigger of the Narcissus: Myth, Mirror, and Metropolis," *Wascana Review*, 2 [1967], 29–41), whose analysis is far more accurate than the standard interpretation by James E. Miller (*"The Nigger of the 'Narcissus':* A Re-examination," *PMLA*, 66 [1951], 911–18). For Torchiana, see above, pp. 275–87.

tient voice calling for him out of a pitiless vastness full of unrest, of turmoil, and of terror. He looked afar upon it, and he saw an immensity tormented and blind, moaning and furious, that claimed all the days of his tenacious life, and, when life was over, would claim the worn-out body of its slave. . . .

While Wait sees, one might think, enough, Conrad allows Singleton a fuller and potentially more shattering perception not merely of his mortality but also of existential chaos, the brevity of life in general, and—a theme to be greatly amplified in "Youth"[5]—the sovereignty of time. Yet Singleton does not allow his perception to impair his seamanship: "at midnight he turned out to duty as if nothing had been the matter." In affirming solidarity in spite of his perception of underlying meaninglessness, Singleton is, unlike almost all of Conrad's other characters, authentically courageous. The uniqueness of his achievement deserves additional consideration.

So much critical attention has been lavished on Wait's symbolic function—though generally he has been treated as an allegorical figure while labeled a symbolic character—that Ian Watt's comment on his deflation bears repeating: "the influence that Wait exercises on the crew is an irrational projection of their own fears and weaknesses . . . Wait is a symbol, not of death but of the fear of death, and therefore, more widely, of the universal human reluctance to face those most universal agents of anticlimax, the facts."[6] Singleton, however, undergoes no such deflation. Of monolithic proportions, his "singleness" is a sure sign that Conrad was unable to give complete humanity to his ideal seaman.

When we first see him, Singleton is the Wise Old Sailor: "he resembled a learned and savage patriarch, the incarnation of barbarian wisdom serene in the blasphemous turmoil of the world." The second time, he is the Wise Old Sailor in Touch with Eternity: "Singleton stood at the door with his face to the light and his back to the darkness. And alone in the dim emptiness of the sleeping forecastle he appeared bigger, colossal, very old: old as Father Time

5. John Howard Weston, " 'Youth': Conrad's Irony and Time's Darkness," *Studies in Short Fiction*, 11, No. 4 (1974).
6. Watt, "Conrad Criticism and *The Nigger of the 'Narcissus*,' " p. 252, above. For others, Wait is "an embodiment of the subconscious, instinctual but regressive quality in man" (Vernon Young,"Trial by Water: Joseph Conrad's *The Nigger of the 'Narcissus*,' " *Joseph Conrad: A Critical Symposium*, ed. R. W. Stallman [(East Lansing): Michigan State University Press, 1960], p. 113; first published in *Accent*, 12 [1952], 67–81), "Our human 'blackness' "

(Albert J. Guerard, *Conrad the Novelist* [Cambridge, Mass.: Harvard University Press, 1958], p. 107), "a symbol of Fate itself" (Adam Gillon, *The Eternal Solitary: A Study of Joseph Conrad* [New York: Bookman Associates, Inc., 1960], p. 100), and "the incarnate symbol of death in the novel" (Leo Gurko, *Joseph Conrad: Giant in Exile* [New York: The Macmillan Company, 1962], p. 73). Watt's insight into Wait's deflation deserves David R. Smith's modification (212): Wait "embodies the narcissistic dwelling upon death and the fear of it, the meaningless and destructive preoccupation, the unanswerable questioning."

himself, who should have come there into this place as quiet as a sepulchre to contemplate with patient eyes the short victory of sleep, the consoler." And just following his identification with Time is Singleton's encounter with a cable-brake: the Wise Old Sailor in Touch with the Spirit of Things:

> Singleton seized the high lever, and, by a violent throw forward of his body, wrung out another half-turn from the brake. He recovered himself, breathed largely, and remained for awhile glaring down at the powerful and compact engine that squatted on the deck at his feet like some quiet monster—a creature amazing and tame.
>
> "You . . . hold!" he growled at it masterfully, in the incult tangle of his white beard.

While "resembled" and "appeared" in the first two quotations prepare us for the possibility that Singleton is not what he seems, as the novel proceeds any doubt evaporates. Alone among the crew incapable of "conceited folly," and consequently suspected by them of stupidity, he proves himself to be as "in touch" as he earlier seemed to be: with "venerable mildness" he admonishes Wait to "get on with your dying . . . We can't help you"; in the storm "He steered with care"; with "unspeakable wisdom, hard unconcern, the chilling air of resignation," he damns Donkin and regains the place for which he cares so little in the crew's eyes; and he finally prophesies what comes to pass, that Wait will die in sight of land. A fully achieved representative figure, Singleton is not, however, a full and rounded character. Nothing can testify more eloquently to Conrad's vision of the essential incompatibility of perception and will than the fact that this, his most notable attempt to have it both ways, constitutes an allegorical ideal, not a symbolic reality.[7]

Wait, on the other hand, is both fully human and fully symbolic; he is, in short, a character in whom Conrad could believe. Less perceptive than Singleton, Wait nevertheless realizes the extinction to which he is subject. And although Singleton's will is not weakened by a deeper realization, Wait's will collapses. He participates so deeply in what he perceives—and his consumption is a physical correlative of his spiritual dissolution—that he succumbs entirely. The most he can do is spin out palliative illusions of indifferent health, malingering, cunning, and official persecution. And in order to reinforce his illusions, the more completely to believe in them himself, Wait does his best to elicit the crew's sympathy. In so doing, he enacts the role diametrically opposite Singleton's in the psychological scheme of the novel.

7. Mudrick (p. 296), who sees "the monolithic Singleton [as] usually persuasive . . . as a kind of Old Man of the Sea," and David Thorburn (*Conrad's Romanticism* [New Haven and London: Yale University Press, 1974], p. 52), who sees him as a "mythic figure," would seem to support my claim.

The second in the triad of opposed pairs, Donkin and Captain Allistoun, present to the crew the political dimension of the sympathy-solidarity dilemma. In his "perfidious desire of truthfulness!" Donkin is sharply perceptive; during the storm only he "lay still with the silence of despair" over his "disregarded right to live." Donkin's aim, mutiny, follows quite naturally from his perception. Imaginative and self-pitying, he sees such existential conditions as storm, calm, and work as capable of reform. Yet in seeking to remake the world according to his imagination, and to eliminate all the ills that flesh is heir to—he inspires the crew to dream of a time when "every lonely ship would travel over a serene sea, manned by a wealthy and well-fed crew of satisfied skippers"—Donkin is also the man who can say of the *Narcissus*: "Let 'er go to 'ell." Allistoun, by contrast, is "here to drive this ship and keep every man-jack aboard up to the mark." Seeming "to have found his taciturn severity in the profound depths of a larger experience" he is, like Singleton, silent, impassive, and impersonal. His juxtaposition with Donkin, "that consummate artist" whose Kurtzian "picturesque and filthy loquacity flowed like a troubled stream from a poisoned source," is a well-structured comment on the widely differing appeals of solidarity and sympathy.[8]

The third of the opposed pairs, the crew as a fragmented collection of individuals and the *Narcissus* as a unitary world, is implicit in the previous discussion. The combined effect of Donkin and Wait dissolves potential solidarity into alienation, self-concern, dissension, and near-mutiny. In their sympathy with Wait the crew feel his intimations of mortality as their own, and pay homage in "the brilliance of a silver shrine [to] a black idol"—a service in which one critic sees "a sacrifice at the altar of death, on which rests the image of the imperilled self."[9] And during their mutinous outbreak the crew's concern with their imperilled selves leads to the imminent peril of the ship. Only with Wait's death, with the disappearance of the object of sympathy, does the crew attain solidarity—"they stepped forward like one man"—and the ship, "relieved of an unfair burden," her life. Without the added burdens of the crew's imaginative sympathy for Wait's weakness, their images of an unattainable state of being, and their yearning for *etwas mehr* ("They knew what they wanted, but they could not find anything worth saying"), the *Narcissus* would have had only external disruption to deal with.

A look at the unification of setting and plot and the schematic

---

8. Though he represents the claims of solidarity to the crew, Allistoun is not, in himself, entirely a figure of will: as Bruce Johnson (pp. 33–34) points out, Allistoun has a moment of sympathy for Wait. Thorburn (115) also notes the Donkin-Kurtz parallel.

9. Torchiana, p. 277, above, to whom I am indebted for my decision of Wait's appeal.

arrangement of characters shows how scrupulously Conrad structured *The Nigger of the "Narcissus"* to embody the dichotomous relation of sympathy and solidarity. In his narrative technique, however, Conrad was considerably less successful. His shortcoming in this regard has nothing to do with the critically belabored shifts in point of view;[1] rather, the difficulty resides in the narrator, such as he is. Because he exists only as a locationless, bodiless being—because he is, in William York Tindall's phrase, "not altogether there"[2]—he presents two problems to a successful discrimination between sympathy and solidarity.

The first problem has to do with the narrator's not being "there" as a participant in the experience he narrates. Obviously he is there in general—but only in general: he lives a mere amalgam of all other lives on the *Narcissus*; he feels the stress of storm and the boredom of calm in the most severely generalized fashion; and he knows the conversations, feelings, and thoughts of others as only an invisible and omniscient being might know them. Incapable of individuality, he seems even to shun it actively, and because he exists no further than the degree to which he is not himself, he *is* only insofar as he shares in the lives of others.[3] Can either "sympathy" or "solidarity" describe this curious creature's relation to the crew? I might preface my response by saying that the question seems to me inappropriate, for I do not see how "relation" can be predicated of a nonentity; unidentifiable apart from the crew—without independent identity—the narrator has not the wherewithal with which to relate.

But even if his sufficient identity is granted, a serious problem remains. In his narration as well as on the *Narcissus* the narrator does his best to avoid self-particularization. An examination of his narrative tactics—he either generalizes an experience in order to validate it, or (presumably) shares and then reports the experience of another—may show how indeterminable his relation to the crew is The first example comes from the storm section:

> There was no sleep on board that night. Most seamen remember in their life one or two such nights of a culminating gale. Nothing seems left of the whole universe but darkness, clamour, fury—and the ship. And like the last vestige of a shattered creation she drifts, bearing an anguished remnant of sinful mankind, through the distress, tumult, and pain of an avenging terror.

1. See Young, p. 119; Mudrick, pp. 291–93; Guerard; and Watt,"Conrad Criticism and the Nigger of the 'Narcissus'."
2. William York Tindall, "Apology for Marlow," *From Jane Austen to Joseph Conrad*, ed. R. C. Rathburn and M. Steinmann, Jr. (Minneapolis: University of Minnesota Press, 1959), pp. 276–77.

3. Watt ("Conrad Criticism and *The Nigger of the 'Narcissus,' "* argues that the success of the novel depends on the narrator's not being a "particularized individual"; while I disagree with his evaluation of the novel, Watt's description of the narrator seems accurate indeed.

Here the narrator generalizes not merely from his sensations to those of others, but from his memory of his sensations to the remembered sensations of others: he effaces himself not once, but twice. In the second example, the scene of Singleton's realization already discussed, the narrator simply reports that seaman's "awakened and groping perception of [the immortal sea's] heartless might"; since the narrator indicates no reaction of his own, he must be said to have none. Beyond a noticeable bent toward narrative depersonalization as marked as that already noted of the narrator in his role as participant, significance is difficult to discover. What Conrad may well have aimed at is a narrator who embodies the "conviction of solidarity," but what he created is a narrator whose relation to the crew is utterly indeterminable. Does the narrator have such "fellow feeling" ("sympathy," *Oxford English Dictionary*) with those whose tale he tells that his relation to them is one of perfect sympathy? Or is he so "perfectly united . . . in interests, sympathies, or aspirations" ("solidarity," *Oxford English Dictionary*) that his relation is one of absolute solidarity? I do not think we can choose.

III

"Sentimentalists," says the Pilgrim's Script, "are they who seek to enjoy Reality, without incurring the Immense Debtorship for a thing done." —*The Ordeal of Richard Feveral*

There is of course nothing inherently wrongheaded in the narrative technique of *The Nigger of the "Narcissus."* It is, however, unsuccessful *in this novel* because, unstructured by the dichotomous values of sympathy and solidarity, it not only weakens the structure by which the plot and setting and the array of characters are informed, but it also, inevitably, weakens the novel as a whole. The specific weakness into which the novel's problematical narrative technique leads it is, I believe, sentimentality. Indeed, if one of the great strengths of Conrad's fiction—its scrupulous weighing of the price paid, in unworldly innocence or in terrible knowledge, for a particular illusion, for a privileged perception—is absent from *The Nigger*, the novel's narrative technique is largely responsible. For although the narrator has Wait's, Singleton's, and (more or less) his own perceptions of personal and universal mortality and existential meaninglessness, they leave him all but untouched: he pays no price, or very little. While the crew, too, are not finally affected, neither do they fully perceive; as the title of the first American publication of the novel indicates, they are "the children of the sea." Unlike the crew, the narrator in his omniscience enjoys Reality to the full—enjoys every vicarious sensation, and enjoys them all, one might add, passively—but he incurs no Immense Debtorship. Through its narrative perspective presenting a world where fearful perceptions can be inconsequentially ignored or repressed, *The Nigger of the "Narcissus"* is Conrad's most nearly sentimental achievement.

What occasions this sentimentality—the narrator's evasion of the claims of perception—originates in his lack of individuality as a participant and his only relative individuality as the narrator. In the last three pages, however, the narrator's individuality comes into clearer focus—an indication that he has gleaned some meaning that prevents him from lapsing back into collective innocence with the crew. His view of London, after he has "separated [him]self gently" from Belfast and, in effect, from the crew as well, shows that he has garnered a bitter harvest indeed:

> The roar of the town resembled the roar of topping breakers, merciless and strong, with a loud voice and cruel purpose; but overhead the clouds broke; a flood of sunshine gleamed down the walls of grimy houses. The dark knot of seamen drifted in sunshine. To the left of them the trees in Tower Garden sighed, the stones of the Tower gleaming, seemed to stir in the play of light, as if remembering suddenly all the great joys and sorrows of the past . . . The sunshine of heaven fell like a gift of grace on the mud of the earth, on the remembering and mute stones, on greed, selfishness; on the anxious faces of forgetful men. And to the right of the dark group the stained front of the Mint, cleansed by the flood of light, stood out for a moment dazzling and white like a marble palace in a fairy tale. The crew of the *Narcissus* drifted out of sight.
>
> I never saw them again.

Seeing that the crew, the Tower, and the sea are of the past, and that Donkin, the Mint, and the earth are of the future, the narrator sees too that "the sunshine of heaven," "like a gift of grace," may as easily illuminate one group as another. Possessed of this dark knowledge the narrator can only retreat into the passivity of retrospection: "on the waters of the forlorn stream drifts a ship—a shadowy ship manned by a crew of Shades. They pass and make a sign, in a shadowy hail. Haven't we, together and upon the immortal sea, wrung out a meaning from our sinful lives? Goodbye, brothers! You were a good crowd."

But there may be one step more to take, a last stop on the journey which begins in collectivity and experience, pauses briefly at relative individuality and retrospection, and concludes in full identity and the artistic task of active engagement with the meaning of past experience. In his 1914 note "To My Readers in America," Conrad wrote:

> After writing the last words of [*The Nigger of the "Narcissus"*], in the revulsion of feeling before the accomplished task, I

understood that I had done with the sea, and that henceforth I had to be a writer. And almost without laying down my pen I wrote a preface, trying to express the spirit in which I was entering on the task of my new life. That preface on advice (which I now think was wrong) was never published with the book.

Thus the Preface constitutes the narrator's emergence into full identity; rather than a preface, it is—poetically as well as chronologically —the novel's coda. By this I do not mean to suggest, however, that Conrad is the narrator of *The Nigger of the "Narcissus."* What is far more the case, I believe, is that the narrator becomes Conrad— and does so by a slow and painful process of individuation. This process is completed in the Preface, not previous to it, and the Preface is, rather than Conrad's first mature statement, his announcement of imminent maturity. The works which soon followed bear witness that his announcement was anything but premature.

The tight links between the novel and its Preface—both are products of the same preoccupation, and the latter is the temporary end point of the process begun in the former—account for the crucial importance of "solidarity" in a work in which it does not appear: it is the antithesis of "pity," "sentimentalism," "compassion"—and of "sympathy." Even so, "solidarity" remains a problematical concept, for while it has become definable by demonstration —one need point only to Singleton—a formal definition is no more possible now than it was at the beginning of this essay; the awkwardness of the narrative stance through most of the novel has made such a definition impossible. But perhaps with Conrad's help we can now discover why "solidarity" is so resistant to definition. Writing to R. B. Cunninghame Graham almost a year after finishing *The Nigger of the "Narcissus"* and four months after completing its Preface, Conrad dealt once more with Singleton. Calling his Wise Old Sailor "that unconscious man" whom "[n]othing can touch . . . but the curse of decay" because "he does not think," Conrad then asks:

> Would you seriously wish to tell such a man: "Know thyself." Understand that thou art nothing, less than a shadow, more insignificant than a drop of water in the ocean, more fleeting than the illusion of a dream. Would you?[4]

In his passionate disagreement with Graham—who had apparently suggested "Singleton with an education" as a sort of human ideal, a combination Conrad found "impossible"—Conrad forgot that Singleton attains precisely that perception in *The Nigger.* More than in his created character, Conrad was true to his understanding in

4. Joseph Conrad, *Joseph Conrad's Letters to R. B. Cunninghame Graham*, ed. C. T. Watts (Cambridge: Cambridge University Press, 1969), pp. 53–54.

his lapse of memory; what Conrad called "consciousness" and I have called "perception" cannot coexist with will. *Either* one affirms solidarity, *or* one perceives its antithetical meaninglessness.

In *The Nigger of the "Narcissus"* and its Preface, this either/or dilemma is not realized; the novel obscures the crucial distinction between will and perception, and the Preface ignores the meaninglessness which makes "the conviction of solidarity" so difficult and so magnificent an achievement. In Conrad's later works, the "solidarity" of *The Nigger* and its Preface will become, by the addition of the all-important "in spite of," what I have earlier called "courage": will *in spite of* perception. But in the present novel "solidarity" is not a human achievement but a monolith's gift, and in the novel's Preface its conviction is not achieved in action but received in reading. Like the novel, its Preface, too, is sentimental; each allows enjoyment without Immense Debtorship. This sentimentality of his literary adolescence is what Conrad outgrew when he put *The Nigger of the "Narcissus"* and its Preface behind him.

PAUL L. WILEY

A Tale of Passion†

The titles or, better, subtitles of Conrad's works suggest his familiarity with a considerable range of narrative forms which today we may either ignore or prefer to cover with the common term "novel." Conrad, in fact, as I have noted in the bibliographical table (pp. 452–59) of the Jocelyn Baines biography (1961), seems to have been rather sparing of the descriptive word "novel"— though it is used, for instance, for *Under Western Eyes*—and often to have attached other tags such as "story," "romance," "confession," and so on. About the implications of these subtitles Conrad seems to have been quite clear, as I think one's reading proves, and they lead to the assumption that he drew upon a store of literary archetypes perhaps quite as potent in their own effects as psychological archetypes in theirs and may well be shown to count in his popularity as a writer. To give weight to the denotation of a particular title may also sometimes help in illuminating certain kinds of textual difficulties.

Several of Conrad's most famous books—in addition, of course, to his shorter fiction—are labeled "tales"—*Lord Jim* (also described in Conrad's preface as "a free and wandering tale"); *Nostromo: A*

† Adapted, revised, and expanded by the author from "Two Tales of Passion,"   *Conradiana*, 6 (1974), 189–95.

Tale of the Seaboard; and *Victory: An Island Tale*—to mention three known to everyone. The word may now sound a little old-fashioned—possibly as dated as the word "passion"—although I am informed that Mr. John Barth at one time recommended the study of tales to beginning novelists. We have been led to regard "tale" as an older alternative to "short story," which overlooks the point that, insofar as the modern short story is concerned, these types are fundamentally distinct, the short story finding its center in a single moment of insight or illumination. Yet if we have tended to lose touch with the tale, this was not so at the start of the century when Conrad and Ford were in full career. A revival of the British tale in the later Nineteenth Century brought to prominence Hardy, Stevenson, Kipling and the early Wells and somewhat further along de la Mare and especially A. E. Coppard who attempted, against odds, to keep the tradition alive. There are reasons, no doubt, why the tale happened to flourish at this time—possibly some influence from the East, in the wake of Burton's *Arabian Nights,* or the often held conviction that the world had become strange or marvelous enough to exemplify those qualities with which the tale has commonly been associated.

In 1897, in this atmosphere, Conrad wrote *The Nigger of the "Narcissus,"* and the word tale was stressed not only in the alternate subtitles "A Tale of the Sea" and "A Tale of the Forecastle" but also in Conrad's dedication to Edward Garnett. The late Professor Morton D. Zabel saw that the work was not a novel by our measurements, and critics on the whole seem to have agreed, at least tacitly. But even closer recognition of the book as a tale brings attention to features about it that appear curious, chief among these being ambiguities or shiftings in the character of the narrator. In considering this work as a "tale of passion" I am aware, however, that I may be falling short of possible expectations.

In India, I have learned, the custom survives of the itinerant story-teller who recites to village audiences tales incorporating a familiar or traditional subject matter. Apparently, too, in our own day this method of narration has been taken over into one of the philosophically centered novels of Raja Rao. In any case, what characterizes the Indian folk tale seems to correspond to essentials of the tale almost anywhere: the oral narration, the primacy of story with an eye to the surprising, including even the magical and mythical, and the assumption of some sort of communal audience. The role of the narrator is quite other than in so many modern first-person novels, being neither autobiographical nor suspect on the score of dependability. Instead the narrator is master of the story, a conjuror free to invent, and thus not bound by psychological consistency or the obligation to act as eye-witness, that concern of a legalistic age. Shahrazade, I suppose one could say, did not risk her head by failing to establish her presence in every bedroom; but her end might have been grim had she neglected to remind the King—to steal a comment from Mr. P. H. Newby in his Introduction to *Tales from the Arabian Nights*—that her hero with the mountain of gold was entertained for a year and a day by forty beautiful damsels with faces like full moons, with lips of coral and bosoms that are temptations to behold.

Despite Conrad's assertion in his note to the American public that on this book he was willing as an artist to stand or fall, *The Nigger of the "Narcissus"* has often been, and to my knowledge of a good many readers still is, censured for technical flaws associated with peculiarities of the narrative method. These objections, frequently traceable to an assumption that Conrad was at this time technically unskilled, can, I think, be allayed through acceptance of the work as a tale, not a novel—indeed a strange tale presumably directed to a communal audience familiar with an English seafaring tradition. But it is a tale more sophisticated, notably in its rhetorical modulations and consciousness of time distinctions, than the ordinary straightforward story. The narrator himself, contrary to the case in many written tales less faithful in simulating an oral method, acquires a recognizable personality and a voice that persist all the way to the solitary "I" figure who bows out at the end.

At the start in Bombay harbor up through the great scene of Baker's mustering of the crew and the startling arrival of James Wait, the narrator's complete grasp of events is fully established; and we are never in doubt of listening to an expert performance. After this point, Wait's coming aboard, the narrative complexity increases, principally because of the often discussed alternations of "we" and "they" in the narrator's point of view. About this important matter more needs to be said; but in one sense at least, and within the framework of a tale, this apparent inconsistency could be seen to enhance rather than detract from the naturalness of the telling. For as one becomes absorbed in the details of even an everyday story and thus self-forgetful, such fluctuations can be taken for granted in oral recollection. "We saw the man struggling in the water, and they really worked to get him out," for instance.

It is to be expected that the obligations of the narrator of a tale are to the effective conduct of the story and that his omniscience in this respect is absolute. He must persuade his audience that his narrative omits nothing vital but not necessarily that he knew everything at first-hand, the latter being, I think, one sign of the turn of the modern novel towards the subjective and autobiographical. How influential this trend has become is reflected in the dissatisfaction over the narrator's lack of direct knowledge of the circumstances of

Wait's death in Conrad's tale, even though this debate lifts these episodes out of an overall context, including sections on the ship's officers, in which the narrator repeatedly testifies not only to what he could not have witnessed but also to thoughts not his own. If, moreover, we charge the handling of the Wait death scenes to Conrad's bungling, we are compelled to face up to the evidence, in the later and surely mature *Nostromo*, that Conrad seems deliberately to set up the death of Martin Decoud so as to exclude any possible human observer. Nevertheless, the controversial scenes in *The Nigger of the "Narcissus"* are surely crucial and provocative not, I would suggest, on grounds of technical after-thought but because they are so inevitable in the pattern of the developing tale and the obligatory fulfillment of expectations aroused in the long and carefully prepared interplay between Wait and Donkin. We reach a phase of culmination in that sealed-off cabin where Donkin preys on Wait but get there, I think, by another route than that of rational demonstration.

These and further questions about the narrator seem to lie at the heart of the book. Even his reliability appears at times in doubt. Of his famous valediction, "Good-bye, brothers! You were a good crowd. As good a crowd as ever fisted with wild cries the beating canvas of a heavy foresail; or, tossing aloft, invisible in the night, gave back yell for yell to a westerly gale," Professor Avrom Fleishman in his *Conrad's Politics* (pp. 131–32) has reasonably asked, though I paraphrase him too bluntly, how we can quite believe this. Simply from a matter-of-fact perspective the notion of "a good crowd" looks somehow at odds with the repeated denunciations in the body of the tale of the crew as childish, sentimental, unreliable, and finally mutinous. Is this narrator forgetful or irresponsible? I believe not, but he has certainly altered his posture from that at the outset of the story with its rather smug adulation of the virtues of the defunct generation of the incorruptible Singleton:

> The men who could understand his silence were gone—the men who knew how to exist beyond the pale of life and within sight of eternity. They had been strong, as those are strong who know neither doubts nor hopes. They had been impatient and enduring, turbulent and devoted, unruly and faithful.

This seeming instability in the narrator is, I believe, an important sign of Conrad's practice not only in *The Nigger of the "Narcissus"* but also in much of his early fiction; and it was perhaps consciously formulated in the famous Preface with its tribute to music as the art of arts, to which Professor Ian Watt has referred in comments on Conrad's style. Whatever subsidiary interests one may find there, *The Nigger of the "Narcissus"* records primarily, I think, an experience of passion—to borrow a usable term from the doctoral dissertation of Mr. Don Dietiker ("Joseph Conrad: The Novel as Process," University of Wisconsin, 1972)—marked to some extent by recurrent images of agony and crucifixion and coming to a peak in the isolated terror of Wait's death. "The watch then on duty, led by Mr. Creighton, began to struggle up the rigging. The wind flattened them against the ratlines; then, easing a little, would let them ascend a couple of steps; and again, with a sudden gust, pin all up the shrouds, the whole crawling line in attitudes of crucifixion." For in the end we are brothers not simply through such rational ideas as those urged by Donkin but through a fundamental capacity for suffering, which, having lived it through, the narrator sums up in his farewell cry that is neither moral nor altogether defensible by common logic. On this point comparison might be made to *Almayer's Folly*, that first novel where the narrative voice slips so unpredictably from its outgoing scorn of a wooly-headed dreamer to its almost lyrical view of Almayer in the final scenes, which Conrad described to Marguerite Poradowska as a solo for Almayer almost as long "as the Tristan solo in Wagner." Here the tonal fluctuations denote the stages in Almayer's unrelieved passion. With the tale form in *The Nigger of the "Narcissus"* Conrad may have succeeded better, since the presence of an actual, if anonymous, narrator would lend more credence to the radical transitions in attitude and feeling.

The strategy for obtaining this effect of passion is most intricate, the narrator turning unexpectedly from a "they" to a "we" association with the ship's company. Understandable as this may be as a trait of oral narration, it is essentially a deeper ingredient in the whole design of the tale. The impression is of parallel and sometimes contrasting states of mind—the one facing outward, the other inward—an approximation to the undulations of mental and emotional activity in the peculiar circumstances of the narrator's inclusion in a collective entity. Broadly speaking, one can recognize two alternating types of rhetoric. In his "they" role the narrator is normally objective but also in places given to praise of the traditional and ideal:

> In the magnificence of the phantom rays the ship appeared pure like a vision of ideal beauty, illusive like a tender dream of serene peace.

But as "we" the narrator becomes personal, excited, and self-tormenting:

> We were trying to be good chaps, and found it jolly difficult; we oscillated between the desire of virtue and the fear of ridicule; we

wished to save ourselves from the pain of remorse, but did not want to be made the contemptible dupes of our sentiment.

Conrad's two voices perform an indispensable function. The mainly dominant "they" outlook maintains the line of story, the order of events, and something of the fabulous air germane to a tale. The "we" mask makes explicit the accompanying strain of a passion that, gravitating toward the great figure of James Wait, invests the tale with its immediately human dimension. As pivotal in the design, Wait connects the two voices, linking the subjective turmoil of the crew with the corresponding progression of narrative events. Thus to the traditional English tale of sea adventure Conrad brought both death and contemporaneity—a new note of modern revolutionary sentiment.

This masterpiece by Conrad was written in a period of transvaluation, in literary as well as social values. His adaptations of the oral tale resulted in a form which, though sophisticated, struck deep into popular tradition and at the same time freely allowed for the enactment of passion, that enduring and most potent transformer of all value systems and of previously accepted public moralities.

EUGENE B. REDMOND

Racism, or Realism? Literary Apartheid, or Poetic License? Conrad's Burden in *The Nigger of the "Narcissus"*†

Part I. The Etiology of Racism in Anglo-Europe

If, in your sociological and linguistic frame-of-reference, *Black* means *Evil/Dirty* and *White* means *Good/Clean*, then you must not overlook *race* and *racism* in Joseph Conrad's *The Nigger of the "Narcissus."* I am betting that *most* readers will subscribe to the foregoing equations; and I am also wagering that, unless they acquire the sharper angle of consciousness-vision needed to bring "color" to an interpretation or analysis of this short novel, few will accept and confront the real "problems" or "burdens" Conrad has ambiguously, and perhaps unconsciously, inherited. Moreover, we can get specific and give bodies and faces to our colors, equating *African* with *Black*, and *European* (especially *English*) with *White*. Our focus now becomes contemporary since many of today's moral, social, and ethical struggles have helped polarize the globe along

† Written especially for this edition.

lines of race and color. (Nearly eighty years ago, the Afro-American thinker W. E. B. Du Bois said that the "Problem" of the twentieth century would be one "of color.")

A full understanding of Du Bois's thesis and Conrad's racism will require the discerning student or teacher—especially if white—to venture down or up from that smug, naïve Parnassus of ornamental exactness and put meat and bones on fancy literary skeletons and devices. If we think of "good" and "bad" things—and associate colors with them—we immediately enter the historical setting of racism. Most of us are acquainted, for example, with "bad" references such as "black eye," "blackball," "blackmail," "black market," and "devil's-food cake," just as we are similarly in touch with "good" references like "white lie," "white sale," "fair day," "whitewash," and "angel-food cake." If these predictable allusions to color-*cum*-quality are still with us in our twentieth-centurized enlightenment, one can imagine the terrors and subliminal machinations that must have haunted the highly self-conscious children of the Victorian Age. The nineteenth century witnessed the biggest European-American takeover of the affairs and resources of other (usually *darker*) cultures—all under the pretense of assuming the "White Man's Burden." This phony self-righteous posture is so blatantly contradictory that, by today's standards, it clearly appears ludicrous. The Monroe Doctrine, the Golden Age of European Colonial Expansion, Victorianism, Realism as an upward swing of the esthetic pendulum from Romanticism, the era when The Sun Never Set on British Soil—these were other assumptions which contributed to the mood that Conrad inherited as a Polish-turned-English gentleman. They are important items to keep in mind when reading "*Narcissus*," for in them can be found the real answers to questions of *race* and *color*.

Conrad's mind-set, however, was not simply a product of the nineteenth century. Actually, he was an apparently willing victim of latent racist thoughts and attitudes developed over several hundred years—years when the colored peoples of the world were subjected to systematic denigration and destruction. Here, again, a multitude of examples can be posited. There is the case of Arnold J. Toynbee, the English historian who claimed that Africans contributed nothing to the development of civilization. Other, contemporary, European historians have said that Africa has no history! If, by the words "civilization" and "history," one is referring to the mere three thousand years that constitute the narrow band of Græco-Roman, European, and Anglo-American culture, then, certainly, such a myopic and prejudiced point of view would not include the ancient or "prehistoric" traditions of Africa, Asia, India, and the Americas. Yet the foregoing are only recent indices to the racism so threaded into the fabric of European culture. Racism, prejudice, discrimination, and apartheid are feelings and positions that grow from long-held attitudes about inferiority and superiority. So one must look at the origins of "Classical" Anglo-European thought in order to determine where all the problems and "burdens" began.

Alfred North Whitehead has said that Western philosophy consists basically of "footnotes" to Plato, who talked, at great length, about the will or soul maintaining "control" over the rest of the personality or *body*. Such mind-over-body orientation (Mind/Body dualism) was subsequently embraced by most of the important philosophers, theologians, religious organizations, politicians, and schools of learning in Europe. What emerged from this orientation was a self-concept or world-view expressed in dualistic terms: either/or, good/bad, heaven/hell, ugly/beautiful, black/white. In science, in art, in theories of work, in literature one sees that dualism was and is a ruling force or concept. But dualism—including dividing life up into poles of *right* and *wrong* or *good* and *bad*—is not indigenous to African, Indian, Asian, or Latin cosmologies. Africans, in particular, view the world holistically, and not as a puzzle made up of compartments and categories. This kind of attitude is difficult for Anglo-Europeans to understand or accept since they are caught up in a regimented, narrow, and (by others' standards) "peculiar" way of looking at things. A restricted, prejudiced view of our multi-cultural world puts the holders of such vision in a "disadvantaged" position as a result of their lack of a point of cultural relativity.

This problem of cultural relativity was apparently unconsciously imbibed into the attitudes of the Europeans and readied for the day when they made contact with Black people. Contributing to the confusion caused by the dualistic view of the universe, and to the whole network of negativisms that were imposed on Africans, was a feeling about the word *black* which is recorded in the *Oxford English Dictionary* in a fully developed form even before the sixteenth century:

> Deeply stained with dirt; soiled, dirty, foul. . . . Having dark or deadly purposes, malignant; pertaining to or involving death, deadly; baneful, disastrous, sinister. . . . Foul, iniquitous, atrocious, horrible, wicked. . . . Indicating disgrace, censure, liability to punishment, etc.

One can now see how the weird web of color-racial-cultural one-upmanship became a literal death-trap, in many different ways, for those dark peoples conquered or colonized by Europeans.

One can also see how Conrad has developed, in James Wait, a straw-man, a scapegoat on whose back he can take a symbolic journey through the world of the White Man's Burden. The ship's crew, triumphant over "evil" and "bad" weather, is also triumphant over Wait's alleged evil nature and doings; and Conrad makes it clear, via sage-*griot* Singleton, that Wait's presence causes the storms. But in daring to suggest that Wait is this omnipotent, Conrad reveals both his own and the white world's love-hate attitude towards Blacks. And it is, finally, this kind of seesaw posture that characterizes Conrad's treatment of the African personality throughout "*Narcissus.*"

While the story is filled with negative references to black and positive references to white, one must keep in mind that Wait *is* Conrad's creation. Whatever our feelings in favor of or against Wait, it is the *white* novelist, Conrad, who has us in his own angle of vision—and we are forced to hate or love Wait in accordance with Conrad's literary, cultural, and racial whims. Wait is set up—during Conrad's seemingly alternate conscious and unconscious states—to take the *weight* or reverse "burden" that the white man perceives darkness or blackness to be; Wait is then held in the fatalistic jaws of a racial fantasy until he loses the last drop of life. A *double-entendre*, the name W*ait* works well as Conrad's ambigious handle for his Black character. Wait is late boarding the ship and is generally depicted as having a "late" (read "lazy" or "niggerish") personality. Still, for Conrad—knowingly or unknowingly—the name W*ait* is even more than *doubly intended*. For aside from the W*ait-late* equation and the W*eight-burden/ed* pairing, James Wait is a threshing floor for all the hearsays, stereotypes, guilts, fears, resentments, ignorances, malignities, and conscience-evoking dramas played out within the broader arena of race and color.

Adding emotional-racial fuel to the feud between himself and James Wait, and the multiple frame of sociological nightmares caused by it, are the writer's own problems with African/European cosmological differences. (These problems, as we observed earlier, are tantamount to racism.) Conrad and the white world are ignorant of the African's use or sense of time and space. At the same time, "uncivilized" peoples are known to be *late* and to "lack responsibility" in the handling of property (a ship, for example) since they do not compute time in the linear (Western) sense or relate to space (property) in the same way as so-called "advanced" Western peoples. Lacking a point of cultural relativity, Europe colonized Africa on the assumption that military and naval superiority were synonymous with moral and spiritual superiority. At the same time, the European had to respect many of the ways and customs of Africans because he, after all, had no choice, and especially since part of the sport of conquest is freedom to relax and romp with the "squaws." Conrad studies this situation in other writings, concluding that the European, in the grip of native intrigue, is destroyed morally because he does not have the watchful eye of ORDER. This ORDER—shrouded in the attraction-repulsion conflict—is what Conrad defends in *"Narcissus."* Having had enough exposure to African and Third World sensibilities to recognize the terrific powers of their intuitive and viscerogenic life-styles, but unable to find a point of reference for them on the human spectrum, Conrad makes James Wait a whipping-boy for his and Europe's insecurities and moral hang-ups. Mind-over-body orientation, a dualistic structure of life, a monotheistic view of religion, exenophobia—all were foreign to the African world-view but part of European cosmology. Most of the fallout from this disparity has persisted up to the present in the form of curious kinds of alterations, guises, and cross-fertilizations such as whites wearing suntans and natural hairstyles when they do not even remotely understand or appreciate where Blacks are literally and figuratively coming from. Most readers, for example, will simply say that Wait is West Indian ("not African"), thereby revealing further cultural ignorance. But these contemporary descendents of Europe's moral and racial maladies do not always appear in cross-fertilized forms, for at this very moment we can predict that "good" guys will be wearing *white* and "bad" guys will be wearing *black* in any image-making context.

Witness, if you will, none other than the spectacular *Star Wars* wherein the Arch Villain, Darth Vader, is dressed, stereotypically, in black, and talks in those "dark" tones. Or return to a cross-fertilized form in the smash hit *Saturday Night Fever*, a neo—minstrel show projecting John Travolta as a near-niggerized white disco hero. The star and his friends admit that they do not believe they can out-dress or out-dance Blacks (when dressed up they are almost "nigger-clean"), but they nevertheless casually throw around terms like *spic* and *nigger. Saturday Night Fever* is an updated commercial exploitation of deep racial-psychological fears and scars that haunt the white world. And whether one views history cyclically or linearly, these same hurts and apprehensions are always there. So the literary historians and critics who claim that Conrad does not subscribe to the prevailing thesis of the White Man's Burden and all the racist implications therein, who claim that he is merely exploring some symbolic profundity which only incidentally has connection to Blackness and Africanity, are either naïve or guilty of a brutal self-deception.

Part II. Narcissus: Self-Love or Self-Hate?

Within our established sociological and historical frame of reference for the time during which Conrad lived and wrote, it is possible to examine *The Nigger of the "Narcissus"* as a "literary" and allegedly "symbolic" piece of writing. Early on in the novel we see that the author jabs a jaundiced pen at many races and nationalities—but it is people of color who get the severest blows. Because of its name, *Narcissus*, the ship symbolizes white Græco-Roman-European culture, so that the intrusion of color creates various emotional and visual disturbances along the range of achromatic "beauty" which reinforces its white self-love. And while, admittedly, Conrad brilliantly deploys colors to develop mood, tone, and setting, he nevertheless concurrently deploys them in the service of racism. The opening of the novel finds "white-clad Asiatics" who "clamoured fiercely for payment." These same men use "the feverish and shrill babble of Eastern language" in an unsuccessful struggle "against the masterful tones of a tipsy seaman." A drunken white man, Conrad tells us, is more coherent and eloquent than Asians whose language consists not of vowels and consonants—but of "feverish and shrill babble." The old man Singleton, who resembles a "cannibal chief" and is an "incarnation of barbaric wisdom," is a consistent tool of Conrad's racist game. He is Black and white ("blackened hands" and "big white arms") and perhaps represents some kind of bizarre compromise on the race question. But the evil Donkin's posture is more obvious; he arrives on the ship as scum, as an "Englishman" who does not live up to English standards. We are told that the "white of his limbs" showed "his human kinship through the black fantasy of his rags." Poor white trash, in Americanese, Donkin does not quite rate being called a *real* white man since he is a failure and embarrassment to his race. Having thus introduced him to the reader, Conrad then proceeds to make Donkin bear his proper "dark burden"—a physical actualization of what everybody aboard the *Narcissus* expects or fears of James Wait.

We anticipate James Wait's arrival, first because of the title and then because of our knowledge that one crew member is "missing." A "Nigger" is supposed to be on board. Suspense overtakes us as we *await* James Wait. Further intrigue develops as Wait repeats his name from the "shadows" before we know he is Black. We hear " 'Wait' . . . 'Wait!' " which we assume to mean something like "Hold it." But no. We behold that a black face belongs to that "sonorous voice" in the dark. *Behold* is the appropriate word because Conrad is setting us up for a number of important events and situations. Wait evokes the greatness of Hannibal, Othello, Ira Aldridge, or Paul Robeson: "The Nigger was calm, cool, towering, superb." He is also eloquent, elegant, and excellent: "The deep, rolling tones of his voice filled the deck without effort." Following these expressions of admiration and awe, however, are clinical descriptions of Wait that are familiar in the annals of *White Over*

Black relations (see Winthrop Jordan [New York, 1968]). Upon getting a closer look at Wait—who arrives late to burden the ship with his *black weight*—Conrad discovers that he possesses "a head vigorously modelled into deep shadows and shining lights—a head powerful and misshapen with a tormented and flattened face—a face pathetic and brutal: the tragic, the mysterious, the repulsive mask of a nigger's soul." In the foregoing passage Conrad's racist instincts override his literary ones. The description of Wait is in fact merged with fantasy, text confused with context, so that what we actually get is a physiognomical and psychological stereotype superimposed on a description from a non-omniscient observer. Mind you, Conrad uses "Nigger" in the title and employs the word throughout the book; so that if we are not sure that the narrator is Conrad, we *know* the author *is*. It goes without saying then that the word has more than just alliterative significance in the title.

In a dualistic world-view—heaven *vs.* hell, good *vs.* bad, ugliness *vs.* beauty, black *vs.* white, and so forth—Podmore the cook's casual revelation that the "devil" is "black" is probably only realistic. This "logic" forces us to assume that the evils visited on the ship are caused by the *black weight*. In the midst of developing his intricate assault on Black humanity, Conrad tells us many interesting (seemingly incidental) things that help make up the larger world of his game. The fact that Captain Allistoun "shaved every morning of his life at 6 o'clock" is in orderly contrast to a motley crew of men and, in particular, to James Wait's goldbricking. But there is, Conrad suggests, a deeper meaning behind the actions of this "casual St. Kitt's nigger" with the "ugly black head." For the love-hate seesaw is ever-present in Conrad the (white) man and novelist. The "Nigger" is a liar, a malingerer, and a sub-human who "was so utterly wrong about himself that one could not but suspect him of having access to supernatural knowledge." This almost unintelligible statement follows and precedes others that reflect confusion and terror in the Conradian literary cosmos. Earlier, for example, the narrator describes Wait as having a "lower lip" that "hung down, enormous and heavy" (cf. Stepin Fetchit) and as being "a pitiful . . . limp . . . hateful burden"; but "even though at the time we hated him more than ever—more than anything under heaven—we did not want to lose him." Within the seesaw vision of humanity and color, the white man is never certain of the Black man's humanness. In bestializing the Black man, Winthrop Jordan tells us, the white man bestialized himself. Hence the White Man's Burden becomes self-imposed and has less to do with "saving and civilizing" colored people than it does with guilt and fear. James Wait, as a Black man, gets placed on the lowest human ring of the European's "Great Chain of Being" but at the same time is the greatest threat to "order." We see this idea consistently played out by Conrad. Wait's presence adds color or contrast and represents a major ingredient in Conrad's distorted symbology. Concurrently, it brings imbalance (disorder) to the Conradian cosmos (tilts the Narcissus paradigm, based, here, on the color white), forcing Conrad, who had not worked out this complex color-racial-mythological puzzle, to alternately view Wait as a kind of Promethean-Samsonian antagonist ("he groaned from his dark hole") and as a sub-human mad thing ("growling angrily like an irritated and savage animal").

In daring to come close to the Black sensibility, Conrad takes other chances: the chance that he will believe Blacks are human, the chance that he will become confused in his own (racial, literary, mythological) sense of order, the chance that he might like Black people, the chance that he might start thinking Black. All of these represented high risks for an English gentleman of the late nineteenth and early twentieth centuries, when the White Man's Burden was, as gleaned by poet, pontiff, and politician, to "save" (read *Christianize*) and "civilize" (read *colonize*) the "underdeveloped" world. In *Saturday Night Fever*, the hero's awe of American Blacks ("I couldn't get no cleaner unless I was nigger-clean") is an extension of Conrad's awe of Wait: "The little place, repainted white, had, in the night, the brilliance of a silver shrine where a black idol, reclining stiffly under a blanket, blinked its weary eyes and received our homage." Conrad had seen the "stiffly" sitting idols and witnessed the incredible power of African sculptures during his visit to the Congo. These were the same art works that inspired new movements in Western art after the turn of the century. He could not have helped witnessing other types and forms of African creative expression (see *Heart of Darkness*): ceremonies, rituals, various religious practices. For he comes close to suggesting that Wait's powers are grounded in Voodoo. In fact, in his 1897 Preface to "*Narcissus*" he expresses—as part of his own aesthetic and philosophy of life—one of the very foundations of African ontology and cosmology when he says that the artist speaks to the "latent feelings of fellowship with all creation— . . . which binds together all humanity—the dead to the living and the living to the unborn." Moving from this self-actuated cue, Conrad, on numerous other occasions throughout "*Narcissus*," excavates the deeper channels and regions of Africanity. The Black personality is merged with fertility figures and other African artifacts the author has seen. But he does not "intellectually" understand either the African or African art. On an intuitive and visceral level, however, he experiences the power and vision of Blackness. But the cerebellum is trained to neutralize (mind-over-body orientation) anything that threatens to subordinate it, so Conrad animalizes his Black human. Even so, the animal-like African is more than animal—and *more* than human!—becoming a sort of "super-nigger."

A random selection of references to, and descriptions of, Wait will point up the inumerable conflicts in Conrad's literary-mythic universe:

The setting sun dipped sharply, as though fleeing before our Negro.

You couldn't see that there was anything wrong with him: a nigger doesn't show.

He overshadowed the ship.

Jimmy . . . screamed piercingly, without drawing breath, like a tortured woman.

"Jimmy darlint'. . . . You bloody black beast!"

He was as quiet as a dead man inside a grave.

infamous nigger

And we hated James Wait.

His heavy lips protruded in an everlasting black pout.

Astounding and animal-like in the perfection of his expectant immobility. A thing of instinct—the unthinking stillness of a scared brute.

his fine baritone voice

His cheekbones glistened as though they had been varnished.

"The man's a man if he is black."

James Wait, stretched out black and deathlike in the dazzling light, turned his head on the pillow.

"One lone black beggar amongst the lot of us, and he seemed to look through me into the very hell. . . . He might have been half a man once. . . ."

Jimmy's steadfastness . . . his untruthful attitude . . . inevitable truth . . . colossal enigma—of a manifestation grand and incomprehensible that at times inspired a wondering awe.

He was absurd to the point of inspiration. He was unique, and as fascinating as only something inhuman could be; he seemed to shout his denials already from beyond that awful border.

a kind of sly, cautious, immobility

Donkin, watching the end of that hateful nigger

Conrad continues this incredible network of mixed metaphors and mixed motives throughout the novel, all of which make one wonder, given his preoccupation with shadows and blackness in other writings, what *really* happened to him during his journey into the Heart of Darkness. Nor does he leave any stereotypical stones unturned: the myth of Black sexuality also emerges from his cluttered aesthetic as Wait tells Donkin a "Canton Street girl would give up any lover for a coloured gentleman." Our antagonist then "dreams" he is "swaggering" up the East India Dock Road.

Prior to Wait's death, Singleton blames the bad weather on the Black man's presence. The crew then begins to feel collectively that, if Wait's death means "fair" weather, so be it. The Newtonian law of "Cause and effect" (as that culture-hero Singleton casually mumbles) prevails—in this highly rule-controlled culture—and so the sighting of land means that Wait's death is inevitable. In Græco-Roman cosmology, disorder anywhere spells disorder everywhere; and the death of Wait brings about the restoration of order. Even here, however, Conrad finds it difficult to have done with the *weight*; for James Wait controls the crew's actions and thoughts after his "death, which like the death of an old belief, shook the foundations of our society." Wrapped in a white blanket, the *weight* becomes too heavy to slide off the planks into the sea during burial services. Although the narrator tells us Wait is "silenced forever," the antagonist is continually spoken of as though he is alive. And, for the first time in the story, he is even made an honorary (circumstantial) human: "Two men made ready and waited for those words that send so many of our brothers to their last plunge." ("Brothers"!?) We have said that Conrad alternately deploys color symbolism in the service of both mood-setting and racism. "To the Black Horse! To the Black Horse!" the crew members cry as they make their way to the pub. Before long, however, Conrad returns to his *dark* equals *dirty*, *white* equals *clean* sensibility: "And to the right of the dark group stood the stained front of the Mint, cleansed by the flood of light, stood out for a moment, dazzling and white, like a marble palace in a fairy tale."

Are Black people human beings? Conrad is not sure; and his uncertainty feeds into a central literary nervous system that breeds racism. He lacks, or rather refuses to establish, cultural relativity. Burdened by a dualistic and perversely ethnocentric English moral outlook, he is unable to find a defensible place for Blacks-as-humans on the spectrum or "chain" of being. He is nonetheless overwhelmed by the Black presence (and this is a major contributor to his stature as a writer)—a presence which he uses profitably, but **also distorts and denies.**

Traditionally, central characters have taken on symbolic significance only after their humanity has been established: e.g., Ulysses, Chaka, Roland, Beowulf, Sigfried, Jody Grinder, Robin Hood, Othello, King Lear, or Roger Chillingworth in *The Scarlet Letter* (another work that equates darkness with evil or sin). At the same time, anti-, non-, or sub-human characters have been identified from the outset so that readers/audiences could follow the attitudes they symbolized: e.g., Cyclops, Grendel, Rumpelstiltskin, the Wolf in "Little Red Riding Hood," and bizarre creatures with several heads, red eyes, or green hair. In *The Nigger of the "Narcissus,"* however, James Wait is a violation of this tradition; he appears in human form, with human possibilities, but, because of his race and color, he is a caricature of Black humanity. Through him, Conrad and the critical establishment practice racism under the banner of realism and symbolism.

Naturally, a number of notable sub-symbols radiate from the social and color combustion aboard the *Narcissus*. But we view them through the eyes of white men, themselves characters drawn by the mind's eye of a white author! Even so, the most salvageable —and socially instructive—of these incidental symbols (i.e., color, race, sexuality, fear, guilt) are overlooked by critics who are also mostly white (men). With few exceptions, the most influential of these men—even today—live in absolute and embarrassing ignorance of major cultural differences between Africans and Europeans, between Afro-Americans and Euro-Americans. Within the gap of ignorance, they concoct "truths" and "explanations" regarding the behavior of Black and other Third World peoples. They are smug men, firmly rooted in a system of thought that views *black* and *blackness* in mostly negative terms. Hence, the evils they unconsciously associate with darkness are smoothly transferred—via elaborate and arrogant theories of literature—onto Black human beings. Atop such a myopic plateau, and in possession of the same dangerous ethnocentric tendencies as Conrad, they remain safe since they can call Wait symbolic and avoid the awful "burden" of considering or accepting his humanity. Such a Narcissistic position allows them to regurgitate racism in the name of realism, and to perpetuate literary apartheid under the cloak of poetic license. At the same time, the white man does, indeed, have a burden to bear; and who knows but that this burden lies deep-deep within the Heart of Darkness, within that unexcavated internal BLACKNESS whose core contains an infinite number of "shadows" and "shadowy" doubts.

Selected Bibliography

I. BIBLIOGRAPHICAL AIDS

The most complete bibliographies on Conrad are Kenneth A. Lohf and Eugene P. Sheehy, *Joseph Conrad at Mid-Century: Editions and Studies, 1895–1955* (1957) and Theodore G. Ehrsam, *A Bibliography of Joseph Conrad* (1969). More helpful to the student, however, are Bruce E. Teets and Helmut E. Gerber, *Joseph Conrad: An Annotated Bibliography of Writings about Him* (1971) and Maurice Beebe. "Criticism of Joseph Conrad: A Selected Checklist," *Modern Fiction Studies*, I (February, 1955), 30–45, revised and updated, X (Spring, 1964), 81–106. George T. Keating, *A Conrad Memorial Library* (1929) describes the largest single collection of Conrad manuscripts, editions, and studies, now at Yale. Thomas Wise, *A Bibliography of the Writings of Conrad 1895–1921* (1921, 2nd ed. 1964) describes both the first English and the first American editions of Conrad's works. The bibliography of Ludwik Krzyzanowski in *Joseph Conrad: Centennial Essays* (1960) corrects and adds to the Polish items in Lohf and Sheehy. The annual bibliography in *Conradiana* may be used to bring all of the above up to date.

II. BIOGRAPHY

Much primary material on Conrad's life is readily available. Of autobiographical value are *The Mirror of the Sea* (1906), *A Personal Record* (1912), *Notes on Life and Letters* (1921), *Last Essays* (1926), and *Conrad's Prefaces*, ed. Edward Garnett (1937). The greatest body of letters by Conrad is in G. Jean-Aubrey, *Joseph Conrad: Life and Letters*, 2 vols. (1927), but other important edited collections are Richard Curle, *Conrad to a Friend* (1928), Edward Garnett, *Letters From Conrad, 1895–1924* (1928), G. Jean-Aubrey, *Letters Françaises* (1929), John A. Gee and Paul J. Sturm, *Letters of Joseph Conrad to Marguerite Poradowska, 1890–1920* (1940), William Blackburn, *Joseph Conrad: Letters to William Blackwood and David S. Meldrum* (1958), and C. T. Watts, *Joseph Conrad's Letters to Cunninghame Graham* (1969). Of testimonial value are two books by Conrad's wife Jessie, *Joseph Conrad as I Knew Him* (1926) and *Joseph Conrad and His Circle* (1935, 2nd ed. 1964), various studies by Richard Curle, the most important of which is *The Last Twelve Years of Joseph Conrad* (1928), and the many reminiscences by literary friends, the fullest of which are by Ford Madox Ford, *Joseph Conrad: A Personal Remembrance* (1924) and *Portraits from Life* (1937). Engaging full biographies are G. Jean-Aubry's 1947 recasting of the biographical part of his pioneer *Life and Letters*, which was translated by Helen Seeba as *The Sea Dreamer*. A *Definitive Biography of Joseph Conrad* (1957), and Jerry Allen, *The Thunder and the Sunshine: A Biography of Joseph Conrad* (1958). Bernard C. Meyer in *Joseph Conrad: A Psychoanalytic Biography* (1967) presents a psychoanalytic approach. To date, however, the excellent work of Jocelyn Baines, *Joseph Conrad: A Critical Biography* (1960), still remains the fullest and most accurate account of Conrad's life.

III. SELECTED SPECIAL STUDIES

In the following list no mention is made of collections, books, studies, or articles already quoted from or referred to in the footnotes of the preceding sections.

Beach, Joseph Warren. *The Twentieth Century Novel: Studies in Technique* (Appleton-Century Crofts: New York, 1932), pp. 348–52.

Biles, Jack I. " 'Its Proper Title': Some Observations on *The Nigger of the 'Narcissus,' " Polish Review*, 20 (1975), 181–88.

Boyle, Ted E. *Symbol and Meaning in the Fiction of Joseph Conrad* (Mouton and Company: The Hague, 1965), pp. 38–59.

Cross, Donald. "On Many Seas," *Times Literary Supplement* (London), September 2, 1965, 761.

Davis, Harold E. "Symbolism in *The Nigger of the 'Narcissus,' " Twentieth Century Literature*, (April 1956), 26–29.

Dowden, Wilfred S. *Joseph Conrad: The Imaged Style* (Vanderbilt University Press: Nashville, 1970), pp. 48–56.

Duffy, J. J. "Conrad and Pater," *Conradiana*, 1 (Summer 1968), 45–47.

Fleishman, Avrom. *Conrad's Politics: Community and Anarchy in the Fiction of Joseph Conrad* (Johns Hopkins Press: Baltimore, 1967), pp. 129–32.

Ford, Ford Madox. "Conrad and the Sea," *American Mercury*, 35 (June 1935), 169–76.

Hammes, Jr., Kenneth W., "Melville, Dana, and Ames: Sources for Conrad's *The Nigger of the 'Narcissus,'*" *Polish Review*, 19 (1974), 29–33.

Jones, Michael P. "Judgment and Sentiment in *The Nigger of the 'Narcissus,'*" *Conradiana*, 9 (1977), 157–69.

Joy, Neill R. "Conrad's 'Preface' to *The Nigger of the 'Narcissus'*: The Lost Typescript Recovered," *Conradiana*, 9 (1977), 17–33.

Kirschner, Paul. "Conrad and Maupassant," *Review of English Literature*, 6 (October 1965), 37–51.

Masback, Fredric J. "Conrad's Jonahs," *College English*, 22 (February 1961), 328–33.

Michael, Marion C., "James Wait as Pivot: Narrative Structure in *The Nigger of the 'Narcissus,'*" *Joseph Conrad: Theory and World Fiction, Proceedings of the Comparative Literature Symposium*, 7 (1974), 89–102.

Molinoff, Katherine. "Conrad's Debt to Melville: James Wait, Donkin and Belfast of the *Narcissus*," *Conradiana*, 1 (Summer 1969), 119–22.

Moyne, Ernest J. "Wamibo in Conrad's *The Nigger of the 'Narcissus,'*" *Conradiana*, 10 (1978), 55–61.

Nelson, Harland S. "Eden and Golgotha: Conrad's Use of the Bible in *The Nigger of the 'Narcissus,'*" *Iowa English Yearbook*, 8 (Fall 1963), 63–67.

Steinmann, Theo. "The Perverted Pattern of *Billy Budd* in *The Nigger of the 'Narcisscus,'*" *English Studies*, 55 (1974), 239–46.

Stewart, J.I.M. *Joseph Conrad* (Dodd, Mead: New York, 1968), pp. 56–71.

Wiley, Paul L. *Conrad's Measure of Man* (University of Wisconsin: Madison, 1954), pp. 44–50.